The

Cranks
Bible

The Cranks Bible

Nadine Abensur

A Seven Dials Paperback

For my parents

First published in the United Kingdom in 2001 by Cassell & Co

This paperback edition first published in 2002 by Weidenfeld & Nicolson

Reprinted October 2003

Reprinted October 2004

Photography by Jason Lowe
Managing Editor Hilary Lumsden
Art Direction Patrick Carpenter
Design Grade Design Consultants
Editors Eluned Jones, Charlotte Coleman-Smith
Food Preparation Ross Dobson

A CIP catalogue record for this book is available
from the British Library

ISBN 1 841 88204 6

Printed and bound by Butler and Tanner in the UK

Weidenfeld & Nicolson
Wellington House
125 Strand
London WC2R 0BB

Contents

Introduction

About 10 years ago, I read an editorial in the now-defunct *Taste* magazine by its editor Drew Smith. I have never forgotten it. He predicted that in a time not so very far away, a chef would be judged by the skill and imagination he (or she) could bring to vegetable dishes, in the same way as he had once been measured by the glory of his sauces. 'Vegetables would take centre stage', he said.

I believe that time is here. I have always been baffled by the reputation of vegetarian food as heavy and brown, and even more so by the kind of cookery that led to that unfortunate stereotype.

Vegetarian cooking should resonate with the abundance and colour of freshly grown vegetables in all their vast array. Organic, seasonal and locally grown or not, one cannot but wonder at the choice. These days, just about the only brown food I can think of is meat. But awareness in the sufficiency of vegetables and in the relatively low need for protein (an adult female needs as little as 36 g of protein a day, an adult male only 50 g) and carbohydrate dawned slowly.

In a way, I am thrilled at the progress made in the realm of vegetarian cooking – certainly, you are rarely fobbed off with an omelette (though *see* p28 for an omelette I would not say no to) any more. But in another way, I am left with a slight disappointment. Excellent and uniquely vegetarian restaurants are still rare and there are very few exclusively 'real' vegetarian chefs. So many have settled for the dubious 'demi-veg' tag that you could be forgiven for thinking chicken an honorary vegetable.

I write this book for all those – and I know that I am in good company – who are fed up of wading through a pile of meat or fish recipes before getting to the (smaller) vegetable chapter. I would like a shift in the balance of power please. I would like more vegetables and I would like meat to take its rightful place as the bit on the side, the occasional treat. I know that not everyone can truly give it up – mostly it gives you up and in my experience this is always accompanied by a growing spiritual, or at the very least aesthetic, awareness. Perhaps you will find a sprinkling of this here and there as you use this book.

Every so often (or should that be increasingly often) a food scare comes along which terrifies people into change. I write this as the horror of the latest Foot and Mouth outbreak rages across the UK with tragic and devastating consequences. The Vegetarian Society is inundated with calls from people anxious to make a long-lasting change, both for their own well-being and because they can no longer ignore the lack of sustainability in modern farming practices.

Even now it seems, many simply do not know where to start, confused as well they might be, by conflicting health claims, not to mention by years of having pretty awful 'non-food' rammed down their throats. Count how many aisles in your supermarket sell 'real food'. And then count them again when you have cooked from this book.

I hope I have presented enough here to whet and satisfy your appetite because above all consideration, food has to be delicious, delectable, psychically as well as physically pleasing. So I hope I have communicated both the detail and the spirit behind this still marginal, though growing way, of eating, while throwing in enough nutritional information to make the diffident brave.

Vegetarians are often accused of taking the moral high ground. Without wishing to do so – you do what is right or true for you in your particular circumstance – I cannot see anything wrong with this. There have always had to be pioneers, cranks and visionaries and we all know that yesterday's folly is today's norm.

So it is an enormous privilege to be writing this book in this, Cranks uncompromisingly vegetarian 40th year, to have been given complete freedom to extract, distil and refine all that is good and delicious about vegetarian food and present it to you in this collection. It has been a hugely enjoyable time, the only difficulty being *l'embarras de choix* (an embarrassment of riches) for every recipe I included I was painfully aware of the many I was leaving out. I could have gone on and on. In the end I hope I came to a balance of old and new – or at least new to you – that will make this book both inspiring and down-to-(the precious)-earth.

spring & summer vegetables

spring & summer recipes

Even if spring is off to a slow start, you'll find artichokes from Italy, locally grown rocket and precious Jersey Royals to take home in proper paper bags. As the pace builds up, revel in bundles of English asparagus and be justifiably proud. Enjoy crisp, sweet peas in the pod and diminutive broad beans. Then, as summer and heaven let loose, I hardly need tell you that apart from the drippingly ripe fruit, there are salad vegetables from the four corners of the earth. Pray for a little sunshine and take it all outdoors, borrowing freely from the inspiration and cooking of the Mediterranean.

Fennel and almond soup
with cardamom

This is my fifth cookery book, so I approach writing about fennel with a sense of trepidation mixed with déjà vu. How can I once again sing its praises with such abandon or recount childhood memories once more? How can I not? I know it has its detractors, those who recoil at the aniseed flavour (so gentle, benevolent and healing when cooked).

I've seen a pendulum swing though, since fennel's slow re-introduction to the British palate. Fewer people than before turn their noses up at it.

I have harboured a passion for fennel since I was very small. I remember it piled high in Moroccan markets, and I would stroke its generous soft fronds – a far cry from the individually wrapped bulbs of modern food emporiums. We never bought it singly, piece by piece, but by the kilo, carried home in multi-coloured rope baskets.

Few things awaken nostalgia in me quite like fennel and, despite the fact that it is now commonly available, it never feels commonplace. This should always be true but I experience a sense of gratitude every single time I cook and eat it: definitely one of my desert island top 10.

Heat the sunflower oil in a frying pan, add the sliced onion and fry until transparent. Add the fennel quarters, garlic cloves and the cardamom, seeds only.

Toss about for a minute and then add half the stock or water. Cover with a lid, bring to the boil and simmer gently for 15 minutes until the fennel is soft and translucent white.

Now add the rest of the liquid as well as the ground almonds and blend until reassuringly velvety smooth. Stir in the cream and add salt and pepper to taste. You can adjust the consistency with a little extra water or stock if necessary.

Serve with a few delicate fennel fronds placed lightly on top.

Serves 4–6

2 tbsp sunflower oil, preferably organic

1 small onion or 1 shallot, finely sliced

600 g/1 lb 5 oz (3 large or 4 smaller) fennel bulbs, quartered, the green fronds reserved

2 garlic cloves

5 cardamom pods

600 ml/1 pint light vegetable stock or hot water with $1/2$ tsp Marigold bouillon powder

25 g/scant 1 oz ground almonds

2 tbsp double cream

Salt and white pepper

Silky soups
Please always take liquid measurements in soups as a guideline. You might need to add a little more or a little less liquid than I suggest. My idea of smooth is super smooth, you might like more texture.

Peppers

When I say peppers, I nearly always mean red, though I like the orange and yellow varieties too and about twice in my life I've eaten a dark purple one. Most of these taste pretty similar, the red being the ripest in the line and also the sweetest.

I cannot stand green peppers and I know only about one person who can. They are indigestible, repeat on you like cheap music and they taste like grass only worse. I was brought up on grilled, charred peppers, lying in slippery strips with very finely minced garlic, a drizzle of oil, sometimes a little lemon. It would never have occurred to us to eat an unpeeled pepper, ratatouille being the one exception I can think of to that rule. Even the most sensitive constitutions can usually handle them thus.

OTHER RECIPES USING PEPPERS

Roasted red pepper soup with aubergine caviar and Greek yoghurt 14

Grilled vegetables in a ring or rough and ready 62

A stupendously good vegetable brochette 152

Puy lentils with roasted vegetables 171

An over-the-top roasted veg lasagne 216

Paella 246

Rouille 278

Roasted red pepper soup with aubergine caviar and Greek yoghurt

Red pepper soup is everywhere now but when I first ate it about 12 years ago at Sally Clarke's in Kensington, it seemed exquisitely novel.

England was just waking up to Mediterranean food and charred vegetables, as if some of us hadn't been brought up on them. I remember the incredulous looks somewhere between horror and fascination on the faces of some of the first people to whom I taught vegetarian classes when I grilled the peppers black. Anyway, I immediately adopted red pepper soup into my repertoire and made it for many a professional engagement.

I served it then, as now, with the accompaniment also first gleaned in that elegant restaurant – aubergine caviar. I like to keep the soup as true to its name as possible though I've seen it cheapened with onion or red lentils, both of which detrimentally affect both the blood-red hue and the intensity of flavour. Occasionally I replace the aubergine caviar with a black olive concasse (see p15), spooned on to the soup or served separately on delicately toasted sliced ficelle.

And sometimes I serve creamy, sharp Greek yoghurt, left plain or scented with a little zest of lime.

Place the peppers under a very hot grill until the skins are charred on all sides, taking care not to overdo them, so that the flesh remains as unblemished a red as possible. Discard any part of the flesh which may have become black. Set the peppers aside to cool in a bowl covered with a clean tea towel or in a polythene bag, so that the rising steam loosens the skin from the flesh. Discard both this and the seeds, though catch what sweet juices you can in a bowl. These are so precious that I don't run the peppers under cold water.

Blend the red peppers, the chopped garlic clove, a dash of Tabasco, a little stock and a pinch of salt to a thick red cream. Transfer to a saucepan and warm gently for a few minutes, adding the rest of the stock and stirring to smooth out any lumps, but don't let the soup boil.

To make the garnish, fry the chopped aubergine in the heated oil, together with the finely chopped garlic and salt and pepper. I let the aubergine disintegrate somewhat so it is a good balance of creamy flesh amply flecked with shiny black skin.

Serves 6

8 red peppers

1 plump garlic clove

A dash of Tabasco

1 litre/2 pints of light vegetable stock and a little more if necessary

Salt and freshly ground black pepper

For the garnish

1 large or 2 small aubergines, cut into rough 1-cm /1/2-inch cubes

60 ml/2 fl oz light olive oil

1 garlic clove, finely chopped

250 g/9 oz Greek yoghurt or soured cream or crème fraîche

2 perfect spring or salad onions, green part only, finely and neatly sliced on the diagonal

Alternative concasse

Simply pit a load of your favourite black olives and chop them very small. There are olive pastes, of course, but I prefer this grainier homemade version. If you want to make it more like a tapenade, add about 2 tablespoons capers to 450 g/1 lb olives, as well freshly ground black pepper and olive oil to bind.

A soup with yellow peppers

Chop the vegetables fairly small and stir-fry in a little hot oil. You can include the yellow peppers here or grill and peel them as in the soup above, but you must take care not to blemish the flesh.

Blend the softened vegetables with the stock until very smooth. Return to a pan and heat but not to boiling point, adding the cream to make it even smoother. Season to taste.

Stir the basil sprig in for a minute and fish out. Both soups are good with a day-old baguette, cut into cubes and fried.

4 yellow peppers, seeded

4 medium-sized potatoes, peeled

1 red onion, sliced

1 carrot

1 stick celery

Garlic, to taste

Extra virgin olive oil

1 litre/2 pints vegetable stock and a little more if necessary

A dash of double cream

Salt and freshly ground black pepper

A sprig of basil

Alternative peppers

For the perfect stuffed pepper I suggest you try the elegant, long Romesco peppers, which are much sweeter. Roast them to just limp no more, not as floppy or sinuous as you would if you were eating them in oil-doused strips. Then make a fresh and last-minute filling either of cannellini beans, slivers of black olives and sunblushed tomatoes, or with a medley of diced summer vegetables.

Roasted tomato soup with garlic cream

People have looked on incredulously when I've made this. I mean, isn't tomato soup supposed to come from a tin? But I can't help it, I love making soups and this is one of my favourites.

What matters most is that the tomatoes are blood red and ripe so really there's not much point in thinking about making this except at the height of summer. Vine tomatoes work well or those 'grown for flavour'. In *Cranks Light* (W&N, 1998) I insist that, despite the preciousness of it, cherry tomatoes actually make the best soup and I still believe this.

But whatever you do, don't end up buying endless little plastic boxes – they are much cheaper bought loose. Some of the baby plum tomatoes are extremely sweet and fragrant and they roast to sugar sweet with a sharp edge. Even a mixture of tomatoes will do to make up the quantity. My garden-grown ones are usually absolutely delicious but the skins are so tough that blitzing them to death like this in a soup is perhaps the best thing for them.

I do sieve. I like my soups velvety smooth but I acknowledge that this is a matter of taste and of temperament. I make (or used to make) plenty of tomato soups by blanching the tomatoes, skinning and deseeding them. But I must say that roasting them on a high heat, as in this recipe, concentrates their sugars and really intensifies the flavours, so the other option is no longer open to me. Plus it's a relief not to have to fiddle about with skin and seed removal. It does mean that the sieving is more crucial than before but it's a price worth paying.

A piece of molten Brie instead of cream dunked in is as good as anything. Serve with some good French bread or some spongy country loaf warmed through to wipe the bowl clean. You could forget about the dairy in the soup altogether and replace it with a glug of the best olive oil you possess.

Serves 6

4 tbsp olive oil

3 kg/6$^{1}/_{2}$ lb cherry or vine tomatoes

200 g/7 oz red onions, chopped

6 garlic cloves

A small handful of fresh basil sprigs

$^{1}/_{2}$–1 tsp caster sugar

A dash of Tabasco

1 tbsp sundried tomato purée

Salt and freshly ground black pepper

Small basil leaves for garnish

6 tbsp Greek yoghurt or crème fraîche or 4 tbsp double cream

For the garlic cream

3 whole heads of garlic, cut in half

Olive oil for drizzling

Sea salt

Preheat the oven to 200°C/400°F/gas mark 6. In a large oven tray, drizzle half the oil over the tomatoes, season with salt and pepper and shake about to coat.

Roast the tomatoes for about 15 minutes in the hot oven until the skins are blistered, shrivelling and charred in places.

Meanwhile heat the rest of the oil in a pan and fry the onion until it is soft and transparent, seasoning it with salt and pepper. Then blitz the lot in a blender (or add the tomatoes to the pan of onions and use a hand-held blender – affectionately known around my home as a 'noisy noisy' – to blend smooth).

Return to a clean pan. Add the peeled garlic cloves, sugar, Tabasco and tomato purée, and, towards the end, the sprigs of basil, left on the stalk so you can fish them out easily.

Simmer gently for 10–15 minutes. By this time the garlic will be as soft as butter so you can leave it where it is. The delapidated basil can come out and be replaced with decoratively small leaves, sprinkled like confetti over each bowlful. The soup will have thickened and reddened. You may need to thin it down with about 200 ml/7 fl oz boiling water or light vegetable stock.

To make the garlic cream cut the whole heads of garlic in half, baste with olive oil and season with a little sea salt. Roast for 30 minutes, wrapped in foil until the garlic is quite soft. Either squeeze out the sweet, pungent flesh yourself into a small dish so people can spread it on warm bread or bring a plate of the roasted half heads to the table and let people get their own hands dirty!

To finish, you can either stir in the double cream just before serving or, if you prefer not to intrude on the perfectly deep red, serve it separately or whirled on top. The yoghurt and crème fraîche are both best added in a thick rounded spoonful to each bowl.

Watercress

Always better in bunches than in sweaty plastic bags (is there anything that is not), these aristocratic leaves, at once peppery and refreshing, succulent and elegant, provide a leaf to be generous with.

And you'll almost certainly be buying British – great fields of it, spring-water-fed, have thrived here since the 19th century. Sybil Kapoor says she stores her watercress by first trimming the stalks, wrapping them in very wet kitchen paper, then placing this in a plastic bag, inflated with air like a balloon and sealed before storing in the salad drawer of a fridge. Otherwise eating on the day of purchase is the best advice I can offer you, short of buying it in ice-packed boxes.

Use watercress as you might use spinach, wilted with butter, in a lightly set tart. My mother often serves it with chicory. It goes well with a mustard dressing and is in fact of the same family. It makes a fabulous fat-slicing pesto for sweet potato or pumpkin gnocchi, as well as for pasta.

It goes as well with Parmesan as rocket does, and is a lot less expensive without being cheap. And, of course, there is the soup, which has to be one of the most sophisticated in the world, a fact not dimmed by its popularity.

OTHER RECIPES USING WATERCRESS

A watercress soup 20

A brilliant green salad 22

Six potato salads 77

Baby broad beans, baby spinach and poached quail's eggs 172

Watercress pesto 266

Cranks wholemeal bread 370

A watercress soup

I only have to hear the word and I am always and without fail transported to a time circa 1986 when I made this for 60 people, and found myself fanatically plucking each leaf from its stalk. And when I say fanatically, I mean fanatically.

I had recurring dreams of watercress for a week. Thank goodness I've loosened up a bit: though I will still exhort you to pluck, I don't expect quite such perfectionism. It's just that I prefer to reserve the stalks for the soup's very own stock and I cannot abide lazy watercress soups, which are more like string than silk.

Pluck the watercress leaves from the stalks and reserve the stalks for the stock.

Place all the stock ingredients, except for the basil, in a large saucepan. Bring to the boil and simmer gently for 1 hour, adding the basil leaves for the last few minutes only.

While that's bubbling away, melt the butter in a heavy-bottomed saucepan and add the potatoes. Sauté gently for 10 minutes without allowing them to turn even the slightest bit brown – they simply need to soften and become waxy.

Season with salt and pepper, stir and add the mound of watercress leaves, one handful at a time, followed by one ladleful of stock and the garlic. Stir, cover with a lid and simmer delicately for 10 minutes, stirring often and adding a little more stock if you see any danger of sticking.

Blend in a food processor until as smooth as a machine can do it and pass through a fine sieve. The soup is now a thick forest-green cream and it needs to be returned to the pan, together with the rest of the stock and stirred gently to stop lumps from forming and for just long enough to touch boiling point. Remove from the heat at that crucial moment.

Stir in the cream at the last moment, adjust the seasoning, warm through and serve.

Serves 6

600 g/1 lb 5 oz watercress

100 g/4 oz butter

450 g/1 lb potatoes, roughly diced

2 garlic cloves, finely slivered

60 ml/2 fl oz double cream, plus extra for garnish

Salt and freshly ground black pepper

For the stock

1 medium onion, sliced

3 spring onions, sliced

A small handful of green beans

3 sticks celery and leaves if possible

1 garlic clove, chopped

Stalks from the watercress

1.8 litres/3 pints water

A few basil leaves

Advance warning

If you want to make the soup in advance, do everything bar adding the cream and it'll keep refrigerated overnight; don't leave it any longer though or it will tarnish. Reheat very gently with the cream and serve, or just remove from the fridge, allow it to mellow and serve cold.

A brilliant green salad

The best green salads do not come out of a supermarket packet. End of story. Any of the fragile leaves you might be interested in will invariably arrive home, bruised and tattered and woe betide you, if you think you can keep a half packet for the next day – they become limp, flaccid and half rotten.

So what's the answer? Well, if designer leaves are what you are after, you had better get growing. Rocket is probably the easiest of all to grow in tubs or flower beds. Just six weeks will give you a harvest. Dandelion grows anywhere and everywhere, just pick the youngest leaves. The same holds true for nasturtiums – they grow with such profligacy, even in a confined box, that you should be well stocked with leaves all summer. Their vibrant flowers, left whole or finely shredded, are sweet and juicy yet have an invigorating kick of hot mustard.

Baby spinach also grows easily, even in my tiny town garden. Again, keep picking the young leaves – when it comes to salads, you should not be afraid to apply some ruthless ageism. Watercress, in thick-stemmed, full-leafed bunches, is usually fantastic. Baby beet leaves are sometimes available from organic vegetable suppliers and their deep ruby red spines look marvellous against the green.

Also worth buying are young heads of chicory, white- or ruby-tipped (rare and exquisite), a still plump oak leaf and, if you are lucky, a thin head of trevise. All this, lightly tossed in some extra virgin olive oil, with a couple of dashes of good balsamic vinegar or a good squeeze of lemon, a few crystals of sea salt crushed between the fingers and a twist or two from the black pepper mill, provides rabbit food fit for a queen.

If the supermarket is your only option, go for the baby gems, *salade de Romaine* or Cos lettuces. Even an iceberg lettuce will do nicely, torn into chunks and spiced up with a thick, yellow, mustard dressing. A meal at my parents' house never ends without this. It's a very good, easily learned habit.

A true Caesar salad

This is the classic Caesar salad, made famous by Caesar Cardini in the 1920s and all but vegetarian to begin with, though you'd hardly know it in these days of bacon or chicken additions.

Use the pale leaves of the lettuce only and save the dark green outer leaves for a separate occasion, braised with petits pois for example or shredded and braised into soup. There are few better first-course salads in my opinion, especially when there's a huge meal to follow, but more to the point I feel bound to provide a starter and I need a little extra time for things to finish off, heat through or set and I want to keep the company occupied as well as whet their appetite. Half moons of avocado at their buttery best are the only addition I might make.

Preheat the oven to 180°C/350°F/gas mark 4.

Separate the inner leaves of the lettuces, wash and place in a colander to drain.

Rub the baguette with the garlic cloves, until softened by the garlic juices. Cut it into bite-sized pieces and coat generously with olive oil. Bake in the oven for about 20 minutes until crisp and golden.

Break the coddled eggs into a large bowl and add the lemon juice and several generous splashes of Worcestershire sauce, if using. Add a good pinch of sea salt, black pepper and the rest of the olive oil and then ever so lightly mix in the croûtons and Parmesan. Transfer the leaves to a salad bowl, then gently mix in the egg dressing and croûtons.

Serve immediately.

Serves 6

3 large, crisp Cos lettuces

1 baguette, sliced, for croûtons

2 large garlic cloves

175 ml/6 fl oz olive oil

2 large organic, free-range eggs, coddled for exactly 1 minute

Juice of 1 lemon

Worcestershire sauce (there are vegetarian brands, otherwise this is optional)

Sea salt and freshly ground black pepper

30 g/1 oz Parmesan, freshly grated

The definitive goat's cheese salad

This is a typical 1990s salad, which has joined ranks with all the great classics. But as always, it must be done properly. Already, it has become debased by the mediocre versions passing under its name. But if you keep it simple and use a good-quality goat's cheese, some thick-leaved, wild peppery rocket, a few fresh wet walnuts (but only in September or October) and a few drops of the delicate but pervasive walnut oil, you'll be most of the way there.

To me, this simplest and excellent version begs for a little acidity, something sharp. So Dijon mustard and a little lemon juice or some good balsamic vinegar go into the dressing and I scatter a few quarters of oven-dried tomatoes over the top. Young baby spinach leaves or watercress can be used instead of rocket.

Preheat the grill to high.

Make the dressing first, by whisking the mustard, garlic, lemon or vinegar and the shallot together. Drizzle in the oils, whisking all the while until you have an emulsion. Season with salt and pepper and set aside.

Place the bread slices under the hot grill until golden brown and, while hot, drizzle with a little of the oils and season with salt and pepper. Place a slice of Chèvre on each piece and return to the grill for about 2 minutes, until the cheese is slightly melted and barely starting to colour – it should be soft and warm but not dry.

Meanwhile, toss the rocket with the parsley and judiciously add the dressing. Turn over very gently so as not to bruise the leaves and divide between six plates.

Carefully place the goat's cheese croûtes on top and serve immediately with a few pieces of oven-dried tomatoes and a few walnuts scattered over the top.

Serves 6

6 slices of baguette, 2-cm/ 1-inch thick

225 g/8 oz Golden Cross Chèvre, cut into slices

450 g/1 lb wild rocket

A small handful of flat-leaf parsley, washed and picked

18 or more pieces oven-dried tomatoes (see p64)

18 wet walnuts, shelled and halved, with whatever skin can be removed (optional)

For the dressing

1 tsp Dijon mustard

1 garlic clove, finely chopped

30 ml/1 fl oz fresh lemon juice or balsamic vinegar

1 shallot, very finely chopped

30 ml/1 fl oz walnut oil plus extra for drizzling onto the bread

30 ml/1 fl oz light olive oil, plus a little extra for drizzling onto the bread

Sea salt and freshly ground black pepper

Nadine's hot Niçoise

Niçoise has taken such an ignominious battering – but how can throwing a few dull olives, a hard-boiled egg and some dried-up tuna on to some insipid cucumber and underripe tomato ever come up to much, even with a few (flaccid) green beans plonked on for good measure? So empty, trash and start again.

Well there's no tuna here but its replacement – good, fat, juicy seared fillets of field mushrooms – more than makes up for it. The egg is gently coddled and all of a warm tremble. Every ingredient is here to do something, say something, contribute something. Assemble with subtly controlled abandon.

Make up the dressing by simply putting all the ingredients in a screw-top jar and shaking vigorously. Set aside.

Prepare the beans, mushrooms and potatoes as described, then blanch the green beans in salted boiling water for 5 minutes. Refresh and set aside. In the same pan, boil the potatoes until cooked. Drain.

Baste the mushrooms lightly in the dressing and add to a hot griddle pan. Cook until lightly charred. It's best to use a heavy cast-iron griddle pan for this. Remove and set aside. Repeat with the green beans, using just a little more of the dressing. Set aside.

Now wipe the pan clean with a piece of kitchen paper and add 2 tablespoons oil to it. Sauté the potatoes till golden, crisp and tender.

Meanwhile bring the eggs to the boil in a pan of water that starts off cold for exactly 6 minutes from the moment it reaches boiling point. The whites should be completely set but the yolks still runny. Refresh under a cold tap, while you shell very carefully.

Separate, wash and pat dry the lettuce leaves. Line a salad bowl with the leaves. Mix the green beans, mushrooms, tomatoes and potatoes together with the remaining dressing and set upon the lettuce leaves. Cut the eggs in half and put on top with the black olives. Serve at once.

Serves 4

300 g/11 oz green beans, topped and tailed

2 large flat open-cap mushrooms, or 3 portobello mushrooms, thickly sliced and brushed with 2 tsp tamari

500 g/1 lb 2 oz new potatoes, preferably waxy, cut in half

Oil for shallow-frying

4 large organic, free-range eggs

2 Little Gem lettuces

20 pieces semi-dried or roasted tomatoes – the equivalent of about 6 whole tomatoes, cut and roasted

12 oily black olives

For the dressing

6 tbsp olive oil

2 tsp English mustard

1$^{1}/_{2}$ tbsp balsamic vinegar

4 garlic cloves, crushed

Sea salt and freshly ground black pepper

Avocado

I first tasted avocado at the age of four, with my father. It was a first for him too and he was eating it with sugar and Cointreau. This extraordinary combination has become a bit of a family classic.

I also make an ice-cream blending in an avocado, sometimes mixed with pistachio *halva* and it is exquisite. Contact with air, as everyone knows, is the greatest enemy of the soft, delicate, buttery flesh. It soon oxidises and goes brown and bitter, so must be eaten immediately or doused in lemon juice or some other citrus, which puts off the offending process briefly.

Avocados can stay on their huge, shiny-leaved trees for up to nine months and begin to ripen 24 hours after being picked. Still, the fruit may take anything between four and ten days to ripen properly and is best done at room temperature, so take them home and nurse them. There is a welcome trend in supermarkets of selling avocados in packs of two, one ready to eat and one not yet quite ripe. The flesh of a perfect avocado should yield slightly to gentle pressure – handle with care and sensitive fingers – especially at the top and there should be no discoloration of the skin.

With all your best efforts, eating an avocado at its peak of perfection can be a bit of a hit-or-miss affair, so though they can be expensive, it is worth buying more than you need, especially if you have an occasion in mind. A bunch of bananas kept in the same bowl speeds up the ripening.

OTHER RECIPES USING AVOCADO

Mango, papaya and avocado salad 27

Avocado action 27

Sweet potato salad with avocado and roasted tofu 81

Flageolet salad with rocket, lemon and feta 169

Rice bites 235

Tamari, lemon and balsamic dressing with chilli and garlic 278

Mango, papaya and avocado salad

I have been making this salad for years and years: proof is that it appears in *The New Cranks Recipe Book* (W&N, 1996) and, even before that, quite similarly in *Secrets from a Vegetarian Kitchen* (Pavilion, 1996). There's nothing worse than becoming self-referential but I am rather attached to it.

It isn't always of these proportions or even quite of these components but usually something like. It has the sensuality of sweet, sharp, bitter, salt, heat. The walnuts should be fresh and wet with skins that peel off like silk. The blueberries must be plump and sweet, the avocado home-ripened, buttery-yellow, soft-green. The mango must be as ripe and bright as a setting sun; the papaya fragrant, perfumed, ripened and pink; the raspberries swollen, sharp, complex, evanescent, English. And the Dolcelatte should be creamy, soft and gently veined.

I am not much of a drinker but I might eat this as a starter with a fine, mildly sweet and fruity wine – even one of the less cloyingly sweet dessert wines.

Cut the mango, papaya and avocado into even slices, the pineapple into cored half or quarter moons of a similar size, and gently mix together with the coriander and black pepper.

Mix the dressing ingredients together, add the reserved, crushed raspberries, and pour over the salad.

Scatter the cheese, whole raspberries, blueberries and walnuts on top. Serve at once.

Serves 2

1 fragrant mango

1 ripe papaya

1 Hass avocado

100 g/4 oz pineapple (optional)

1 small handful fresh coriander, loosely picked off in small sprigs

60 g/2 oz Dolcelatte, crumbled

60 g/2 oz raspberries, including half a dozen to crush into the dressing

60 g/2 oz blueberries

60 g/2 oz shelled walnuts, wet

Freshly ground black pepper

For the dressing

2 tbsp olive oil

200 ml/7 fl oz fresh orange juice

1 generous tsp grain mustard

The reserved raspberries

Avocado action

Avocado with vinaigrette may be a cliché but is popular for the simple reason that it works and is delicious, though a good olive oil, salt and pepper is often all you need. Also try blending the flesh of ripe, untainted avocados with a little water and light olive oil, lemon juice and crushed garlic, some salt and pepper. Not a guacamole but light, creamy, mousse-like and an exquisite shade of soft green.

Sourdough bread is good with it as, rather bizarrely you might think, is a sprinkling of ground cumin, especially added to a light vinaigrette.

Tossed in perfect half moons with wide leaved organic watercress and cherry tomatoes – yellow and red – as well as a few crushed walnuts and some cumin-marinated olives for good measure, this is another full-flavoured salad and one open to your creative potential. Slivers or strips of warm, lightly blanched celeriac, fried mushroom slices, chargrilled peppers, whole roasted, honeyed cloves of garlic, even crumbly cubes of feta – all would go well with a cumin dressing (*see* p271).

Finally, as yet another alternative to conventional vinaigrette, blend the ripe avocado and seasonings as above but this time instead of stopping with the water when it resembles a mousse, continue till it is of pourable consistency. You can add a very finely chopped spring onion or two or a handful of finely snipped chives.

Petits pois omelette

Am I having a laugh? Well actually I am deadly serious. This is a tribute to all the poor souls who, when they ask for a vegetarian option, are endlessly presented with an omelette: and generally one that is far removed from this pale, fluffy, light as goose down and dangerously wobbly affair.

First blanch the petits pois for about 3 minutes and drain, reserving the cooking water.

Melt the butter in a small saucepan, add the shredded lettuce and the peas as well as a spoonful or two of the reserved cooking liquid. Season with salt and pepper and set aside but keep warm.

Crack the eggs into a large bowl, add the cream, salt, a touch of pepper and a sprinkle of snipped chives. Use an omelette pan or a 20-cm/8-inch non-stick pan and melt a small knob of butter in it, swirling it about in the pan a little. Place it on the smallest ring of your stove, on the lowest heat and drop half the mixture into the pan: it takes about a ladle and a half.

With a rubber spatula, start to lift the edges gently, allowing the uncooked egg to flow into the space. The egg should wrinkle slightly as you move it, tear and quickly heal again. At no point should you increase the heat. In barely a minute, the egg has formed a soft, fragile, pale pancake on the bottom with a foamy, frothy top – *baveuse*, as the French say.

Makes 2

4 large organic, free-range eggs

6 tbsp double cream

1 tsp chives, snipped

2 knobs butter

Salt and white pepper

For the filling

4 tbsp petits pois

A knob of butter

2 lettuce leaves, finely shredded

Salt and freshly ground black pepper

Lift the pan to within inches of the heat, hovering above it, like
a psychic with healing hands. Add 2 tablespoons petits pois and begin
to fold the omelette over, moving it to the edge of the pan and on to the
plate as you help the final fold along. The omelette is a primrose yellow,
barely marbled with a delicate golden vein.

Transfer it to a warmed plate and quickly start on the second while
someone stands or sits close enough for it not to matter if they finish
theirs as you start yours. Making an omelette this delightfully precarious
for more than two is too much heartache unless you want to make one
large one in which case you need a bigger pan, a little more patience
and a little more practice.

An all-white meal

I've made this as part of an all-white meal which, far from being
boring or insipid, is elegantly and elatedly perfect. First take some baby
leeks, cut into three, blanch until tender and serve with a classic
vinaigrette (*see* p266).

Peel some new, earthy-skinned potatoes (allow 1–2 per person), child
fist size, cut into 5-mm/$1/4$-inch slices. Place in a small pan just covered
with water and 2 tablespoons olive oil and a good pinch of Marigold
bouillon powder added. Boil these furiously for a minute, then reduce the
heat to a moderate simmer till the water is all but evaporated and the
potato slices waxy, syrupy and still pale with a hint of marigold yellow.

A lightly dressed green salad – or, if you want to take me at my word,
some pristine white leaves of chicory – and a glass of well chilled
white wine round off the perfect kitchen supper.

Artichokes

The cooking of artichokes, that most aristocratic of vegetables, is at its most elevated in Italy. There are recipes for this sweet, lingering delicacy dating back to the Renaissance and before that to the Romans who cultivated them.

Sicily is sometimes cited as their place of origin, though perhaps it is North Africa, given that artichokes feature just as grandly in the cooking of the Arab world. The common French way with vinaigrette, though delicious, does seem rather prosaic when placed alongside the deep-fried or stuffed recipes, the risottos and salads or the golden-fried dishes, partnered with broad beans or almonds, saffron and lemon.

Unfortunately, small purple artichokes, where everything including the leaves themselves and the choke can be eaten, are not readily available in Britain and it is only the labour-intensive huge globe artichokes that seem to make it to the British table, even though they come from the same plant.

Tiny artichokes can be grown in Britain despite the unpropitious weather. So perhaps it is with the home gardener that the future lies.

Choose a crisp, tightly closed all-green or purple head with a firm, snappy stem. Using vinaigrette makes sense – the acidity is just what artichoke needs to balance the chemical cynarin. This, as most people attest, makes other foods taste sweet. Provide little bowls of warm water with a slice of lemon on top to dip fingers. Also, plenty of napkins.

OTHER RECIPES USING ARTICHOKES

Artichoke with sundried tomatoes and preserved lemon dressing

This is a Mediterranean hybrid. I doubt that you'll find sundried tomatoes and preserved lemon in one dish elsewhere, but even though it might sound like too much of a good thing, I promise you it isn't. It's just intensely redolent of an Arab souk and an Italian market all in one.

The French *fond d'artichaux* sounds a good deal more appetising than 'artichoke bottom', but anyway, those preserved in oil are available from good Middle Eastern shops and I've used them several times. Find the best sundried tomatoes you can: some in jars are excellent, smooth-skinned and tender.

Make the dressing by liquidizing the lemon with the rest of the dressing ingredients.

If you are using fresh artichokes, cook them first in plenty of salted acidulated water – an immersed cut-up lemon is good. If your fingers become tannic black from handling the artichokes, rub them with a cut lemon: they will soon come right again, if a little shrivelled looking. The artichokes will take about 45 minutes to become tender.

Remove the leaves and prepare (*see* p35). Heat the olive oil and, on a fairly high heat, fry the slices of artichoke for about 5–8 minutes or until they are golden-brown all over.

Halfway through, begin to add the saffron stock and the sliced garlic, stirring all the time until the liquid is mostly absorbed but creating a smooth unctuous sauce with the olive oil and bits of dissolving artichoke. The rest will be lightly coated in this delicious sauce.

Add the olives and sundried tomatoes to the warm pan, then add the preserved lemon dressing, adding a little hot water if necessary.

Remove from the heat and garnish generously with the toasted pine nuts and the chopped parsley. Eat with warmed bread and a gutsy, peppery-leaved salad. Pine nuts provide all the protein needed, but if you want more, Parmesan shavings on top go beautifully well.

Serves 4–6

6 artichoke bottoms, freshly cooked, or artichoke bottoms preserved in oil, sliced 1-cm/ 1/2-inch thick

2 tbsp olive oil or oil from a jar of sundried tomatoes

Saffron stock made by infusing a pinch of saffron in up to 200 ml/7 fl oz boiling water

1 garlic clove, finely sliced

20 black olives, preferably rich and oily

12 pieces sundried tomatoes in oil

Salt

For the dressing

1 small preserved lemon

6 tbsp extra virgin olive oil

1 garlic clove, finely sliced

1 tbsp hot water

A dash of Tabasco or a fine pinch of cayenne

To serve

2 tbsp pine nuts, dry-toasted

1 tbsp finely chopped fresh parsley

Parmesan (optional)

Preserved lemons

Here is an easy, manageable recipe that will last you up to several weeks. Serve the lemons with cold drinks, chopped into green olives, or simply on the side with any of the Moroccan- and Moorish-inspired recipes in this book. Blended with olive oil and a little crushed garlic, they also make a delicious and unusual dressing.

3 whole lemons, thick skinned and unwaxed

3 tbsp sea salt

Juice of 3 lemons

Cut the lemons, but not all the way through, into quarters, so they are still attached at the stem end. Fill them with salt and place in a preserving jar – with a rubber seal, if possible. Add any remaining salt on top.

Leave for 3 days. By then they will have begun to soften and weep some of their juices. Cover them with the juice of the other 3 lemons.

Reseal and set aside in a cool dark place for about a month before you use them.

Artichokes simmered in tomato with broad beans

I have eaten this so often in my local Greek restaurant that I eventually braved the lengthy artichoke prep time and didn't find it so hard. After all, you can do an awful lot in the 45 minutes it takes them to cook. So this has become a regular recipe at home. I once added a *soupçon* of non-Greek harissa based on the confident assumption that a dish like this must have close North African cousins. It added depth, not searing heat, and the practice has stuck. The acidity of the tomatoes works well with the sweetness of the artichoke. As a main course, I'm sure you can eat two although they are very filling, but as a starter one each is good and leaves you wishing you had had just a little more.

Serves 3–6

6 whole globe artichokes

1 lemon

500 g/1 lb 2 oz fresh tomatoes from the vine, plus 6 whole ripe, red vine tomatoes

475 g/1 lb 1 oz frozen broad beans

4 tbsp olive oil

6 shallots, finely sliced

3–4 large garlic cloves, finely sliced

1 small carrot

400 g/14 oz tin tomatoes

3 bay leaves

1/2 tsp cumin powder

1/4–1/2 tsp harissa

Sea salt and freshly ground black pepper

Trim your artichokes of any old-looking leaves and cut off the pointed tops. Also remove the stems if they are at all woody.

Fill your largest pan with cold water and, once it has boiled, add plenty of salt and the whole lemon cut into quarters to acidulate the water. This is much more effective for neutralising the effect of the tannic acid than just adding juice to the water, and it's tastier too.

Push the artichokes under as if to drown them and hold them down with a weighted plate if necessary. Boil them pretty ferociously for 40–45 minutes – an outer leaf should peel off easily as an indication that the heart is going to be soft and yielding enough.

Bring a second smaller pan of salted water to the boil and first plunge in the 500 g/1 lb 2 oz vine tomatoes until the skins split. Remove them with a slotted spoon and set aside. Then add the broad beans to the same boiling water and cook for about 10 minutes or until tender – this will depend on their age and size and will invariably take longer than the instructions on the back of the packet suggest. Once again, drain and set aside.

Meanwhile, heat 2 tablespoons olive oil in a pan and gently soften the shallots, garlic and carrot. Add the blanched tomatoes, cut into quarters (removing the seeds if wished). Fry for several minutes, before adding the tinned tomatoes, bay leaves and cumin powder, if using.

Continue to cook slowly for about 20 minutes until the sauce is properly thickened but you can still see discernible pieces of fresh tomato. Towards the end, add $1/4$ teaspoon harissa or more depending on your taste-buds.

The real fun starts when the artichokes are cooked. First run them under cold water for a couple of minutes. Then begin carefully to remove the leaves, until you come to the hairy choke which you can pull out quite easily if the artichokes are still fairly young, or cut out with a small pointed knife if they are older. You should end up with 6 perfect artichoke bottoms. Reserve the leaves for another dish (see p36).

Add the broad beans to the tomato sauce. Cook them together for 5–6 minutes and then add the artichoke bottoms, and the 6 quartered vine tomatoes, cooking together so that the flavours and seasonings are given a chance to merge. You can leave the whole thing in the pan like this, off the heat, until you are ready to serve. At that point, warm through again, finishing with 2 tablespoons olive oil and fill the artichoke bottoms with the sauce and broad beans. Either sit them in the same pan on top of the remaining sauce, or transfer them and the sauce to a neater though preferably fairly rustic-looking dish.

Eat at once with saffron rice (see p232) and warm crusty bread or flour tortillas, fried on each side in a little olive oil.

Artichoke purée with garlic and Dijon mustard

What follows is a labour of love tinged with a touch of waste not, want not morality. Faced with the enormous leftover mound of artichoke leaves from the recipe above, I then scraped every single leaf (bar the ones I couldn't resist eating) with a teaspoon, then blended the not inconsiderable amount of flesh with olive oil, mustard, garlic, salt, pepper and a little water to loosen until smooth.

Garnished with a few flakes of sweet dried red pepper and an obligatory swirl of extra virgin olive oil, this is a thing to be eaten with reverence. It lasts a good week or more in a cold fridge.

Flesh scraped from the leaves of 6 cooked artichokes

4 tbsp olive oil, plus extra to finish

1/2 scant tsp Dijon mustard

1 garlic clove, finely chopped (optional)

1–2 tbsp water

Sweet dried red pepper flakes

Sea salt and freshly ground black pepper

Artichokes with saffron and green olives bound with cream in a puff pastry pie

This dish marries classic European flavours: the cream, Middle Eastern: the saffron and Mediterranean: the artichokes and olives – ah for such brotherhood elsewhere. You will need to cook the artichokes either in batches or in two large pans. But if you feel you simply cannot go to these lengths for just 8 artichokes, then you'll have to go hunting the Arabic food stores for the ready-prepared varieties, stored in jars with oil, or for frozen ones, which are pretty good as long as you fry them straight from frozen.

As an alternative to the puff pastry, use filo. Brush each layer – about 4 or 5 – with melted butter, leaving an overhang. Fill with the artichokes, olives and potatoes, bring the overhang to the top and finish with a couple of sheets, scrunched up like fine chiffon. Brush with more melted butter and bake as if you were using puff pastry.

Preheat the oven to 200°C/400°F/gas mark 6. Divide the pastry in two, one part slightly larger than the other. Roll out on a lightly floured surface into two discs. Use the smaller disc to line the base of a 20-cm/8-inch lightly buttered and floured pie tin. Prick it all over with a fork and bake it for about 20 minutes until golden brown, and risen to multi-layered flakiness. Set aside to cool while you carry on with the rest.

Serves 4

500 g/1 lb 2 oz puff pastry

8 artichokes

1 lemon, cut into quarters

250 g/9 oz new potatoes

250 ml/9 fl oz water with a pinch of Marigold bouillon powder

A good pinch of saffron dissolved in 2 tbsp boiling water

6 garlic cloves

4 tbsp olive oil

100 g/4 oz green olives

125 ml/4 fl oz double cream

1 tbsp lemon juice

1 tbsp chopped parsley

60 g/2 oz almonds, slivered and toasted, or pine nuts

Salt and freshly ground black pepper

1 egg for glaze

Trim the pointy ends from the artichokes and immerse them in a pan (or pans) of cold, acidulated water, using the quartered lemon. Weigh them down with a plate, over which you've placed a heavy weight (a tin of beans will do). Cook for 40–45 minutes until an outer leaf comes away easily from the core.

Meanwhile, peel the new potatoes and slice them to the thickness of pound coins (*see* p118). Place them, the water, saffron, half the garlic, 2 tablespoons olive oil and salt and pepper into a large pan and cover with a lid. Simmer at first vigorously, then after a couple of minutes more gently for another 20 minutes or so, until the potatoes are beautifully tender and bathed in a golden-hued sauce. Set aside.

Run the cooked artichokes under cold water and remove the leaves and choke. (Reserve the leaves for another recipe, *see* p36). A small pointed knife or teaspoon does the trick neatly. Slice each into 3 or 4 thick slices. Heat another 2 tablespoons olive oil in a large frying pan and fry the slices until turning a caramel-gold around the frayed edges, then the rest of the garlic, taking care not to burn it, and the olives. Cook together for a few minutes, breaking the olives up a little with a wooden spoon.

Add the potatoes and sauce to the artichokes or vice versa, stirring with care. Bind with the cream, lemon juice, seasoning and, if it is looking too oily, a little hot water. This will have the effect of bringing it back to smooth homogeneity. Bring back to the boil, immediately reduce the heat and simmer for another couple of minutes.

Remove from the heat and add the chopped parsley and the toasted slivered almonds or pine nuts. Turn this filling into the tin and cover with the pre-cut lid. Make small indents all over the top with the point of a small sharp knife.

Brush with the beaten egg and bake for about 25 minutes until the pastry is risen and deeply golden. Serve at once either still in the tin or, if you're feeling brave, by turning it out on to one plate and then on to another so that it ends up the right way up. Serve with a tomato and red onion salad and something green. I like either spiky-leaved wild rocket or watercress.

Asparagus

Mention of asparagus dates back to Roman times and the prized vegetable had arrived in France by the 15th century. There are different types – thin stemmed and thick; white, green or purple.

The French, Belgians and Germans favour the white, the English and most of the Italians the green. I love them all equally. But you won't catch me elaborately tying it in bundles and cooking it in specially-designed pots.

A successful method of Madhur Jaffrey's involves lying them down horizontally in only a few tablespoons of salted boiling water. When the water is all absorbed,it is cooked and the flavour kept where it should be and not leeched out into the water. Otherwise I just blanch them in plenty of boiling salted water, having first peeled fat stalks and snapped off the woody stem, at the point where they break off easily.

Asparagus is classically served (warm) with melted butter, with Hollandaise sauce or vinaigrette in France. But a Chinese seasoning of soy sauce, sesame seeds, garlic and a little finely chopped chilli goes very well with fine-stemmed asparagus, stir-fried and still crunchy. Another favourite method of mine is to baste thick stems (cut down the middle if they are really thick) with olive oil and balsamic vinegar and to throw them on to a hot griddle for a couple of sizzling minutes so they are just charred all round. Garlic and soy are optional extras.

OTHER RECIPES USING ASPARAGUS

Asparagus with Hollandaise

I break every seasonal taboo in the book except one – this one. Waiting for the new season's asparagus crop and buying exactly as much as I think I really need and not how little I think I can afford. I allow 5 or 6 good, fat, tightly tipped spears per person, or a mound of finer ones, or a bowlful of the string-thin lengths of sprue. Always trim any woody ends off the asparagus – you'll find that they have a natural 'snap' point below which soup is the only sensible use. I love nothing better than a good, yellow, mustard-rich vinaigrette, with or without the mouli-grated hard-boiled egg of my childhood. But once a year, maybe twice, I adore this.

Hollandaise dresses blanched broccoli florets as well as it does asparagus. Indeed a platter of just blanched baby spring vegetables with it is heavenly. Use a good *beurre d'Isigny* or *de Charente* and organic, free-range eggs. You can make the Hollandaise in a bowl set over boiling water but if that involves a panic over which pan and which bowl, then brave it the other way. You do need a small heavy-bottomed saucepan and you need to take it slowly, one step at a time, but it really doesn't deserve its fearsome reputation. Try it and enjoy its delicate charm.

Cut 180 g/6 oz of the butter into small pieces and melt it slowly over a gentle heat or put it in a bowl placed in a warm oven until just melted but not oily. Meanwhile, place the egg yolks in the heavy-bottomed pan and whisk them well with a small wire whisk. Add the lemon juice, the white wine and a pinch of salt, then beat again.

Now add 15 g/$^{1}/_{2}$ oz of cold butter and place the pan over a very low heat, stirring steadily with the whisk. Continue until the egg yolks are creamy, thickening and beginning to coat the whisk.

Take the pan off the heat and beat in another 15 g/$^{1}/_{2}$ oz of cold butter. Then, pretend you are making mayonnaise and add the melted butter to the eggs one drop at a time until the sauce is really thick. Only then can you dare to add it a little more rapidly. Quite soon the sauce will be a thick, glistening bowl of sunshine.

Season with salt and pepper and lemon juice to taste. If you feel it's too thick, thin down with a little water. Keep it warm over a pan of hot water. It does reheat, if you take it gently – no more than a couple of spoonfuls first and then the rest added a little at time – but I really prefer to make Hollandaise no longer than 1 hour before I need it.

Plunge the trimmed asparagus into boiling water for 5–8 minutes until cooked, drain and smother in the sauce.

Serves 4
20 fat asparagus spears

For the Hollandaise
200 g/7 oz best butter

3 organic, free-range egg yolks

1 tbsp lemon juice, plus extra to taste

1 tbsp dry white wine

Salt and white pepper

Asparagus with morels in an easy tart

Perhaps this should be called an easy peasy tart. All you do is pour some beaten egg and cream over layers of filo or puff pastry rolled to thinly fit a large oven tray, Then cover the surface with quickly blanched asparagus and 2 or 3 fat, foresty morels, sliced into suckered rings.

Bake for 25 minutes in a medium hot oven and carry to the table as it is. It can be one of several things you knock out quickly for a party or informal gathering. In that case, cut it into as many as 12, or, if it's a main course, as few as 4 pieces. People will polish it off in first inquisitive, then amazed mouthfuls.

Preheat the oven to 180°C/350°F/gas mark 4.

Place the double cream in a bowl, add the garlic and leave to infuse for about 10 minutes. Blanch the asparagus in salted boiling water for a couple of minutes and refresh under cold water. Soak the morels in the wine, the water, a spoonful or two of the scented double cream and set aside for now.

Brush the tray with melted butter and line with the filo sheets, in turn brushing these with melted butter, going up the sides and a little over, the better to accommodate the filling later. Bake for about 10 minutes until it turns the gentlest camel colour. Leave the oven on.

Meanwhile, transfer the morels and liquid to a frying pan, snipping them into fine rings. Set over a gentle simmer so that the wine and cream are reduced to about half and are headily scented with the woody, physical smell of the fungi. Add the asparagus and toss in the wine-cream sauce.

Transfer to a bowl with the beaten eggs and the rest of the cream. Season with salt and pepper and pour into the filo casing, tidying up the spears so they completely cover the entire surface in neat rows. The morels should be evenly distributed throughout, they are the prize in every mouthful.

Bake for 15–20 minutes until gently set, and serve.

Serves 4–6

6 tbsp double cream or crème fraîche

3 garlic cloves, finely sliced

250 g/9 oz thin-stemmed asparagus, trimmed as necessary

3 or 4 large dried morels, or fresh if you are very blessed

3 tbsp white wine

3 tbsp hot water

30 g/1 oz butter, melted

8 sheets filo pastry

6 large organic, free-range eggs

Salt and freshly ground black pepper

Griddled fat asparagus spears with sesame seeds and tamari

We think so much of asparagus in its English or French context that I wanted to show it in an altogether different Asian light. It is stunning like this served with softened, exploded wild rice (not a minute less then 45 minutes slow cooking) and extra dressing.

In *Cranks Light* (W&N, 1998) there is a recipe like this, which also has pan-fried or griddled slices of artichoke. Keep the window open as you work to let out the smoke and serve straight from the pan.

Toss the asparagus in the olive oil, then throw on to a very hot griddle pan (a proper cast-iron one is best for the job) and wait until the asparagus is charred on all sides, tossing the pan about as necessary.

Add the garlic slices only when the asparagus is very nearly ready. Stir in the sesame seeds and toss vigorously for a hot sizzling moment, adding the tamari, ginger juice and chopped chilli just before removing from the heat.

Serve straight from the griddle pan and pass around the lime wedges for a good fresh and lively squeeze. Asparagus served like this does not wait for anyone!

Serves 4

900 g/2 lb fat green asparagus, trimmed and peeled as necessary

3 tbsp light olive oil or groundnut oil or a mixture of both

2 garlic cloves, finely sliced

2 tbsp toasted sesame seeds

2 tbsp tamari

2-cm/1-inch piece of ginger, grated and squeezed, with the resulting liquid reserved

1 small piece fresh red chilli, chopped very finely

To serve

Lime wedges

Modern asparagus

You know the thing – a *salade composée* served in one of these super-sizrd, white, flat soup plates; crisp asparagus falling like pick-up-sticks on a towering heap of red-veined, claret, almost purple lettuce leaves and soft, yellow, baby lettuce hearts, Californian shavings of Parmesan, aged balsamic vinegar and estate-bottled olive oil.

Extras can include thin, ficelle croutons, delicately poached quail's eggs and tiny, shrivelled-skin new potatoes.

Aubergine

Aubergines are believed to be of Indian origin. Their Sanskrit name *vatin gana* becomes *badingen* in Persian, *albadingen* in Arabic, *albadingena* in Spanish, then *aubergine* in French, which in an etymological nutshell sums up their migration from east to west.

The first types to reach Europe were egg-shaped – hence the name eggplant. In southern Italian markets, they sit alongside much larger white ones, the more common elongated purple ones, and the beautifully marbled purple and white or green and white, as well as some miniatures. When I was a child, the latter were served *confites*, sweet, slowly cooked and exotically spiced. Smooth, glossy, unblemished skins promise a good firm inside but one which weighs heavy in the hand is best avoided – it probably contains far too many of the bitter seeds.

Aubergines absorb oil in what my aunt Ninette used to describe as 'industrial quantities', but it is this capacity which facilitates the extraordinary transformation of the aubergine from its inedible raw state to the voluptuous, when cooked. The simplest and endlessly popular *baba gannush*, demonstrates this excellently.

Salting aubergines used to be a necessary ritual to draw out bitter juices that caused terrible rashes in some people. These days, the tendency to bitterness has been bred out – no more bitter juices, no more rashes.

OTHER RECIPES USING AUBERGINES

Aubergine purée with cumin pitot

This is everyone's favourite aubergine purée, the kind we all end up eating in Greek restaurants. I know it's often made with mayonnaise (which is an unnecessary modern perversion) but I think it's quite rich enough and cleaner tasting just with olive oil.

These dishes make great starters if you can exercise any kind of self-restraint. Otherwise it is better to be honest and to make an entire lunch of it, going back for more to your hunger, greed or heart's content. You won't need more than a room temperature minced garlic and onion tomato salad with it and a generous bowl of olives.

The cumin pitot come from further east than Greece, but many of these recipes appear in one guise or another from the Mediterranean to the Middle East. Pitot is simply the Hebrew plural for pitta.

There are two methods to this recipe. You can either cut the aubergine into chunks and fry in the hot oil until soft and golden, add the garlic and onion and the rest of the ingredients, then purée until smooth. But then you will need more olive oil than the above ingredients suggest, as you'll still need to add some as you blend the aubergines.

Or, you can baste the aubergine in the olive oil and roast it at 220°C/425°F/gas mark 7 until it is soft and deeply golden. Some people peel off the skin but I always leave it on, I like the texture and flavour it adds. Blend till smooth, adding the olive oil as you would to an emulsion. It will expand quite considerably.

Add the garlic, chopped onion, lemon juice and cayenne and blend again. When light and creamy, stir in the chopped herbs.

Cut the pitot into quarters and brush with olive oil on both sides. Sprinkle with the cumin seeds. Place in a hot oven for 6–8 minutes and serve to dunk into the purée.

Serves 6

1 large aubergine

3 tbsp extra virgin or other olive oil

2 garlic cloves, finely chopped

1 small onion, very finely chopped

1 tbsp lemon juice

A small pinch cayenne pepper

2 tbsp finely chopped parsley or coriander or a mixture of both

6 pitta breads

Extra olive oil for brushing

1 tbsp cumin seeds

Salt and freshly ground black pepper

Flame-smoked aubergine with olive oil, lemon and garlic

My first editor and good friend Laura Washburn first introduced me to this quick, easy and, more importantly, stunning and delicious way of preparing an aubergine. While it's ideal for the barbecue, I've dedicated an oven rack to the purpose and it is now warped beyond recognition from having been set upon a naked flame so very many times. But my need has been commercial as well as domestic.

I occasionally cook for people's parties, birthdays, weddings and so on, and one summer, I got it into my head that these would make a simple and dramatic offering.

Over the course of a few months, I smoked literally hundreds and hundreds of aubergines. I attempt to find small aubergines because I like to serve one per person whether on a buffet laden with other Moorish dishes or as a starter with chermoula and fried tortillas.

The skins are charred to coal black which, despite any carcinogenic risk, doesn't seem to deter me or many I know from eating them. But be prepared that they may be just too strange for some and expect the skins to be left on the side of the plate or do as I do when I'm being professional and remove them fairly informally first – bits here and there won't matter.

Place a wire rack or oven shelf (an old one that you don't care too much about) over a high flame and put a washed and dried aubergine on top. The skin will soon start to char. Regularly turn the aubergine over for about 7 minutes so that it becomes charred and black all over.

Prick with a fork to test that the flesh is completely soft inside – it should offer no resistance at all. Hold the aubergine at one end while you cut 1-cm/1/2-inch thick slices into the flesh with the point of a sharp knife. Don't cut all the way through though – this is just a way of introducing direct heat right into the flesh of the vegetable.

Remove from the heat as soon as you are satisfied that the aubergine is softly unctuous and yielding. Continue with further aubergines while you generously douse the ready one with olive oil, lemon, garlic, salt and Tabasco. You can mix all these ingredients together before pouring if you choose.

Garnish with fresh herbs and serve with chermoula (*see* p268) or chickpea salad (*see* p176) or both.

Serves 4

4 long, quite thin aubergines

4–6 tbsp olive oil

Juice of 1 lemon

2 large garlic cloves, very finely chopped

Sea salt

Tabasco

A few basil or coriander leaves, shredded

Smokin'

How many aubergines, you can successfully smoke at one time depends on how large your stove rings are. I am assuming for this exercise that your stove is gas. It is possible to carry this out on a small ring but obviously since the flame won't be as large or strong, it will take longer and you'll have to shift the aubergine about to cover all aspects.

Aubergines with smoked Ricotta

I always hesitate before including a recipe for which I think you will have trouble finding the ingredients. I don't want to write a book for the privileged few who can get to Harvey Nichols or some rarified West London deli. But occasionally I like to push the boat out.

I once bought my smoked Ricotta in a Venetian Christmas market and brought it back to London hidden in the depths of my cavernous bag. Smoked Ricotta, like the more readily available smoked Mozzarella, which I suggest you use as an alternative, is drier and firmer than its conventional virginal counterpart and doesn't melt but only slightly softens under heat.

You will need a whole individual Ricotta, about 250 g/9 oz, per generously sized aubergine and this should feed two people. The result is rich and meaty.

Preheat your oven to its maximum setting.

Chop the tomato into small pieces and fry lightly in a little hot olive oil. Season with salt and pepper and set aside.

Slice the aubergine at 5-mm/$\frac{1}{4}$-inch intervals from stem to tail, slicing all the way through but keeping it attached at the top, and lay it a little splayed out on a sheet of foil cut big enough to wrap around it. Brush each aubergine side abundantly with the olive oil, sprinkle with salt and pepper and insert the thinly sliced Ricotta between each layer. Also introduce the cooked tomato. Baste with any remaining oil, hold tightly together and make a parcel of the foil.

Lift into the oven and bake on a high heat for 35–40 minutes. Unwrap the foil – the aubergine should be soft right through by now – and continue to bake for another 10 minutes or thereabouts so that it browns a little. You can do this last under the grill but keep an eye on it.

Lift the parcel (you can seal it again if you want to surprise) on to a plate and serve. There's no point in trying to lift the aubergine out of the foil as it will just fall apart. Serve with tabbouleh (*see* p185) or just warm bread and a green salad.

Serves 2

1 large tomato

3 tbsp light olive oil, plus extra for frying

1 large or 2 small aubergines

250 g/9 oz smoked Ricotta

Salt and freshly ground black pepper

Tian d'aubergine with crème fraîche

Tian is an earthenware dish lending its name to anything cooked in it. A traditional Provençal *tian d'aubergine* contains slices of grilled aubergine and a béchamel sauce using crème fraîche. The Italians layer the aubergines with Mozzarella and tomato sauce.

My version is a hybrid. I use fresh, cooked beef tomatoes and insist that the aubergines are well and truly golden, not pale and insipid looking. I have a horror of such aubergines and hope to instil the same horror into you.

Preheat the oven to 190°C/375°F/gas mark 5.

Prepare the aubergine slices as described and immediately squeeze half the lemon juice over them. This cuts through the oil to make them less cloying. Also sprinkle with salt.

You should find that you can fry the tomato with half the garlic and salt and pepper in 1 heated tablespoon olive oil while the aubergine slices are under the grill.

Next, simply place the aubergine slices in a dish, reserving one-third for the final layer. Add the seasoned, cooked tomato, another layer of aubergines and finally a layer of crème fraîche mixed with the remaining lemon juice, remaining raw sliced garlic, salt and pepper.

Sprinkle the Parmesan on top and bake for 20 minutes. Eat with warm bread and green salad – a ubiquitous choice, but unmatchable.

Serves 4

3 aubergines, sliced into 5-mm/^{1}/$_4$-inch thick slices, brushed with olive oil on one side and grilled on both

Juice of 1 lemon

1 beef tomato, chopped into 8 pieces

2 garlic cloves, thinly sliced

1 extra tbsp olive oil

6 tbsp crème fraîche

1 tbsp freshly grated Parmesan

Salt and freshly ground black pepper

Baby spinach with mango, crispy tofu and pink ginger cordial

I'm sorry but I've been raiding previous books again – some old favourites just go on and on and should be included in any Bible of Cranks recipes. This one, with its Pacific Rim overtones (or should that be undertones) needs to be made with sharp precise intention.

The flavours are unusual and the combinations unexpected, but you must aim for something scintillatingly fresh and alert, not a clashing mish-mash.

First dip the tofu slices into the tamari and set aside.

Heat 1 tablespoon olive oil in a frying pan. Add the tofu and sesame seeds and fry until the tofu is golden-brown all over, crisping up in places and amply covered in the seeds. Remove the tofu from the pan, adding any remaining sesame seeds to it.

Heat the rest of the olive oil in the same frying pan. Add the mango and quickly sauté for a few seconds on both sides so that it becomes beautifully seared and caramelised. Remove the mango and keep the pan to one side.

Toss the spinach quickly in a hot saucepan until it wilts, then squeeze out any excess liquid. Add the onion to the spinach, reserving some for garnish. Season lightly with salt and pepper and a dash of olive oil. Keep all the components warm while you make the dressing.

To the same frying pan that you used for the tofu and mango, add the ginger cordial or syrup and sugar and warm over a gentle heat until the sugar is completely dissolved and the liquid just begins to bubble, which will only take a minute or two. Quickly stir in the squeezed ginger juice and Tabasco. Remove from the heat.

To serve, divide the spinach between two plates. Top with the mango slices, the sesame-covered tofu and sprinkle with the reserved onion. Pour the dressing over and around and serve immediately.

Serves 2

275 g/10 oz firm tofu, cut into about 12 quite thick slices

1 tbsp tamari

2 tbsp olive oil, plus extra to finish

1 tbsp sesame seeds

1 smallish mango, ripe, sweet and firm, cut into about 12 slices

250 g/9 oz baby spinach, washed

Half a small red onion, sliced paper-thin

Sea salt and freshly ground black pepper

For the dressing

1 tbsp pink ginger cordial or syrup from a jar of preserved ginger

1 tbsp soft brown sugar

2-cm/1-inch piece of ginger, grated and squeezed, and the resulting liquid reserved

A dash of Tabasco

Chicory braised with sundried tomatoes and slivered garlic

I'm the only person in my (small) household who likes chicory but I give you a recipe for four because I live in hope. Maybe it is my *dosha* (Ayurvedic mind-body classification), but I often seem to crave a slight bitterness; even without exactly liking it, it seems to satisfy some deep need in me.

Sometimes I buy the chicory intending to create this recipe or something similar, only to find that I've devoured most of it on my way home. If you need to add sweetness to the bitter chicory flavour, add a tablespoon or two of crème fraîche at the last minute. A simpler way is to cut the chicory in half and braise the pieces in a little oil and water until they sear to golden and are coated in few spoons of syrupy sauce. You can do this on the stove or in the oven.

Slivers of garlic can go in with them. Walnuts, shelled and broken up, are the traditional addition, but sometimes just a good squeeze of lemon or a sharp dose of vinegar is all you need.

Remove any leaves that are not scintillatingly fresh from the chicory and cut into 4 long quarters.

Heat the olive oil in a heavy-bottomed pan and add the chicory. Fry for a few minutes until beginning to brown, then add the garlic and fry for a couple more minutes.

Add the water and bouillon powder. Bring to a fast boil, then reduce the heat to a steady simmer and cover with a lid. Braise for about 8 minutes, checking against burning or drying out.

Uncover and add the sundried tomatoes, cooking for a further couple of minutes until softened. The liquid should be reduced by a good half, but there should be enough deeply-flavoured sauce for you to mop up with bread or some simply cooked rice.

Stir in the basil leaves until wilted but remember to do this only at the last minute.

If using Gruyère, you can sprinkle on top and flash under a hot grill. With Parmesan you can simply sprinkle on top just before eating.

Serves 4

4 heads chicory, tightly packed and fresh looking

3 tbsp olive oil

4 garlic cloves, thinly sliced

250 ml/9 fl oz water with 2 tsp Marigold bouillon powder

8 pieces sundried tomatoes in oil

A small handful of basil leaves

40 g/1 1/2 oz freshly grated Parmesan or Gruyère (optional)

Sea salt and freshly ground black pepper

Grilled courgettes with Greek yoghurt and lemon

This has become one of my most oft-prepared summer vegetable dishes and the quantities are pretty generous because they get eaten in appreciative first, second and third helpings. I first got the idea from Claudia Roden but have changed some of the details.

Preheat the grill or a large griddle pan. Top and tail the courgettes, then slice lengthways – 5-mm/¼-inch thick. Brush the courgettes on both sides with olive oil and a little crushed sea salt. Spread out on a baking sheet and grill, or cook on the hot griddle, until pleasantly browned or charred on both sides. Transfer to a plate lined with a double layer of kitchen paper.

Meanwhile, mix the yoghurt with the lemon and garlic, adding the lemon a little at a time so as not to curdle the yoghurt and to stop before it's too runny.

Season the courgettes with salt and pepper and allow them to cool down a little (or the yoghurt will run). Then place them side by side, 4 or 5 slices at a time on a dinner plate or shallow serving dish, spooning on enough yoghurt to cover. Continue to layer like this until it is all used up.

Mint is the traditional garnish but, given the choice, I always opt for basil, so authenticity be damned. The pine nuts or pistachios are also my addition and they are meant to be only a gentle intrusion. Let the layers rest for a while if you can, even a few minutes makes them more sliceable than spoonable.

Serves 4

4 large or 6 medium courgettes

3 tbsp light olive oil

350 g/12 oz Greek yoghurt

Juice of half a small lemon

1 garlic clove, crushed

Fresh mint or basil to garnish

1 scant tbsp pine nuts, or pistachios, lightly toasted and, in the case of the pistachios, roughly broken

Sea salt and freshly ground black pepper

Courgette koftas with an almond and tomato sauce

Courgettes are funny vegetables. In themselves they are often not very special, either a little bland, or a little bitter. And yet, grilled they become sweet and succulent, dripping with juice. Or try briskly stir-frying them in the macrobiotic way – cutting across the courgette, at alternate 45-degree diagonals. This, by going with the direction of growth, is said to preserve the yin-yang ratio. I love the theory of macrobiotics, and though my cooking is a million miles away from the food usually served up in its name, I hope there is some of its spirit and balance there.

Seized and seared by the fierce heat, then splashed with tamari and generously sprinkled with toasted sesame seeds, courgettes take barely a minute to cook – as clear an expression of fresh, simple vegetable cooking as you could wish for. Or cut into slightly smaller chunks they can be fried in 1 tablespoon olive oil with a cleavered clove of garlic. To this you can add a bunch of top-and-tailed, blanched green beans, a heap of baby spinach leaves, even a deconstructed and wilted pak choi or two for an all green plate, either enhanced with tamari or with a little sundried tomato purée.

I can eat a whole bowlful with a handful of cooked quinoa or couscous scattered on top. If you want extra protein, add your favourite toasted seed or cheese – Mozzarella to melt into elastic thread, Ricotta to dissolve and soothe or Parmesan for a sweet sharp pucker.

Then there are these koftas, like super-sized Indian gnocchi, fragrant with the spicing of a different continent, a different sensibility. They have a delicacy all of their own. I am indebted to Julie Sahni for them. I can't say that I cook Indian food all that often these days. There are only so many meals a person can cook, much less eat, and I do have a life beyond the kitchen. But when I do and I feel that I need help, it is always to her that I turn. I lived in India for a year both in the south and right up in the Himalayas. Cooking was not high on my agenda in those days so unfortunately I brought back only olfactory memories. Julie Sahni decodes them into practical recipes for me (see her *Classic Indian Vegetarian Cooking*).

I have made the sauce alone and kept it refrigerated in a screw-top jar. It can be stirred into bean soups and purées and most usefully in a spontaneously conceived and executed laksa.

Serves 6

750 g/1 lb 11 oz courgettes, grated

1 medium onion, very finely chopped

90–100 g/3–4 oz chickpea flour

1 tsp paprika or red pepper flakes

2–4 hot green chillies or 2 bird's eye chillies, finely chopped

3 tbsp chopped fresh coriander

1/4 tsp baking powder

1 tsp sea salt

For deep-frying

Sunflower oil, about 1 litre/2 pints

For the sauce

6 medium tomatoes, roughly chopped

4–6 hot green chillies, or to your taste

4-cm/2-inch piece of ginger, grated and squeezed and the resulting liquid reserved

2 tsp ground cumin

1 tsp turmeric

3 tbsp ground almonds

2 tsp bright red paprika

2 tsp garam masala

A pinch of freshly grated nutmeg

6 tbsp groundnut or sunflower oil

A small bundle of fresh coriander

Salt

Squeeze the grated courgette of its excess liquid, one handful at a time. Then place all the kofta ingredients in a large bowl and mix well with your hands. Heat the oil in a large saucepan so it is about 6-cm/ 3-inches deep. Add more oil if necessary.

Use two tablespoons to drop the fragile mixture into the hot oil, a few koftas at a time. You can roll the mix in the palms of your lightly floured hands if you like, but it is best to lower the koftas into the oil with a spoon or heaven knows what danger you may face.

Turn them over carefully with two forks so that they are golden all over, which will take 2–3 minutes. Remove and drain on layers of kitchen paper. You can eat them as they are with salt and lemon juice or the cumin, coriander and garlic cream (see p271). It's a bit cross-cultural this one, but it works. A garlic-rich yoghurt is good too.

To make the sauce, start with the unusual step of blending the tomatoes, chilli, ginger and spices to a smooth purée. Salt to taste.

Heat the oil in a frying pan and add it all in. Fry over a quite high heat for a few minutes, stirring all the time, then lower the heat and simmer for 30–35 minutes or so adding about 125 ml/4 fl oz water to loosen the sauce and more as the sauce cooks. Julie Sahni says you should let the sauce rest for several hours or overnight, then measure it, topping it up with water if necessary so that you have 800 ml/1½ pints. Since I cook it for longer than she recommends, use more tomatoes and add water while the whole thing cooks, I am able to avoid this step.

When the sauce is hot, gently add the koftas and heat together for 3–4 minutes. Garnish with fresh coriander, leaves plucked off the stalks, and serve with warm naan bread or Basmati rice, egg-fried or plain. I also serve plain yoghurt as a cooling agent next to the chilli.

Additions

There is no garlic in the original Brahmin recipe as it is forbidden to them, but if your conscience lets you, add a finely minced clove to the sauce. I have added grated paneer to the kofta mix and even about 200 g/ 7 oz grated Haloumi – making the koftas even lighter and more delicious.

Alternatives

The sauce is fantastic as a dip for raw vegetables or with cannellini bean purée and served with warm flour tortillas.

If you can't be bothered to make the koftas, you can fry the courgette mix like a thin Indian farinata (see p179). It will make two, fried in 1 tablespoon oil in a frying pan set over a medium heat for about 5 minutes on each side. Make sure to cook on both sides.

Tamari

People always rail at me for referring to this obscure word. Why can't I say soy sauce like everybody else? Why? Because tamari is what I use, of course.

Ok, so it's basically soy sauce but with the proviso that it is wheat free. Now this isn't for some fanatical exclusion diet, but because I sincerely prefer the taste. It is purer, as was originally intended before commercialism set in, is deeper, darker, fuller, richer and can be diluted to suit the vagaries of your palate or the dish in question or simply used with a more conscious hand.

Tamari is always available in health-food shops and finally, 23 years after I first started using it, it is available in supermarkets. Buy the biggest bottle of it you can: it works out less expensively and keeps forever. And don't restrict it to Asian recipes. A drop here and there adds body, depth and character to just about everything.

OTHER RECIPES USING TAMARI

Griddled fat asparagus spears with sesame seeds and tamari 42

A spinach soup with a page-full of alternatives 75

A vegetarian gravy 76

Broccoli sautéed with shiitake mushrooms and tofu 91

Green beans with butternut squash, goat's cheese and a maple syrup glaze 111

Mushroom Wellington 127

Field mushrooms with black polenta 134

A stupendously good vegetable brochette 152

Rice bites 235

Tamari, lemon and balsamic dressing, with chilli and garlic 278

Griddled filled courgettes with Ricotta, almonds and tomato sauce

There are not many occasions where I wouldn't find these eminently suitable. So please don't throw up your hands in horror with the adage that life's too short to stuff a mushroom (let alone a hollowed-out courgette) emblazoned on your psyche like a curse. The filling is childishly easy to make, so is the sauce. And the coring, either with a small knife or an apple corer, is no great chore either.

Choose medium-sized courgettes about 4 cm/2 inches in diameter and cut them in half so you end up with stumpier tubes. I like to season the hollowed-out tubes before filling them, so I push oil, salt and pepper into them with my index finger, then stuff them full to overflowing.

Preheat the oven to 200°C/400°F/gas mark 6.

Cut the courgettes in half to make two tubes, hollow out the flesh and chop it roughly. Heat half the oil in a pan and fry the shallots and garlic. Add the chopped courgette flesh. Soften for 7 minutes on a medium heat, stirring often.

Stir in the Ricotta, Parmesan, bouillon powder, chopped almonds, breadcrumbs and herbs, and season with salt and pepper.

Season the courgette tubes inside and out with salt, pepper and oil. Then stand them on a board like soldiers and push the filling into them, using a teaspoon and your thumb.

Heat the remaining oil in a griddle pan. Fry the courgettes all the way round till the skin starts to char, shrivel and visibly soften and bits of the cheese are slipping out into the pan forming crisp to nutty delectable golden nuggets.

To make the sauce, heat the second lot of oil in a frying pan. Add the garlic and onion and soften until translucent. Add the tomatoes and fry for about 8 minutes. I leave the skins on but you can blanch the tomatoes in boiling water first for a minute and remove them, chopping them and removing the seeds at the same time. Do catch all the juices though and add these to the tomatoes. When the sauce is nearly ready, add the chopped olives. Season to taste.

Transfer the sauce to an ovenproof dish and place the hot griddled courgettes on top. Place in the preheated oven for 10 minutes or so, so that the whole dish comes together bubbling hot. Scatter a few basil leaves over the top and serve extra Parmesan on the side if you like.

Serves 4

3 courgettes, long, generous but not fat (they'll weigh about 500 g/ 1 lb 2 oz between them)

4 tbsp olive oil and more for the insides

2 shallots, finely chopped

1 garlic clove, finely chopped

100 g/4 oz Ricotta

1 tbsp freshly grated Parmesan, plus extra for serving

$1/2$ tsp Marigold bouillon powder

30 g/1 oz whole almonds, roasted for 8 minutes and chopped into thin slivers

2 tbsp fresh white breadcrumbs

1 tbsp chopped fresh basil or $1/2$ tbsp basil, $1/2$ tbsp chives

Sea salt and freshly ground black pepper

For the sauce

4–6 tbsp olive oil

2 garlic cloves, finely chopped

1 small red onion, finely chopped

500 g/1 lb 2 oz tomatoes, roughly chopped

8 black olives, stoned and chopped (optional)

Salt and freshly ground black pepper

To serve

A few small basil leaves

Both the Romans and the ancient Greeks held fennel in a hallowed place and used it extensively in their cooking. Wild fennel is grown for its seed, sweet fennel also for its seeds and leaves which are used as a herb and in infusions.

The round, compact, bulbous vegetable is also called *finocchio* or Florence fennel and it is this we eat as a vegetable. It is widely used by the Italians, the French are fond of it and it is used prominently in various parts of the Middle East. Fennel's flavour is mildly aniseed when raw, but this is greatly softened by gentle braising. It is reputed to be both a digestif and a diuretic, and its seed is a component of gripe water, given to soothe the delicate stomachs of babies. I love it.

I recently picked up some cheap horoscope gismo in a bookshop and turned to Aquarian foods. There they all were, my passions spelled out, fennel and cumin among them. I can't escape.

It makes wonderful, fresh, crisp salads, old-fashioned creamy soups, elegant risotti, robust sautées, succulent braises and delicate gratins. It is good sliced thin and griddled until lightly charred, then oiled and lemoned, and it roasts beautifully with aubergines, red peppers, courgettes and a little balsamic vinegar. I'm thrilled to see how it has gained in popularity over the last few years having previously gone into undeserved decline. This is the Age of Aquarius after all.

OTHER RECIPES USING FENNEL

Carpaccio of fennel with black olives and tomato

The fennel in this recipe needs to be paper-thin or as close to it as possible. I use the cheapest of plastic vegetable slicers, but a mandolin would work a dream as would the thinnest blade attachment on your food processor.

In the same vein, I make another salad with baby courgettes, sliced similarly delicately and mixed with paper-thin red onion and thin to transparent radish slices. (200 g/7 oz baby courgettes, 1 small red onion, a handful of radishes, dressed as below.) A mound of each is a sharp summer starter, dressed in a light vinaigrette, and with the vegetables well marinated until soft. Only the tomatoes and black olives have to be added at the end.

Slice the fennel lengthways into very thin slices and arrange them on a summery plate.

Pour the mixed dressing ingredients on top at least 1 hour before you want to serve the salad and store it at room temperature, unless it is a very hot day, in which case bring it out of the fridge a good half hour before you need it.

Scatter the tomato crescents, the minced garlic and the black olives all over and eat soon.

Serves 4

2 fennel bulbs, fronds and tough bits removed

4 tomatoes, about 300 g/11 oz, ripe but firm, quartered, deseeded and sliced into thinnish crescents (reserve the juice)

2 garlic cloves, finely minced

50 g/scant 2 oz black olives, stoned and thinly sliced

For the dressing

2 tbsp good-quality wine vinegar

Reserved juice from the tomatoes

4 tbsp extra virgin olive oil

Sea salt and freshly ground black pepper

Fennel braised with tomatoes and Pernod

The idea for this recipe owes nothing to me at all. I stole it lock stock and barrel from Annie Bell who got it from French chef Alain Ducasse.

All I have done is tweak it here and there. I stew the sauce a little longer than she does, use vine tomatoes instead of small and add garlic – how can I not? I leave it sweet and delicate and serve it with roasted new potatoes or a new potato salad (Jersey Royal by preference), with the skins removed and turned gently in 2 tablespoons of watercress pesto (see p266). At the end I add a handful of shredded Gruyère, like fine-tangled silk threads, in a feather-light heap on top of the tomatoes. I put the lid back on the pot again and let the cheese meld with them.

Preheat the oven to 200°C/400°F/gas mark 6.

Take half of the tomatoes and cut them in half. Drizzle over 2 tablespoons olive oil and crush some sea salt over them. Then add a twist of ground black pepper. Place on a baking tray in the oven until the skins shrink and the juices are concentrated, sticky and sweet.

Meanwhile, roughly chop the rest of the tomatoes and blend them until smooth – they should look pale, almost pink, and lush. Rub them through a fine sieve and collect the slippery juices in a bowl.

Trim the fennel bulbs and keep the fronds aside for use later. Cut the bulb through the top and then into even strips.

Heat the remaining olive oil in a heavy-bottomed pan. Add the garlic, turning until it becomes transparent and then add the fennel, crammed-in and well seasoned with salt and pepper.

Holding the lid tightly on the pan, give it a good shake and then leave the fennel to soften on its own for 5–6 minutes. Then add the tomato juice, season again and simmer for another 10 minutes until the fennel is soft and dressed in the thick sauce.

Remove the roasted tomatoes from the oven and place them over the fennel. Warm the Pernod in a ladle over a gas flame, or in a small saucepan. As soon as it ignites, pour it on to the tomatoes (it helps if you have an audience, so you can marvel together) and wait for the flames to subside before adding the Gruyère, replacing the lid and waiting a while.

Serve with new potatoes, simply buttered or as described above or with some warmed crusty French bread. Hand around the olive oil for those who want more.

Serves 4

750 g/1 lb 11 oz vine tomatoes

4 tbsp extra virgin olive oil, plus extra for serving

1 large fennel bulb or 2 smaller ones, white and firm with healthy fronds

1 large garlic clove, finely sliced

60 ml/2 fl oz Pernod

60 g/2 oz Gruyère, finely grated

Sea salt and freshly ground black pepper

Fennel gratin

My unending passion for fennel reveals itself again. Even here, where it is covered in cream, I feel sure that its digestive properties shine through. Braising is a two-way process – the taste of the vegetables into the sauce, the sauce flavour into the vegetables – and the result is so much greater than the sum of its parts. The fennel can be as soft as can be – don't fall into the trap of thinking it needs bite – this is vegetable in soothing mode.

Heat half of the olive oil in a heavy-bottomed pan and fry the trimmed fennel quarters over a fairly high heat until they turn golden in places. Cover with the remaining oil, garlic and stock. Bring to the boil, reduce the heat to low and simmer gently for 10–12 minutes or until the fennel is tender, the liquid reduced by three-quarters to a syrupy sauce.

Meanwhile, sauté the mushrooms, if using, in a little light olive oil. Add a dash of tamari when they are nearly done and set aside.

Now, turn your grill on high and, while it is heating up, stir the cream into the fennel, bring back to the boil and immediately remove from the heat.

Stir in the mushrooms, if using. Sprinkle with the grated Parmesan and place under the hot grill until just bubbling. Serve at once.

Serves 2

5 tbsp light olive oil, plus a little extra

2 fennel bulbs, cut in 4 lengthways

2 garlic cloves, finely sliced

300 ml/10 fl oz hot vegetable stock, made with $1/2$ tsp Marigold bouillon powder

60 g/2 oz chestnut mushrooms, finely sliced (optional)

A dash of tamari (for the mushrooms)

100 ml/$3^1/2$ fl oz double cream

30 g/1 oz Parmesan, grated

Grilled vegetables in a ring or rough and ready

It's a sad fact that we are influenced by fashion in food as in all else, even when we think we are not. The only freedom is in wearing, eating and sitting on what suits you, but that is unbelievably difficult to do given all the ego-driven manifestations to the contrary.

So if you can live with the deep unfashionability of this ring, please make it. If you can't, then place the vegetables abundantly on a large plate in a laid-back and unpretentious style, or so the theory goes.

Marinate the Mozzarella slices in a third of the olive oil with salt, pepper, Tabasco and some of the crushed garlic. Set aside.

Make the sauce by stirring the olive oil into the sundried tomato purée, then adding the warm water, Tabasco, balsamic vinegar and basil leaves.

Preheat the grill. Baste all the vegetables, except the peppers, with the remaining olive oil and sprinkle with salt, pepper and the remaining crushed garlic. Lay the aubergine slices on a baking tray and grill on both sides until well-browned. Repeat with the fennel, then the courgettes and the spring onions. Take care with the latter as they brown quickly.

Place all the vegetables in a bowl, add the balsamic vinegar and allow to cool.

Layer the vegetables inside a 25-cm/10-inch ring mould. Begin with the aubergine slices so that the sides are well covered and there is some overhang; reserve a few for the final layer. Follow with the sliced Mozzarella and the rest of the vegetables, completing with the courgettes and peppers as the final layers. Fold any protruding aubergines over and finish with the remaining slices. Press the vegetables down and refrigerate for several hours.

Place an upturned plate on top of the mould and turn so the plate is right-side up. Carefully remove the ring – when you cut into the vegetables, the many colours will be revealed. Garnish with loosely scattered basil leaves and serve with the sauce, chunks of olive bread and green and black olives.

Serves 6–8

2 Mozzarella cheeses, cut into 8 slices each

125 ml/4 fl oz olive oil

A dash of Tabasco

3 garlic cloves, crushed

2 large aubergines, cut into 5-mm/ 1/4-inch slices

2 bulbs fennel, cut into 5-mm/ 1/4-inch slices

3 medium courgettes, cut lengthways into thick slices

2 bunches spring onions, trimmed

2 red and 2 yellow peppers, grilled, peeled and cut into 6 pieces (*see* p14)

1 tbsp balsamic vinegar

Salt and freshly ground black pepper

Basil leaves, for garnish

For the sauce

100 ml/3 1/2 fl oz olive oil

100 g/4 oz very red sundried tomato purée

4 tbsp warm water

A dash of Tabasco

A dash of balsamic vinegar

A few small basil leaves

Spring vegetables with butter, lemon and parsley

Spring heralds all manner of young, sprightly, snappy vegetables requiring little that is rich or elaborate. Baby courgettes and baby carrots, the size of a finger, young delicate asparagus, marble-sized turnips, skinny leeks barely bigger than a scallion, finger-nail-size broad beans, peas succulently sweet and tiny Jersey Royal potatoes.

You need do hardly more than plunge them, suitably cut, hard ones first, into a pot of salted water all of a frantic boil or even steam them. Then drain and toss them in plenty of butter, lemon juice, snipped chives or finely chopped parsley, sea salt and freshly ground black pepper. If you want to give the vegetables a more Mediterranean feel, crumble a few dried saffron threads on to the cooked vegetables and the hot water that clings to them, replace the butter with olive oil, add a little freshly minced garlic and sprinkle with a few lightly toasted cumin seeds. Otherwise, enjoy these clean, hopeful young vegetables in all simplicity.

Start with a large pan of salted boiling water and plunge in the potatoes, moments after the carrots and whole garlic cloves, if using. They should become butter soft. Then after 4 minutes or so, add the rest of the vegetables for little more than another few minutes, Test that they are ready before draining well in a colander.

Meanwhile make the sauce by placing the butter, lemon juice, herb or herbs of your choice, salt, pepper and honey, if using, in a summery bowl and immediately add the hot vegetables. Toss carefully and serve at once in generous mounds on top of the watercress and wild rocket mixed together.

A bowl of fromage frais or soft goat's cheese is pleasantly easy and makes a light lunch of this bright plate.

Serves 4

200 g/ 7 oz Jersey Royal potatoes, scrubbed

2 bunches baby carrots, trimmed, left whole if tiny enough or peeled and cut on the diagonal

6 garlic cloves (optional)

200 g/ 7 oz baby courgette, trimmed and cut on the diagonal

150 g/ 5 oz young, fresh peas

150 g/ 5 oz baby broad beans

1 bunch skinny leeks, trimmed

2 bundles asparagus, trimmed

For the sauce

50 g/2 oz butter

Juice of half a small lemon

1 small handful parsley or chives, chopped very finely

Sea salt and freshly ground black pepper

1 tsp honey (optional)

To serve

100 g/4 oz watercress

100 g/4 oz wild rocket

Oven-dried tomatoes with sea salt and olive oil

I recommend vine tomatoes for this recipe as they are usually redder, juicier and sweeter than others, so often picked unripe. Besides I cannot think of a better way to cook a tomato.

Preheat the oven to 150°C/300°F/gas mark 2.

Generously coat the tomato pieces with the other ingredients and place them cut side up in an oven tray to roast for up to 1¹/₂ hours until very soft. Then switch off and leave in the oven to cool.

In an airtight container, they will keep for a couple of weeks in the fridge. Use them in sauces and salads or add to pasta. You can either leave them as they are to brighten up a rocket pesto linguine (see p209) for instance, or blend them to a rough sauce in their own right.

Alternatives

Add about 125 g/4¹/₂ oz Ricotta to half the quantity of tomatoes and serve with pasta.

A spoonful or two of double cream added to the deeply flavoured tomato paste makes an easy but 'classy' sauce.

Or, just blend with a handful of pine nuts or 8 tablespoons of basil pesto – this will dress pasta for about eight.

Serves 4

850 g/1 lb 14 oz vine tomatoes, halved, or quartered if they are a larger size

6 tbsp olive oil

3 tbsp balsamic vinegar

1 tsp sea salt flakes

1 tsp dried basil

2 garlic cloves, finely minced

A pinch of soft brown sugar

autumn &
winter
vegetables

autumn & winter recipes

The colder seasons are a perfect invitation to patient braises, comforting food and good old-fashioned stodge – which doesn't have to mean an endless round of carrots, cabbage and potatoes. Turn East, near and far, for intense, hot, blood-warming spices and take a fresh look at the weird and wonderful – celeriac, Jerusalem artichokes, pumpkins and squashes, even the under-estimated beetroot and turnip. Marvel and be cosseted as prosaic fare turns to manna. This is the time for convivial lunches; linger over mile high pies, soups, cobblers, fragrant apples and pears, contorted tubers, honey-sweet roots and woodsy wild fungi.

Celeriac soup with bouillabaisse seasonings and rouille

This is an extravagant soup with an incredible depth of flavour. Served with Gruyère toasts and rouille it's also quite substantial.

Occasionally I remember a certain flavour, associated with a long-ago meat or fish dish, and realise that an important part of that flavour is still available to me in the guise of aromatics and other seasonings. I then seek to create a version which 'hits the spot' in the same way.

Some vegetarians don't feel right about doing this, it's a bit like wearing fake fur. I don't like meat substitutes or our instinctive carniverous hauntings, but there are times when the taste memory is so deeply ingrained that it fuels a zealot's search. It might take hours to mix, but like searching for the perfect colour once you've got it you know. Don't despair at the long list of ingredients – prep time is minimal.

To dry the orange peel, place it as thinly peeled as possible in a medium hot oven for about 40 minutes. It will release a wonderful essential oil.

Heat 3 tablespoons olive oil in a large, heavy-bottomed saucepan and fry the cleaned sliced leeks. Then add the carrot, sliced garlic, red pepper and black pepper. Fry for about 10 minutes until the vegetables yield and soften.

Next, add the fennel seeds, orange peel, saffron, tomato purée, soft brown sugar, celeriac and chopped basil and fry for about 5 minutes until the celeriac is well coated in all the aromatics.

Add the hot stock and 1 tablespoon olive oil. Stir well and cook on a brisk simmer for 30–35 minutes until the celeriac is completely soft.

Around 7 or 8 minutes before the end, stir the wine and 2 tablespoons chopped parsley into the pot.

Blend most of the soup until very smooth, first in a blender and then through a fine sieve. Then add the remaining soup so there are some chunky pieces. Return the soup to the pan and stir in the remaining parsley and olive oil as well as the double cream if using. The soup should be voluptuous in texture and flavour.

Adjust the seasoning and let the soup rest and ease into its full flavour. Serve with the toasts topped with the threaded Gruyère, and with spoonfuls of rouille (*see* p278) and see how this brings it to life.

Serves 6

8 pieces dried orange peel (from about half an orange)

6 tbsp extra virgin olive oil, plus extra to serve

2 thin leeks, cleaned and sliced

1 carrot, peeled and chopped

8 garlic cloves, thinly sliced

1 small red pepper (about 150 g/ 5 oz), chopped

1 tbsp fennel seeds

1 tsp saffron threads

1 tsp tomato purée

1 tsp soft brown sugar

1 large head celeriac (about 1 kg/ $2^1/4$ lb), peeled and chopped into 3-cm/$1^1/2$-inch pieces

2 litres/ 4 pints vegetable stock made with 1 tbsp Marigold bouillon powder, plus extra if necessary

250 ml/9 fl oz dry white wine

6 tbsp finely chopped parsley

2 tbsp double cream (optional)

Half a very fresh baguette or ficelle, cut into rounds and lightly toasted

60 g/2 oz Gruyère, freshly grated

Sea salt and freshly ground black pepper

Cauliflower and corn chowder

I wish I could claim a connection between this and the first chowders, cooked in clay pots by wandering immigrants to the New World. But at least the soup is rich, pale and creamy, all requisites of the original, stuffed full of clams though that may be.

Buttered crackers would take you a step closer, but slices of toast cut thinly from a wholemeal loaf are delicious to break into small pieces and dunk into the soup. It is endlessly soothing with an underlying sharp high note that keeps you on your toes.

Discard the outer leaves from the cauliflower (young tender leaves can be kept) and break the cauliflower into smallish florets.

Heat three-quarters of the butter in a large pan, watching that it does not brown. Fry the onion and leek, if using, until transparent, then add the garlic and cauliflower florets. Fry for 5 minutes on a medium heat, stirring all the time.

Then cover with the hot stock and simmer quite rapidly for about 15 minutes until the cauliflower is soft but not mushy. Although you are going to blend it, you want to preserve all its flavour and some of its texture.

Blend with a hand-held whisk until smooth though with a touch of grainy texture to it.

Stir in the sweetcorn (keeping a little back for garnish), Dijon mustard, cream, salt, pepper, nutmeg and half the sorrel. Stir well and simmer very gently for another 10 minutes or so, adding a little stock or hot water if it seems to be going too thick.

Finally transfer to a soup tureen and stir in the remaining butter. Sprinkle over the rest of the sorrel, more grated nutmeg, the spring onions or chives, if using, and seasoning.

Serves 4–6

1 medium cauliflower

40 g/1^1/$_2$ oz butter

1 medium onion, roughly chopped

1 leek, trimmed and finely sliced (optional)

3 or 4 garlic cloves, thinly sliced

750 ml/1^1/$_4$ pints vegetable stock, made with Marigold bouillon powder if you wish

200 g/7 oz frozen sweetcorn or the kernels from 2 cobs

1 tsp Dijon mustard

2 generous tbsp double cream

A grating of fresh nutmeg

1 sorrel leaf, shredded (optional)

2 spring onions, finely sliced, or a few snipped chives (optional)

Salt and freshly ground black pepper

Sensational sweetcorn

If you are using fresh sweetcorn, blanch it for a couple of minutes first and then fry it in a spoonful of sunflower oil so it catches brown in places. Frozen sweetcorn does not need to be blanched but is greatly improved by this almost dry-frying method. Add it to the creamy soup, reserving some for the garnish.

Soupe à l'oignon flambé

I promised myself that I wouldn't include any recipe in this book, the introduction for which couldn't begin with the words 'I love this'. So here goes, I love this. I just love it.

Peel the onions and slice them very thinly. Place a large pan over a gentle heat and melt the butter and oil. Fry the onions for about 15 minutes in the lidded pan until soft, golden and shiny. Then sprinkle with the salt, pepper and sugar and stir for a few more minutes, by which time the onion will be a deeper, darker more fulgent gold.

Add the hot stock and then the tamari, Tabasco and wine. Simmer with a loosely fitting lid on top for about 45 minutes, the ever richer aroma filling every nook of your house.

Preheat the oven to 200°C/400°F/gas mark 6. Slice the ficelle or baguette into rounds and toast them in the hot oven for a few minutes until they are just crisping up and turning a delicate shade of gold.

In an ideal world, you'll be able to turn the soup into a warmed earthenware tureen or into individual pots, each with its own lid and add a scant sprinkling of herbs if you wish.

Float the bread slices on top, sprinkle with cheese, dot with butter and place under a hot grill for a couple of minutes to melt, bubble and brown gently.

Warm the brandy and set a match to it. You can pour a little on to each serving or into the tureen. I sort of pour it around the cheese floats. I've heard a rumour that you can't flambé if you are putting cheese on top. Poppycock! It is alight so gently and fleetingly that the toasts are barely tinged by the blue flames.

Serves 4

700 g/1 lb 9 oz onions

40 g/1^1/$_2$ oz butter, plus extra for the bread

1 tbsp olive oil

1 scant tsp soft brown sugar

Salt and freshly ground black pepper

2 litres/4 pints good strong stock

A dash of tamari

A dash of Tabasco

175 ml/6 fl oz dry white wine

1 ficelle or baguette

150 g/5 oz Gruyère

6 tbsp brandy

Herbes de Provence or oregano (optional)

Parsley soup

There's not much point in attempting this with those mean-spirited little packets containing a small handful of parsley and a fistful of plastic. The whole point is to grab the opportunity when you come across a gargantuan bunch. Mine was a whopping 540 g/1 lb 3oz before removing the toughest of the stalks. In fact that only left 175 g/6 oz but that's still a mountain when it comes to parsley. Weigh your bunches and reckon on losing about half, though you'll use that in the stock.

This is so quick to make that I suggest you do so soon before serving, as reheating does not do it any favours. Like other green things it will oxidise and turn black, which is a great pity when you see the fabulous colour it starts off with.

I rather like a spoon of thick Greek yoghurt with this.

To make the stock bring to the boil gently and simmer for at least an hour before straining and using. Also good as a hot drink.

To make the soup heat the butter in a large pan and fry the potatoes and garlic over a low heat for about 15 minutes, stirring occasionally until they are nearly soft.

Add the parsley and pour the stock over, a ladleful at a time. Add the bouillon and simmer for another 10–15 minutes depending on how thick the leaves are, as they might wilt in seconds or take longer.

When the potatoes are completely tender and the parsley quite collapsed, blend smooth and adjust the seasoning. I always end up adding a dollop of crème fraîche or thick yoghurt to a bowl of this but it's up to you. Buttered rye bread, not too dark, is perfect for mopping up.

Serves 4

60 g/2 oz butter

300 g/11 oz potatoes, cut into chunks

2 garlic cloves, finely chopped

175 g/6 oz parsley leaves

12 ladles parsley stock

1 tsp Marigold bouillon powder

Salt and freshly ground black pepper

For the stock

The parsley stalks

1 onion, chopped

1 carrot, peeled and chopped

3 whole garlic cloves

Water to cover

A spinach soup with a page-full of alternatives

I am rarely without spinach. At least one bag of the ready-washed baby leaf goes into my weekly shopping trolley so this soup is a regular, usually last-minute, occurrence. It can take 101 embellishments, with things that could all be described as common-or-garden store-cupboard staples. If the worst comes to the worst (and if that's the worse it gets, things can't be that bad), there's always frozen leaf spinach, crammed beside the frozen petits pois and the frozen broad beans.

I go for the ready-washed bags these days. I know that if I don't the spinach will stay there all week, slowly rotting away and end up in the bin.

Besides there's so much wastage with the stuff that seems cheaper, so buying the fuss-free, lazy kind is a win-win solution. Like the watercress soup (*see* p20) this demands to be eaten *prontissimo*.

Serves 2–4

1 litre/2 pints light vegetable stock or water and Marigold bouillon powder

2 tbsp light olive oil

1 small onion, chopped

2 garlic cloves, finely slivered

1 bag, usually 225 g/8 oz ready-washed baby spinach

A pinch of grated nutmeg

Salt, or Herbarmare (herb salt, *see* p362), and freshly ground black pepper

Set your stock to boil, even if it's only composed of water and bouillon powder, so that you can add it to the spinach already boiling hot. You want the green chlorophyll trapped in by the searing heat, not allowed to leach out slowly while the soup comes to the boil.

Heat the oil in a large pan and fry the chopped onion and garlic until transparent. Add the spinach and stir quickly to wilt in the heat.

Add a ladleful of the boiling stock and blend. This is a soup that can take quite a bit of rough with the smooth so don't get too carried away. Add the rest of the boiling liquid, adjust the seasoning with salt or Herbamare, pepper, and nutmeg. Simmer for a few minutes to concentrate the flavours and serve.

Alternatives

Add a drained 400g/14 oz tin borlotti or cannellini beans to the soup and heat through. Fry 4 finely sliced chestnut mushrooms in a minimum of hot oil until browned and dry. Season with half a teaspoon tamari, fry a little longer and add just before serving.

Replace 400 ml/14 fl oz of the stock with a tin of unsweetened coconut milk, a finely chopped lemongrass stick, a dash tamari and the same of Tabasco.

Add a generous gloop of mascarpone and the zest of 1 lemon.

Add a handful of arborio rice to the fried onion, simmer gently in the stock for about 20 minutes before adding the spinach. Finish with transparent shavings of Parmesan.

Grate some strong Cheddar or Caerphilly into a tub of Ricotta, together with finely shredded Parmesan, some toasted almond slivers and a spoonful of chopped chives. Shape into quenelles with 2 spoons and plop one on top of each serving.

Add a diced potato (or a chunk of butternut squash or a sweet potato) and fry with the onion until tender before adding the spinach and stock.

Fry thin slices of tamari-marinated tofu and place on top.

Melt Gruyère on to rounds of baguette and float on top.

Add a handful of orso (the pasta that looks like rice) to the hot stock, again before adding the spinach.

Add spoonfuls of thick Greek yoghurt and finely sliced spring onion.

Use a mixture of some of the above.

I think that will do for now, though I'll probably think of another 20 or so variations, and so will you.

A vegetarian gravy

To make the gravy, melt the butter in a large frying pan set over a delicate flame. There must be no browning whatsoever. Then soften the shallot, garlic and carrot for a few minutes, stirring steadily all the while with a wooden spoon.

Now add the dark stock, into which you have first reconstituted the dried porcini and continue to stir, for a moment quite vigorously, then more lazily, though no less attentively, adding the red wine and tamari at any time. This leasurely activity lasts a good few minutes by which time the sauce is reduced slightly to a glisten.

In the last few moments, add the sugar – it's a tiny amount, hardly more than a pinch but it makes all the round difference, especially once you have added the chilli and black pepper.

When satisfied that the sauce tastes just right, stir in the arrowroot dissolved first in 1 tablespoon cold stock or water and continue to stir until no trace of flouriness remains.

It is now ready to serve with a pie or Wellington, or simply a plateful of stickily, crispily starchy, well-roasted roots.

Serves 2–4

50g butter

1 shallot, very finely chopped

1 garlic clove, finely sliced

1 very small carrot, thinly sliced

200 ml/7 fl oz dark vegetable stock

Several pieces dried porcini

1 dsp tamari

1/2 tsp soft brown sugar

50 ml/2 fl oz red wine

A small piece red chilli, chopped to a fine speck

1/2 tsp arrowroot

A few chives, very finely snipped

1–2 basil leaves (optional)

Freshly ground black pepper

Six potato salads

I don't really know what makes these qualify as salads, as none of them are served cold, but I suppose it's the fact that the uncooked seasonings are all simply added to the cooked potatoes, rather than cooked with them. Left-over potato salads I tend to throw into a pan with a little hot oil and fry into a kind of rough rösti, breaking them up with a wooden spoon and even turning them over on to the other side. At the very least, I leave any left-overs out in the kitchen, covered with a clean tea towel to eat the next day. Fridge-cold potato salads are a big no no.

with celery and capers

Let the cooked potatoes cool down slightly and mix gently with the rest of the ingredients. This is also successful and more traditional made with old potatoes, cut into chunks. Scrub the skins well and remove them altogether if they seem tough.

Serves 4

500 g/1 lb 2 oz new potatoes

3 tbsp thick, homemade mayonnaise

Salt and freshly ground black pepper

1 stick celery, finely sliced

1 tbsp capers (optional)

with olive oil

Boil 500 g/1 lb 2 oz potatoes for longer than you might think clever so that they are on the edge of breakdown.

Turn them out into a bowl, pour olive oil on top and roughly continue their onslaught with a fork, lots of sea salt and freshly ground pepper. They will be broken but not destroyed.

Shred some basil on to them or a few leaves of coriander or some finely sliced spring onion. Serve at once.

with chives, lemon and garlic

You hardly need a method for this, just don't forget that the potatoes need to be tender right the way through. Drain them well and toss them into a bowl into which you have already poured the cream, salt, pepper and chives. Stir well and serve.

I love this dish with the lemon, which you can use alone or with the garlic. Or you can use the garlic on its own. And you can replace the cream with extra virgin olive oil if you prefer. That's just one recipe, but even that is like a lexicon – see how many variations you can come up with, given a limited number of ingredients.

Serves 2–4

500 g/1 lb 2 oz small new potatoes

5 tbsp single cream

Sea salt and freshly ground black pepper

Snipped chives, lots

Juice of half a small lemon (optional)

1 small garlic clove, very finely chopped (optional)

with green beans and feta

Cook the potatoes.

Meanwhile, top and tail the green beans and blanch them until they still have a little bite. Refresh them immediately under cold water and add them to the cooked, drained potatoes.

Toss the feta into all this and pour on as much olive oil as you are happy with (*ie* lots). Crush salt and grind black pepper on top. A grilled and peeled red pepper, well cleaned and sliced into sinuous strips is good in this salad too. Green beans, grilled red pepper, feta, olive oil and a dash of balsamic vinegar, with or without a few fresh walnuts is one of my favourite salads.

Serves 4

500 g/1 lb 2 oz new potatoes

200 g/7 oz green beans

150g/5 oz feta cheese, roughly broken up

Extra virgin olive oil

Sea salt and freshly ground black pepper

with Moorish overtones

This recipe features in *Cranks Fast Food* (C&C, 2000) and is quite a departure from anything you would usually associate with a potato salad, so I don't mind including it here again.

Apart from being an obvious easy lunch, I think it is best served as part of a mezze platter. This can include quickly prepared items such as spinach, raisins and almonds (*see* p141); oven-dried tomatoes (*see* p64); green salad (*see* p22); smoked aubergines (*see* p47); or simply a plate of grilled peppers, doused in lemon juice, olive oil and crushed garlic. There are lots of possibilities.

You need a floury potato such as King Edward, which is all the better to absorb the dressing with. Serve warm, with a slab of feta cheese, cut into thin morsels to place on top of each potato slice. Serve with tiny dabs of harissa for a potato salad with pep.

Boil the potatoes in plenty of salted water until they are very soft and are almost at breaking point. Drain well. Put them in a bowl and pour over the olive oil, add the coriander and season with salt and pepper. Mix very gently.

Lay the potato slices flat on a plate and pour the excess olive oil dressing on top. Sprinkle with paprika.

Toast the cumin seeds for a few seconds in a dry frying pan and let these be your finishing touch.

Serves 2

2 large potatoes, cut into slices about 1-cm/1/2-inch thick

3 tbsp olive oil, quite green and rough

A small handful of coriander leaves, chopped

Sea salt and freshly ground black pepper

A pinch of paprika

1/2 tsp cumin seeds

To serve

Olive oil for frying

2 or more flour tortillas

Feta cheese, cut into slabs

Harissa

To serve, make a quick imitation of a real Arabic bread (or *melawah*) that is difficult to find and notoriously difficult to make (or so I had always been told). In fact, it is really a fried disc of puff pastry, but I think I rather prefer this less oily version. Heat a little olive oil in a frying pan and fry the tortillas for about 30 seconds on either side until they puff like a gigantic Indian pouri – mottled brown, gold and even black. With the feta cheese, oil-drenched potatoes and the harissa you'll be transported to the Middle East in one mouthful.

I like to take it one slice at a time, a thin slab of feta on top and a dash of harissa on top of that.

with watercress pesto

Believe me when I say there are times when your potatoes need to be as smooth and white as an egg. So even if you have scrubbed them first, once they are fully tender and you can taste their soft waxiness, remove any shred of skin that remains, even if it means burning your fingers a little. Just blow and carry on. It is so worth it.

You just need 500 g/1 lb 2 oz new potatoes, the new-season crop of Jersey Royals would be the very best you can do here, scrubbed clean and boiled in a pan with plenty of salt until as soft and pale as described. Cut them in perfect half ovoids and dress them gently in a couple of tablespoons of the watercress pesto (*see* p266).

Four peoplw will eat well from this.

Tofu

I am an apologist for tofu, unashamedly. So why is it that I can devour practically a whole block of it at one sitting and yet I rarely hear a good word said about it elsewhere? What's the secret?

Marinade, macerate, steep, soak, immerse – call it what you will. Tofu loves its close relation, tamari (they are both soya after all). Add red wine, garlic, chilli, even ginger juice to it and let the tofu soak it all up. Then baste it in a light olive oil and fry it over a moderate heat, or roast it in a hot oven until it is uniformly browned, crisped and sticky with the concentrated juices. This is a westernised version, but it banishes bland. Its pale, delicate, silken Japanese and Chinese versions can be served in desserts, with a sugar syrup, or, to introduce another western turn, honey or maple syrup. It makes a good cheesecake as long as you use the silken variety. Indeed, tofu from ground-up, water-soaked, drained and pressed soya beans has much in common with cheese or at least cheese-making.

It is highly rich in protein but in a form that is more accessible and more easily digestible than the bean it comes from. Its growing significance in Japan coincided with the emergence of Zen Buddhism and its vegetarian principles in the 12th century. To this day, tofu is eggs, cheese and meat to committed vegetarians and in China and Japan it comes in a hundred different forms – spiced, smoked, hard, soft, just as cheese does here.

OTHER RECIPES USING TOFU

Sweet potato salad with avocado and roasted tofu

This started life as one of those 'what have I got in the fridge?' moments, and I associate it in my mind with so-called Pacific Rim cooking. I suppose this is because of the sweet potatoes, which are a strong feature of Australian and New Zealand cuisine – the indigenous people had already cottoned on to them as a serious culinary contender.

Mixing sweet potatoes with both Asian and European ingredients gives this salad some cross-continental intrigue. Good orange-fleshed specimens are required here, the colour being half the fun, and because they are not just sweet in name, but sweet by nature, the salty, sharp dressing makes for a truly delicious contrast.

The avocado must be perfectly ripe and it will add to the dressing's creamy fullness. If you can possibly do it, please don't use supermarket-own-brand of yellow bean paste, which is far too thick; or, if you have no other choice, then water it down first.

Marinate the tofu in the teriyaki sauce and the yellow bean paste for about 20 minutes. If you can do this sometime in advance, then you can do both of the following manoeuvres at the same time.

Preheat the oven to 200°C/400°F/gas mark 6 and bake the sweet potatoes for about 25 minutes until tender. Allow to cool, peel and cut into slices just under 1-cm/^{1}/$_2$-inch thick and set aside. Roast the marinated tofu for 15 minutes or so until well browned.

Make the dressing by mixing the olive oil, mustard and vinegar together, then gently toss with the sweet potatoes, avocado, tomatoes and tofu. Place a mound of the leaves on large plates and loosely deposit the potato salad on top. Serve at once.

Serves 2–4

125 g/4^1/$_2$ oz tofu, cut into thick strips

3 tbsp teriyaki sauce

2 tbsp Blue Dragon yellow bean paste

2 sweet potatoes

1 ripe Hass avocado, peeled and cut into chunks

125 g/4^1/$_2$ oz baby plum tomatoes, halved

250 g/9 oz mixed leaves or just wild rocket and coriander

For the dressing

2 tbsp olive oil

1 tbsp wholegrain mustard

1 tsp balsamic vinegar

Jerusalem artichoke

I love this knobbly tuber with its strange, convoluted and interesting etymology that is neither an artichoke nor yet comes from Jerusalem.

Its flavour does bear a passing resemblance to artichoke, albeit crossed with potato and perhaps a hint of Brazil nut, but it is in fact a relative of the sunflower and has similar large bright flowers. It hails from North America, though it is less used there than over here, these generalisations, however, changing with the greater globalisation of food.

In the 17th century Jerusalem artichokes were more noted for their use in sweet rather than savoury dishes but this is now rare.

They make lovely, nutty salads – great mixed with wild rocket or mildly bitter radicchio and, even better, delicious, gooey, sticky roasts with whole garlic cloves, red wine and olive oil. They make great slow braises as well as velvety soups and purées. They take well to cheese and cream as well as mushrooms. As with other roots and tubers, it is always best to choose firm, freshly dug examples with smooth skins and this is more likely if you buy organic. I usually peel them but not always. Sometimes the sweet, soft insides with the crisp shrivelled skins, are just perfect.

As for their other reputation – I think you know the one I mean – they don't have that effect on everyone (me for instance) and even if they did, so what?

OTHER RECIPES USING JERUSALEM ARTICHOKE

Jerusalem artichoke, lemon and parsley salad with green olives and pistachios 83

Jerusalem artichoke soufflé 83

Stoved roots 145

Jerusalem artichoke, lemon and parsley salad with green olives and pistachios

If you don't mind sullying the pristine white crispiness of sliced Jerusalem artichokes, just a splash of a light soy sauce will do wonders for the dressing. You can also add wild rocket or very thinly sliced radicchio to this salad. Either mix them in or pile them in a teetering mound on top of each serving.

Peel the artichokes and place in a pan of water acidulated with one of the half lemons. Salt and bring to the boil, cooking the artichokes for 8–10 minutes until tender.

While they are still warm, slice them to 3-mm/^{1}/$_8$-inch thickness and put in a bowl with the rest of the ingredients, including the juice from the rest of the lemon (at least 4 tablespoons). A sprinkling of reserved pistachios is attractive on top. The generously garnished artichokes are best eaten warm or at room temperature with 1 or 2 other salads – why not try grilled oil-doused red peppers, a bowl of olives, pungently dressed mushrooms or sharp watercress for something green.

Serves 6

1 kg/2^1/$_4$ lb Jerusalem artichokes

1^1/$_2$ lemons

4 tbsp olive oil

2 garlic cloves, very finely chopped

5 spring onions, finely chopped

60 g/2 oz radishes, very finely sliced

2 tbsp chopped toasted pistachio nuts, reserving some for decoration

12 green olives, stones removed and finely chopped

A dash of Tabasco

1 tbsp chopped parsley

Sea salt and freshly ground black pepper

Jerusalem artichoke soufflé

This is a lovely recipe for Jerusalem artichokes – they are so collapsible and turn so easily to a purée. I have added all kinds of things to them to bring out an unexpected depth.

Jerusalem artichokes can be very delicate and have a subtle sweetness and nuttiness, boiled blandness is not the point here. So, don't hesitate to add strong tastes such as red wine and garlic and be liberal with the Parmesan. As a result, the flavour from this strange-looking tuber is rounder, more pronounced and much richer than you would think possible.

First make a parchment paper collar about 4-cm/2-inch high for the 1-litre/2-pint soufflé dish. Butter the inside and dust with alternating teaspoons of breadcrumbs and Parmesan. Set aside.

Preheat the oven to 200°C/400°F/gas mark 6, with a baking sheet inside.

Peel or scrub the artichokes depending on their condition, place them in a pan with the onion and garlic, add the salt and bouillon and cover with water. Lid the pan and bring to the boil, lowering the heat just slightly and removing the lid if you need to. Cook until tender.

Drain, reserving the water and push the vegetables through a sieve to make a thick purée. A blender would also work here. You need to end up with 200 g/7 oz of purée – any left over can be added to a soup or livened up with more seasoning and spread on bread.

While the artichokes are cooking, melt the butter in a small pan, add the flour to make a roux and cook until thickened. Add the hot vegetable water (or cooking liquor), stirring to form a smooth paste, then the milk and finally the red wine and bay leaf.

When thick and smooth, add the artichoke purée. Beat the egg yolks and add them in a little at a time. Add the herbs, chilli, salt and pepper (you'll have to taste despite the raw egg) and the Parmesan. Finally fold in the whisked egg whites, in large circular movements using a metal spoon. Don't worry if it doesn't all break down, what matters is sweeping the air in.

Pour the mixture into the prepared soufflé dish. Place the paper collar around the rim to hold the rising soufflé in place and sit on the hot baking sheet to better transmit the heat. Cook for 30 minutes in the preheated oven. Don't peek once, unless it is through a glass door.

When the soufflé is well risen, open the oven door, but let it sit there for a couple of minutes before taking it out. A soufflé will tolerate no late-comers so make sure your people are waiting for you and not the other way round.

Serve with a generous green salad, some garlic croûtons and, if you are not too cheesed out, some cubes of any vegetarean blue cheese; if you are, a few sliced toasted hazelnuts scattered over the leaves will marry well with the subtle nuttiness of the Jerusalem artichokes and provide a contrast to all that comforting creaminess.

Serves 4

60 g/2 oz butter, plus extra for greasing

1 tbsp fresh white breadcrumbs

375 g/13 oz Jerusalem artichokes

1 medium onion, peeled and quartered

6 whole garlic cloves, peeled

A pinch of Marigold bouillon powder

50 g/2 oz plain flour

125 ml/4 fl oz artichoke cooking water

125 ml/4 fl oz milk

30 ml/1 fl oz red wine

1 bay leaf

4 organic, free-range eggs, separated, plus 1 extra egg white

4 tbsp chopped parsley or chives, or a mixture of the two

A good pinch of chilli powder

Salt and freshly ground black pepper

4 tbsp freshly grated Parmesan, plus 1 tbsp for dusting the soufflé dish

Borscht with accessories

This recipe is for Alankar, who loves it, and for Volodyo, who first showed me how to make it nearly 20 years ago – he was luckier in this than in his attempts to teach me the violin. I absolutely adore this soup for its sheer opulent vulgarity, its bucolic use of vodka and its unabashed sensuality.

Wash and trim the beetroot and bring to the boil in a pan with the stock. Cook for about 45 minutes until it is tender but still just firm enough not to have leached its colour. It's a curious fact that if you continue to cook beetroot for long enough, the cooking water becomes ever darker, while the beetroot itself becomes almost bleached white and tasteless. I only know this because I was once asked to make borscht by some Polish people who insisted that their version remain a clear bouillon, every bit of colour and flavour deliberately transferred from vegetable to stock. Only a little julienne of beetroot is allowed into their soup, but the Russian version given here is by far my preferred one.

With your fingers, slip the skins from the cooked and cooled beetroots, chop them into quarters and set them aside, reserving the cooking liquid.

Heat the oil and fry the onion until transparent and then add the diced potatoes, carrots, salt, pepper, Tabasco and chopped garlic and continue to sauté for about 5 minutes. Add the beetroot and cook this medley for another 2 minutes. Pour in the reserved beetroot liquid and simmer gently for another 10 minutes, still carefully protecting the beetroot's colour. Stir and remove from the heat. You may need to add more liquid. If you are preparing this soup in advance hold back on the lemon or lime juice and the vodka and only add them as you reheat or they lose their sharp astringent effect. Otherwise add them now.

Blend until smooth. If using a hand-held electric whisk, be careful or drape a tea towel over your hand and the pot; it would be a pity to have it splurt gorily all over the place. Check the seasoning.

For the garnish, the potatoes can be served the lazy way, simply boiled and tossed in a little butter, or, as yet another Russian showed me, par-boiled, thoroughly drained, and then deep-fried in the hot sunflower oil. Serve at once with a bowlful of yoghurt or soured cream, the herbs and chopped spring onion. I don't use the other traditional garnish of chopped hard-boiled egg, but you can if you want to.

Serves 6

1 kg/2^1/$_4$ lb small fresh raw beetroots

1.3 litres/2^1/$_4$ pints vegetable stock

60 ml/2 fl oz sunflower oil

1 large onion, peeled and diced

500 g/1 lb 2 oz potatoes, peeled and diced

90 g/3^1/$_2$ oz carrots, peeled and cut into chunks

A dash of Tabasco

3 garlic cloves, finely chopped

Juice of 1 small lemon or lime

100 ml/3^1/$_2$ fl oz vodka

Salt and freshly ground black pepper

To serve

350 g/12 oz potatoes, diced into 1-cm/^{1}/$_2$-inch cubes

1 litre/2 pints sunflower oil for deep-frying

150 ml/5 fl oz Greek yoghurt or soured cream

1 tbsp chopped parsley

1 tbsp chopped dill

6 spring onions, trimmed and finely sliced

Aloo gobi

If the thought of using ghee (clarified butter) fills you with trepidation, you can do one of two things – replace it with a mixture which is half butter and half sunflower oil (pale and unobtrusive), or you can be reassured by the great health claims made for it by Ayurvedic doctors and use it anyway. A fair-sized supermarket will stock it.

To imitate the nutty taste of ghee, I sometimes add a few almonds to the frying oil and butter medium but remove them before serving. People are often put off by the sheer quantity of ghee and, if that is your reservation, simply use a little less. In this particular recipe I have been as restrained as I can without compromising the integrity of the dish.

The tomatoes in this are a nod to the Indian restaurants that feel they need to add a little freshness and colour at the end. If you feel it detracts from the pallid softness of the dish, leave them out.

This feeds four if you are serving other dishes or makes a generous main meal for two people. If you like a fiercer heat, have a green chilli handy so that you can chop it up finely and add it in towards the end.

For all the stories about curries developing over time and their great keeping qualities, there is nothing like a curry just made, fairly singing with delicate and full-bodied notes.

In a large saucepan, heat the ghee and fry the cumin seeds, keeping a watchful eye on them so they don't burn. Add the potatoes and stir-fry them for about 8 minutes until they start to soften; stay vigilant and add a little of the water now if you need to. Remove them from the pan for a moment while you deal with the cauliflower.

Now toss the florets in the pan until they start to catch and go brown in places. Then return the potatoes to the pan, cover them with a lid and let them soften over a medium heat for about 5–6 minutes, again adding a little water to prevent too much sticking.

Add the chopped chilli and the rest of the spices, stirring in large but careful movements so as not to break up the vegetables. Simmer for a further 8–10 minutes with the lid on, sneaking a peek now and again to check all is as it should be, until the cauliflower is cooked with just a little firmness left to it and the potatoes are perfectly tender. Keep adding judicious spoonfuls of water and adjusting the heat as you need to.

Stir the tomato quarters in, barely longer than needed to warm them through. Season with salt and pepper and liven up with fresh coriander. Serve with thin, warm chapati or Basmati rice, simply boiled or egg-fried.

Serves 2–4

6 tbsp ghee, or half butter, half light olive oil or sunflower oil

1 tbsp cumin seeds

540 g/1lb 3 oz small new potatoes, peeled and cut in half

About 125 ml/4 fl oz water

540 g/1 lb 3 oz cauliflower florets (equals 1 good-sized whole cauliflower, separated into florets)

1 green chilli, chopped

1 dsp ground cumin

1 dsp ground coriander

1 garlic clove, finely sliced (optional)

1 tsp turmeric

1 tsp cayenne

2 tomatoes, cut into quarters (optional)

Salt and freshly ground black pepper

1 small handful fresh coriander (optional)

Beetroot in sour cream

I love this densely herbed, generously dressed, resplendent salad. Beetroot divides people so no guesses which side of the fence I'd plant my flag on. And a splendid crimson it would be too.

Use baby beetroots you have cooked yourself or buy them still steaming hot on the rare occasions that you might see them like this on the shelves of a greengrocer that hasn't (yet) been overtaken by a heartless chain. Or use a vacuum pack – not as romantic but very reliable.

Mix all the ingredients together, reserving a little of each of the green things to scatter on top. The beetroot will colour the cream a shocking pink and since there's no way on earth to avoid this, don't try but enjoy the over-the-top vulgarity of it.

Eat with a thick slice of soda bread, buttered or plain.

Serves 4

500 g/1 lb 2 oz beetroots, liquid drained, cut into 8 pieces

125 ml/4^1/2 fl oz soured cream

A dash of Tabasco

2 tbsp finely snipped chives

4 spring onions, cleaned and finely sliced

1 tsp lemon juice

2 tbsp chopped parsley

Sea salt and freshly ground black pepper

Beetroots with green beans and Haloumi

If you can find tiny bunched beetroots, still with their delicious tops on, that would be great (add the cleaned leaves, very lightly blanched, to the salad at the end). They are so small that they don't need blanching first and still take on a shrivelled, juicy eatability when grilled. If you can't find these, then use unvinegared baby beetroots or larger ones, blanched and cut into pieces.

Grill them with the Haloumi while it reaches its part-molten, part-crisp, golden ideal. You could replace the green beans with purple sprouting broccoli during its precious short season. If you need to make more of a meal of this, try the skorthalia (*see* p279).

Preheat the grill. If using baby beetroots place them and the Haloumi on a metal baking sheet. Baste with 2 tablespoons olive oil and grill for about 5 minutes if raw, about 2 minutes if already cooked, turning regularly so that the Haloumi is golden and crisp on the outside and still soft inside and the beetroots are wrinkled without and tender within. Larger pieces of beetroot will need to be grilled, roasted or even griddled for longer than the Haloumi.

Put the cumin seeds alongside and remove as soon as they start to darken. Even ready-cooked beetroots, similarly basted, benefit from being stuck under the grill for a couple of minutes. It's amazing what a quick blast of intense heat does to bring out the flavour, natural sugars and syrup of so many vegetables.

Meanwhile, bring a pan of water to the boil. Blanch the green beans until tender, refresh under cold running water and set aside.

Mix the remaining ingredients together to make a dressing. Add the beetroots, green beans and Haloumi and mix gently. Sprinkle the cumin seeds on top. Serve at once with chunks of warm bread.

Serves 2

275 g/10 oz baby beetroots, cooked, or 350 g/12 oz bunched baby beetroots, cut in half if necessary

125 g/4^1/$_2$ oz Haloumi, cut into 5-mm/^{1}/$_4$-inch thick, finger-size strips

3 tbsp olive oil, plus extra if needed

1–2 tsp cumin seeds, lightly toasted

125 g/4^1/$_2$ oz green beans, topped and tailed

1 tsp balsamic vinegar

A dash of Tabasco

Sea salt and freshly ground black pepper

Broccoli

This is another probable import from Asia, also beloved of the Romans, who passed on a passion for it and therefore an abundance of recipes to their Italian descendants.

Botanically indistinguishable from cauliflower, despite their obvious colour differences, the vegetable we know as broccoli comes originally from Calabria and is more accurately called *calabrese*. The smaller-headed, leafier variety of purple sprouting broccoli (in fact the heads can also be green or even white) is a brief springtime treat and is sometimes known as poor man's asparagus. Both enjoy the same company – lemon, garlic, mustard, olive oil, butter and Parmesan are particularly apt companions and they have plenty of other friends of their own.

Orange and almonds go well with broccoli as do ginger and tamari, in simple stir-fries which keep it crisp and vibrant. Choose broccoli with firm, fat heads and bright-green stalks, with no woodiness and no splitting. Any yellowing indicates age and an unpleasant deterioration of flavour. Broccoli is rich in vitamin C and beta-carotene and is often quoted as a natural anti-carcinogen. The stalks are better peeled, but either way they are delicious, eaten raw or very lightly blanched.

OTHER RECIPES USING BROCCOLI

Broccoli sautéed with shiitake mushrooms and tofu 91

Broccoli with chicory, Dolcelatte and walnuts in a rich tart 93

Soft polenta with broccoli 133

Olive oil and lemon dressing 277

Broccoli sautéed with shiitake mushrooms and tofu

As it happens, I made this on the same day as I made the French onion tart (*see* p109), and since someone had to eat it, it went on the plate with the tart. The tofu was a bit *de trop* but the shiitake and broccoli went with the tart surprisingly well. So, on days when a green salad isn't enough, why don't you stir-fry some mushrooms and broccoli?

On reflection, I think it's the tamari that does the trick. Its dark saltiness contrasts really well with the sugar sweetness of the onion, and both are complemented by a bit of crunch from the broccoli.

Cut the tofu into thick square slices or chunky cubes and place it in the marinade for at least half an hour. Strain the marinade and keep in the fridge where it will last a few days. You can use it for other stir-fries and soups, or freeze it for a later date.

You can peel and slice the broccoli stems into sticks or rings or, if you think they spoil the look of the dish, reserve them for soup or to eat raw, cut into chip-size fingers.

Drop a small puddle of oil into the hollow of the wok and heat to searing, smoking (just) fearsomeness. I do crazy things such as put the empty wok over a large and naked flame for a few seconds before pouring in the oil, just to make sure it's hot enough. You have to play on the edge here, without taking foolish risks unless you know your limits pretty well.

Quickly add the broccoli on a furious heat, grabbing the wok handle with confidence and shaking it fearlessly back and forth for a couple of minutes. Also add a splash or two of water until the broccoli is part-fried, part-steamed to a tenderness that has attitude — *ie* not soggy.

Add the shiitake mushrooms and garlic slices and fry for 2 minutes, adding a mere splash of water if the pan dries out too much, as well as the ginger juice and stir, still with the same speed and vigor.

In the same pan, add the tofu, with a little more oil if necessary, and fry to a burning gold on both sides, again working on a high heat and moving the pan back and forth over the flame. Remove from the heat and add the Tabasco or chilli as well the tamari, tossing and turning the vegetables as you do so.

Pour into a wide Chinese bowl and eat slurpily with chopsticks, the shiitake sliding down like satin.

Serves 1–2

150 g/5 oz tofu, marinated

175 g/6 oz broccoli, separated into florets

1 tbsp groundnut oil

5 tbsp water, or as appropriate

125 g/4^1/$_2$ oz shiitake mushrooms

1 garlic clove, finely sliced

2-cm/1-inch piece of ginger, grated and squeezed and the resulting liquid reserved

A dash of Tabasco, or 1 small bird's eye chilli, finely chopped

1 tbsp tamari

For the tofu marinade

1 tbsp tamari

60 ml/2 fl oz water

A dash of Tabasco

A small piece of fiery red chilli, chopped very small

Steaming action

If you want to do more with this you can. You could toss in a few quick-cook noodles, keeping the balance very much in the vegetables' favour. Or you could add a little left-over rice or even a spoonful or two of coconut milk. Perhaps you will first have made a bowl of egg-fried rice and it will be sitting there, all of a steam, waiting for you.

Please note, this is not one of those thick, glossy-sauced stir-fries. If that's what you're after, dissolve a little cornflour or arrowroot into a little cold water and pour it into the boiling juices. Stir very well until thickened and remove from the heat.

Ways with woks

When you first buy your wok, it is likely to be coated in a rather foul-smelling industrial oil, straight off the steel press. Scrub this off with warm soapy water, dry well and place it over a gentle heat.

Pour 2 tablespoons of sunflower oil into the wok and wipe the whole surface with it using a piece of kitchen paper. Now heat it slowly for about 15 minutes. Wipe the surface again. You will see that the paper is now black. Keep going, once again wiping the surface with oil, heating and wiping as many times as you need until the paper comes away clean. A properly seasoned wok will darken with age.

To clean your wok, wash it with water and a soft cloth and dry it thoroughly over a low flame for a couple of minutes so it is really bone dry. If rusty bits do appear, you'll have to start the whole process again.

Broccoli with chicory, Dolcelatte and walnuts in a rich tart

Three potentially quite bitter flavours – the Dolcelatte, the walnuts and the chicory – end up being rich, refined and with a hint of caramelised sweetness. Don't overcook. In this, as in other eggy tarts, the filling needs to wobble vulnerably and to continue to firm up in its own heat once you have removed it from the oven. You shouldn't even need to add salt as there is sufficient saltiness in the cheese and the bouillon powder. There are few better lunches than this soundly flavoured tart.

First make the pastry, going as short as you dare, and chill. I end up adding very little water indeed, 2 ice-cold tablespoons at most, because I've pushed the butter content as far as I possibly can.

Preheat the oven to 200°C/400°F/gas mark 6.

Roll out the pastry on a lightly floured surface and use to line a buttered, floured loose-bottomed 28-cm/11-inch tart tin. Chill again and then bake for 15 minutes, either with an overhang which will shrink to fit or blind-baked with all the parchment and dried beans paraphernalia that entails. Remove and allow it to cool before adding the filling, otherwise the warm pastry will absorb anything you add to it and lose all its crisp charm.

Meanwhile, warm the butter in a saucepan and add the chicory pieces, with the white wine, sugar and bouillon powder. Bring to the boil, then reduce the heat and simmer steadily for about 10 minutes until the chicory is soft and lightly browned.

Set aside to cool while you blanch the broccoli in salted boiling water until tender but not soft. Drain and refresh under cold water, shaking out all of the excess liquid.

Beat the eggs, cream and broken-up Dolcelatte together, stir in the broccoli florets and pepper to taste. When you have just covered the pastry base with a layer of braised chicory, pour the broccoli and egg mixture all over. Dot the walnuts over the surface so they are partly exposed. Bake in the oven for about 15–20 minutes.

Serve with a simple tomato salad, lightly dressed in olive oil, balsamic vinegar and a little finely chopped red onion.

Serves 6–8

200 g/7 oz pastry (*see* p305)

30 g/1 oz butter, plus extra for greasing

Plain flour for dusting

175 g/6 oz chicory, about 3 heads, each cut into 8 long strips

60 ml/2 fl oz white wine

A pinch of soft brown sugar

A pinch of Marigold bouillon powder

450 g/1 lb broccoli, separated into florets

4 large organic, free-range eggs

8 tbsp double cream

225 g/8 oz Dolcelatte, crumbled

50 g/scant 2 oz shelled walnuts, the fresher and younger the better

Salt and freshly ground black pepper

Butternut squash, spinach and walnut tortilla

Before you turn the page, let me reassure you. There is nothing dried-up or bland about this tortilla. The colours, textures and tastes are all there and in gloriously generous terms. I like it best at room temperature when it has had time to settle and ease into itself. It keeps well for several days wrapped in foil and kept in the fridge.

However, I think it is best for a friendly gathering, served with vinaigrette-dressed salads and, though you may not at first see why, beetroot (the Moroccan way with cumin, red onion and a dash of vinegar) included among them. The rich creaminess welcomes a sharp note. You are not misreading the amount of cream.

Preheat the oven to 220°C/425°F/gas mark 7.

Crack the eggs into a bowl and whisk with the double cream. Season with salt, pepper and the garlic.

Leave to infuse while you both peel and chop the butternut squash into 2-cm/1-inch chunks. Baste them in an oven tray with the olive oil, tamari and Tabasco. Then bake in the preheated oven for about 20–25 minutes or until tender, golden and crisp in places. Transfer the butternut squash to a large, preferably non-stick frying pan.

On a medium heat, add the spinach to the squash until it is wilted, stir well and pour the egg mixture on top. The egg and cream should reach to at least two-thirds of the way up. Still on a moderate heat, adjusting it as you see fit, let the egg begin to set.

Over the next 15–20 minutes, use a knife or spatula and cut into the tortilla, letting the uncooked egg flow like tributaries into the valleys and crevices, so that it is eventually all set, cooked parts lifted up as the rest flows beneath and cooks. Don't stir or mix but move the pan gently from side to side.

When it is all but done, set the walnut pieces loosely into the still softish top. Remove from the heat and if you can cover with a lid, do so, so that the tortilla's last cooking is done in its own heat.

Allow to cool for 15 minutes or more and eat in generous and shimmering wedges.

Serves 6

12 large organic, free-range eggs

250 ml/9 fl oz double cream

Sea salt and freshly ground black pepper

4 plump garlic cloves, finely minced

1 butternut squash, about 900 g/2 lb

2 tbsp olive oil

1 tsp tamari

A dash of Tabasco

225 g/8 oz baby spinach

5–6 walnuts, shelled and roughly broken up

Carrots braised with cumin, saffron and garlic

I make this often with organic carrots, their green tops still attached. I once read that pesticides lurk most stubbornly in the tops of carrots and I really resented this, as I am very fond of the dark-green, iron-rich leaves.

There are times when I'll grab the nearest out-of-season thing, knowing it can only have grown by means of huge interference. But choosing carrots is not one of them and bunched organic carrots are graciously easy to find.

Braising brings out all the natural sugars, so they end up sweet, yet earthy and pungent because of the cumin, and they dissolve softly on the tongue without any of the sogginess that so often characterises cooked carrots.

Wash the carrots thoroughly and peel them carefully, leaving their tops attached. If they are large, cut them in half lengthways though not all the way, so that they stay attached at the top.

Place the carrots in a large saucepan (I use an oval, cast-iron pan which is perfect for the job) together with the olive oil, the ground cumin, cumin seeds, water, saffron, bouillon, garlic, salt, pepper and Tabasco. Make sure the carrots are lying as flat as possible in the pan and that they have all been well doused in the spicy oil.

Cover with a lid and simmer for about 20 minutes, checking occasionally to see that they are not sticking – though some catching on the bottom is a good thing as they should brown a little in places. Keep turning them over gently and shake the pot about now and again to distribute the flavours and the emerging sauce. Add a little water if it seems to be drying out too quickly. When they are ready, the tops will be completely wilted and the carrots covered in a sticky, saffron, garlic, cumin sauce. You will see carrots in a different light forever, I promise.

Serve with the lemon wedges and either the Middle Eastern rice (*see* p245) or broad bean pilaff (*see* p240).

Serves 4

500 g/1 lb 2 oz bunched carrots

4 tbsp olive oil

1 tsp ground cumin

1 tsp cumin seeds

150 ml/5 fl oz water

A generous pinch of saffron

$1/2$ tsp Marigold bouillon powder

4 large or 6 small garlic cloves, finely sliced

A dash of Tabasco

Sea salt and freshly ground black pepper

Lemon wedges to serve

Carrots glazed with shallots and almonds

Carrot tops can be really delicious; although the stalks themselves are tough and inedible even after long braising, the leaves are delicate and flavourful. Even if you decide to remove them before serving, they're worth keeping on during cooking for the extra flavour.

This makes carrots almost a sweetmeat, instead of the flaccid, dull vegetable you may have come to expect of a cooked carrot.

Wash the carrot tops thoroughly to remove any grit but keep them attached to add extra colour and flavour.

Heat the oil in a large saucepan or casserole and add the shallots. Brown briefly on a high heat, adding the whole carrots and letting them catch slightly on the bottom of the pan. Turn a few times and add the sugar and garlic. Add the water and bouillon, and bring to a steady simmer. Cover with a lid and cook for about 20 minutes until about three-quarters of the liquid is either absorbed or cooked out and the carrots are lying in a sweet sticky, oniony sauce, with some of the shallot collapsed and soft, the rest still quite whole.

Adjust the seasoning, adding salt and pepper as necessary and, only a few minutes before the end, add the blanched almonds to the simmering vegetables. Add a dash of Tabasco to round off the taste.

Serve garnished with the chopped parsley (not really necessary if you have kept the carrot tops on but more important if you haven't).

Serves 4

500 g/1 lb 2 oz bunched carrots, peeled and left whole

1 tbsp olive oil

175 g/6 oz shallots, peeled

2 tsp soft brown sugar

3 garlic cloves, finely sliced

200 ml/7 fl oz water

A pinch of Marigold bouillon powder

60 g/2 oz almonds, blanched and skins slipped off

Salt and freshly ground black pepper

A dash of Tabasco

To serve

1 tbsp chopped parsley

Carrots with parsley, garlic and lemon in a walnut pastry tart

Just about any vegetable can be set in a cream-rich egg custard, though the prosaic carrot may not usually spring to mind. It works in the way that sweet and savoury flavours often do, creating a multi-layered experience, much more intricate than you would expect. On another occasion, a dish of sliced carrots, cooked in lemon and butter like this, would be a treat, served with mashed potatoes and some green vegetables.

The simplest carrot preparation of all is one that features weekly on my mother's table (and so often on mine). It is simply finely grated carrots – I use the fine julienne blade of a food processor – dressed with a delicate olive oil or something even lighter, a dash of lemon juice or vinegar, a little mustard and salt and pepper. My grandmother sometimes added cumin or chopped flat-leaf parsley or went the whole hog with a salad from her childhood in Mogador (now Essaouira), adding oranges and black olives, cumin, garlic and paprika. My mother doesn't do this, but you could!

If parsley is not 'interesting' or 'important' enough for you, use thyme – see, I do use English herbs sometimes.

Preheat the oven to 200°C/400°F/gas mark 6

Make the pastry as instructed, adding the walnut pieces just before the water. Bring together into a ball and refrigerate for at least 20 minutes. Proceed to line a 23-cm/9-inch loose-based tin with it, chill again and blind-bake.

Melt the butter in a large frying pan or sauteuse pan and, without letting it brown in the slightest, add the carrot slices and some salt and pepper. Stir over a gentle heat for about 4 minutes before adding the chopped garlic. The pale yellow and orange are as sunny and soothing as grown-up nursery food.

Continue to simmer the carrots for about 8-10 minutes until tender. Then add the lemon and parsley. Remove from the heat and allow to cool slightly before combining with a mixture of double cream, Gruyère if using and beaten eggs.

Bake in the oven for 20 minutes until set to a gentle, tremulous wobble.

Serves 8–10
For the pastry
(*see* p124) and add 60 g/2 oz walnuts, shelled and chopped quite small

For the filling
40 g/1$\frac{1}{2}$ oz butter

500 g/1 lb 2 oz carrots, peeled and sliced to the thickness of one pound coin (*see* p118)

3 garlic cloves, peeled and very finely chopped

Juice of half a lemon

30 g/1 oz parsley, finely chopped

284 ml/10 fl oz double cream

30 g/1 oz Gruyère, finely grated (optional)

3 large organic, free-range eggs, beaten

Salt and freshly ground black pepper

Braised celery

Celery is another divisive, love-it-or-hate-it vegetable, but like fennel I'm sure it's just that people have forgotten what to do with it. I think they mostly throw it into a soup and hope for the best or eat it raw, which is honourable enough, especially with a slice of blue cheese. I only hope that it doesn't just end up on some plate of curled crudités.

I love raw vegetables but the sight of a plate of them cut into batons makes my heart sink. It's nearly always someone's unimaginative 'let's keep them quiet' ploy, a tub of indifferent shop-bought hummus plonked in the middle. It's too depressing. So much work for so little.

Carrot sticks marinated in a little ume-su and tamari, peppers properly cleaned of pith and cut into pert chunks, celery disencumbered of its tough string, cucumber in seed-removed half moons, plump and super-crunchy radishes with their green tops still perkily erect, a few lightly pickled green chillies and a handful of oily, broken olives might be ok. More than ok.

Wash the celery and remove the strings from the outer part, pulling them from top to bottom. Then cut each celery head in half and place closely in a comfortably sized pan in which you have just heated the oil. Toss and turn until the celery catches slightly on the bottom and lightly browns in places.

Cover with the water, bouillon powder, slivered garlic and pepper. You shouldn't really need salt because of the bouillon powder and because of the celery's own natural saltiness.

Put the lid on the pot and bring to the boil, then reduce the heat and simmer gently for about 15 minutes, topping up with a little water if the liquid dries out before the celery is soft.

Remove the lid and continue to cook until all the liquid has evaporated and there is a little sauce coating it, sticky and syrupy.

Alternatives

I eat this happily as a starter but with the cream and Gruyère added at the end and cooked just long enough to bubble, and flashed under a hot grill, then I can happily make a whole meal of it. Blue cheese is reputedly good with celery, so you could melt a lump of it into the hot creamy sauce instead of the Gruyère.

Serves 4
For basic braised celery

3 whole celery heads

50 ml/1$^{1}/_{2}$ fl oz light olive oil

600 ml/1 pint water

A pinch of Marigold bouillon powder

3 garlic cloves, finely slivered

Freshly ground black pepper

For fancy braised celery
Add 6 tbsp of double cream and, if you want a gratin, 75 g/2$^{1}/_{2}$ oz finely shredded Gruyère or 3 tbsp freshly grated Parmesan.

Venerable vegetables
The big difference about the use of vegetables in the vegetarian kitchen is simply this. We eat them in far greater quantity. We'll make a meal of a gratin instead of having it as a prissy afterthought on the side of the plate. Any of the starches, such as organic, short-grain rice, can accompany this dish. Or why not try some pappardelle or some new potatoes roasted in the skin, basted with sea salt and olive oil? Wonderful.

Celeriac

Celeriac is the round, knobbly, rough-skinned, cultivated root or, more precisely, the swollen stem of wild celery and has a distinctive taste like a creamy celery, though sweeter and milder.

It is most famously used in the French celeriac rémoulade or *celery rave à la rémoulade* and has been used extensively in French cooking since at least the 15th century. The large roots that we know as celeriac are a result of cultivation; in the wild the roots are much smaller and the celery that sprouts from them is hollow and leafy, but the similarities are clear. Britain has woken up late to celeriac's charms but now we use it in gratins with porcini, sliced in juliennes and mixed with potato to make a more interesting rösti, in soups or simply cooked in butter. Two delicious Middle Eastern, braised preparations mix celeriac with carrots in a lemon sauce and also with fennel, lemon and parsley, both gently sweetened with a little caster sugar (*see The Book of Jewish Food* by Claudia Roden [Viking, 1997]). I love it in all these guises.

Choose firm, pale roots and always peel before cooking. The firm white insides should smell like freshly cut celery hearts. Don't let celeriac sit in the vegetable basket for too long or it will become woody. Like potatoes, celeriac discolours quickly on exposure to air and must be quickly rubbed with lemon, or kept in acidulated water once peeled.

OTHER RECIPES USING CELERIAC

Celeriac soup with bouillabaisse seasonings and rouille 70

Celeriac gratin with porcini 102

Celeriac rémoulade 103

Celeriac gratin with porcini

It's always a little difficult to decide how many something like this should feed, but as someone who happily makes a meal of a single vegetable (dish, that is), I can't see that four people would have the slightest problem wolfing this down. However, if you want to serve a starter and a separate main-course pie or suchlike with it, then it will comfortably stretch to six.

Put the porcini into a measuring jug with a little hot water to cover.
Heat the oil in a large frying pan or sauté pan. Add the onion and sweat for 2 minutes. Add the celeriac, 800 ml/1½ pints water and the bouillon powder, garlic, lemon juice (if using) and a little pepper. Bring to the boil and bubble rapidly for 20 minutes, turning the celeriac regularly, until the liquid has evaporated and the celeriac is cooked.

After about 15 minutes, add the porcini and their strained soaking liquid to the celeriac, followed immediately by the cream. Continue to simmer briskly until the sauce is reduced to the consistency of double cream. Preheat the grill to high.

Sprinkle the grated Gruyère over the creamy celeriac and porcini and place under the hot grill for about 2 minutes. Sprinkle with chives or parsley and serve with a green salad.

Serves 4–6

20 g/¾ oz dried porcini mushrooms, sliced

2 tbsp olive oil

1 onion, very finely sliced

1 celeriac head, about 600 g/ 1 lb 5 oz, peeled and sliced very thinly, either with a mandolin or with a very sharp knife, no more than 3-mm/⅛-inch thick

1 tsp Marigold bouillon powder

3 garlic cloves, very finely sliced

1 tsp lemon juice (optional)

Freshly ground black pepper

100 ml/3½ fl oz double cream

60 g/2 oz Gruyère, grated

A few chives, finely snipped, or 1 tbsp chopped parsley

Celeriac rémoulade

The British have coleslaw, the French have this. Need I say more?

Peel the celeriac. There's no way around this: the peel is inedible, tough and woody and it will take a little effort with a potato peeler to get it all off. Then, cut the celeriac into large pieces and rub each with one half of the lemon to stop it going black, which it will otherwise do alarmingly quickly. Grate or shred finely on the finest grating blade of a food processor so that it comes out like fine string or fine julienne.

Transfer the grated celeriac to a bowl with the rest of the lemon squeezed over it and the salt. These may have the effect of making the celeriac weep its excess liquid, which you can then discard. It is better to do this now than after you have added the mayonnaise or the whole thing will become waterlogged and lose some of its distinctive appeal.

Add the mayonnaise (mixed with mustard if necessary – the homemade version should have enough), a spoonful at a time. The quantity depends entirely on the size of your celeriac and on how much liquid you have extracted from it.

Mix well. Stop as soon as the celeriac looks well coated and creamy. Some people like it left as virginal as this. I like a small amount of very finely chopped parsley and a little freshly ground black pepper on top.

Serve with crusty bread and a bowl of black olives.

Alternatives

Celeriac partners well with mushrooms so a bowl of garlicky, parsleyed mushrooms, brushed with olive oil, blasted under a hot grill until gently blistered, is delicious. So are sliced mushrooms fried in a modicum of hot oil, splashed with tamari, a drop of Tabasco, a finely minced garlic clove and a handful of closely chopped parsley or coriander. By the way, a simply prepared quinoa moistened with olive oil and a dash of tamari seems invented for this.

One day, because I was starting to feel as tyrannised by the keep-it-simple mindset as by any more finicky approach, I took a large biscuit cutter from my box of tools, set it upon a plate, filled it with the rémoulade almost to the top, then added the sliced cooked and warm mushrooms on top. I then rained the lightest dusting of freshly chopped parsley to lighten the look. Next, I drizzled some olive oil and lemon dressing (see p277) around with a few slivers of black olives and a few of sundried tomatoes.

Serves 4–6

1 medium head celeriac, about 600 g/1 lb 5 oz

1 small lemon, cut in half

1/2 tsp salt

About 90 ml/3 fl oz mayonnaise, homemade (see p275)

1/2 tsp mustard (optional)

Freshly ground black pepper

1 tbsp finely chopped parsley (optional)

Couscous

Couscous is unusual in being the unique preserve of North Africa, with one Sicilian recipe being the single exception, though no prizes for guessing where that came from.

I have watched aunts sprinkle water on to ground wheat grain, sweeping and raking with splayed-out fingers of the right hand and rubbing it into little balls against the sides of the bowl. They spread these in a *tamisier* – a large fine-meshed, wooden-rimmed sieve to dry. No self-respecting Moroccan household is without a couscoussier, the special double boiler which holds the broth and vegetables and usually the meat while the couscous steams in a lidded pot above, bound together with muslin to make sure that none of the vital steam escapes.

The couscous is loosened with two forks at regular intervals – fingers for the brave – and moistened with a light oil or butter. After several repetitions, it is fully plumped and is served with the rich broth, vegetables, chickpeas etc. It is always, followed by a green salad.

Couscous is served in huge mounds, folklore being that it initially fills you to bursting but leaves you quickly hungering for more. I don't know about that. These days, even the most purist and traditional of cooks resort to the much simpler reconstituting with boiling water or light stock. In my family this has turned couscous into a regular pleasure.

OTHER RECIPES USING COUSCOUS

A typical Algerian couscous

I've told you this before in *Cranks Fast Food* (C&C, 2000), but I simply have to tell you again. To eat this the authentic way, take a little couscous in the palm of your hand. Place a chickpea or raisin in it and roll into a small ball. Then (are you ready for this?) flick the ball with your thumb into your open mouth!

Heat the oil in a large, heavy-bottomed saucepan. Add the leeks and sauté until golden. Remove and set aside.

In the same pan, add the onion and fry over a medium heat until just browned. Add the garlic and some salt, then add the cumin and cook for a further 3–4 minutes, loosening with a little of the saffron water.

Add the carrots and sauté until just beginning to soften. Add the courgettes and sauté for a further couple of minutes. Then add the sautéed leeks, chickpeas, tomatoes (breaking them up a little with a wooden spoon) and the rest of the saffron water. Finally, stir in the raisins.

Simmer for about 10 minutes, until the vegetables are tender, even soft, but not soggy. If the sauce seems too thick – it should be more of a broth than a sauce – add a little more hot water. Season with salt and pepper to taste and sprinkle the chopped parsley on top.

Cover the couscous with the hot stock. Add the butter or oil. Stir once and set aside until plump and tender.

Serve the vegetables and their broth with the couscous, fluffed up with two forks and your fingers if you can take the heat. Melt another knob of butter into the couscous or drizzle a little extra olive oil as you do so.

Harissa or chermoula (*see* p273, p268) should be served on the side. Follow with a crisp, simple salad of iceberg torn into chunks or gem lettuces, both thickly dressed in a mustard vinaigrette (*see* p267).

Fluffy couscous

I generally find that couscous requires slightly less water than packet instructions suggest. It needs to be light and fluffy, not wet and sticky.

Serves 4

3 tbsp olive oil

500 g/1 lb 2 oz leeks, trimmed and chopped into 2-cm/1-inch pieces

275 g/10 oz onion, finely chopped

4 garlic cloves, sliced

Sea salt and freshly ground black pepper

3 tbsp ground cumin

A pinch of saffron in about 3 tbsp hot water

500 g/1 lb 2 oz carrots, cut into 2-cm/1-inch thick chunks

500 g/1 lb 2 oz courgettes, cut into 2-cm/1-inch thick chunks

400 g/14 oz can chickpeas, liquid included

400 g/14 oz can tomatoes (not chopped), liquid included

2 tbsp raisins

1 tbsp chopped parsley to garnish

For the couscous

400 g/14 oz good-quality couscous, medium to large grained

400 ml/14 fl oz hot vegetable stock, made with 1 tsp Marigold bouillon powder

1 tbsp butter or olive oil

Moroccan pumpkin couscous with a prune and onion confit

I'm sure this made-up combination doesn't exist elsewhere. The prune confit is traditionally served with lamb but it is far too good to miss out on, so try it here.

The pumpkin is a nod in the direction of the wonderful, elaborate Moroccan Couscous Royale, where seven vegetables are served first in a savoury fashion, cooked in the saffron broth which sits in the bottom of the couscoussier. It sends its steam upwards to soften the couscous in the traditional manner.

In the broth remain other foods (not the subject of this book), and also chickpeas and onion. The vegetables are lifted out when tender, set in an ovenproof dish and roasted to Asiatic gold with oil and chopped garlic.

Meanwhile, pumpkin, carrots, baby onions, raisins and a few cooked chickpeas are sprinkled with sugar and cinnamon and cooked in a hot oven until completely tender and caramelised.

Combining the two notions creates an unbelievably exotic, sweet dish best eaten in moderation and ideally followed by the inevitable green salad and/or preceded by a Lebanese *fattoush* – a sort of Middle Eastern bread salad (*see* p108).

Serve a dish of warm flaccid green beans, finger-sized courgette pieces and sliced garlic. The vegetables, cooked in a way that is more Italian than Middle Eastern, either blanched or steamed, seasoned with salt and, most uncharacteristically for me, a little chopped fresh mint, are then doused with olive oil and provide another fresh tasting foil.

Preheat the oven to 200°C/400°F/gas mark 6.

First plunge the shallots in a pan of boiling water for 1 minute, as this makes them so much easier to peel and saves your tears for when you might really need them. Set aside.

Prepare the pumpkin or butternut squash by removing the seeds and cutting into about 18 crescents, 2-cm/1-inch thick. Baste them in olive oil, together with a little salt, pepper, Tabasco, soy sauce, sugar and cinnamon.

Roast in the oven for about 25–30 minutes until browned and caramelised. Heat the olive oil in a pan or deep frying pan. Add the peeled shallots and fry them until they are brown and golden.

Season with a little salt and pepper and add the whole garlic cloves,

Serves 6
For the prune and onion confit
500 g/1lb 2 oz small round shallots, peeled

900 g/2 lb pumpkin from a very good Italian orange-fleshed pumpkin with a green carapace, try Crown Prince, or 900 g/2 lb butternut squash

2 tbsp light olive oil or sunflower oil, plus extra for basting

Sea salt and freshly ground black pepper

A dash of Tabasco

A dash of soy sauce or tamari

1 tsp soft brown sugar

1/2 tsp ground cinnamon

4 garlic cloves,

400 g/14 oz soft prunes, stones left in

A handful of whole almonds, blanched and skins slipped off

For the couscous
500 g/1 lb 2 oz couscous

Boiling water to cover

A pinch of saffron

Marigold bouillon powder

A knob of butter

1 tbsp finely chopped parsley, to garnish

then add the prunes and enough water to just cover. Simmer on quite a fierce heat, until it is all absorbed, adding water a little at a time, until the shallots become golden and caramelised all the way through but still maintain much of their shape, and the prunes are soft with some dissolving into the sauce. The whole thing should take about 20–25 minutes. A few minutes before the end, add the blanched almonds and heat.

Reconstitute the couscous in a volume of boiling water roughly equal to its weight and seasoned with the saffron first as well as a good pinch of bouillon. When the water is fully absorbed, fluff up with two forks and melt a knob of butter through it. There must be no lumps whatsoever, so use your fingers too if necessary.

Transfer the couscous to a tagine or large plate and cover with the prune and onion confit and roasted pumpkin crescents on top too, with any remaining juices poured in. Scatter with a little very finely chopped parsley and serve.

Lebanese fattoush

Rip up 2 thin oven-crisped pitta breads into small pieces and mix them with about 4 firm, chopped tomatoes; a roughly torn Cos or a couple of Little Gem lettuces; roughly chopped onion; a little finely minced garlic; a sweet, crisp and snappy baby cucumber or two, cut into densely seeded chunks; and a few black olives.

Drench all this with olive oil, the juice of a lemon or some white wine vinegar, a little salt and allow to sit for a while, sprinkled with a little chopped coriander and parsley. The bread will start to become impregnated with the oil and will look for all the world like the kind of item which sends a certain type of vegetarian, running to the trades description office or the poor beleaguered Vegetarian Society, muttering 'It said it was vegetarian but …'.

French onion tart

'For it is every cook's opinion,
No savoury dish without an onion'
Green Leeks by Jonathan Swift

I love to cook and eat recipes that were a part of my childhood. I avoid nostalgia where I can, but through food we are often transported to a time we like to imagine as more innocent.

How much better apples tasted then. Everything was sharper when it was new; the world was made real to us through sense impressions, smells, tastes, non-verbal signals and stimuli.

Tarte à l'oignon was one of my mother's regulars and, having always inclined towards vegetarianism, it was one of my favourites. She made it with a béchamel base, while I make it the classic French way with eggs and double cream. But the sentiment is the same. Perhaps frying the onion to deep golden brown betrays the Moroccan influence, but recipes for this with the onion left barely coloured, leave me cold.

This serves six, though four of us polished it off without any difficulty.

First lightly butter and flour a 28-cm/11-inch loose-based tart tin and preheat the oven to 190°C/375°F/gas mark 5.

Make the pastry and, while it is chilling, begin to make the filling.

Heat the oil and butter in a large frying pan and add the finely sliced onion. Fry for about 25 minutes, stirring regularly until quite a dark, jammy, golden-brown, adding the tamari (apt, though very non-French) and red wine, if using, for the last few minutes. Tamari, used like this, is simply to intensify and enrich, not in any way change, the character of the dish or to indulge in some misplaced cosmopolitanism. By a dash I mean just half a teaspoon. You can add the nutmeg, garlic and pepper at any time, but only season with salt at the very end.

Meanwhile, in a bowl mix the egg yolks with the double cream. Then add in the fried onions. Adjust the seasoning one last time.

Roll out the pastry and lift into the tin, pressing into the sides, then chill again for the usual 15–20 minutes. Bake blind or as it is but with a pastry overhang of about 1-cm/1/2-inch which will probably shrink quite precisely to size. You can pick at the golden crisp overhang later if it's still there. Little morsels like that are always good for keeping hungry mouths quiet until the time comes. I always keep a small lump of raw pastry aside and fill any gaps between pastry and tin if I need to or

Serves 6

60 g/2 oz butter, plus extra for greasing

Flour for dusting

200 g/7 oz shortcrust pastry (*see* p112)

4 tbsp olive oil

4 large Spanish onions, finely sliced

A dash of tamari (optional)

A dash of red wine (optional)

A pinch of freshly grated nutmeg

3 garlic cloves, finely chopped

4 large organic, free-range egg yolks

300 ml/10 fl oz double cream

Sea salt and freshly ground black pepper

indeed repair any other breakages. It's as well to be safe rather than sorry and I am not at all ashamed of such primitive precautions. Maybe it's because I didn't ever formally train as a chef, but I cheat all the time.

Allow the baked pastry to cool, then return it to the safety of its own tray on the oven shelf, before filling it with the gloopy onion, egg and cream mix. Push the shelf gently back into the hot oven and bake for 20–25 minutes until softly, unctuously set.

Remove and serve with a good green salad and a glass of wine.

Green beans braised with tomatoes and garlic

I often make a whole pan-full of this for myself. Some people will tell you that, of all vegetables, green beans must be *al dente*. How I disagree. I'm not saying they should be flaccid, although, to tell you the truth, I prefer that to crunchy.

This is not a neat buttoned-up dish but one that revels in its sauce, like a rich ratatouille, and should be eaten with wedges of warm white loaf, Knives and forks are quite superfluous to the peasant roughness of this dish. Wipe the bowl clean with a piece of bread and enjoy the sun, wind and fresh-air appetite of it. Some dry-fried, brown and chewy mushroom slices or some black olives can be added to the sauce.

This serves two if you're feeling greedy, or four as an accompaniment.

Serves 2

200 g/7 oz green beans, topped and tailed

4 tbsp olive oil

1 small red onion, cut into wedges

4 garlic cloves, roughly chopped

5 tomatoes, cut into quarters

A dash of Tabasco

Sea salt and freshly ground black pepper

Bring a saucepan of salted water to the boil and blanch the beans for about 7 minutes until they are tender.

Heat the oil in a frying pan. Add the onion and garlic and cook until translucent. Add the tomatoes and beans, some salt and pepper and the Tabasco. Cook over a generous heat and add an occasional spoonful of water to loosen the sticky, flavourful juices.

Keep adjusting the heat as you see fit, until you have a thick sauce and the beans are tender. Eat within about 3 days, hot, cold or inbetween.

Green beans with butternut squash, goat's cheese and a maple syrup glaze

I give you the recipe of the title, and also an alternative with a quick-fried tofu which gains the dark intensity of lengthy marinating and simply through brisk cooking in plenty of oil and tamari.

Preheat the oven to its highest setting.

Mix together 1 tablespoon olive oil, the Tabasco and a little salt and pepper. Put the butternut squash, garlic and onion quarters into a roasting tin and baste them with the olive oil mixture. Tuck the onion and garlic among the squash so that they don't burn. Roast for 25 minutes, until browned and tender.

Meanwhile, bring a small saucepan of salted water to the boil with a little olive oil. Add the beans and boil for 7 minutes. Drain and refresh under cold water. Set aside.

If using tofu, heat 2 tablespoons oil in a small saucepan. Add the tofu and fry for a minute over a high heat, then add 2 tablespoons tamari, reduce the heat slightly and continue to fry on all sides until the tofu is well browned all over and crisp in places. It will stick to the bottom of the pan but that is how it cooks best. Use a metal spatula or spoon to turn it over carefully. The tofu will take about 10 minutes to cook.

If using Chèvre, in the last 7 minutes or so of roasting the butternut squash, add the tamari, Chèvre, almonds and green beans. Mix carefully as you add the maple syrup. Return to the oven. The almonds should crisp and caramelise slightly in the maple syrup.

If you are using tofu instead of Chèvre, add it to the rest just a minute or two before the end.

Serve with a bowl of sharply dressed watercress.

Serves 2–4

3 tbsp olive oil, plus a little extra

A dash of Tabasco

Sea salt and freshly ground black pepper

1 good-sized butternut squash, about 900 g/2 lb, seeds removed, cut into 8 crescents

2–4 garlic cloves, unpeeled

2 small red onions, cut into quarters

150 g/5 oz green beans, topped and tailed

100 g/4 oz thickly sliced Golden Cross Chèvre, or 275 g/10 oz tofu, cut into 16 cubes

Tamari

30 g/1 oz whole almonds, chopped into slivers

1 tbsp maple syrup

Homity pies – the new way

Homity pies represented the essence of Cranks for many years. Then came a time when the very idea of potato and wholemeal pastry filled anyone seriously interested in food with dread. I was among those who considered such food a sad travesty of what it meant to be a vegetarian. It didn't help that the pastry was of door-stop thickness or that the herbs were rarely fresh. Homity held absolutely no charm in my eyes.

By the time I joined Cranks, the pastry had disappeared and it had become nothing more than a mashed potato bake. To the committed, this was comfort food personified, but I still couldn't get into it. For a start, it was not prepared or presented in an acceptable manner. Worse was to follow with its bastardisation into a light, low-fat version for which I sadly and reluctantly have to accept responsibility. But they made me do it...honest gov!

All this returns full circle to a point I feel sure must have existed somewhere, if only in someone's imagination. Here, therefore, is a homity pie where the potatoes are sautéed first, not mashed but left in tender golden chunks, the mushrooms are browned to meaty depth, the cream and cheese bubble and meld in that inimitable way that cream and cheese do, and the herbs are zinging fresh. As for the pastry, I've left it wholemeal, as the quality of such flours nowadays is much finer than before. I add butter with a generous (rather than exact) hand, ice the water with ice cubes, salt adequately, rest at length and, most important of all, roll it out as thinly and delicately as I possibly can. If it tears, I patch it up.

Lastly and only because I happen to have them, I make them in heart-shaped metal tins (rescued from my loft and scrubbed up nicely). I think homity pies are restored to prime position and save me in all kinds of situations, not least those involving small children.

To make the pastry, first read my tip on perfect pastry (see p114). Sift the flour and salt into a bowl, folding the bran back in. Rub the butter into it and add the water. Once you have brought the dough into a ball, wrap it loosely in cling film and leave it in the fridge for 30 minutes or the freezer for 15 minutes.

Makes 6
For the pastry

175 g/6 oz wholemeal flour, plus extra for dusting

Salt

100 g/4 oz butter, plus extra for greasing

2 tbsp iced water

For the filling

600 g/1 lb 5 oz potatoes, chopped into chunks

40 ml/1^1/$_2$ fl oz olive oil

375 g/13 oz onions, finely chopped

3 garlic cloves, finely chopped

125 g/4^1/$_2$ oz mushrooms, sliced

A dash of tamari (optional)

A splash of Tabasco (optional)

100 ml/3^1/$_2$ fl oz double cream

125 g/4^1/$_2$ oz mature Cheddar, grated

1 tbsp chopped parsley

1 tbsp fresh marjoram leaves

Sea salt and freshly ground black pepper

Preheat the oven to 220°C/425°F/gas mark 7.

Butter and dust the tins, each 10-cm/4-inches in diameter, with flour. Roll out the pastry to a dangerous level of thinness, cut it out into squares to line the base and sides of each tin and carefully lift it in, pressing into the sides. Then prick all over with a fork and return to the fridge or freezer. After this second rest, bake for 10 minutes in the oven, lining with baking parchment and baking beans.

Meanwhile make the filling by frying the chopped potatoes in 1 tablespoon olive oil. As for most tasks, I use my large, non-stick, deep-sided frying pan. Although it comes from a catering supplier (these exist in every town), it is extraordinarily cheap. Go about it fairly slowly, so that the potatoes don't reach the golden apex of their perfection on the outside only to remain somewhat under-done on the inside.

Separately, fry the chopped onion to golden-brown in a second tablespoon of oil, adding the chopped garlic halfway through. Add the potatoes to this and fry together over a steady flame for a couple of minutes, then transfer to a bowl while you fry the mushrooms in the same pan with an extra teaspoon or so of oil. They should remain dry so the flame must be high this time, to catch the juices and seal them in. You can add the tamari and Tabasco to give them a little more body.

Mix the lot together in the pan and add the double cream, then remove from the heat and add half the cheese. Season with salt and pepper, add the fresh herbs and allow to cool to a tepid temperature before pouring into the pastry cases.

Scatter the remaining cheese generously all over and bake for 15–20 minutes in the oven. Remember how tongue-searingly hot cheese can get, so allow to cool slightly before eating. The pies make perfect freezer food as long as you bake them straight from frozen the next time you want them. In memory of the tomato slices traditionally placed on each homity, eat with a tomato salad, aromatically dressed.

Perfect pastry

First and foremost, the pastry must be made with light, cool fingers. In my view, nothing affects the success of a pastry more than your own body's temperature. I have a good friend who is a gifted masseuse and an all-round healer of wounded souls. Once, with hundreds to feed, I asked her to help out and set her upon the task of making the pastry for me. I was staggered by the sight of the dough, literally running through her fingers, molten in her natural body heat. Needless to say I set her to a different task. My hands on the contrary are ice cold for about nine months of the year so chilblains are the price I pay for being a born pastry maker. You can take precautions though – chill your bowl and your butter, dip your hands in cold water and use ice-cold water to bind. I promise it all helps.

Kale gratin

Preheat the oven to 200°C/400°F/gas mark 6.

First remove the tough stems, then place the kale into the salted boiling water. The leaves should take about 6–7 minutes to become tender. Meanwhile, sparsley butter a 1-litre/2-pint soufflé dish.

Drain well and either slather with butter or do the following: season the double cream with salt, pepper, nutmeg and garlic. If you are making this with the mile high pie (see p118) add the 2 remaining egg whites, lightly beaten. If not, just add the whole beaten egg. Mix and pour into the prepeared soufflé dish and add the grated mature Cheddar on top.

Bake in the oven for about 20 minutes until the egg is tremulously set, the cheese thickly melted. Allow to sit for a few minutes before serving. If you are making this with the pie, put it in the oven about 10 minutes before the pie is due to come out. By the time they have sat about for the desired time, they'll both be ready for the table.

Green scene

There are other spinach-like greens, such as red-veined Swiss chard and cavolo nero that you can use in this or some other context.

Swiss chard is by far the softer of the two, taking only 3 minutes to turn to a crumpled mass in salted boiling water. Now don't laugh, but the lightly salted red-hued water is delicious. I drink it like a cleansing tonic. But if that's not your idea of fun, you can just stir-fry the Swiss chard in a little melted butter.

Cavolo nero takes 10 minutes, again in salted boiling water. Well drained, you can replace it for the kale in the gratin above or serve it with polenta, butter, freshly grated nutmeg and some shaved Parmesan. Unless I am serving it as a side vegetable, simply dressed, I tend to cut it into more humanly manageable pieces.

To any of these, you can also add drained borlotti or cannellini beans. I usually go for equal amounts of bean and leaf. A whole 400 g/14 oz can drained and mixed with 250 g/9 oz of hot wilted Swiss chard is wonderful with 2 tablespoons olive oil and lemon dressing (see p277).

Alternatively add tamari, Tabasco, more olive oil and a few stoned black olives. To make a whole meal of it, just for yourself, mix 125 g/4^1/2 oz greens with 125 g/4^1/2 oz fresh pasta (weights are before cooking). Again dress with olive oil, lemon juice, finely minced garlic, 1 tablespoon double cream and some grated Parmesan.

Serves 2–4

325 g/11^1/2 oz kale

2 litres/4 pints water

Butter for kale (optional), plus extra for greasing

100 ml/3^1/2 fl oz double cream

A pinch of nutmeg

1 garlic clove, finely chopped

1 organic, free-range egg, beaten

60 g/2 oz mature Cheddar, grated

Sea salt and freshly ground black pepper

Kale tale

Tough, fibre-rich (but never fibrous) dark, curly, green leaves like spinach gone mad and requiring a little taming to make it right – that's kale.

Leek and mushroom buckwheat crêpes

You can substitute the basic recipe for crêpes (*see* p117) for the buckwheat ones, if you think you might prefer something delicate and familiar to something dark and nutty. I rarely make a batch of crêpes without making two – one for now and one to freeze. I sit them on a frying pan on top of a pan of boiling water and they thaw in the steam, ready for a Sunday brunch served with cooked apple and maple syrup.

When I was growing up, we were always allowed to choose our birthday suppers and, until I left home, I always pleaded for pancakes filled with a mushroom sauce. Other members of the family asked for quite different things when their turn came, but the vegetarian in me looked for any opportunity to eschew meat even then.

Allowing the batter to rest in the fridge then stirring in melted butter just before cooking gives crêpes their characteristic laciness. A well-seasoned iron pancake pan is perfect for making crêpes – it's cheap and lasts a lifetime. This recipe makes six crêpes.

To make the crêpes sift the flours and salt into a large bowl and make a well in the centre.

Beat the eggs and pour them into the hole then, beating vigorously with a fork or wooden spoon, work the flour into the eggs until they are amalgamated into a thick, sunny-yellow paste.

Pour the water and milk in slowly, still beating, so that you have a batter of a consistency barely thicker than single cream. Add salt to taste, and let it rest for 1 hour in the fridge. Then add the melted butter and stir it in. Adjust the consistency with a little more water or milk if you need to.

To fry the pancakes, heat the pan to very hot, even with a hint of smoke, wiping it first with a little oil. I do, this the inelegant way by lightly dipping a piece of kitchen paper into the oil and wiping the pan with it. Test to see that the pan is hot enough by dropping a few drops of the batter on to it. It should set and sizzle rather than spit and splutter. Adjust the heat as necessary.

Then use a ladle, measuring jug or cup measure to pour just enough mixture into the pan to cover it – too much and you'll get a thick gooey mess; too little and the mixture won't cover the pan. Run a spatula around the rim and flip the pancake over with the help of your fingers if necessary to cook on the reverse side. Pile the pancakes on a plate kept close by.

To make the filling, first preheat the oven to 200°C/400°F/gas mark 6.

Serves 4
For the crêpes
30 g/1 oz buckwheat (or rye) flour

30 g/1 oz plain flour

1/4 tsp salt

2 organic, free-range eggs

125 ml/4 fl oz water

125 ml/4 fl oz milk

1 tbsp melted butter or light olive oil, plus extra for frying

For the filling
6 young thin leeks or 4 fatter ones

8 chestnut mushrooms

60 g/2 oz butter

1 whole garlic clove

100 ml/3^{1}/2 fl oz milk

1 bay leaf

2 tbsp plain flour

100 ml/3^{1}/2 fl oz double cream plus a little to pour on top

A pinch of freshly grated nutmeg

Freshly ground black pepper

1 tbsp finely snipped chives, to garnish

Slice the leeks finely as far up as you can. If they are very young you might be able to use much of the green. Rinse the mushrooms and slice fairly thinly.

Melt half the butter in a frying pan and fry the finely chopped leeks, together with the chopped garlic clove until transparent and delicately coloured. In an ideal world, I would fry the mushrooms separately and add them to the leeks. They brown better with the barest minimum of liquid and I like the concentrated flavour you get this way, but you could add them to the not-quite-there leeks and fry them together for a few moments if you can't wait.

While they are frying you can start on the béchamel sauce. Pour the milk into a small pan and infuse it with the bay leaf and garlic while it warms slowly through. Next melt the remaining butter in another pan and stir in the flour to make a roux. Little by little, pour in the scalding milk and stir until smooth. Remove the bay leaf and garlic clove, add the cream and season with salt, pepper and a pinch of nutmeg. Add the leeks and mushrooms and stir through for a minute. The sauce will be abundant with vegetables.

Butter an ovenproof dish. Fill each crêpe with the vegetable mixture, then either roll up or fold into a *panequin* – a little square parcel – and arrange snugly in the dish. Drizzle a little double cream on top and warm the pancakes through once more in the oven. Serve with a snippet of chopped chives and a smattering of freshly ground black pepper.

A plain crêpe batter

Use half milk and half water for the batter, it makes for lighter, thinner, more delicate crepes.

Follow the method as described on the previous page. This quantity will make around 16 crêpes.

4 organic, free-range eggs

100 g/4 oz plain flour

200 ml/7 fl oz water

200 ml/7 fl oz milk

1 tbsp olive oil or melted butter

A pinch of salt

A pinch of sugar (optional and only if making a sweet filling)

Mile high vegetable pie in a hot-water crust

What a marvellous thing this is with its thickly crimped and fluted rim and its well-set layers, at once comfortingly mellow and sharply tinged. The hot-water crust breaks every rule you ever thought you knew about pastry. Still, it comes out exotically golden, curiously crisp, friable and firm.

I strongly suggest that you make the fillings first and then the pastry, working it into the sides of the spring-form tin while still hot enough to handle. If you do it the other way round, the pastry has a slippery, slidy way of falling down the sides and sabotaging your best efforts. How do I know? How do you think?

Make sure to cut the potatoes into thick slices. The day I can come up with a comparison that describes a slice a little less than 5-mm/¼-inch thick, I'll be happy. Nigel Slater uses a fitting comparison to the thickness of pound coins for a slice half as thick as the one I'm imagining. I have had my head in my hands over this one, but I suppose I could ask you to slice to the thickness of two one-pound coins. Ah well.

The potatoes are braised in saffron and garlic to melting golden, buttery tenderness, the spinach is nutmeggy, mustardy and creamy, the leeks are ultra-soft and the mushrooms are deeply flavoured and well browned. Serve this majestic pie with a gravy as old-fashioned as a vegetarian gravy can be. If you must have more greens, serve the kale gratin (see p115).

Afterwards or before, serve cherry or baby plum tomatoes, halved, mixed with slivered salty black olives, a little snappy young cucumber, a finely minced red onion, loosened with balsamic vinegar and a pinch of soft brown sugar, all held in a green glug of olive oil. You might not expect it to go together, but it does. You see how many this feeds, so it stands to reason you'll be expecting a crowd. This will keep them happy. Very happy.

For the potato layer, melt the butter over a gentle heat and soften the papery shallot for a moment or two – there must be only infinite gentleness here. Add the potatoes to the same large pan – a pressure cooker is absolutely ideal. Cover with 200 ml/7 fl oz water.

You may need to add the rest in dribs and drabs, you may not – it will depend on your pan and the quality of your heat. Also add the garlic,

Serves 8–10
For the potato layer
40 g/1½ oz butter

1 shallot, sliced paper thin

500 g/1 lb 2 oz new potatoes, thickly sliced

About 300 ml/10 fl oz water

3 plump garlic cloves, finely sliced

A pinch of saffron

Sea salt and freshly ground black pepper

1 large organic, free-range egg, beaten, plus 1 yolk

125 g/4½ oz mature Cheddar

For the spinach layer
350 g/12 oz spinach

A knob of butter

A pinch of freshly grated nutmeg

1 tsp grain mustard

1 garlic clove, finely chopped

1 large organic, free-range egg, beaten, plus 1 yolk

75 g/2½ oz mature Cheddar

Sea salt and freshly ground black pepper

saffron, salt and pepper. Cover with a lid. I use the pressure cooker lid, half turned so it seals without activating the pressure valve. Another lid is fine but I like the hermetic seal of this – it allows for the other meaning of hermetism – alchemy. That's what it's all about, *n'est-ce pas*? Bring this to the boil and quickly reduce to a simmer.

When they are there – about 20 minutes, the pan moved about fairly regularly over a medium heat throughout – and all that remains of the liquid is a slippery saffron glow, add the beaten egg and egg yolk as well as the cheese. Turn with care and set aside.

The spinach happens more pragmatically. Simply add it to a knob of just melted butter and let it wilt for an exact 6 minutes. Then let it cool and squeeze out what liquid you can without squeezing it to death. Season with salt and black pepper, nutmeg, grain mustard and garlic. Add the beaten egg, egg yolk and cheese.

For the mushrooms, melt the butter in a frying pan – it could be the one you've just done the spinach in – and add the mushrooms, each cut into 3 fairly chunky slices. Toss them in the butter until well coated and fry them on a high heat – they'll release liquid so quickly that the butter shouldn't burn. Keep moving the pan about briskly. After a brief minute of this, add the tamari and brandy and keep going a bit like a Chinese wok fryer, fast and furious. The mushrooms should still be firm, dark with soy sauce and seared in places. Finish with the Tabasco to give them a kick and, at the last, a handful of the herb of your choice – anything from sweet to musty. If any liquid remains in the pan, add it to the gravy if you are making it. If not, then drain it off.

Finally, for the leeks, melt the butter and soften the leeks, then season with the other ingredients. They will take 10 minutes over a gentle heat but should not colour.

While all this is happening – and all of the above three steps can be done in the time it takes the potatoes to come to their best – place the 5 large eggs in a pan of cold water. Bring to the boil and from that moment on, time for exactly 3 minutes. Immediately remove them and refresh under cold water, peeling them carefully.

While the fillings cool down a bit make the pastry. Place the butter and vegetable shortening (if using) in a pan with the water and bring to the boil. Pour this straight into a bowl containing the flour and salt.

For the mushroom layer

20 g/³/₄ oz butter

350 g/12 oz chestnut mushrooms

1 tsp tamari and more

1 tbsp brandy

A dash of Tabasco

A small handful of basil, tarragon or marjoram

For the leek layer

30 g/1 oz butter

1 kg/2¹/₄ 1b leeks, washed, trimmed and tough green leaves removed, 1-cm/¹/₂-inch slices

1–2 tsp grain mustard

A pinch of freshly grated nutmeg

Salt and freshly ground black pepper

For the eggs

5 large organic, free-range eggs

For the pastry

225 g/8 oz butter, or half butter, half vegetable shortening

250 ml/9 fl oz water

600 g/1 lb 5 oz plain flour, plus extra for dusting

1 tsp salt

1 large, organic, free-range egg, beaten

For the glaze

2 large, organic, free-range egg yolks

A pinch of salt

3 tbsp double cream

Add the beaten egg and mix to a soft, sensually textured dough. Allow to cool slightly and cut off three-quarters of the pastry, reserving the rest wrapped in cling film until later.

Place the first lot in a 30-cm/12-inch spring-form tin and press it up the sides and over to leave a 2-cm/1-inch overhang. I roll it out sometimes first, but it tears easily so it's easier to do as I first suggest.

Preheat the oven to 190°C/375°F/gas mark 5. Then begin the pleasurable process of layering, first the potatoes, then the spinach, a layer of mushrooms then the eggs softly snuggled in, the leeks heaped around and over and in between until they reach the top of the dish.

Now lightly roll or press the remaining pastry on to a lightly floured surface and cut a lid from it. Lift it over a flour-dusted rolling pin on to the pie and then roll the overhang over, pushing with the index finger of one hand, the thick wedge of pastry between the thumb and index finger of the other. Do this all the way round to make a thickly crimped and fluted rim.

For the glaze, beat the egg yolks, salt and double cream together lightly and brush the top and edge and tiny crevices with this abundant glaze, keeping a little back for the decorations. Make a finger-sized hole in the middle of the lid – start with the point of a small knife, then burrow your finger into the pie. You can use one of those ceramic birds with an open beak if you want to and if you have one.

Sway the pie gently from side to side, letting the deliberately over-generous yellow cream glaze flow into the hole, pouring any excess in there yourself if you need to.

Last but not least, roll the trimmings to a long piece, cut 2-cm/1-inch-wide strips from it and from this, several diamond shapes, which when turned, roughly veined with a sharp knife and twisted make passable-looking leaves to stick on top of the pastry. A 5- or 6-petalled configuration looks pretty. Brush with the remaining glaze.

Bake in the oven for about 1½ hours until the top is as rich and warm as expensive gold. Leave in the tin for a good 15 minutes before you open the spring-form rim. The sides will also be golden and the pie will sit proudly on any platter. Present at once and cut into wedges with a finely serrated knife.

Sexy simmering
The French for simmer is *mijoter*. Time and time again, I want to use it. Maybe it's just my linguistic pathways, first formed in French, that give the word its extra resonance, but it's also the barely restrained passion of the word that does it for me. This is what is happening to the potatoes and especially at the end when they have just melted.

Moussaka

The national dish of Greece has long been a part of the vegetarian lexicon. There's no need to replace the meat of the original with any *ersatz* thing, soya mince being the obvious no no. I've had many a moussaka made with mushrooms, but this is too far from true for my liking (and I don't like the combination of aubergine and mushroom anyway – it's all too soft and mushy for me). Besides, I really think it's rich enough as it is, as well as amply filling and, to use a word I hate, nutritious.

Slice the aubergines a shade under 1-cm/^{1}/$_2$-inch thick and brush them generously with olive oil on one side, but grill them on both sides. You will see that the oil seeps through from one side to the other, doing away with the need to oil on both. Immediately sprinkle them with salt, which is taken in by the hot oil and soft flesh more effectively by far than salting them once they have already cooled.

A few drops of Tabasco are good but not the lemon juice you might out of habit add to fried aubergine – their later pairing with tomatoes make it unnecessary.

Next make a good, well-reduced tomato sauce, keeping going until there's not a trace of wateriness. In a large frying pan, fry the onion in the hot olive oil, then add the chopped tomatoes, juice and all, as well as the garlic and the bay leaf.

Cook on a medium hot flame for 30 minutes, but do stir regularly to stop it sticking to the bottom of the pan. Depending on the quality of the tomatoes, you may need to add a pinch of soft brown sugar.

Add the fresh basil about 3 or 4 minutes before the end; adding it any earlier tends to spoil its delicate sweetness and turns it noticeably metallic. Adjust the seasoning with salt, pepper and a pinch of caster sugar and remove the inedible bay leaf as well as the wilted basil.

Preheat the oven to 200°C/400°F/gas mark 6. Meanwhile place the potato slices in a pan of salted and oiled cold water, bring to the boil and cook for 5 minutes or until tender but not falling apart. Drain them well and set aside for a moment.

Finally make the béchamel by first melting the butter, then adding the flour and stirring until well amalgamated and slightly nutty. Add the warmed milk and stir vigorously until it is all absorbed, the sauce nicely thickened and completely smooth. Remove from the heat before adding the grated cheese, then gently beat in the egg yolk. Season with salt, pepper and grated nutmeg.

Serves 4–6
For the aubergines
2 large or 3 medium aubergines, weighing about 750 g/1 lb 11oz in total

Olive oil for grilling

4 garlic cloves, chopped very finely

A dash of Tabasco

Sea salt and freshly ground black pepper

For the tomato sauce
1 onion, about 150 g/5 oz, thinly sliced

4 tbsp olive oil

1 large can chopped tomatoes, 800 g/1 lb 12 oz

2 garlic cloves, finely chopped

1 bay leaf

Soft brown sugar to taste

A handful of fresh basil

Sea salt and freshly ground black pepper

For the béchamel
40 g/1 ^{1}/$_2$ oz butter

40 g/1 ^{1}/$_2$ oz plain white flour

500 ml/18 fl oz milk, warmed

60 g/2 oz Gruyère, grated

1 egg yolk, beaten

Freshly grated nutmeg

Sea salt and freshly ground black pepper

You are now ready to assemble the moussaka, starting with a double-thick layer of half the aubergine slices, a layer of half the potatoes, followed by a layer of half the tomato sauce, then of half the béchamel. Repeat in this order a second time, finishing with a blanket of béchamel, sprinkled over with grated cheese.

Bake for 30 minutes in the oven until bubbling and golden on top and allow to cool for a few minutes first before serving.

Serve with a Greek salad (omitting the feta cheese if you don't want to overdo it on dairy products) and some gently warmed pitta bread.

For the potato layer
600 g/1 lb 5 oz potatoes, peeled, sliced 5-mm/$\frac{1}{4}$-inch thick and boiled in salted water until tender

A splash of olive oil

For the top
60 g/2 oz Gruyère, grated

Filled field mushrooms in a golden cage

Saucer-sized mushrooms beg to be heaped with goodies, here a confetti of diced, colourful vegetables.

Remove the stumpy stalks from the mushrooms and chop them roughly. Grill the red pepper till charred so that the skin peels off easily, then deseed and cut into long, thin strips.

Sauté the fennel in 1 tablespoon olive oil with the tamari, Tabasco, and 1 garlic clove for 2–3 minutes. Remove from the pan and replace with the mushroom stalks and the courgette, which you must also sauté quickly over a high heat. Set aside with the other vegetables while you briefly sauté the red pepper, simply to tinge it black here and there.

Return all the vegetables to the pan, give them a good stir and add the spinach so it wilts. Finally stir in the spring onion. Season with salt and pepper and set aside while you slowly fry the mushrooms in oil, tamari and garlic, until tender but still holding their shape.

Remove the mushrooms, squeezing out and reserving any excess liquor. Heap each one with the vegetables and set aside to cool.

Reduce the sauce liquid and butter over a gentle heat for around 10 minutes, stirring with a small whisk to amalgamate the butter.

Preheat the oven to 220°C/425°F/gas mark 7. Roll out the pastry on a well-floured surface and roll again with a lattice-work pastry cutter. Cut the lattice into 10-cm /4-inch square pieces, stretch to reveal the lattice and place carefully over each mushroom, trimming any excess. Glaze with beaten egg and bake for about 30 minutes or until risen and golden.

Serve with the sauce, dotted with pomegranate seeds.

Serves 4
4 very large portobello mushrooms (they shrink!)

1 medium red pepper

1 small fennel bulb, trimmed and diced

2–3 tbsp olive oil

1 tbsp tamari, plus another $\frac{1}{2}$ tsp

$\frac{1}{2}$ tsp Tabasco

2 garlic cloves, very finely chopped

1 medium courgette, diced

1 large handful baby spinach, plus 225 g/8 oz extra to serve

1 spring onion, finely sliced

Salt and freshly ground black pepper

175 g/6 oz puff pastry

1 small egg for glazing

For the sauce
All the mushroom liquor, plus 100 ml/3$\frac{1}{2}$ fl oz red wine or Port

1 small shallot, finely chopped

60 g/2 oz butter

1 ripe pomegranate, seeds only

Freshly ground black pepper

Mushrooms

Of the 5,000 types of wild mushrooms that grow in Europe, about one quarter are believed to be edible, about 30 toxic, some fatally so and about the same liable to cause unpleasant symptoms.

Only a famous handful are considered 'prized'. They are *boletus* or ceps chanterelles, blewits, horn of plenty, the rare and more highly prized (and priced) morels, oyster and, of course, the king of them all, truffles. More common are the dark and sultry field mushrooms with their inky, dark juices, aptly referred to as a liquor, as well as the cultivated button that you have to treat as a blank canvas and veritably pour the flavours on to.

Most Europeans enjoy the simple but sophisticated dishes that can be made from wild mushrooms, fried with butter and garlic, a little lemon juice to the lighter ones. I prefer a little tamari on the already pungent ones.

For the French, Italians, Swiss, Russians and Scandinavians, the mushroom season (September to November) is a highlight of the kitchen year, almost religious. Many of the more delicate and rare mushrooms are harvested and dried which increases their otherwise short shelf life and intensifies their flavour so that a few transform a dish.

A ragoût of mixed wild mushrooms is a classic of the vegetarean kitchen. Perfect with pasta, with soft polenta, with a potato gratin, on toast, inside an omelette, in a risotto, I salute the 'magic' mushroom.

OTHER RECIPES USING MUSHROOMS

A Christmas mushroom pie

This is a ceremonial pie, with a delicate, nutty, ethereal pastry, Christmas being the most obvious, but by no means only, occasion for it. It is less labour-intensive than the mushroom Wellington (*see* p127) but has all of its deeply flavoured, mushroom appeal.

You can also make it in a vegetable suet crust and eat it when it is just cooked, still light-textured, friable and tempting. Around $4^1/2$ hours before you want to eat, place a large pan of water on the stove and bring to the boil. When the water starts to boil, mix 400 g/14 oz self raising flour in a bowl with 200 g/7 oz vegetable suet, a good fat pinch of salt, a teaspoon of baking powder and a little powdered English mustard.

Add just enough very cold water to bind it – about 2 $^1/2$ tablespoons, maybe a tad more. Keep about a quarter of the dough aside to make a lid, roll the rest out on a floured surface to a thickness of about 5-mm/$^1/4$-inch and line a well buttered 1-litre/2-pint pudding basin with it, leaving a 3-cm/$1^1/2$-inch overhang.

Fill with the cold filling, leaving a 2-cm/1-inch gap at the top, and roll out the remaining pastry to make a lid. Place it on top, moisten the edge with a little milk or water and seal with the overhang (you will probably be left with a child-friendly lump of dough for small hands to play with).

Cover the pudding with a layer of well buttered foil, pleated in the middle to leave room for expansion and tightly held with string.

Place the pudding in the boiling water so that it reaches two-thirds of the way up the pudding bowl, and cook on a regular simmer for at least 4 hours, checking water levels occasionally and topping up as necessary. When cooked, the pastry dissolves on the tongue like the most buttery shortbread.

If you do go for this suet option, use only 750 g/1 lb 11 oz mushrooms, 15–20 g/$^1/2$–$^3/4$ oz dried porcini, soaked as in the main recipe, 1 fried onion and 3 garlic cloves. Apart from leaving out the spinach, follow the same procedure as for the pie filling.

Either serve traditionally wrapped in a napkin or tea towel that you have used to lift the pudding out of the water, and spoon out. Or turn out the pudding on to a large, deep plate or rimmed dish and watch as it groans, gently collapses, the crust cracking like dried mud, oozing with thick brown juices.

Serves 8–10
For the pie
350 g/12 oz plain white flour

60 g/2 oz wholemeal flour

$^1/2$ tsp salt

225 g/8 oz butter, cold and cut into small pieces

150 g/5 oz whole walnuts, shelled to yield about 60 g/2 oz kernels, roughly chopped

15 g/$^1/2$ oz fresh chives, finely chopped

5 tbsp ice-cold water

1 beaten egg for glazing

Preheat the oven to 200°C/400°F/gas mark 6.

Sift the flours and salt together, stirring any bran back that's been left in the sieve. Lightly and deftly rub in the butter, adding the roughly chopped walnuts and finely chopped chives. Bring the pastry together by slowly adding 1 tablespoon of cold water at a time. I dissolve an ice-cube or two into the water to make it cold enough. I don't often measure the water – it can depend on how hot or cold your hands are, the quality of your flour and the weather. But in this case, it did take exactly 5 tablespoons.

Shape the pastry into a ball with the palm of your hand, wrap it in cling film and refrigerate for a good 30 minutes or place in the freezer for 15 minutes.

Roll out two-thirds of the pastry on a lightly floured surface and carefully lift into the lightly buttered and floured pudding basin. Press into the sides, leaving a slight overhang. Refrigerate it again for another 30 minutes. Bake in the oven for about 20 minutes until golden and crisp. Set aside to cool so that it doesn't go soggy when you add the filling.

Meanwhile, from the remaining pastry (reserving some for decoration), roll out 1 circle for the lid, using the pie tin as a guideline and set aside. Make some pastry holly leaves and a long strip to fit all the way round. Set aside.

Then make the filling by heating the butter and oil in a large frying pan and adding the chopped onion. Fry on a gentle heat for a good 20 minutes, stirring frequently, until the onion is soft and starting to turn golden. Add a little salt only when the onion is of the desired hue, or it may never get there.

About halfway through the frying, add the sliced garlic, but keep a watchful eye on it; it should turn transparent but not brown. Now add the chestnut and shiitake mushrooms, briskly washed of any earth, to the pan of fried onions and fry for about 15 minutes on a medium to high heat. Salt them lightly, remembering that they are going to get an intense hit of soy sauce or tamari a little later on. They will weep some of their deeply flavoured juices, but as you carry on frying, these will start to dry out and intensify in flavour. You may need to shift the heat up a gear or two first.

For the filling

60 g/2 oz butter

1 tbsp walnut or light olive oil

2 medium onions, about 150 g/5 oz each, roughly chopped

5 garlic cloves, thinly sliced

1 kg/2^1/$_4$ lb small chestnut mushrooms or include about 150 g/5 oz shiitake to make up the amount

30 g/1 oz dried porcini, soaked in 150 ml/5 fl oz hot water, a dash of soy sauce and a dash of brandy or Marsala

1 tbsp tamari or soy sauce

Leaves from 5 stalks tarragon, or 4 sprigs thyme, leaves only

5 tbsp Marsala, or red wine or Guinness

4 tbsp double cream

2 tbsp ground almonds

2 tbsp finely chopped parsley

300 g/11 oz baby spinach

Freshly grated nutmeg

A dash of Tabasco, or 1 small crushed dried red chilli

Sea salt and freshly ground black pepper

Strain the softened porcini to remove any grit (rub them with your fingers to be sure), reserving the soaking liquid. To your frying pan, add the porcini, the strained liquid, the tamari or soy sauce, half the tarragon or thyme, the Marsala and the double cream and cook together for 4–5 minutes.

Using a slotted spoon, fish the mushrooms out and set aside while you pump up the heat again, to reduce the sauce by at least half, so that it is thick and creamy, not watery at all. It will go from milky coffee colour to black with a dash of cream.

Return the mushrooms to the sauce, discarding any extra liquid that may have wept in the meantime and heat through, adding the remaining tarragon or thyme, and stirring in the ground almonds to thicken the sauce. Finally add the chopped parsley.

Transfer the mushrooms and their sauce to a bowl. In the same frying pan, using any droplets of sauce that cling there, wilt the spinach for about 3–4 minutes on a moderate heat. Season with salt and pepper, a good pinch of finely grated nutmeg and the Tabasco or crushed dried red chilli.

Loosen the cooled spinach with your fingers and place on the pastry base to completely cover it. Now pile in the mushrooms and sauce and cover with the reserved circle of pastry. Show a little artistic flair with the pastry leaves. Place the strip around the top, gluing it with a little beaten egg and crimp to a fluted crown all the way round.

Glaze the pie abundantly and bake in the oven for 35–45 minutes until golden and crisp.

Let it rest for 10 minutes, then carefully turn out the heavy pie onto a grand serving plate and serve ceremoniously to an attending fanfare of oohs and aahs.

Mushroom Wellington

There's no way around this. Mushroom Wellington takes time and you need a good food processor, the blade of which still has some zip to it. But the beauty is that you can prepare it to baking stage weeks in advance and bake it straight from frozen. At this stage glaze the pastry with beaten egg and put it in a hot oven to cook for 45 minutes until puffed, golden and as festive looking as possible. I like to have a centre of attraction on my table on Christmas day, something I can ceremoniously carry forth, that shows I've cared and that everyone can share.

I don't believe in mean individual portions, especially on an occasion like this. This has to be about abundance and there has to be a certain sense of ritual. I've been making this on and off for 17 years and it has stood the test of time. For the gratin, you can slice the potatoes the day before and keep them in cold water. Just drain them and dry them well on the day and proceed with the recipe as set out below. If you want a completely stress-free morning, you can even cook the gratin the night before and simply reheat it in the same oven as the Wellington, covered with a piece of buttered foil or baking parchment to stop it from burning. Or to make life even simpler, use good roast potatoes, which means not stinting on the oil – there's no such thing as a virtuous roast potato. They must cook on a very high heat for 1 hour until crisp and golden, par-boiled first if you are truly dedicated.

I include a simple braised fennel recipe here (*see* p130) because it could have been designed as an accompaniment to this. The fennel gratin on p61 is best kept for a less gargantuan affair. Also the carrots and parsnips, dressed up a bit for Christmas and cranberry sauce are ideal alongside.

Something else you can do with this wonderful mixture is treat it like a pâté. You'll see just how much it looks like one. As it is will do fine but if you want something really spectacular, fold a spoonful or two of whipped cream into it, a little more Marsala or brandy and turn quenelles through it with 2 dessertspoons.

In *Secrets from a Vegetarian Kitchen* (Pavilion, 1996) I serve the pâté with an apricot and shallot confit and a few home-fried vegetable crisps (the packet ones are foul). If that sounds like too much hard work, then served plain with some thin crisp toast will be divine enough. One final thought, you can add texture with a few fried sliced mushrooms.

Serves 12–16 (makes 2)

500 g/1 lb 5 oz puff pastry

60 ml/2 fl oz sunflower oil

675 g/1^1/$_2$ lb onions, chopped

4 garlic cloves, crushed

450 g/1 lb chestnut mushrooms, left whole

2 tbsp fresh tarragon

4 tbsp soy sauce or tamari, or replace 1 tbsp with Marsala or sherry

Salt and freshly ground black pepper

320 g/11^1/$_2$ oz broken cashew pieces

175 g/6 oz fine, freshly made breadcrumbs, white or wholemeal

320 g/11^1/$_2$ oz ground almonds

1 egg, beaten for glazing

Drying tarragon

Dried tarragon is the only dried herb I keep and this Wellington is the only thing I sometimes use it in, having once too often found myself with no fresh tarragon and it is an essential of this very particular flavour. Try a freeze-dried, still very green-looking batch. Anything dull looking will taste it.

Roll out the pastry on a lightly floured surface into two rectangles, 30x23-cm/12x9-inch each and set aside, covered up in the fridge until required.

To make the filling, heat the oil in a large pan and fry the onion with half the garlic for at least 20 minutes or until coloured deep, dark browny gold. This is crucial as pale onions will give an insipid mix. Remove from the pan and set aside. Add the mushrooms to the same pan with the rest of the garlic and half the tarragon and cook on a fairly high heat. Halfway through cooking, add the soy sauce or tamari and alcohol, using. Continue until the mushrooms are cooked through; there should be no white centre left when you cut one open.

Season with salt and pepper. Set aside, reserving all the mushroom liquor – the intensely flavoured liquid wept by the mushrooms.

In a food processor or blender, blend the cashews with the reserved mushroom liquor to a fine, smooth purée, adding a little water or even more of whichever alcohol you are using until you have a smooth, paste or pâté. Remove from the blender and also blend first the onions, then the mushrooms until they are also perfectly smooth.

Mix all the blended ingredients together in a bowl, adding the breadcrumbs, ground almonds and the remaining tarragon. The mixture should gently hold its shape when formed with the hands.

Preheat the oven to 220°C/425°F/gas mark 7. Remove the pastry from the fridge and place on a lightly floured surface. Separate the two rectangles and place one amount of filling onto one of the pastry pieces, shaping it with your hands as you go to make a long rectangular shape about 28-cm/11-inches long, 6-cm/3-inches wide and 5-cm/2-inches high.

Now with the thin point of a sharp knife, make diagonal cuts at a 45 degree angle, starting from the left-hand corner of the pastry towards the pâté mixture. Repeat on the other side, this time starting at the top right-hand corner and cutting down towards the centre. The strips should be about $1^{1}/_{2}$-cm/$^{3}/_{4}$-inch wide. Fold the end pieces in first. Then draw a strip over from the left, then one from the right, crossing them over. It's OK to tug at the strips slightly if needed, so the mix is snugly wrapped up.

Repeat for the second Wellington. Either freeze at this stage or glaze generously with beaten egg. Place on a floured tray, using 2 fish slices or the loose base of a tart tin, slipped underneath to help you.

Bake in the oven for 35–45 minutes until golden. Allow to cool for a few minutes before attempting to lift on to a serving dish. Run a blade underneath to loosen it completely from the tray.

Allow two festive slices per person, cut with a sharp serrated knife or, better still, an electric knife.

To serve, place the Wellington on your largest platter, surrounded by roasted vegetables and braised fennel (*see* below).

Braised fennel

Reserve the fine feathery fronds from the fennel. Heat half the oil in a heavy-based saucepan and add the fennel quarters. Fry them on all sides until catching and burnishing in places. Add the water, bouillon powder, the remaining oil, the garlic, salt and pepper.

Cover with a lid and bring to the boil. Reduce the heat and simmer gently for 10–12 minutes or until the fennel is tender, the liquid is reduced to three-quarters and is thickened to a coating sauce.

This can be made the day before and reheated slowly. It will serve four to six people.

4 fennel bulbs, trimmed of their green fronds

4 tbsp sunflower or light olive oil

300 ml/10 fl oz water

1 scant tsp Marigold bouillon powder

3 garlic cloves, finely sliced

Salt and freshly ground black pepper

Roasted vegetables

For the carrots and parsnips, allow one of each per person. Peel and cut into half or quarters lengthways and mix with a light olive oil to coat, a tablespoon of maple syrup, squeezed ginger juice (obtained by grating a 5-cm/2-inch piece of ginger and squeezing out the juice with your fingers), a dash of Tabasco, salt and pepper and a sliced mango – allowing about 1 small mango per six portions of vegetables.

Roast in the oven with the Wellington for about 30–40 minutes until the vegetables are crisp and caramelised on the outside and soft inside.

Accompaniments

You can make a quick sauce if you wish although the gratin is creamy enough and the vegetables will have given off juices of their own. However a few thinly sliced button mushrooms with a few wild ones added, slowly fried in a knob of butter and seasoned with a little white wine, salt, pepper and thickened with a dash of cream would be delicious poured over the Wellington slices. Add some finely snipped chives or shredded watercress for colour and sharp contrast

Good old-fashioned cranberry sauce goes well too, made by boiling an equal weight of cranberries and sugar, the juice of an orange, a touch of grated nutmeg and an optional clove or two. It will only take about 10 minutes.

A ragoût of mushrooms with vermouth

What can you not eat this with? Oversized homemade pappardelle ribbons at their slurpy, slippery best? Mashed potato, light and fluffy with butter, milk, cream (yes, all three), or soft and silken with olive oil? On a split and toasted brioche? In a puff pastry pie? Stirred into some soft yet nutty brown rice? With polenta in any guise – soft gnocchi or fried finger-fat chips of it? As a luxurious filling for a pale and fluffy omelette? Cooked in a risotto with the cream as an optional, utterly indulgent extra? On its own, with bread, your fingers? And, well, see below.

Melt the butter in a frying pan over a low heat and gently soften the garlic, stirring all the while.

Add the mushrooms (though keep aside the soaked dried mushrooms and the chanterelles and enoki to fry separately and return to the pan later), a dash of tamari, Tabasco, salt and pepper and cook for a further 3–4 minutes until the mushrooms are tender and release their liquor, at which point, reduce the heat to a minimum so it doesn't dry out.

Add the cleaned, soaked reconstituted dried mushrooms and their soaking liquid – about 150 ml/5 fl oz – strained of any grit. Add the vermouth and herbs and reduce to about half, then add the cream, the separately fried chanterelles and enoki and stir. When the ragoût is ready, remove from the heat and serve in any of the ways mentioned above.

Or serve on its own in a deep soup plate, a heap of wilted greens within easy reach and a loaf of bread, warmed right the way through with which to wipe every drop of the sweet, alcoholic, meatily mushroomy sauce. Plate-licking is entirely permissible under the circumstances.

And finally, the ragoût can be served with a Jerusalem artichoke mash (part potato, part tuber) softened with butter and spiked with snipped chives. Dress it up with tight, thumb-thick heads of sautéed fennel, braised turnips so minuscule they are not so much baby as embryonic, and tiny pointy carrots, fried to a golden-tinged, mellow softness. Short stumpy asparagus spears, first blanched then browned in butter, and finely chopped garlic can join this medley or be served on their own. Butter-mashed swede is yet another option, either in a rustic bowlful or – and perhaps prettier – in spoon-turned quenelles.

Serves 2–4

75 g/2^1/2 oz butter

2 garlic cloves, finely chopped

1^1/4 kg/2 lb 14 oz mixed mushrooms, to include button or chestnut; a few shiitake, thickly cut; pieds bleu; trompettes des morts; about 30 g/1 oz dried porcini or morels, soaked for 20 minutes and drained; wild chanterelles and a few extra-terrestrial looking enoki

Tamari

A dash of Tabasco

4 tbsp vermouth

A sprig of tarragon (optional)

Leaves from 4–5 sprigs thyme

A small bunch of basil or a sprinkling of very finely chopped parsley

3–4 tbsp double cream

Salt and freshly ground black black pepper

Enoki escapades

The enoki usually comes in thick clumps. You are better off slicing them across into as many as 3 thinner slices and frying them in a little butter. When they are softening, add 1 dsp tamari and continue to cook on a moderate heat until they become darker, silkier and tastier.

Polenta

Maize reached Italy via Spain and the New World and was enthusiastically adopted by the Venetians who found it grew well on their soil.

Picture this – a woman (invariably) stands over a huge, unlined copper pan filled with polenta and boiling water hanging over an open fire. She holds a very long, wide, wooden paddle-like spoon and stirs. And stirs. For up to 2 hours till it is cooked. The golden polenta meanwhile heaves and swells and sputters. Then it is poured on to a large wooden board, set in the middle of the table. The assembled company cuts away at it with a long thin wire. Perhaps there is an aromatic stew close by too. Such scenes may be rare now but surely it is to capture something of their essence that so many of us turn to rustic dishes.

For those who simply don't have the patience, let alone the time, there is a polenta *svelta*, pre-cooked so you don't have to do as mama did. On the premise that you get what you pay for, this is a limpid imitation which lacks texture. But, big but, you can make it good. Add indecent amounts of Parmesan, butter, salt and pepper, olive oil, fresh basil, and even soft semi-dried tomatoes. Now see if it doesn't get eagerly torn at, wolfed down. Finally, if this really does seem beyond the pale to you, then invest in a heat diffuser – a cheap thing. You'll hardly need to stir at all and 30 minutes later the polenta should be thick and smooth.

OTHER RECIPES USING POLENTA

Soft polenta with broccoli

Forty minutes of patient stirring – a clear indication that proper polenta is one of my favourite foods. I like it as liquid as I have eaten it in Florence in a restaurant owned by Benedetta Vitali, a pioneer of the slow-food movement. It was the palest primrose yellow, thin and creamy, soothing and deeply sophisticated. I like it firm, cut into 'gnocchi', baked with butter and served with translucent slices of Parmesan.

If 40 minutes of stirring seems too dedicated, there is a pre-cooked polenta which takes as little as 8. It lacks the texture of the best and some of its flavour, but with more Parmesan and butter than you might think prudent, with plenty of freshly torn herbs and abundantly seasoned, it can be a useful understudy, especially if there are children around.

Fill a pan with the water or stock. Salt and bring to the boil. Stirring with one hand, pour in the polenta in a steady slow stream with the other. Once it is all in, reduce the heat and continue to stir patiently for 40 minutes or so until the polenta starts to move away from the sides of the pan. Stop sooner than this if you want it runny and start with a little more water in the first place. Stir in the Parmesan, butter and herbs.

If you want to be rustic, pour straight on to a wooden board so you and your companions can serve yourselves from it as you please.

Blanch the broccoli in plenty of salted boiling water for 3 minutes. Strain and run quickly under cold water to seize and capture the chlorophyll and its vibrant green.

Heat the olive oil in a pan and fry the garlic until transparent. Add the broccoli and generous seasonings and sauté slowly, adding a dash of water if necessary. Shake the pan about a bit – it doesn't matter if the broccoli begins to fall apart; in fact it will be absolutely delicious like this. Serve it next to or on top of the polenta with more Parmesan if required.

Polenta pancake

To make a polenta pancake, make a quantity of the quick-cook polenta. Season it to your heart's content and pour it thinly into a large frying pan, with 1 tablespoon olive oil. Fry on both sides till golden and crisp around the edges. Serve straight from the pan, cut into wedges.

To turn it over, slide on to a plate, cooked side down and quickly flip back into the pan. Or simply give the uncooked side a quick blast under a hot grill. Serve with roasted vegetables.

Serves 4
For the polenta

1.6–1.8 litres/2^1/$_2$–3 pints boiling water or light vegetable stock, depending on consistency required

800 g/1 lb 12 oz polenta, quite coarse, organic if possible

Sea salt and freshly gound black pepper

60 g/2 oz Parmesan, finely grated, plus extra for serving

30 g/1 oz butter, cut into small pieces

A handful of basil, roughly torn

Sundried tomatoes, black olives and extra olive oil added to taste

For the broccoli

350–500 g/12 oz–1 lb 2 oz broccoli, cut into florets, stems peeled and trimmed

1–2 tbsp olive oil

1 garlic clove, very finely chopped

Sea salt and freshly ground black pepper

Field mushrooms with black polenta

This was inspired by a plateful of polenta with cuttlefish which my husband and some friends ate in Venice. The polenta had been cooked in the ink and I could see the dramatic blue-black intensity that had them so enthralled. No one but no one will ever have me cooking cuttlefish.

But something about the impact of the black polenta appealed and I resolved there and then to try a version with field mushrooms. Old ones, ragged about the gills, work best. They need to release the blackest of inks and do so best on a low heat. Together with garlic, Marsala, tamari and a little black olive paste, the juices are sweet, intense and inkily dark.

These are not huge portions, but they are so rich and deeply flavoured that any more would be too much. If time isn't a concern do use the good-quality coarse grained polenta.

Soak the porcini in 150 ml/5 fl oz hot water, 1 tablespoon tamari and 1 tablespoon Marsala. Set aside until reconstituted.

Heat 1 tablespoon olive oil in a frying pan and fry the shallots until soft. Add the mushrooms and soften for about 8 minutes. You should be able to collect a good 125 ml/4 fl oz of their liquid. When the mushrooms have begun to soften, add the garlic, tamari, black olive purée and 2 tablespoons Marsala.

Add the plumped-up porcini – cleaned of grit, strained and their soaking liquid reserved – as well as the basil, and stir for a minute or so. Now collect all the mushroom juices from the pan and mix with the reserved porcini liquor. If a couple of pieces of mushrooms get left behind, snip them with scissors, they'll add texture to the polenta.

Pour into a small pan and bring to the boil. Pour the measured polenta in a thin stream into this dark mushroomy stock, stirring vigorously all the while. When it is thickened to a sloppy paste, spread it 1-cm/1/2-inch thick into a straight-sided buttered dish and allow to cool.

When you are ready to serve, cut it into 6 wide fingers and fry them on both sides, back in the frying pan you originally used for the mushrooms. If the pan is large enough you might be able to reheat the mushrooms, with the knob of butter and the remaining Marsala and fry the polenta at the same time. If not, do one and then the other, keeping the polenta hot in a warm oven.

Wilt the spinach, pour a little olive oil over it, season and divide between two shallow bowls. Place 3 polenta fingers and half the mushrooms on top of each and serve hot.

Serves 2

4 large field mushrooms, cleaned and cut into thick slices

30 g/1 oz dried porcini

2 tbsp tamari

4 tbsp Marsala

2 tbsp fruity olive oil, plus extra

1 shallot, finely sliced

5 garlic cloves, chopped small

1 tbsp black olive purée

1 tbsp basil

90 g/3 1/2 oz (8-minute) polenta

A knob of butter

225 g/8 oz spinach

Salt and freshly ground black pepper

Mushy business

Usually, I just chuck the mushrooms into a big colander, run water over them and toss them quickly with my hands, then shake them out. In a recipe like this one, I positively want the mushrooms to weep, so don't mind if they become flabby. Sometimes though, if I can see that it's just a bit of earth here and there, I flick it off and don't worry too much about it. Whatever you do, don't let yourself be guilt-tripped into brushing the mushrooms clean. You'll be there all day, cussing and cursing instead of getting on with the sexier business of cooking them.

Potatoes

I think the most useful thing I can do here is to give you a list of which are best for what. Personally, I think it's the most useful thing I ever cut out of a newspaper article – I think it was by Michael Bateman. I laminated it and kept it in my otherwise messy-beyond-words filofax for ages.

The general rule is to use fluffy-fleshed, floury potatoes for anything that needs to crisp up on the outside and remain light and crumbly within. So for roasted potatoes, chips or sautéed (which we don't seem to make often enough) use a King Edward (particularly good for mash as it breaks up on boiling), a Maris Piper, or the Dutch all rounder Wilja – these at least should be very easy to find. For a great baked potato, try a fluffy Golden Wonder with its delicious skin. Estima is easy too and looks good but tastes of nothing so I avoid it if I can.

I also break the rule and use a floury potato for some types of potato salads, cut into thick slices and served not in a bowl but flat on the plate so they don't completely collapse. I like the way they absorb the olive oil and herbs I slather them with.

For a gratin – and I think this is where it most matters which variety you use – try the waxy, yellow-fleshed La Ratte, the similar-tasting, nutty Pink Fir Apple or the excellently textured Charlotte. All of these are also great in olive-oil-rich salads or with mayonnaise or just warmed cream and snipped chives.

OTHER RECIPES USING POTATOES

Middle Eastern potatoes with saffron and raisins

This lies somewhere between a stew and a braised dish and you've got it right when the potatoes are gloriously radiant with the copper-hued saffron and waxily, meltingly tender because of the oil. I know we baulk at dishes swimming in oil, so I don't go totally mad... just mad enough.

Some people think you cannot get the same deeply cooked onion from a stainless-steel pan as you can from an old-fashioned aluminium one, its bad press notwithstanding. I know why they say this – a thinner metal with such great heat-retaining properties will sear and hold the juices in, yet brown the onion much more quickly than a pan where the onion has to go through a sort of wishy-washy phase first.

Still I cannot put my hand on my heart and ask you to use an aluminium pan and I don't believe any of you would listen to me if I did. The point is that you don't need your best heavy-bottomed pan, but you do need to be there, stirring and keeping an eye on things.

Heat the oil and fry the sliced onion until brown and sweet. Add the sliced garlic and fry for a few minutes before adding the potatoes. Fry them for a few minutes too before adding the saffron stock, as well as salt, pepper and most of the chopped chilli.

Add water in 5 or 6 goes, allowing it to be absorbed into the potatoes – these thicken up the vegetable juices as they begin to collapse, to give a translucent coating sauce which will appear saffron-coloured and glistening with the oil.

Only when the potatoes are halfway cooked, add the celery pieces so that they retain a little bite, as the potatoes become waxily tender and rich with oil and intense seasoning. The raisins can be added for the last 10 minutes or so, releasing their sugars into the sauce. Under no condition should this end up watery or bland, so keep cooking until you achieve the right, gorgeous, slow-cooked consistency and adjust the seasoning accordingly.

Scatter the chopped coriander and the remaining chilli on top and serve when you are ready.

Serves 4

4–5 tbsp light olive oil

1 large onion, thinly sliced

2 garlic cloves, finely sliced

500 g/1 lb 2 oz salad potatoes, cut in halves or large chunks

A good pinch of saffron, dissolved in 4 tbsp hot water

1 bird's eye chilli, chopped very small

2 sticks celery, roughly chopped

30 g/1 oz plump raisins

2 tbsp chopped coriander

Salt and freshly ground black pepper

Gratin Dauphinois

Everyone but everyone loves gratin dauphinois, sometimes against their better judgement, or rather guilt over the lashings of double cream. But they cannot resist. Apart from being utterly, wickedly, indulgently divine, it is about the most useful vegetarian recipe on the planet. I don't believe there's a single one of you out there who doesn't have a recipe for it already, but it is a dish I almost revere. For me, this is the recipe that makes all others obsolete, those with more cream as much as those with less.

There are other ways of making it, some involving eggs and milk, and modern versions with ceps or slivers of fennel, or mixed with thin slices of celeriac. The original *pommes de terre à la dauphinoise* is made with no cheese at all, the cream setting to a golden, bubbling top as it slowly bakes (even without the cheese). If I'm serving the gratin with something rich and filling in its own right, then I opt for that. But if it's to be the main part of the meal, I like the double indulgence of this recipe, cheese and all.

The dish it goes in should be shallow – a lasagne dish is perfect – and the potatoes should be as firm and as waxy as possible. New potatoes are fine for these reasons – even cut very thinly by hand or in a food processor, they won't fall apart on you.

When it is ready, the potatoes are bathed in cream, gentle notes of garlic and nutmeg wafting through. I serve it on its own (though quite often with the extra-tasty morsels I mentioned earlier) or as an accompaniment to a no-holds-barred mushroom Wellington (*see* p127) and an all-the-trimmings feast. This has been my vegetarian Christmas lunch for about 17 years as well as being the vegetarian meal I am never afraid to serve my parents nor indeed anyone who stills recoils at the idea of an all-vegetarian meal. It wins them over every time.

Preheat the oven to 180°C/350°F/gas mark 4. Then peel and slice the potatoes thinly – I aim for 3-mm/^{1}/8-inch thin and either do this by hand, with my trusted vegetable chopper or the thinnest blade of my food processor. Pat the slices dry with a tea towel and immediately mix them in a basin with the cream, nutmeg, garlic, salt, pepper and finely sliced onion, if using.

Butter an ovenproof dish about 6-cm/2^1/2-inches deep, and press most of the potato mixture firmly into the dish, finishing up with the remaining slices placed neatly on top. Hide the onion in the mixture, though, or it will burn. Sprinkle with the Gruyère and bake in the hot oven for about an hour, until the top is molten gold and the potatoes soothingly tender.

Serves 6

1 kg/2^1/4 lb waxy potatoes

560 ml/scant 1 pint double cream

A pinch of freshly grated nutmeg

2 garlic cloves, chopped very finely or sliced thinly

1 shallot or small onion, sliced very fine (optional)

20 g/^{3}/4 oz butter

100 g/4 oz Gruyère, finely grated

Salt and freshly ground black pepper

Looking good

I used to place the slices one by one in neat concentric layers, pouring a little of the seasoned cream over each layer. Then I discovered that mixing the whole lot together still gave me an elegant multi-layered look when cut, so I stopped.

Potatoes with tomatoes and red onions

This was a regular feature of my mother's table, she makes it as an accompaniment to baked fish. I might add a little Gruyère to the softened, oil-absorbed potatoes. They do go well with griddled aubergine slices rolled around Mozzarella, or strips of Haloumi then brushed with pesto, warmed and brushed with lime or lemon juice and chopped corriander. They also go well with a braised vegetable such as fennel or celery.

The potatoes must be scalloped – that is sliced very thinly with a sharp knife, a mandolin or the finest blade of a food processor.

Preheat the oven to 170°C/325°F/gas mark 3. Slice the potatoes thinly and, unless you are going to use them immediately, immerse the slices in a bowl of cold water until you are ready. Then you can dry them between 2 clean tea towels and continue.

In a bowl, mix the potatoes well with the oil, salt, pepper and garlic. Pack them tightly into an ovenproof dish, and intersperse the red onion and tomato slices into the top layers, so that they are only partly revealed (they will burn if they are overexposed).

Cover the dish with a lid or a piece of baking parchment but not foil as this can react with the tomatoes and turn the whole dish black.

Bake in the oven for 45–50 minutes. Remove the lid and turn the heat up to 200°C/400°F/gas mark 6 for a further 10 minutes until the top layer is gently crisped.

Serve at once, garnished with the basil. With a little cheese melted on top, this may well make the most significant part of a meal. Green salad is an imperative accompaniment.

Serves 6

2 kg/4$\frac{1}{2}$ lb small potatoes, thinly sliced, 3-mm/$\frac{1}{8}$-inch thick

100 ml/3$\frac{1}{2}$ fl oz olive oil

1 garlic clove, finely slivered

1 red onion, cut into thin wedges

8 tomatoes, cut into quarters

Salt and freshly ground black pepper

Basil to garnish

Sudanese potatoes

My friend Kerry, a professor involved in some cutting-edge medical research, spent two years travelling around the Sudan. She tells me that she ate this dish, cooked slowly in a clay pot, in every village she stopped at. When she was describing it to me, she mentioned several times the masses and masses of garlic, either left whole or chunkily cut.

She also told me that in most villages, the casserole is served with a feta-like cheese crumbled on top, then squirted with lime juice. I wondered about fresh coriander, which she had not seen in Sudan, but we agreed that if it were available, it would be welcomed here. So I chopped a handful on top too and it goes perfectly. I also added a little garam masala and ground coriander, knowing it not to be strictly authentic but I suggest it as an aromatic, successful addition. You can use canned tomatoes or the equivalent weight of fresh.

When it is ready, the sauce must have all the piquancy of chilli, softened by the sweetness coaxed out of the tomatoes and added to with a pinch of sugar if necessary. I played around with this quite a bit, making it both on top of the stove in a deep, lidded, wide-based pan or in a covered casserole dish in a slow oven. Either way it takes a good 2 hours and in both cases the potatoes are as tender as butter, the sauce thick, smooth, voluptuous. The typical side dish is not one I think I could handle – a millet-like grain made into a glutinous pancake, or fried okra which I have had to relegate to my list of kitchen rejects.

I could not find the need – or the space – for any accompaniment, but if you think you need more I can't recommend anything more tempting than the fried tortilla (*see* p94) and the spinach and almonds (*see* opposite) however tenuous the connection.

Preheat the oven to about 160°C/325°F/gas mark 3.

Fry the onion until transparent in a little olive oil, heated in a large pan. Add the spices and tomatoes, which you can roughly break up with a wooden spoon.

Add the potatoes to the tomatoes. Also add the garlic cloves, either left whole or chunkily cut – I quarter them, that's all. Stir a couple of times and make sure that the potatoes are fully immersed.

Cover and set upon a gentle flame for about 2 hours, stirring occasionally. Do exactly the same if you want to make this in a casserole dish though you will need to fry the onion and start the casserole on top of the stove. Cook for about 2 hours.

Serves 4

1 good-sized onion, roughly chopped

2 tbsp light olive oil or more

1/2 tsp garam masala

1/2 tsp ground coriander

1/2 tsp dried chilli pepper flakes or more, even much more to taste

800 g/1 lb 12 oz canned or fresh tomatoes, plus 2 ripe tomatoes

500 g/1 lb 2 oz potatoes, waxy if possible, thickly sliced

6 or more plump garlic cloves

100 g/4 oz feta

Juice of half a lime

A small bunch fresh coriander

Salt and freshly ground black pepper

When the potatoes are completely soft and a knife slides through with no resistance, serve, with a little feta crumbled over each portion, a little lime juice and a scattering of fresh coriander. Even (or especially) if you are using canned tomatoes, complete with a couple of good firm but ripe tomatoes, roughly chopped and cooked through for the last few minutes. This is deliciously fresh and alive when first made but reheats well the next day too, by which time the flavours are rounder if less perky.

Spinach with slivered almonds, raisins and fried onion

You'll need 2 whole bags of supermarket ready-washed spinach to serve two if this is a main recipe or four if it's one among other side dishes, such as mushrooms sautéed in olive oil, garlic and lemon, or cumin-braised carrots (see p96). I'm assuming that you're going to enjoy this so much that any less will not do. Besides, the way spinach shrinks is legendary.

I have never got into the habit of blanching spinach; it just seems insane to me when wilting it in its own moisture, with or without a little butter or olive oil, does the job so remarkably well.

I am beginning to serve vegetable dishes like this as a course in their own right; I love vegetables too much to be satisfied with a spoonful on the side – I want whole delicious mounds of them. They are not the afterthought but the *raison d'être* of my cooking. If you need any other excuses, then the healthier French and the Italians have been doing this forever, they taste great, they fill you up, they're supremely good for you and they don't make you fat. What more do you want?

Serves 2–4

3 tbsp olive oil

1 large Spanish onion, finely sliced into half moons

1 tbsp cumin seeds

60 g/2 oz large juicy raisins, soaked in hot water for about 10 minutes and drained

1 garlic clove, finely chopped

500 g/1 lb 2 oz baby spinach, picked over to remove any limp bits

Fresh nutmeg, grated

40 g/1^{1}/2 oz almonds, slivered and toasted for 8 minutes

Sea salt and freshly ground black pepper

Heat the olive oil in a large, heavy-bottomed frying pan, add the onion and fry until golden brown and crispy, but watch continuously and keep stirring, so that it does not blacken and spoil your good intentions.

Add the cumin seeds and fry with the onion for about 30–40 seconds, followed by the softened raisins and the garlic as well as some salt and pepper. Keep stirring for a minute or two before adding the spinach.

You will need to do this in stages, adding more as the last lot has collapsed. Keep pushing it down and turning it over, adding the grated nutmeg at any stage. You will have to work quickly and on a fairly high heat which evaporates the water leaked out by the spinach, as it's important you don't let this savoury-sweet marriage become wet and soggy or metallic and overcooked.

When the spinach is all wilted and you have a luscious mound before you, add the almonds. This must be at the last moment before you are ready to serve so that they provide the necessary crisp contrast. Eat with saffron rice, a warm legume salad and a dollop of Greek yoghurt by the side or some feta crumbled on top.

Spinach gnocchi with a rich tomato sauce

There aren't many shortcuts to boosting your self-esteem, but making a supremely easy dish that still makes people think you are a genius. It is practically impossible to go wrong and because they are a thousand times nicer than the little bullets most people are used to, they always elicit praise and approval – who can't do with a bit of that now and again?

As usual it is the little tricks that help. If you are making this for more than four people, have two pots of boiling water on the go or you'll be fishing about blindly in the opaque water. Gnocchi like plenty of space to boil and generally dance about in. Also, if you can't face cooking the gnocchi at the last minute, then bring them to the boil first and remove them with a slotted spoon as soon as they rise to the surface. Keep the pot simmering and simply keep the par-boiled gnocchi ready to dunk back into boiling water for just another minute or so, before serving.

Working backwards, I also shape the gnocchi to the walnut stage as much as the day before, lay them on a large plate lined with lightly floured baking parchment (in layers if necessary), cover them loosely with cling film and keep them in the fridge until needed. Don't give yourself a panic attack or be on tenterhooks until the last. Test one in advance and if it seems too collapsible, add a little flour and a little extra cheese. Finally taste the mixture and season it to your taste-buds' delight. Just because the gnocchi will be accompanied by a delicious sauce, it doesn't mean they should be bland and boring. Leave that to the factory-made stuff. When each component part of a meal is as

delicious as you can make it, you know that the final result is going to be 'A1 OK'. Taste, balance, taste. The tomato sauce is as rich and aromatic as they come. To be honest, I stopped measuring the olive oil when I got to about 100 ml/3^1/$_2$ fl oz. Sometimes I want a simple, light tomato sauce, barely more than a concasse of tomatoes only very loosely bound with olive oil; at other times I like it thicker, oilier and jammier, and this was just such a time.

Start by soaking the porcini in a little hot water and add a dash of tamari if desired.

Wilt the washed spinach in a large pan. Again only the water clinging to it is necessary. Squeeze it of any excess and season it with salt, pepper, a grating of fresh nutmeg and the chopped garlic.

Let it cool down completely before adding the Ricotta, flour, grated Parmesan and reconstituted porcini, chopped small. Stir it all together with a fork (or your fingers) to a soft, malleable mix which shapes easily in your lightly floured palms. Keep dipping your fingers into a little flour before breaking off lumps and forming into 36 small walnut shapes.

You can start on the sauce while the spinach is cooling down. First heat a couple or more tablespoons olive oil in a large frying pan and fry the onion on a medium heat until quite well browned. Add the chopped garlic about halfway through and the salt at the end. You can season with pepper at any stage.

Meanwhile, cut the fresh tomatoes in half, sprinkle them with a little salt and pepper and 1 tablespoon olive oil. Place them in a preheated oven set to about 180°C/350°F/gas mark 4 for about 40–50 minutes.

While those are doing, you can continue with the rest of the tomato sauce. Add the canned tomatoes to the fried onion and a copious amount of olive oil – nearly all the rest can go in now. Simmer first quite violently for a few moments, then on a gentler steady roll. Add the tomato purée at any stage.

Cook this sauce for a good 40 minutes – certainly the whole time the fresh tomatoes are roasting. When these are browning and shrivelling and the surfaces starting to dry out, blend them as smoothly as you can in a food processor or with a hand-held whisk.

Add this purée and the olives to the simmering tomato sauce. Continue to simmer for at least 10 minutes. If you feel that the sauce is too thick, add a little water or very light stock or some red wine or Marsala or a combination of these. Stir the sprig of basil in for the last few minutes only and remove it before serving. You can use a few baby

Serves 6–8
For the gnocchi
15 g/^{1}/$_2$ oz dried porcini

Tamari (optional)

600 g/1 lb 5 oz fresh spinach

A pinch of freshly grated nutmeg

2 garlic cloves, finely chopped

225 g/8 oz Ricotta

90 g/3^1/$_2$ oz plain flour or Farina 00

40 g/1^1/$_2$ oz Parmesan, freshly grated

Sea salt and freshly ground black pepper

For the tomato sauce
1 large Spanish onion, roughly chopped

150 ml/5 fl oz olive oil

6 garlic cloves, finely sliced

500 g/1 lb 2 oz ripe vine tomatoes

800 g/1 lb 12 oz good-quality canned tomatoes, in thick juice rather than red water

2 tbsp sundried tomato purée

18 or so top-quality olives, stones removed, but left whole

Stock, red wine or Marsala

A good-sized sprig of basil

To serve
Extra Parmesan

leaves scattered over as garnish. Make a pile of Parmesan shavings, kept covered somewhere cool with a tea towel or a piece of baking parchment until you need them.

Place the soup plates in a hot oven for a few minutes, taking them out with a thickly wrapped tea towel or an oven glove when needed.

Meanwhile make sure you have a pot or two of boiling, salted water on the go, with a few drops of oil added in. Drop the gnocchi into the boiling water for 1 minute if you've cooked them previously or for about 3 minutes if not. Once they have risen to the surface they need only a minute or so.

Spoon the thick, bubbling tomato sauce into each soup plate and arrange 3 or 6 gnocchi on each depending on whether this is a starter or main course. Drop shavings of Parmesan artlessly over and serve at once. If you can't bear the thought of plating anything in advance, just warm a large flattish bowl or deep serving plate and fill that with the sauce and gnocchi instead. Serve at the table and hand the Parmesan around. Serve with plenty of warmed bread.

Stoved roots

As you probably know by now, I consider braising to be the apex of culinary practices and it works gloriously with potatoes. I'll give you a basic recipe but, needless to say, you can customise it with Eastern, Middle Eastern and Mediterranean seasonings.

This is particularly apt for Jerusalem artichokes, where you can add garlic and freshly diced chilli, or for baby turnips, add thyme, rosemary and a drop of soy. You can also do it with small onions, though you will need to adjust the cooking time.

Stoved potatoes

I make these potatoes with olive oil as easily as with butter, though their Scottish forebears would never have come near the first. Optional additions include whole garlic cloves (I add these in every time), cumin or black mustard seeds from the beginning, basil or coriander folded in at the end, a few filaments of saffron in the water or light stock.

Some people, Jane Grigson among them, think you should on no account allow the potatoes to brown. They are tender, waxy, pale-yellow and very, very buttery. Others make a virtue of browning them. Indeed you have to be quite determined to stop them catching on the bottom of the pan. So I tried both ways but I am not going to pass judgement.

The appeal of the pale, buttery potatoes is quite obvious, but the browned, or golden, potatoes have the most delightful flavour. They do begin to brown about halfway through, unless you make a special point of not letting them do so by turning the heat down to the barest flicker and moving the pan about pretty much constantly, even adding a very little water now and again. I looked at the quantities at first rather incredulously and wondered that four people could eat their way through the whole lot. But we did. By this time the water was all but gone and the potatoes were swimming in hot, pale golden butter, and the garlic cloves were as soft as ripe avocado, delicately tinged with copper tones.

We poured the butter on to the hot potatoes. It was a while before anyone said very much except 'oh my god these are so delicious', and 'oh ok just one more'. We ate them for lunch but I strongly recommend that you keep them for supper. It is hard to stir yourself after such pampering. A huge bowlful of soft, well salted, well-peppered broccoli is the simplest, best thing to serve with these.

Place the butter, if using, in a pan with the water and heat until it is melted, or add olive oil instead.

Peel the potatoes and pack them tightly with the garlic cloves, if using, in the pan. Season with salt and pepper. Cut a piece of baking parchment to fit snugly over and cover with a closely fitting lid – this ensures the liquid does not dry out too quickly.

Cook on a very gentle simmer for about 40 minutes, shaking the pan now and again to stop the potatoes from sticking. Serve immediately.

Serves 2–4

90 g/3^1/$_2$ oz butter, or 90 ml/ 3^1/$_2$ fl oz olive oil

700 g/1 lb 9 oz small new potatoes

90 ml/3^1/$_2$ oz water or light stock

4 garlic cloves, peeled (optional)

Salt and freshly ground black pepper

Stoved turnips

How these melt. How they turn from animal fodder to rich, golden, old-fashioned baubles, all buttery and oniony – in little more than 20 minutes.

Peel the baby turnips – how much is not crucial but peeling them helps the sauce to penetrate deep into the body and fibre of the vegetables. Then soften the onion in 30 g/1 oz of the butter, all this on a gentle heat until brown. Add the turnips and cover with the water, bouillon, white wine, Vegemite or Marmite and the remaining butter.

Add the rosemary or thyme and garlic, if using.

Season with salt and pepper. Cover with a piece of baking parchment cut to size and seal with a well-fitting lid. (I use my pressure cooker pan for its perfect size and lid but not under pressure.)

Bring to the boil and leave like this for a minute before reducing the heat to a more manageable medium. Shake the pan about to loosen any catching on the bottom. By the time you remove them from the heat, the turnips will be softened, ready to break. If one or two do, it will only make things better. They will be sitting in a sauce so thick and rich, deep and, of all words to use of a turnip, exotic, that you will wonder if someone slipped something in while you weren't looking.

Gently add the chilli. I happened to have a lump of mature Cheddar sitting on the counter. I grated it coarsely and chucked it in. What else was I going to do with it? With the lid back on for a moment, it melted to a thick pale cream. I served the turnips like this, straight from the pan, with a little extra-finely chopped chilli and a smattering of parsley.

Serve with a glass of white wine.

Stoved Jerusalem artichokes

These can be prepared in exactly the same way as the turnips, though I prefer red to white wine this time and red to ordinary onion. I am also more generous with the garlic and use about 1 teaspoon tamari instead of the Marmite. Let them become completely soft and caramelised.

Unless they are very knobbly, you won't even need to peel them and the skin will shrivel and crisp wonderfully. The nuttiness of Gruyère echoes that of the Jerusalem artichokes, so I usually grate a fine netting of it on top.

Stoved or braised salsify

Salsify is a rare treat in England but as I was brought up with it and am very fond of it, I include a recipe here, in the hope that you might be tempted. It is closely related to the Italian *scorzonera*, which is fatter and straighter than the thin, twisted, bark-like salsify. You treat them both in the same fashion, though.

The peeled roots – a potato peeler does the job best – turn black very quickly but you can guard against this by immediately immersing them in acidulated water as you go, cut into 2 or 3 lengths depending on their size. You can also leave them whole if this appeals.

Serves 2–4

800 g–1 kg/1 lb 12 oz–2^{1}/$_4$ lb baby turnips (size of a golf ball)

1 medium onion

90 g/3 oz butter

400 ml/14 fl oz water

A pinch of Marigold bouillon powder

60 ml/2 fl oz white wine

^{1}/$_2$ tsp Vegemite or Marmite

1 sprig rosemary, or a small bunch fresh thyme

1 garlic clove (optional)

1 bird's eye chilli, chopped very small

30 g/1 oz mature Cheddar (optional)

Maldon sea salt and freshly ground black pepper

Parsley

Take a good pinch of saffron and, if you happen to have something else cooking on the hob, place it on a piece of foil and sit this on top of the lidded pot for a few minutes until the filaments are dried out. This makes it easier to crumble to a powder and gives you an even more intensely flavoured dish.

I don't usually specify this but it does make the saffron go further. It is also worth remembering this little tip for using in the other recipes that use saffron.

Then put the salsify – about 1 kg/2^1/$_4$ lb – in a large pan with 2 tablespoons light olive oil, a couple of garlic cloves, thinly planed, a good squeeze of lemon juice and water about 1-cm/^{1}/$_2$-inch deep, a pinch of Marigold bouillon powder and some salt and pepper.

Bring to the boil, then reduce the heat and simmer for 20 minutes until tender and the liquid evaporated to a mop-uppable sauce. Some may go softer much more quickly than this so keep an eye on them, though again a few collapsed ones won't harm.

Finish off with a scattering of very finely chopped parsley or tiny thyme leaves. If you want cheese, Parmesan is the best here, and if you want a fuller dish, add about 6 tablespoons double cream or crème fraîche. Finally, and in the same vein, you can replace the olive oil with butter.

Root action

Salsify also makes a delicious, creamy soup. Use about 500 g/ 1 lb 2 oz to 1 litre/ 2 pints stock; 1 onion, roughly chopped and softened in 3 tablespoons butter or light olive oil; a clove or two of sliced garlic; a pinch of saffron if desired; and a small peeled, diced potato. Add the stock, cook until tender and blend until very smooth, finishing off with 150 ml/6 fl oz double cream or crème fraîche, finely chopped parsley and more salt and pepper if necessary.

Peeled salsify also roasts in the same manner as parsnips, though you have to blanch them till tender first. It is a bit of work, but the unusual and delicate flavour is the reward.

Roasted vegetables with mango and tamarind

I have been going through a phase of not being able to roast a tray of vegetables without sticking a sliced ripe mango into the tray at the same time. I don't think I'm likely to grow out of it for some time yet – it's wonderful. When a mango isn't available, a fragrant Cox apple hints at the same effect.

Preheat the oven to its highest setting. Place a roasting tin in the oven to heat up while you get on with your preparations.

In a large bowl, mix together the tamari, olive oil, Tabasco and half the tamarind paste. Add the chopped vegetables, mangoes and garlic and toss with your hands or a wooden spoon.

Tip the vegetables into the hot roasting tin and roast for 20 minutes. Check now and again to make sure nothing is burning or drying out too much. If necessary, add a drop or two of water or stock or even brandy to keep the vegetables moist. A couple of minutes before the end of the cooking time, add the remaining tamarind paste.

Meanwhile, place the pumpkin seeds in a heavy-bottomed pan with some crushed sea salt and toast in the oven or in a dry pan until they begin to brown slightly and some begin to pop. A warning – they take only moments.

Serve the seductively sweet roasted vegetables on warmed plates, sprinkled with the pumpkin seeds and chopped coriander.

Serves 4

1 tsp tamari

3 tbsp olive oil

A dash of Tabasco

1 tbsp tamarind paste

4 sweet potatoes, scrubbed and cut into slices less than 1-cm/$1/2$-inch thick

1 smallish butternut squash, peeled, seeds removed, then cut into chunks

16 or so small new potatoes, cut in half or sliced if necessary

16 or so shallots, blanched and peeled

1 large or 2 small mangoes, perfectly ripe and sweet

4–8 whole garlic cloves, unpeeled

2 tbsp pumpkin seeds

Sea salt

A sprig of coriander, chopped, for garnish

Root vegetable casserole with herb dumplings

It is impossible not to be deeply warmed and satisfied with this on a cold winter's day, sometime in January, when parsnips are still around – your appetite and affection for them rekindled by the recent Christmas celebrations.

Preheat the oven to its highest setting. Toss the parsnips with 2 tablespoons olive oil. Season with a little salt and pepper and roast for about 25 minutes, until golden brown. They may be ready a little before the stew, in which case take them out and set aside.

Heat the remaining oil in a large, heavy-bottomed saucepan. Add the shallots and garlic and fry for 2 minutes, stirring occasionally. Add the carrots and turnips and sauté for about 4 minutes, then add the mushrooms and sauté for a further minute.

Meanwhile, make the dumpling mixture. Lightly mix all the ingredients together and season with salt and pepper. Add about a tablespoon of water to bring it together to make a soft dough. Form into about 16 small walnut-sized balls and set aside.

Add the vegetable stock to the vegetables, along with 175 ml/6 fl oz of the cider and the bay leaf, and let the stew bubble steadily for another 5 minutes, stirring occasionally. Now dissolve the cornflour in the remaining cider, add to the stew and boil to thicken.

As soon as it has thickened, place the dumplings in gently, so that they are about three-quarters immersed. Cover with a lid and simmer slowly for 15–20 minutes, until the dumplings are risen, the stew looks rich and the vegetables are meltingly soft. If you have not already done so, remove the parsnips from the oven and scatter them over the top.

Serves 4

300 g/11 oz parsnips, smallish, cut lengthways into 4

6 tbsp olive oil

Sea salt and freshly ground black pepper

8 shallots, cut in half

2 garlic cloves, sliced

350 g/12 oz carrots, peeled and cut into 3-mm/$1/8$-inch slices

350 g/12 oz turnips, cut into 2-cm/1-inch chunks, or in half if using baby ones

175 g/6 oz button mushrooms

1 strong vegetable stock cube, dissolved in 350 ml/12 fl oz water

200 ml/7 fl oz or more cider

1 bay leaf

$1^1/2$ tsp cornflour

For the dumplings

125 g/$4^1/2$ oz self-raising flour

60 g/2 oz Cheddar, grated

3 tbsp chopped fresh parsley

60 g/2 oz butter

Salt and freshly ground black pepper

A stupendously good vegetable brochette

Please don't be alarmed at the extravagance, both in quantity and type. I go to this length quite deliberately because I am so fed up with fabulous-sounding things, which appear on the plate as two shrivelled mushrooms, a couple of fork-scored chunks of courgettes and a soggy cherry tomato – in other words, about a mile short of any brochette I'd ever be on nodding terms with.

But if this is all too much for you, stick to a selection only or make several different types of brochette. If you do go the whole hog, you'll need extra-long kebab sticks, preferably good and thick so they don't splinter threateningly. Since there is always a slight danger of the wooden skewers catching alight under the hot grill, I soak them in water for half an hour beforehand and it seems to make all the difference.

Try these on a barbecue or even on a solid cast-iron griddle pan and redefine skewer, brochette, and especially kebab forever.

Mix all the marinade ingredients together and allow the flavours to mingle and merge for as long as you can – a good hour is ideal.

Meanwhile prepare the vegetables. Leave all the baby vegetables whole, you don't even need to remove the stalks. Cut the pumpkin and papaya into slices about 2-cm/1-inch wide and 10-cm/4-inches long. Leave the skin on both, but discard the seeds.

Cut the red pepper into 6 large strips, removing every last trace of white pith and seeds. Choose fat, juicy asparagus spears, trimmed to about 12 1/2-cm/7-inches long. Remove any brown leaves from the chicory and cut into quarters. leave the pattypan whole.

Blanch the shallots in boiling water for 1 minute and then peel. Wash the tomatoes, but leave whole. Make shallow incisions into all the vegetables except the tomatoes and mushrooms so that they can absorb the marinade through every surface.

Place all the brochette vegetables in a shallow dish and pour half the marinade over them. Mix well, cover and leave to marinate and tenderise for at least 1 hour or overnight.

Makes 8
For the marinade
150 ml/5 fl oz olive oil

4 tbsp tamari

1 tbsp Tabasco

1 tbsp grain mustard

1 heaped tsp ground cumin

1 tbsp paprika

Juice of 1 1/2 limes

2 garlic cloves, crushed

1 red chilli, finely chopped

For the brochette
8 baby aubergines

8 baby courgettes

500 g/1 lb 2 oz small pumpkin

1 papaya

1 red pepper

16 thick asparagus spears

4 heads chicory

8 shallots

8 tomatoes

100 g/4 oz shiitake mushrooms

100 g/4 oz oyster mushrooms

16 yellow and green pattypan

To prepare the rice, place in a pressure cooker with the lightly salted water. Bring to pressure, then reduce the heat and cook for a good 35 minutes. Remove from the heat but do not remove the lid for a further 5 minutes.

Meanwhile, prepare the vegetables for the rice. Remove all seeds and pith from the peppers and slice into the thinnest and longest possible slivers, not unlike noodles. Repeat with the courgette, carrot and leek. Slice the corn kernels off the sides of the cob.

Then heat half the reserved marinade in a wok or large pan. First add the carrot, seconds later the leek, then the corn, and finally the pepper and courgette. Sauté on a high heat for a minute, taking care not to burn either the marinade or vegetables and retaining the redness of the paprika throughout. Set aside.

Back to the brochettes.

Preheat the grill. Skewer the vegetables and papaya on to large sticks. Really pack them in. Brush copiously with the remaining marinade and place under the hot grill for about 15 minutes, turning over at least once and removing only when all the vegetables are charred and sizzling on all sides.

Meanwhile add the rice to the fried vegetables and continue to sauté for 2 minutes on quite a high heat, stirring all the time until it is hot. Remove from the heat and immediately add the chopped parsley and coriander. Taste and add more salt, Tabasco and lime juice if you wish. Set aside and keep warm for a moment while you wait for the kebabs.

Heap the rice onto a large plate and stack the brochettes on top, scattering generously with the remaining coriander. A Greek yoghurt spiked with minced garlic and finely chopped herbs is great served on the side.

For the rice

500 g/1 lb 2 oz Italian short-grain brown rice

1 litre/2 pints lightly salted water

2 red peppers

175 g/6 oz courgette

1 large carrot

1 fine leek

1 corn on the cob

1 heaped tbsp finely chopped parsley

1 heaped tbsp finely chopped coriander

Tabasco (optional)

Lime juice (optional)

To serve

Several sprigs very fresh coriander, to garnish

Salt

Vegetable cobbler

This is winter comfort food at its warming, reassuring best, the scone dough 'cobbles' making it so much more than just a pie. The sauce should be copious and rich, the better to be mopped up by the golden, polenta scones, a tip I picked up in an article by Nigella Lawson. I even persuaded my three-year-old to eat an adult-sized portion by convincing him that it was cake.

You have all the carbohydrate, protein and vitamins that you could hope for in one dish but if I were tempted to serve anything at all with this, it would have to be a bowl of old-fashioned greens, soft and buttered.

This recipe happily satisfies six hungry people.

Begin by preparing the vegetables. Then heat the oil and butter in a large pan. Add the blanched and peeled shallots and cook with the lid on for about 5 minutes until they are not only soft but catching the bottom of the pan in places and tinged with coppery tones.

Add the chunks of potato, carrots and garlic as well as the cauliflower, cumin and coriander, allowing a couple of minutes between each addition of a new vegetable. Cover with a lid again and cook on a medium heat for another 15 minutes, shaking the pan about a bit occasionally. Still on a medium heat, add the mushrooms until they slightly brown and soften.

Preheat the oven to 200°C/400°F/gas mark 6.

To make the béchamel for the sauce. Melt the butter and add the flour on a low heat, cooking for a few minutes and stirring continuously to make a roux. Add the hot vegetable stock (1 teaspoon Marigold bouillon powder in 500 ml/scant 1 pint hot water is a good guideline). Whisk it in to smooth out the lumps and then add the double cream, the pinch of nutmeg and the bay leaf.

Turning up the heat slightly, carry on whisking to thicken and cook out the floury taste. At this stage, add the red wine, if using. Next, stir in the soy sauce and season with salt, pepper and the merest dash of Tabasco. Fish out the bay leaf and pour the sauce over the vegetables.

Mix well and pour into a buttered dish measuring about 30x20-cm/ 12-x8-inches. At this stage keep the vegetables hot by covering them with foil and placing the dish in the oven. The flavours will develop while you make the cobbler.

Serves 6
For the vegetables

275 g/10 oz shallots, blanched in boiling water for 1 minute and peeled

450 g/1 lb potatoes, cut into bite-sized chunks

450 g/1 lb carrots, sliced in half, then cut into 2-cm/1-inch thick diagonal chunks

3 garlic cloves, finely sliced

540 g/1 lb 3 oz cauliflower florets(1 medium cauliflower)

1/2 tsp ground cumin

1 tsp ground coriander

450 g/1 lb chestnut or button mushrooms

1 tbsp light olive oil or sunflower oil

30 g/1 oz butter

Salt

For the sauce

60 g/2 oz butter

2 tbsp plain flour

500 ml/scant 1 pint vegetable stock

300 ml/10 fl oz double cream

A pinch of freshly grated nutmeg

1 bay leaf

1 tbsp red wine (optional)

2 tbsp light soy sauce

A dash of Tabasco

Salt and freshly ground black pepper

For the cobbler – which makes 16 rounds – melt the butter, then leave it to cool slightly. Sieve the flour, polenta, baking powder and bicarbonate of soda as well as some salt and the sugar together. Mix the cooled butter with the buttermilk or natural yoghurt and 2 of the beaten eggs and pour this mixture into the dry ingredients. Stir lightly with a fork until it becomes a malleable dough.

On a lightly floured surface, roll this out to 1-cm/$\frac{1}{2}$-inch thickness and cut rounds with a 5-cm/2-inch cutter.

Increase the oven temperature to 220°C/425°F/gas mark 7.

Remove the vegetable dish from the oven and uncover it. Pack the rounds snugly over the top, in neat rows without overlapping which would cause the unexposed bits not to bake. Lightly glaze the mounds of dough with the remaining beaten egg and return the dish to the oven for another 15–20 minutes or until the cobbler is well risen and golden brown.

Easy way out

The cobbler recipe assumes that you have time on your hands, but if that's far from the truth then you can still make it as easy as pie! We all love a good pie after all

Fill a dish with the vegetables and sauce, and cover with rolled out pastry – puff, short or even filo, it doesn't matter; and shop bought, why not?

For the cobbler

125 g/4$\frac{1}{2}$ oz butter

225 g/8 oz self-raising flour, plus a little extra for dusting

125 g/4$\frac{1}{2}$ oz polenta or yellow cornmeal

2 level tsp baking powder

1 level tsp bicarbonate of soda

2 level tsp sugar

3 large organic, free-range eggs, beaten

4 level tbsp buttermilk or natural yoghurt

Salt

Ginger

Ginger has never been found in its wild state but evidence of its cultivation goes back to early Roman times and, though they used it in cooking, it was more prominently used medicinally.

To this day it is much used by Chinese medicine. A ginger infusion is often recommended to pregnant women to alleviate the symptoms of morning sickness. Southern Italian recipes sometimes call for ginger, reflecting the Arabic influence. But in the rest of Europe, especially England where it was once widely used, it remains almost exclusively a flavouring of bakery products and always in its powdered form – a very different phenomenon. As children, we ate the French *pain d'épices*, drier than English ginger bread and made with honey instead of golden syrup.

Ginger has re-entered the kitchens of the West through the huge influence of the East. Fine grating or chopping is usually advised for this fibrous rhizome, but I find grating it and squeezing to extract the juice more satisfactory and you don't get the fibrous bits stuck in your teeth.

Try ginger with chocolate, orange, apples, plums, most fruit in fact. It finds its apogee as an essential ingredient of Chinese stir-fries and Thai curries, imparting its strong, peppery, deeply aromatic, astringent qualities. Choose large, smooth-skinned, pale brown examples, which should reveal a juicy flesh.

OTHER RECIPES USING GINGER

Baby spinach with mango, crispy tofu and pink ginger cordial 50

Thai green curry 157

A quick, aromatic laksa 204

Dried figs caramelised with kumquats, Mascarpone and ginger 295

Roasted plums with orange water and crystallised-ginger crème fraîche 308

Chocolate tart with crystallised ginger 344

Thai green curry

I love all the flavours that are so typical of this dish – coconut; coriander; the in-your-face citrussy (some people say soapy) fragrance of lemongrass; and lime, which in its right place, gives one of the cleanest, freshest tastes on the planet. I don't go overboard on chilli, as I don't have the constitution for it, but it adds the necessary fire.

I cannot abide the little ropy pieces of ginger bark that lurk in the sauce and get stuck in your teeth, so I just squeeze the grated ginger as hard as possible. I have a similar problem with lemongrass, which is why it is important to choose fresh, young stems, remove the outer leaves and then slice it as finely as you can with your very sharpest knife.

Alternatively in cooked dishes, just smash the stems, still keeping them attached at their base and fish them out when you are ready to serve.

To make the green curry paste, place all the ingredients in a food processor, ideally in the small herb-chopping attachment. Otherwise, do it all by hand, using a very sharp knife or *mezzaluna*. The quantities above will give you a little more than you actually need, but I found it difficult to process with less. You will need 5 tablespoons of the mixture, more if you like a hotter version than I do. Any left over can be refrigerated for a couple of weeks or even frozen in ice-cube trays if that makes things easier and added into a soup.

Heat the groundnut oil in a heavy-bottomed saucepan. Add the cauliflower florets. Toss them in the hot oil for 2–3 minutes, until they begin to brown prettily all around and to soften slightly. Add the carrots and repeat the process, then the courgettes.

Next add the shiitake mushrooms and sauté for a minute or so. Now add the coconut milk and most of the stock as well as 5 tablespoons green curry paste, the tamari and Kaffir lime leaves, lightly crushed but not torn to release more of their distinctive aroma. Finally add the green beans.

Simmer for a couple of minutes over a gentle heat, then add the remaining stock. Stir gently for another couple of minutes to allow the flavours to mingle.

Garnish with fresh coriander and serve with Basmati rice or Thai jasmine rice.

Serves 4
For the green curry paste

2 stalks lemongrass, tough outer leaves removed, the rest chopped very finely

2 shallots, finely diced

Juice and zest of $1^1/_2$ limes

3 green chillies

1 tsp ground coriander

1 tsp ground cumin

5 garlic cloves

1 bunch coriander, about 60 g/2 oz

1 dsp Thai 7 spice (optional)

4-cm/2-inch piece of ginger, grated and squeezed, resulting liquid reserved

For the curry

3 tbsp groundnut oil

250 g/9 oz cauliflower, cut into 4-cm/2-inch florets

250 g/9 oz carrots, peeled, cut in half lengthways, then into half moons on the diagonal, slightly less than 1-cm/$^1/_2$-inch thick

250 g/9 oz courgettes (as carrots)

200 g/7 oz shiitake mushrooms, thickly sliced

400 ml/14 fl oz unsweetened coconut milk

150 ml/5 fl oz stock, made with Marigold bouillon powder

$1^1/_2$ tbsp tamari

8 Kaffir lime leaves

100 g/4 oz fine green beans, topped and tailed

A small handful of coriander

beans
& pulses

beans & pulses recipes

We have been eating beans and pulses since earliest times, both fresh and dried, which preserves all their goodness. They are low in fat, high in protein and fibre and have been shown useful in controlling diabetes and in combating several cancers. Eaten with whole grains, they provide the body with all its essential and non-essential amino acids, allowing it to create new protein. None of this is by way of an excuse. They are also fantastically delicious with robust flavours that take to abundant, complex seasonings in salads, soups, purées and slowly simmered casseroles. And they are even good from a can.

Harira – chickpea soup

This recipe was given to me by my cousin Ginette, who faxed it over from Washington in the USA. Hers included meat – marrow-bones actually. I add a dark vegetable stock cube, cumin and Tabasco and it is as rich and exotic as any I remember from my childhood.

The traditional soup is made with dried broad beans, however using fresh (as seen in the picture) adds a good dash of colour.

It is the fast-breaker for Ramadan and though I would find it too heavy a thing to break a fast with, I don't recommend that you eat heavily on either side, as it is colossally filling. You can make a quick version with canned chickpeas. Replace the chickpeas in the recipe with a whole tin, including the liquid. The slow cooking and the simmering Levantine spice will fill the house with anticipation and stimulate your appetite wonderfully which is just as well.

Follow with a finely chopped Arabic salad of finely chopped cucumber, tomato and celery mixed with olive oil, lemon juice, garlic and capers; and a side dish such as the grilled courgette with yoghurt (see p52).

You will appreciate something cool and calming after such a blow-out.

Heat the oil in a saucepan, add the onion and fry until transparent. Add the lentils and cook for a few minutes, stirring continuously. Then add the chickpeas and the broad beans as well the tomatoes, celery, saffron stock, cumin, crumbled vegetable stock cube, garlic and some black pepper.

Cover with the water, lid and simmer aromatically for a good hour until the pulses are quite soft. In a small bowl, add just enough water to the flour to make a smooth paste and add a ladle of hot soup, stirring it briskly to avoid any lumps from forming. Return it to the pan, bring the soup back to the boil, stirring vigorously until it thickens.

Add the lemon juice and adjust the seasoning with salt and extra pepper and/or cayenne if necessary. Add the parsley and coriander, stir through and remove from the heat.

Serve with fried tortilla bread. You may like to have a small dish of harissa (see p273) nearby for an extra dab of fiery heat.

Serves 6

60 ml/2 fl oz light olive oil

1 medium onion, roughly chopped

100 g/4 oz brown lentils

100 g/4 oz chickpeas, soaked overnight

100 g/4 oz dried broad beans soaked overnight

500 g/1 lb 2 oz tomatoes, roughly chopped

1 whole celery head, including any green leaf, chopped

A good pinch of saffron strands, dried (see p149) and soaked in 2 tbsp boiling water for 10 minutes

1 dark vegetable stock cube, crumbled

2 tsp ground cumin

2 garlic cloves, finely sliced

2¹/4 litres/scant 4¹/2 pints water

2 tbsp plain flour

Juice of half a large lemon

A pinch of cayenne pepper

1 large bunch parsley, finely chopped

1 large bunch coriander, finely chopped

Salt and freshly ground black pepper

Lentils

Lentils are a staple food of India and the Middle East, their high protein content and cheap price making them important for the poor. They are also very filling.

Nutritionally they are much appreciated by vegetarians, albeit the butt of deprecatory humour. They can be large brown or green or small pink (called red lentils), brown or grey. The tiny green French Puy lentils are the most prized, with their ability to hold their shape even when cooked.

I use lentils in the same way that they are used in much of the Middle East and Mediterranean – mostly in soups and casseroles. Blending them smooth with Cognac or black olive purée makes a rich, dark spread for crostini or it can be lightened with a little whipped cream. Either way it is a versatile thing and I also like stirring it into a nest of linguine or a small bowl of rice. cumin and mushrooms are other close friends.

OTHER RECIPES USING LENTILS

Lentil soup with porcini

You might think of lentils as the plebs of the earth, porcini as the aristocrats, but oh my, when you put them together, who cares? They are both divine essences of Mother Earth. And before you say 'Oh for goodness sake, it's only mushrooms and lentils', try this recipe, then tell me about it.

Begin by browning the onion in 2 tablespoons olive oil. Then add the chopped garlic, the chopped celery, the carrot and the bay leaves. Toss the pan about so the vegetables are fully coated in the oil and cook until they begin to colour lightly.

Add the whole garlic cloves and the lentils, also coating them in the oil. Amply cover with about 2 litres/4 pints of water and bring the lidded pot to the boil. Reduce to a simmer for about 45–50 minutes until the lentils are tender. You may read elsewhere that Puy lentils can be cooked in 30 minutes but remember that, for culinary as well as digestive reasons, the longer cooking time is preferable. A soup of all things should be easy on the senses and the digestion. What matters is that they cook on a slow and gentle heat so that the skins also soften. Otherwise you get mush in a leather coat.

While the soup is cooking, you'll have plenty of time to soak the porcini in 150–200 ml/5–7 fl oz hot water. In fact, 5 minutes is all you need, as they will continue to soften in the soup. Strain them through a piece of muslin, which will catch most of the grit though you will have to use the tips of your fingers to detect the rest. Then add the strained liquid to the soup for the strong flavours to marry.

For the last 5 minutes, add the mushrooms themselves, then they will expand to their full size in the simmering soup; plus the tomatoes.

Finally, stir in the tablespoon of tamari – being essentially composed of salt it has been kept to last, otherwise it will hinder the softening of the lentils.

Before serving, swirl 4 tablespoons olive oil into the soup and shower a little chopped parsley on the top for both colour and flavour. Adding some lemon juice to suit your taste rounds it off.

Serves 6

1 medium onion, sliced

6 tbsp olive oil

6 garlic cloves, 3 chopped fine and 3 left whole

2 sticks celery, chopped

1 medium carrot, chopped

2–3 bay leaves

500 g/1 lb 2 oz Puy lentils

30 g/1 oz dried porcini

1 tbsp tamari

2 tomatoes, chopped

To serve

Extra olive oil

1–2 tbsp chopped parsley

Lemon juice

Split pea soup with spinach, mushrooms and lime-scented yoghurt

Okay, so the split pea soup is a childhood favourite. The spinach, mushrooms and lime yoghurt are my adult extras. I prefer green split peas to yellow though, to be honest, I'm not sure there is any difference in flavour. I think it's habit more than anything.

Beware the phenomenal ability of split peas to absorb water. The 2 litres/4 pints or so of stock are just right for getting it to cook and soften to the desired velvety consistency, but let it stand for even a few moments and you'll find yourself needing to add more.

Once it's gone completely cold, it will look like pâté rather then soup. Warming it will turn it back to liquid but not without further addition of stock. Save this and other pulse soups for a hand-rubbing, feet-stamping cold day. You can soak the split peas overnight, then cook them for 20 minutes or so, or do as I do and bung them, stock and all, in the pressure cooker and let them do their collapsible best for 40 minutes.

Peel and roughly chop the onion: there's no need to stand on ceremony here as it's going to get blitzed anyway.

Heat 2 tablespoons oil in a pressure cooker pan and throw in the onion. Add the roughly chopped garlic and fry for about 10 minutes until the onion is softened and starting to catch brown. Heat up the stock.

Add the cumin, stir quickly with a wooden spoon for a couple of minutes and add the split peas. Give them a good going over too and pour the hot stock in, spitting and spluttering against the hot oil. I love that sound, the sight of the rising steam and the volcanic bubbling.

Fix the lid on and adjust the weight until the pan comes to pressure. Now tame the heat and let the soup slowly, gently and safely come together. Some 40 minutes later, turn off the heat and let the pan ease slowly back to normal. Remove the lid, give the soup a good stir and blend until very smooth.

Meanwhile you can have added the lime zest and juice to the yoghurt and fried the sliced mushrooms in the remaining oil. When they are cooked through, quickly add the tamari, and take the pan off the heat immediately (or the tamari burns) and continue to stir the mushrooms in the heat. Stir the mushrooms into the piping hot soup together with the baby leaf spinach. Serve at once into warmed bowls, swirling a little of the lime yoghurt into each.

Serves 6–8

1 generously sized onion

3 tbsp olive oil

3 fat garlic cloves, roughly chopped

2 litres/3½ pints dark vegetable stock, or water and Marigold bouillon powder

1 tbsp ground cumin

500 g/ 1 lb 2 oz split peas

100 g/4 oz chestnut or button mushrooms

1 tbsp tamari plus a dash more for the mushrooms

Tabasco

Salt and freshly ground black pepper

2 handfuls of baby leaf spinach

For the lime yoghurt

8 tbsp bio yoghurt or Greek yoghurt

Zest of 1 lime and juice of half a lime

Cheese

A hard (cheese) lesson to learn this, but unrequited passions are best left alone; however strong the attraction, you know you'll get hurt in the end.

So there are only gentle flirtations with cheese in my recipes – a delicious frisson here and there but never a full-blown love affair. Now if you are differently constitutioned and cheese positively does it for you, then you can do no better than pay a visit to Neal's Yard Dairy in London's Covent Garden where the following cheeses are all made with vegetarian rennet.

You will find Single Gloucester from Gloucestershire and Double Gloucester from Shropshire; Ardrahan from Ireland (a twice Gold Medal winner at the British Food Awards) and sharply so; a Beeleigh blue from Totnes and a Corzier Blue from Ireland; a soft ewe's Wigmore from Reading, a Colston Bassett Stilton from Nottinghamshire – the list just goes on and on.

Flirt to your heart's content.

OTHER RECIPES USING CHEESE

The definitive goat's cheese salad 24

Aubergines with smoked Ricotta 48

Beetroots with green beans and Haloumi 88

Flageolet salad with rocket, lemon and feta 169

Linguine with walnuts, Dolcelatte and Marsala or Port 206

Dried figs caramelised with kumquats, Mascarpone and ginger 295

Bulgarian filo coil with three cheeses 356

Feta and sunblushed-tomato scones with black olives 361

Goat's cheese, olive and sunblushed-tomato muffins 362

Flageolet salad with rocket, lemon and feta

These delicately flavoured, summery beans are hugely under-used and underrated, I suppose because the canned ones are so dead looking – just compare the shades of green – and because we still seem to have a resistance to actually soaking and cooking beans, even though really most of the work does itself. I think this salad is pretty enough, fresh enough and interesting enough to tempt you, however.

Buy a new season batch of flageolets, from a good deli and you'll substantially reduce your cooking time. The beans when cooked must be tender – they should give when pressed against the palate with the tongue. Please don't take any notice of any recipe that says cooked beans should be nutty. All that will achieve is agonising indigestion and murderous thoughts towards vegetarians. Much wiser to listen to people for whom bean cooking has been part of the culture for millennia.

Avocado is another delicate and delicious partner for flageolets, and a salad of the two is definitely worth remembering and trying.

Soak the beans overnight and include the bay leaves and a half lemon.

Change the water and bring to the boil, leaving in the bay leaves and lemon half and adding 6 of the garlic cloves, which will all but dissolve into their intrinsic, slowly released sweetness, and 1 tablespoon olive oil.

It is not an old wives' tale that says salt inhibits the softening of cooking beans, so on no account add any until the beans are cooked (30–60 minutes depending on their age). Do salt them when they are cooked though.

Make the dressing by roughly smashing the feta together with the juice from the whole lemon, the remaining olive oil and black pepper. Then stir in both the basil and parsley and mix into the warm beans.

Let them sit there for a good 30 minutes before adding the rocket and serving.

Serves 6

300 g/10 oz dried flageolet beans

2–3 bay leaves

1^1/$_2$ lemons, large and unwaxed

8 garlic cloves, peeled

6 tbsp extra virgin olive oil

100 g/3^1/$_2$ oz feta

1 tbsp finely shredded basil or chives or a mixture of the two

1 tbsp chopped parsley

75 g/2^1/$_2$ oz rocket

Sea salt and freshly ground black pepper

Puy lentil salad with baby spinach and grilled goat's cheese

As I've warned before, you cannot add salt to the lentils while you cook them without turning the skins to leather, so it's as well to imbue them with as much alternative flavour as you possibly can.

The salad is substantial enough for a lunch, nothing added, and you can set the lentil temperature according to the weather. The goat's cheese is flashed under the grill until oozing and barely coloured.

As for the sunblushed tomatoes, served with this dish, I don't know whether the description is romantic or downright sentimental. We both know that they are simply very slowly cooked in a mildly hot oven. That's not to say that the sun would not do a perfect job of the slow drying. For years I have been meaning to give it a go. Sundried tomatoes, however, are what they say they are.

Place the lentils in approximately 850 ml/1½ pints water, together with the olive oil, Tabasco, whole peeled garlic cloves, onion and lemon quarters and the bay leaf.

Bring to the boil, then reduce to a fast simmer and cook for about 40–45 minutes until the lentils squeeze easily between the fingers. Then add the tamari and mix well. You decide whether you want just to drain the lentils so a little of their thick cooking juice stays, or rinse them under cold water. I like them with a little of their cooking juice so I don't rinse through. They may not look as neat or restaurant perfect this way, but they'll be wetter and tastier.

Flash the goat's cheese slices under a hot grill for a couple of minutes on both sides. Remove and set aside while you mix the lentils, first with the vinaigrette then with the baby spinach. Top with the slices of goat's cheese – 2x1-cm/½-inch thick slices per person is generous – and scatter over the tomato. Serve at once.

Golden goat's cheese

Dip the slices in beaten egg, then in freshly made breadcrumbs and deep fry until crisp and golden on the outside, softly molten inside.

Serves 4

200 g/7 oz Puy lentils

1½ tbsp olive oil

A dash of Tabasco

3 garlic cloves

1 small red onion, cut into quarters

1 lemon, cut into quarters

1 bay leaf

2 tsp tamari

To serve

225 g/8 oz goat's cheese log, cut into thick slices

4 tbsp vinaigrette of your choice (see p266–7)

100 g/4 oz baby leaf spinach

20 pieces sunblushed or oven-dried tomatoes

Puy lentils with roasted vegetables

You can make this as a restorative, warming, convivial winter supper or as a simple and light summer dish. In the first instance, you'll make the lentils soupier and more intensely flavoured; in the second, it will be restaurant neat with the vegetables grilled instead of roasted and served cold instead of piping hot. Despite its hot-weather origins cumin is a warming spice, so you may want to leave it out in the summer months, adding more lemon or balsamic vinegar or even a little grain mustard.

I've been quite liberal and not very precise with the vegetable quantities here because you know better than I what will precede, accompany or follow.

To cook the lentils, fry the onion in the olive oil until transparent, then stir in the lentils, cumin, lemon quarters, crushed garlic and Tabasco or dried chillies. Add the water and bring to the boil, then reduce the heat and allow to simmer gently for about 25 minutes, adding a little more water if necessary.

When the lentils are tender, remove from the heat, add the chopped coriander and parsley, then season with salt and pepper. Push the spinach into the lentils at the end and stir in until wilted. In the winter you may like this more soupy, and in summer, in a more discreet mound. Lighten the look before serving with some long thin strands of lemon peel.

Preheat the oven to 220°C/425°F/gas mark 7.

Chop the winter vegetables into sizeable pieces as appropriate, place in a roasting pan with the whole, peeled garlic and baste them with the olive oil and the other seasonings and roast in the oven for 35 minutes or more until tender, shrivelled and with the flavours deeply concentrated. The mushrooms will become chewy and meaty which I love but you can add them in a little later if you prefer. Serve piled on top of the lentils.

For the summer vegetables (*see* overleaf) generously baste the vegetables with olive oil – the aubergine need only be brushed on one side – and lay flat on a tray under a very hot grill. Turn over so that both sides are deeply golden, tinged with patches of black. In the case of the peppers, char all the way round and, when they are black, place them in a bowl, covered with a tea towel, so that the steam arising from them loosens the inedible skin from the luscious flesh. Discard the skins.

Douse with more olive oil, the finely minced garlic, balsamic vinegar and some salt and pepper. Serve with a dish of the lentils.

Serves 6

1 red onion, cut into wedges

3 tbsp olive oil

250 g/9 oz Puy lentils

1 tbsp ground cumin

1 lemon cut into quarters, plus the zest of another

1 garlic clove, crushed

1–2 crushed dried chillies or a good dash of Tabasco

750 ml/1¼ pints water

1 tbsp finely chopped coriander

1 tbsp finely chopped parsley

Salt and freshly ground black pepper

450 g/1 lb fresh spinach or red Swiss chard (optional)

For winter roasted vegetables

6 small carrots

18 or more chestnut mushrooms, left whole

12 or more whole baby onions or shallots

3 or more courgettes

1 small or half a medium butternut squash

6 garlic cloves

1 tbsp olive oil or more

1 tsp tamari

A dash of brandy, Marsala or red wine

1–2 crushed dried red chillies

A sprig of fresh thyme

Salt and freshly ground black pepper

Mushroom magic

A roasted field mushroom, dripping with garlicky juices, a heap of deeply flavoured, purple-green Puy lentils and a grilled, peeled and lemony red pepper, with a roughly latticed pastry on top, makes a good starter, easy to prepare in advance and served on a large dish with a rocket and parmesan salad beneath.

A tomato concasse, spiked with tiny basil leaves or even a red-pepper sauce – basically a thicker version of the red pepper soup (*see* p14) – also works wonders

For a last alternative, about 10 minutes before the end of cooking, add 50 ml/scant 2 fl oz each of sherry vinegar, Cognac and Madeira as well as a few prize dried morels or porcini and an extra spoonful of light olive oil. Reduce until the lentils are tender and glazed in the rich and sharp sauce. Leave out the cumin if you choose to do this.

For summer grilled vegetables

1 aubergine, cut into 5-mm/ 1/8-inch slices

4–6 red onions, cut into wedges

2–3 fennel bulbs, sliced into 5-mm/1/8-inch slices

2 or more courgettes, sliced fairly thickly lengthways

2 red peppers, left whole

1 yellow pepper, left whole

Olive oil

2 garlic cloves, finely minced

2 tsp balsamic vinegar

Salt and freshly ground black pepper

Baby broad beans, baby spinach and poached quail's eggs

This is a salad in miniature and all the more beguiling for it. Once again, it takes next to no time and makes a good first course or a seductive lunch for two.

Start by whisking the olive oil, lemon juice, garlic and salt and pepper to make the dressing and set aside.

Mix the baby spinach leaves with the broad beans in a large bowl and set aside while you prepare the quail's eggs.

Place an inch of salted water in the bottom of a small saucepan and bring to the boil. Reduce to a simmer and crack the quail's eggs very carefully into the water, do 2 or 3 at a time. Give them 45 seconds for the egg whites to set and the yolks to remain soft and fish them out carefully with a slotted spoon.

Now quickly pour the dressing over the leaves and beans, mix gently and lower the quail's eggs on top. Shave Parmesan all over. Add a little freshly ground black pepper and serve immediately.

Serves 2
For the dressing

3 tbsp extra virgin olive oil

1 tbsp lemon juice

1 garlic clove, very finely chopped

Sea salt and freshly ground black pepper

For the salad

2 good handfuls baby spinach, carefully washed and picked over; use rocket or watercress if spinach isn't your taste

450 g/1 lb baby broad beans, blanched and peeled

6 quail's eggs

30 g/1 oz Parmesan

Broad beans

Fear and loathing seems to have surrounded this bean for centuries. There was a fear that the soul was expelled from the body together with the wind they are apt to create, and a tiny proportion of people, indigenous to their countries of origin, suffer a jaundice-like allergy to them.

This said, they remain an enduring pleasure for me and for many. The young ones have a delicate yet earthy flavour, which makes them delicious even when simply served, and the bigger ones are great in hummus-like purées called bissara.

Broad beans freeze remarkably well but everyone should give themselves the pleasure, at least once a year, of removing fresh ones from their pods. Last century's chore is this one's luxury.

In the Middle East they are often accompanied by cumin, paprika and olive oil. In the West they are more likely to be partnered with cream or butter and lemon and, in Italy, the tiny, tender, new season's crop are most often eaten raw.

OTHER RECIPES USING BROAD BEANS

Broad beans with goat's cheese

I rarely find very young and tender fresh broad beans; the best and smallest specimens are bought up by suppliers of frozen vegetables. So it's a sad irony that in order to eat these particular delights you are likely to have to turn to frozen, unless you are a vegetable gardener in which case I envy you.

You can use Ricotta or fine Mozzarella instead of the goat's cheese. I can make a meal of a salad like this but it's also good as a no-fuss starter. I give you two methods, one simpler than the other. But do remember the Middle Eastern origins of such a dish, it is another gentle braise. At home we would have eaten it without the cheese, either as a side dish or among other Moorish antipasti.

Serves 4

4 tbsp olive oil

1 large onion, chopped

1 kg/$2^1/_4$ lbs fresh young broad beans or 500 g/1 lb 2 oz frozen, skins removed

Sea salt and freshly ground black pepper

250 g/9 oz soft goat's cheese

Heat the oil and fry the onion until golden. Quickly blanch the broad beans in salted water. They don't have to be tender at this stage but thawed enough to peel. Preheat the grill to high.

Add the skinned broad beans to the onion and pour in just enough water to cover them. Season with salt and pepper and simmer for about 7 minutes until the liquid is absorbed and the beans are tender.

Turn the beans and their sticky, golden onion sauce out on to a plate. Scatter with the cheese and flash under a hot grill to warm.

Serve immediately.

Simply beans

Even more simply you can take 500 g/1 lb 2 oz tender beans, cooked and shelled to reveal the lively green, and dress them with 3 tablespoons olive oil, juice from 1 small lemon, 1 clove finely chopped garlic, salt and pepper and as much goat's cheese as you want, broken up on top.

It's vibrant, fresh, delicate but with an edge and makes a lovely, summery lunch. You can top it with Parmesan (or Pecorino, if you are not religious about your rennet source).

Chickpeas

A bowl of new-season chickpeas, soaked overnight, then cooked patiently for as long as necessary to render them soft as pulp to the palate, warm and drenched in green olive oil and paper-thin garlic, now that is a fine thing.

A bowl of chickpeas, insufficiently cooked, all leather skin and bullet flesh, now that is a vile thing. Even tinned chickpeas vary in size and quality and it's worth buying them from a Middle Eastern shop, an Italian deli or anywhere where someone might be able to advise you as there is a surprisingly large choice. Price might be a good index. Some are small and mean and would have been better used ground-up in flour or to make hummus.

Others are the size of marbles and really splendid, whether eaten plain or as part of a couscous, *chana masala* or in a rice dish. If ever you are in an Indian supermarket ask if it is the season for green chickpeas, the young two-in-a-pod precursor of the later dry, brown pulse we think of as chickpea. They are usually served raw, crunchy, earthy and delicately spiced. And if you are in a chickpea-growing region of Italy in late summer, you might ask the same.

Chickpea salad with coriander, sunblushed tomatoes and Haloumi

This uses canned chickpeas – go for good-quality plump ones. The recipe is so quick to do, taking hardly more than 10 minutes, so I included it in *Cranks Fast Food* (C&C, 2000), but you'll see when you make it why it's become a bit of a standby, so forgive me for including it here.

It looks fabulous as part of a summer table, abundantly heaped on a large Mediterranean platter. The Haloumi needs to be done at the last minute and served still hot and molten. Whether you are making it for lunch or supper, serve it in large flat soup plates, the better to hold the herbed dressing.

There is nothing to stop you using home-cooked chickpeas, but I just have the sneaking feeling that you won't.

Preheat either your grill or a griddle pan. In a bowl, mix the chickpeas with the lemon juice, parsley, coriander, olive oil, garlic, tamari and Tabasco, the onion, if using, and salt and pepper. Allow the flavours to develop and to sink into the absorbent chickpeas.

Cut the Haloumi into 5-mm/¼-inch thick slices. Baste with a little olive oil, then grill or griddle for about 1 minute on each side until golden and crisp outside, molten and warm inside. Griddling gives it a pretty, ridged effect.

Make a mound of rocket leaves on each plate. Divide the chickpea salad between the plates and garnish liberally with the olives and tomato quarters, the Haloumi slices placed on top. Drizzle any remaining dressing over and eat immediately.

Serves 2–4

2 x 400 g/14 oz canned chickpeas, drained

1 tbsp fresh lemon juice

2 tbsp each chopped parsley and coriander

2 tbsp extra virgin olive oil, plus a little more for basting the cheese

1 garlic clove, finely cleavered

A dash of tamari

A dash of Tabasco

Half a small red onion or shallot, very finely chopped (optional)

Sea salt and freshly ground black pepper

225 g/8 oz Haloumi

100 g/4 oz wild rocket

100 g/4 oz oily, herbed black olives

24 pieces slow-roasted tomato quarters or shop-bought sunblushed tomatoes

Chickpea fritters with tikka yoghurt sauce

Like falafel, these fritters are better using soaked chickpeas mixed with cooked, but see below for a cautionary tale. They are a good starter or light lunch, and any of the sauces and dips in chapter six would work well with them.

To make the tikka paste, mix all the spices together and add the water and then the oil. Mix thoroughly to a smooth aromatic paste. Add the garlic, tamarind, chilli paste and coriander. Mix well and set aside in a covered bowl or lidded jar.

To make the fritters, rinse the soaked chickpeas in several changes of water, place them in cold water and bring to the boil for a good 10 minutes. This is to neutralise the possibility of indigestion. Since the fritters are fried, I had never bothered with this step, until someone wrote to say that they had been unwell after eating them. So better safe than sorry. (Falafel is always made at least in part with uncooked chickpeas.)

Drain well and place in a food processor. Pulverise for 15 seconds until broken down but still gritty in consistency.

Mash the cooked chickpeas with a fork or potato masher until almost smooth but with just a few chickpeas nearly whole. Mix with the ground chickpeas. Stir in 2 tablespoons tikka sauce mixture, the red onion, lime juice, fresh coriander and salt and pepper. Mix well and set aside, covered with cling film, for 20 minutes for the flavours to develop.

Work the fritter mixture with your fingers for a few seconds to make sure it holds together properly, and form into rough patties about 7 1/2-cm/3-inches in diameter and 1-cm/1/2-inch high. If it seems too soft or too wet, add a smidgen of flour (chickpea flour if you happen to have some). Heat the oil and fry gently for 2–3 minutes on each side until golden brown and crisp. Drain on kitchen paper and sprinkle with salt and a squeeze of lemon.

Just before serving, stir the yoghurt into the tikka sauce. Serve the fritters while they're still hot with the sauce to drizzle over, together with a sprig of fresh coriander and a wedge of lemon.

Serves 6

For the tikka paste

1 heaped tsp ground ginger

1 heaped tsp ground coriander

1 heaped tsp ground cumin

1 heaped tsp turmeric

2 heaped tbsp very red paprika

1/2 tsp dried chilli powder, very red, or 2 crushed dried chillies

5 tbsp water

3 tbsp sunflower oil

2–3 garlic cloves, crushed to a smooth paste

1 heaped tsp tamarind paste

Half a large chilli, chopped or blended very finely to form a paste

25 g/scant 1 oz fresh coriander, chopped

6 tbsp yoghurt

For the fritters

250 g/9 oz chickpeas, dry weight, soaked overnight in water

500 g/1 lb 2 oz cooked chickpeas

1 large red onion, diced

Juice of 1 lime

A small bunch fresh coriander, chopped

Salt and freshly ground black pepper

100 ml/3 1/2 fl oz light olive oil or sunflower oil for frying

To serve

Fresh coriander

Lemon wedges

Chickpea farinata

This is a southern Italian speciality, but I had to hunt down the chickpea flour in an Indian supermarket. Though there is not an egg in sight, the farinata falls somewhere between a pancake and a frittata or tortilla. It is like batter to begin with but sets in thick slabs that look and cut like a frittata. It is wonderfully easy to make and, apart from the setting aside time, so very quick that I experimented with several vegetable additions for this recipe. I give you two.

The *River Cafe Cook Book Green* (Ebury Press, 2000) suggests using small purple artichokes, which I am sure are perfectly divine, but I wanted to show just what an everyday sort of a meal this could become and have kept my options rather more prosaic (*see* overleaf).

Though the farinata is delicious hot, it also tastes fine when eaten cold and is one of the few things my husband bothers to cut up, wrap and take to work with him. I expect it's pretty good for a picnic too. The cumin is obviously not Italian, but since we're talking southern Italy with its Arabic influences I didn't think I could go wrong and, to me, it's the secret ingredient which brings the farinata to life.

Serves 6

250 g/9 oz chickpea flour

750 ml/1^1/$_4$ pints warm water

Maldon sea salt

Lemon juice to taste

6 tbsp olive oil

2 tbsp fresh herbs, such as basil or marjoram

1 tsp ground cumin

Freshly ground black pepper

^{1}/$_2$ tsp dried red pepper flakes (optional)

Preheat the oven to 230°C/450°F/gas mark 8.

Sieve the chickpea flour and add it to the warm water in a large bowl, whisking all the time to prevent lumps from forming. Add a tablespoon of salt, cover the bowl with a cloth and leave it in a warm place, above a boiler or in an airing cupboard for at least 2 hours. Meanwhile prepare your vegetables (*see* p181).

When the batter has rested, stir in 5 tablespoons olive oil. Then pour the remaining oil into a large double-handled frying pan or large round earthenware dish or the closest equivalent. Place the dish in a hot oven until the oil is just smoking. Pour in the batter, about 1-cm/^{1}/$_2$-inch deep. Add the black pepper and dried red pepper flakes, if using.

A deeper farinata will take longer to cook and, although not particularly authentic, I rather like it thicker sometimes.

Then add the vegetables and bake for about 15 minutes until golden and crisp on the outside. Allow to cool slightly before serving.

Cumin

Cumin is far and away my favourite spice. I love its deeply pungent, highly aromatic, even slightly sweet earthiness. It is the most intensely sensual smell I can think of outside the human body and, to me, has an ancient quality, which makes its Biblical associations romantic, mysterious and apposite.

As Ayurvedic doctors will tell you, it warms the constitution. It is pivotal to the multi-layered cooking of the Middle East and, known as *jeera*, to that of India where, though it makes few lone appearances it forms part of all sorts of pastes, sauces and spice mixes including, in its rarer black-seed form, garam masala. It is of the same umbelliferous family as fennel – one Indian dish mixes the two to delicious effect with green beans, potatoes and tomatoes. It is also a gloriously central ingredient of chermoula, the magnificent Middle Eastern sauce designed for fish, but which elevates all manner of vegetable dishes.

In Morocco, we used it in thick-lentil or chickpea soups and often with otherwise simple beetroot or carrot salads. A teaspoon of cumin transforms a conventional vinaigrette and anything you pour it over is transposed to another continent, so don't feel you have to wait to be in the mood for elaborate cooking before you turn to it.

OTHER RECIPES USING CUMIN

Aubergine farinata

Baste the aubergine in the oil. Salt and roast in a hot oven (*see* p179) for about 20 minutes or until tender and golden. Add a splash of Tabasco and add to the chickpea pancake. Scatter with baby basil leaves or finely chopped parsley.

1 large aubergine, cut into chunks

1 tbsp olive oil

Salt

Tabasco

Baby basil or parsley, chopped

Tomato farinata

Deseed the tomatoes, cut into chunks and fry in the hot oil with the finely sliced garlic so they only just begin to disintegrate. Season and add the fresh basil and olives. Add these to the chickpea pancake.

You could, of course, use a mixture of these two recipes.

2 large tomatoes, red and ripe

1 tbsp light olive oil

1 garlic clove, finely sliced

Salt and freshly ground black pepper

Fresh basil

A handful of black olives

Bissara – Moroccan broad bean purée with cumin

Hummus is so much the ubiquitous bean purée, that it's easy to forget that equally delicious purées can be made with any of the other beans. Serve in the same shallow plates with a sprinkling of cumin on top and olive oil generously swirled through. Why not serve it with grilled aubergines, peppers and courgettes, also abundantly dressed with olive oil, lemon, garlic and fresh coriander; warmed Arabic bread torn in chunks and a bowl of olives. It is so easy to invoke the spirit of the Mediterranean. You can make the purée more or less coarse as desired, so either a potato masher or a blender will do.

Blend the broad beans together with the chopped garlic or mash them together with a potato masher, using a little of the cooking liquid to achieve a smooth purée.

Slowly add the olive oil, reserving about half to swirl on top at the end. Also add most of the paprika and cumin, keeping some cumin back for later. Season with the salt and cayenne. Then scatter the coriander over and sprinkle with the remaining spices and serve with lemon wedges.

Serves 4

500 g/1 lb 2 oz frozen broad beans, boiled until tender

4 garlic cloves, chopped

150 ml/5 fl oz extra virgin olive oil

2–3 tbsp cooking liquid

1 tsp paprika

1 tsp (generous) ground cumin

Sea salt to taste

A pinch of cayenne

A small handful of chopped coriander (optional)

Wedges of lemon to serve

Butter beans (gigandes) with tomato and olive oil

These Spanish butter beans are magnificently plump, generous offerings and they deserve to luxuriate in good-quality olive oil, accompanied only by gently softened, ripe tomatoes. That's pretty much it except for the olives and bread on the side and the knowledge that a tapas rarely looks this good.

The irresistible combination of bean with tomato will have me look for every possible permutation, but this is simply one of the best.

On another day, you can leave out the tomatoes altogether and simply drown the beans in an intense blend of olive oil, sharp garlic, salt and pepper. Very finely chopped parsley is easy in this.

Warm the olive oil in a pan, add tomatoes and stir gently for 2–3 minutes to soften and lightly colour them.

Add the beans with 1 or 2 tablespoons reserved liquid, the reserved tomato juices, chopped garlic, tomato purée, salt and pepper. Either discard what you don't use of the rest or add it to a soup. Simmer gently for not much more than 5 minutes, depending on the quality of your tomatoes.

Transfer to a deep plate and drizzle with extra olive oil, a few basil leaves and a twist or so of black pepper. Wipe the bowl clean with a piece of bread. It's child's play.

Serves 6

3 tbsp olive oil

350 g/13 oz ripe tomatoes, seeded and quartered, juices reserved

350 g/13 oz jar Gigandes butter beans, liquid strained but reserved

1 garlic clove, very finely chopped

1 tsp sundried tomato purée

Sea salt and freshly ground black pepper

A few small basil leaves to garnish

Falafel

I just couldn't write a vegetarian cookery book with any pretensions to being Biblical without including a recipe for falafel. I know it is a vegetarian cliché, but you can now buy so many ready-made versions – when the whole point is to eat them fresh, sizzling from the hot oil – that I just wanted to remind you what a simple, fashion-defying thing they can be. If all you've ever had are the ready-made apologies, please don't be put off, have a go at these.

You can add more cumin and coriander but not less and don't be mean with salt and pepper either. I learned to make these from an Israeli friend, Tova. On more than one occasion, we made falafel for hundreds of people at a time, deep-frying them in pots the size of a small bath and only just keeping up with demand.

Have the salad and other accompaniments ready before you launch into the deep-frying operation. Preheat the oven to 180°C/350°F/gas mark 4.

Place the soaked chickpeas in a food processor and grind to a coarse, gritty mass. Add the cooked chickpeas, the Tahini and the rest of the seasoning, coriander and garlic. Pulse through the processor a couple of times so that the mix holds together when you roll it in the palm of your hand. In this way, roll 40 or so walnut-sized round balls.

Heat the oil and when it is very hot drop a few of the balls at a time into it. Turn the heat down a bit, or it will boil to overflowing and you will have a disaster on your hands. Wait until they are deeply golden and crisp, then remove using a spider (a long-handled flat sieve) or slotted spoon or two forks. Try just one to begin with to test you have both the consistency and the heat right.

Transfer to a plate or sieve, copiously lined with kitchen paper, and immediately sprinkle with salt and lemon juice. This cuts through the fat and is absorbed into the body of the falafel in a way that adding them any later just doesn't achieve. Keep the falafel hot in the oven while you work. Alternatively, you can use a larger pan with more oil than I suggest above and work in bigger batches, having them all ready in two ticks.

Make the oriental salad by made by chopping, tomatoes, cucumber, celery, and white cabbage very small then salting and adding capers.

Stuff the warm slit pitta breads with as many of the falafel and as much of the garnishes as you can. You want absolutely nothing mean, neat or held back about this.

Serves 4–6

250 g/9 oz dried chickpeas soaked for at least 2 hours, preferably longer

400 g/14 oz canned chickpeas, drained of all but 2 tbsp liquid

1 tbsp Tahini, runny variety

Tabasco

1 tsp ground cumin

A handful of fresh coriander, chopped

4 garlic cloves, crushed

1 litre/1$\frac{3}{4}$ pints groundnut or sunflower oil in a small saucepan, enough for frying

Juice of half a lemon

Salt and freshly ground black pepper

To serve

An oriental salad

Warm pitta bread

Tahini (as above)

Whole pickled green chillis

Chilli sauce or Tabasco

Hummus

Clean frying

When frying these, I keep the pan handle turned in and have everything within easy reach so I don't have to leave the pan unattended. I also wear a shower cap – it's not very becoming but it's better than coming out smelling like a chippie.

Garlic

Garlic crosses the whole gamut of taste from sweet and gentle, to in-your-face pungency. These two extremes manifest themselves in various ways.

Take the appearance of garlic for instance. The youngest could not look more delicate, its many layered, silky white leaves, opening out like petals while the oldest has fine parchment skins that fall apart in papery flakes. Then bang – you cut into a clove and crush it and all hell's let loose.

Even the way you cut it makes a difference. Slice it fine and the smell is quite well-behaved, crush it with the back of a knife to make a purée and the pungent oils start to be released. Fry it and you're onto another level. Brown it and you add depth and warmth but watch – it's a fine fine line. Burn it and the acrid, bitter smell and taste will put you off for life.

Fresh, young, raw garlic, either summer young or drier and more intense is the stuff of countless dressings and sauces. Providing you chop it very small, it perks everything up and turns the dullest thing vibrant. Think of chermoula, skorthalia, aïoli, gremolata. The whole Mediterranean is awash with sauces to explode your taste-buds, to set the juices flowing. The Jains are right to exclude it from their diet. You cannot keep an upright, quiet countenance with garlic around.

OTHER RECIPES USING GARLIC

Roasted tomato soup with garlic cream 16

Chicory braised with sundried tomatoes and slivered garlic 51

Carrots braised with cumin, saffron and garlic 96

Carrots with parsley, garlic and lemon in a walnut pastry tart 99

Green beans braised with tomatoes and garlic 110

Cannelini and garlic purée with tabbouleh 185

Cumin, coriander and garlic cream 271

Roasted garlic and other tales 277

Tamari, lemon and balsamic dressing with chilli and garlic 278

Cannellini and garlic purée
with tabbouleh

Here I go with a can again, although if you read on I give you a simple treatment for freshly cooked cannellini and you can do either. Despite the specification here, you can do this with any white bean, haricot or fat gigandes butter beans coupled with the more mellifluous-sounding cannellini. The tabbouleh can be as herb-based as you like, but I'll start with a less threatening balance that you can play around with and accentuate in whatever way pleases you. Make sure the tomatoes are window-sill-softened rather than fridge-cold.

On another occasion, you could warm the freshly cooked, well-seasoned beans through first, leaving out the additions, and serve with grilled or roasted vegetables, in particular red pepper, courgette and aubergine, succulent with their heat-extracted juices. Halved heads of roasted garlic – soft, pale and creamy go well with this either served on a separate plate or half a head squeezed out and blended with the cannellini.

When I do this, I also add finely chopped parsley, not so much as a breath-freshening antidote as for herbal harmony.

Drain the beans, retaining 1 or 2 tablespoons of the cloudy, viscous liquid. Place this, the beans and the olive oil, cream, garlic, lemon juice, Tabasco or chilli, salt and pepper into a herb chopper or blender and process to a smooth and aerated purée. You can replace the double cream with extra olive oil.

Roughly chop the sundried tomatoes, the stoned black olives and scrape them and any oil dripping from them into the purée. Pulse it all together for a couple of seconds, then transfer to a bowl and stir through the roughly torn basil leaves.

To make tabbouleh for four people, soak the bulgar wheat in the seasoned water and let it soak for about 15–20 minutes. Drain properly, then fluff it up with two forks, add the tomatoes and let it absorb the juices for a good half an hour. Add the rest of the ingredients as well as the olive oil and season with salt and pepper. Mix gently.

Have some of the lettuces, cleaned and pulled apart, piled in a bowl and use them to scoop the salad and the purée.

Serves 2–4

400 g/14 oz canned cannellini beans

1 tbsp olive oil

1 tbsp double cream

1–2 plump garlic cloves, roughly chopped

Juice of half a lemon

A dash of Tabasco or a fine mincing of fresh red chilli

Sea salt and freshly ground black pepper

3–4 very good-quality soft, oil-drenched sundried tomatoes

8 black olives, stoned

About 8 basil leaves

For the tabbouleh

200 g/7 oz coarse bulgar wheat

400 ml/14 fl oz cold water, seasoned with a pinch of Marigold bouillon powder

500 g/1 lb 2 oz firm but ripe tomatoes, chopped

A very large bunch of flat-leaf parsley, roughly chopped

60 g/2 oz of either fresh mint or coriander, chopped

6 tbsp extra virgin olive oil

Sea salt and freshly ground black pepper

To serve

Small Little Gem lettuces, organic

Pasta e fagioli

If you have been to Venice in the winter, you will know how cold and bone-chillingly damp it can get. Perhaps you've even had to wade through St Mark's Square knee-deep in water. I saw perfectly ordinary Wellington boots there selling for a colossal £70.

So it makes complete sense that the toe-warming and cheap cure the Venetians have come up with is this soup. I don't know if it's any good for rheumatism, but it will warm the cockles of your heart. Borlotti is the most typical bean and I think its nuttiness particularly suits the earthy heartiness of the soup, but cannellini is also used.

I've had *pasta e fagioli* made with small conchiglie (tiny pasta shells) and with sorpresine which I think prettier, even though prettiness isn't exactly the aim. Ditalini is good too. Some people just break up good-quality egg pappardelle but this doesn't seem to me to have enough substance next to the robust beans. So you should stick to a short stumpy pasta, added just 14 minutes before you are ready to eat. Please note, the sorpresine takes only 7 minutes. If there's going to be a delay, wait and add the pasta only once you have reheated the soup; much as the beans improve on keeping, the pasta doesn't.

The stock for something like this really does need to be good and strong and I know how impractical it can seem to make your own. You can buy good ready-made vegetable stock, but if you must turn to Marigold bouillon powder, it's worth a little extra work: place a pot of water with the bouillon powder dissolved in it over a medium heat and add into it the carrot peelings, a stick of celery, a chopped leek, a bay leaf or two, a few mushrooms or anything else that is easily to hand and simmer gently for about 20 minutes.

Even that will be better than nothing.

There's really no reason why you shouldn't make a quick after-work supper of this and use canned borlotti beans. But if you do get the chance, this does seem a perfect opportunity to do things properly. Soak the beans overnight and cook them for about 40–45 minutes until tender, or use a pressure cooker to speed things up.

Better still – though this is likely to be only a rare pleasure – see if you can find fresh borlotti beans still in their red-flecked pods. If you want a supper that cooks itself, place the vegetables, beans, herbs and stock in a large earthenware or other type of lidded casserole and place in a slow oven. Some 3 hours later the soup will be thick and deeply aromatic.

Serves 6

300 g/11 oz dried borlotti beans, or 2 x 400 g/14 oz cans

1 medium onion, chopped

1 leek, sliced

2 tbsp olive oil, plus some extra virgin for drizzling

4 garlic cloves, roughly chopped

1 small sprig thyme

1 small sprig rosemary

1 small sprig sage or basil

600 ml/1 pint vegetable stock

2 carrots, chopped

1 medium potato, chopped

1 stick celery, chopped

200 g/7 oz conchiglie, ditali or rigatoni pasta

2 tomatoes, each divided into 6 pieces

Salt and freshly ground black pepper

To serve

Parmesan, finely grated

Meanwhile, you need not even have been there except at the end to add the pasta. This soup is at its best when very unsophisticated, so don't go for blending the beans. However, one version of *pasta e fagioli* sees the pasta cooked in the watered-down, sieved bean purée. I only mention it so that you can play around with it if you like.

The last time I made this – and I'm sorry but I didn't measure it – I added white wine to the soup. Suffice it to say that it was with a liberal hand, some at the beginning, some in the middle and some at the end and it made the most wonderful difference. I also used a bulb of fennel instead of the celery and about 200 g/ 7 oz sliced mushrooms. You can ring the changes endlessly. What isn't an option is the Parmesan at the end. Provide a bowl or a block of it.

Soak the dried borlotti beans overnight.

Fry the onion and leek in a little olive oil with the garlic. Add the beans, most of the herbs and stock. Bring to the boil, then reduce the heat and simmer for 40–45 minutes until the beans are tender.

About a third of the way through cooking, add the rest of the herbs (you can reserve just a little for garnish) as well as the carrot, potato and celery. When the vegetables and beans are tender, add the pasta, stirring it in a couple of times and making sure that there is enough liquid for it to cook properly. Add a little stock if necessary. Add the tomatoes shortly after the pasta. Adjust the seasoning, transfer to a warmed earthenware dish or tureen and drizzle extra virgin olive oil on top.

Serve with plenty of Parmesan. Venetian flooding and damp, optional.

Better beans

If you are using canned beans, fry the onion and leeks as before but also add the rest of the vegetables and fry the lot together for 7–8 minutes. Then add the tinned beans and simmer gently for about 15 minutes. I know it's common to discard the liquid but it can be useful in bulking up the stock and its thickness can be just the thing this soup needs. Be careful when seasoning if the beans are ready salted. If you use canned beans, it really is best to cook the pasta separately, adding it to the beans for a final 5 minutes of joint cooking.

pasta
& some alternatives

pasta recipes

Basic pasta dough

I go through phases of wanting to make my own pasta. I can't say that it's more than a sometime occurrence, but each time I am pleased to have overcome my inertia. Firstly, there is nothing complicated about it. Secondly, watching that pile of flour and eggs turn into silk-thin sheets is quite empowering. And thirdly, homemade pasta opens up new avenues. I use it especially for large pouches – sometimes a single one to serve as a magnificent starter, filled with truffles or wild mushrooms or asparagus or other things you are only likely to find in the most upmarket delis and then never with the abundance and generosity you can afford yourself.

Then there are the slippery squares and odd-shaped pieces and the super-wide pappardelle which need only the simplest of sauces and yet are luxury and feast.

For those of you swayed more by pragmatism than poetry, making your own pasta is a good deal cheaper than buying its namesake. Using half and drying the rest (you can do this by simply leaving it out in the air for a couple of hours, draped over the backs of chairs, or just twisted into nets and knots) does not defeat the object either. You are unlikely to find a commercial brand as egg-rich and delicious in its own right. Use the best Italian flour and absolutely the largest, freshest organic eggs you can buy.

Any of the pasta dishes that follow, I hardly need say, are meals in themselves, with a green salad on the side. But recently, I have cottoned onto the Italian way of things and occasionally serve a much-reduced portion as a starter to a two-course meal though never to a three.

The following is a basic pasta dough; there are much eggier versions, but I think this is the most versatile.

Mix the flour and eggs, either by hand (in which case, break up the eggs slightly with a fork first) or in a food processor until the mixture is smooth, silky and elastic. By hand this will take about 8–12 minutes of steady kneading, in the processor only about 3 minutes, though you will have to work it with your hands for a couple of minutes anyway and faff about with blades and cleaning. Besides, it is much easier to develop a feel for it using your hands.

Then wrap the dough in cling film and allow to rest for about 30 minutes. If I am not going to use it immediately, I keep it in the fridge for an hour or so; I have even kept it there overnight, it darkens a bit but is still fine to use.

Serves 6 and more

500 g/1 lb 2 oz pasta flour (Farina 00)

5 very fresh, large, organic, free-range eggs

1 tsp sea salt (optional)

Semolina flour for dusting

Divide the dough into two balls. Cover one of them with cling film or a clean tea towel until you are ready for it and proceed with the other. Flatten it slightly with the palm of your hand on to your semolina- or flour-dusted worktop and begin to roll it out with a rolling pin – a heavy marble pin is good. Always roll, or more accurately, push, the pasta away from you and keep turning it at a 90° angle each time.

Continue to do this until the pasta sheet is very thin – they say it should be as thin as silk scarves and amazingly it can be, and certainly I aim for no more than 1-mm/less than $1/16$-inch thick. Repeat the process with the second ball. Remember that any excess can be rolled, dried and used later.

Alternative

I do have a pasta machine and it's true that, with a little practice, you can make even thinner pasta with it. Some have attachments for making ravioli as well as the more obvious linguine or tagliatelle. If yours has been languishing at the back of a cupboard for months or years, now is the time to dust it down and start playing with it.

This time divide the dough into four and cover three pieces while you work on one. Flatten the dough as before and introduce this flattened piece into the pasta machine on its thickest setting. It will come out like a thick sheet. Put it through again, another 3 or 4 times until it is as wide as it can get.

Dust this by now thinner, longer piece on both sides with flour or semolina and run it through the machine again, this time on a thinner setting. You will be able to continue doing this until you are on the machine's thinnest setting. Then you can cut it to the shape that suits you best. If I've bothered to make it in the first place it's because I want to do something special. I love pappardelle but it's quite difficult to get and the packets are never big enough, so I consider making my own worthwhile. Besides, you can make the strands a generous 2-cm/1-inch wide which looks splendid. I can't say I ever make my own linguine or tagliatelle.

Customising pasta

Part of the fun of making your own pasta is to be able to customise it. I add spinach purée or sundried tomato purée or a mottled herb medley. Substitute a whole bag of baby spinach, wilted and squeezed of excess liquid, then chopped very finely and use instead of 2 of the eggs in the recipe. Or add 2 tbsp of sundried tomato purée instead of 2 of the eggs. For a herb pasta, add 4 tbsp of finely chopped basil, marjoram or chives, either singly or a mixture of all of them.

A proper Thai noodle salad

I could drink this sharp, fragrant dressing, and I love the salad, resplendent with life-packed, multi-coloured, crisp vegetables. Soon enough, vegetarians and all those deliberately seeking the power punch of fresh foods (organic if possible) will be known by their radiance and sheer *joie de vivre*. Old notions about anaemic vegetarians overfed on stodgy foods will be seen as a temporary false start. The real stars of the kitchen are vegetables, and these should make up 70 per cent of a diet. Grains and cereals need only feature as minority ingredients, and there is no excuse for dullness.

Cook the noodles in plenty of boiling water, either conventionally salted or, as I do for these Asian dishes, with a dash of soy sauce instead. Most very fine noodles are cooked in 4 minutes so watch carefully. Refresh well under cold water and drain properly.

Meanwhile, wash the spinach and wilt in a pan set over a low flame. Only add a splash of water if the spinach is ready-washed and looks bone dry. Allow to cool, and squeeze out any excess liquid, but don't be so zealous as to bleed the poor leaves to death. Season with a dash each of tamari and Tabasco.

Toss the cucumber and carrots in the rice vinegar – a little goes a long way. Mix the dressing ingredients together.

Mix the refreshed noodles, most of the macerated carrots and cucumber and the red pepper with the dressing. Then, heat the oil in a large non-stick pan or wok and add the mangetout and spring onions. Stir-fry for about 20 seconds over a strong heat, then reduce the heat to a whisper and add the remaining tamari and Tabasco.

Even if your sesame seeds are already toasted, it's as well to toss them for a few moments in a dry frying pan over a gentle heat to bring out their flavour.

To serve, twist the noodles with a large fork and place each mound into four individual large soup plates. Be liberal in your garnishing using the remaining vegetables, including the mangetout and spring onions as well as the wilted spinach.

Finally, sprinkle each plate with the toasted sesame seeds and garnish with small sprigs of coriander, a smattering of diced chilli and any remaining dressing, and serve.

Serves 4–6

250 g/9 oz egg thread noodles

200 g/7 oz fresh spinach

1 tsp tamari, plus a dash

A couple of dashes of Tabasco

Half a cucumber, peeled and cut into thin batons

2 small carrots, peeled, cut in half and sliced on the diagonal

1 tsp rice vinegar

1 red pepper, seeded and finely sliced into thin strips

1 tbsp groundnut or sunflower oil

100 g/4 oz mangetout

4 spring onions, sliced diagonally

I tbsp toasted sesame seeds

A small bunch of coriander

1-cm/1/2-inch piece of fresh chilli, diced small

For the dressing

125 ml/4 fl oz teriyaki sauce

100 g/4 oz light yellow bean sauce

Juice of 1 lime

1 stalk lemongrass, very finely chopped

1 garlic clove, chopped very finely

5-cm/2-inch piece of fresh ginger, grated, juice squeezed out and the resulting liquid reserved

Cold Japanese noodle salad with Thai overtones

The traditional way to serve this salad is to keep the dressing separate and to twist the noodles into nests, each to be dipped in the dressing by the deft handling of chopsticks. Though I rather like this restrained elegance, taste-wise, I prefer to mix the dressing into the noodles. Rather than a mouthful of bland noodles with a bit of piquant sauce, you get one of perfect balance. But if you do mix, then serve at once – any delay and the noodles lose the cold firmness that's essential to this simplicity.

Umeboshi paste is made from the pickled plums of the same name. It is available in health-food shops and some supermarkets. I try not to be without it and though I don't use it all that often, it sometimes adds the perfect astringent note not just to Japanese dishes but anything similarly inspired.

A little added to cooked brown rice, for instance, is an alternative to adding lemon juice, providing a hint of sourness with its own very particular note. I also like to tell you of things, which I know are good for the general functioning of the body, and umeboshi plums are reputedly good at reintroducing equilibrium to the acid/alkaline relationship.

Also, nori (dried seaweed) is rich in iodine – good for metabolic and liver functioning. Sesame seeds are rich in the antioxidant vitamin E, and ginger is an all-round toner, cleanser and purifier. Oh, and buckwheat is good for lowering blood cholesterol. You should glow.

Serves 4

250 g/9 oz soba noodles (try to find 100 per cent buckwheat)

1–2 sheets nori

4 tbsp light soy sauce

1 tbsp mirin or white wine vinegar

1/2 tsp umeboshi plum paste, loosened in 1 tbsp hot water

2-cm/1-inch piece of ginger, grated, the juice squeezed out and the remaining liquid reserved

1 stalk lemongrass, finely chopped

1 tbsp toasted sesame seeds

2 tbsp chopped spring onion

Salt

Cook the soba noodles in plenty of salted boiling water according to packet instructions, in my case 7 minutes. Drain and refresh thoroughly in cold water until all excess starch is well and truly flushed away.

Meanwhile, hold the sheet or 2 (depending strictly on your taste for this power food) of nori over a naked flame and wave it like a black sail, not close enough to burn, but close enough to crisp and shrink slightly.

Blend together the light soy sauce, mirin, umeboshi paste, ginger juice and lemongrass to make a light dressing. Pour over the noodles and mix well. Then add the toasted sesame seeds and the chopped spring onion and mix, leaving enough of each to sprinkle on top. Finish off with pieces of torn seaweed and serve at once.

Spinach and Ricotta cannelloni

This is much better made with fresh pasta but you can stuff a pile of uncooked, ready-made tubes if you prefer. It had been ages since I made these, but my son is just approaching the age when he can be enticed to eat by the sight of anything bubbling with melted cheese. As a friend of mine always says, 'Give them tomato sauce and cheese and they'll eat it.'

There isn't a section especially devoted to children in this book, but I try to let you know when I think you are going to be on to a winner. Older children may prefer the Mascarpone, lightened with *smetana* which is a light sour cream. If you cannot find it, use Greek yoghurt instead. All children love béchamel (*see* p217), so you can use it instead.

Preheat the oven to 200°C/400°F/gas mark 6. Make the tomato sauce by heating the oil in a frying pan and frying the onion until transparent.

Add the tinned tomatoes and break them up with a wooden spoon.

Add the garlic, salt, pepper and bay leaves and cook on a gentle heat for about 25 minutes, adjusting the heat as necessary and finishing off with a blast of strong heat if it looks at all watery.

Taste and add the sugar if it seems too tart. Also, dunk the basil leaves into the sauce for a couple of minutes, then remove them and the bay leaves. Either remove from the heat or maintain on a slow simmer until you are ready to use it.

Place the spinach and a little salt and pepper in a pan set over a low heat for 1 minute until wilted. Drain thoroughly and add the nutmeg. Chop roughly and set aside to cool.

Heat the olive oil and, when it is very hot, add the onion and sauté for 5–6 minutes. Then add the sliced mushrooms, garlic and tamari. Sauté for 1–2 minutes until browned. Mix with the spinach and set aside to cool. Then mix with the Ricotta, smashed eggs, if using, and Parmesan.

To assemble the cannelloni, lay each pasta sheet on a dry chopping board and place a heaped tablespoon of the filling, shaped roughly like a sausage, along the long end. Roll to make a tube with very little overlap. Trim the ends and any excess pasta with a sharp knife and proceed in this way until all the pasta sheets and filling are used up.

Place half the tomato sauce in an ovenproof dish and arrange the cannelloni side by side in two lines. Cover with the remaining tomato sauce and then with the *smetana* and Mascarpone, or béchamel, if using. Finally add the grated Cheddar and bake in the preheated oven for about 25 minutes until golden brown. Serve as soon as possible.

Makes 12
For the tomato sauce
30 ml/1 fl oz olive oil

1 medium onion, diced

400 g/14 oz canned chopped tomatoes

2 garlic cloves, finely sliced

2 bay leaves

1/2 tsp sugar

1 large handful basil

Salt and freshly ground black pepper

For the cannelloni
350 g/12 oz fresh spinach, washed

A scraping of fresh nutmeg

1 tsp olive oil

Half a small red onion, diced

100 g/4 oz chestnut mushrooms, sliced

2 garlic cloves, crushed

1 tsp tamari

250 g/9 oz Ricotta

2 organic, free-range eggs, hard-boiled, peeled and roughly smashed (optional)

30 g/1 oz Parmesan, grated

1 quantity fresh pasta (*see* p193); or 12 sheets vacuum-packed, fresh lasagne sheets, trimmed to two-thirds their length – about 9 cm long (freeze the trimmings).

250 g/9 oz *smetana,* or sour cream

250 g/9 oz Mascarpone

100 g/4 oz Cheddar, grated

Salt and freshly ground black pepper

Farfalle with aubergine, fennel and tomatoes

I love the way the aubergine and tomato in this begin to dissolve, then lightly coat the pasta and anyway I like the combination of the melting, dissolving aubergine on the still-just-firm fennel.

A big bowl on its own with ribbons of Parmesan and a wedge of warm bread is yet another of the all-vegetable dishes which I happily make a whole meal. Although it's served here with pasta, rice (Basmati or well-cooked brown), soft-to-runny, sunny-hued polenta or potatoes with olive oil and crushed sea salt would all be just as good. As for the choice of pasta, anything short will do – penne or one of those corkscrew twisted types or skinny rolled Genovese trofie.

Heat the olive oil in a pan and fry the garlic until transparent and just beginning to colour. Immediately add the fennel and fry on a fairly high heat for about 5–6 minutes, stirring constantly.

Add the aubergine and continue to sauté for about 12–14 minutes or until the aubergine is well softened and browned. Season with salt and pepper. At first, the aubergine will seem impossibly dry, but persevere and it will release its own juices. Even so, you may add a splash of water to the pan as the vegetables start to catch and this, as it unites with the aubergine, will give you the deeply flavoured sauce you are looking for.

Finally add the tomatoes, chilli and half the basil, leaving the tiny sprigs for decoration. Stir on a fierce heat until the tomatoes soften slightly but are still pretty much intact. Remove the basil.

Meanwhile, bring a large saucepan of water to the boil and cook the pasta according to packet instructions. Drain the pasta and add to the vegetable sauté. Stir, adding sea salt and freshly ground black pepper to taste. Serve with the tiny basil sprigs pinched from the plant and plenty of grated or shaved Parmesan.

Serves 6

150 ml/5 fl oz olive oil

3 garlic cloves, finely chopped

2 fennel bulbs, cut into 3-cm/ 1½-inch chunks

500 g/1 lb 2 oz aubergine, cut into 3-cm/1½-inch chunks

500 g/1 lb 2 oz ripe tomatoes, cut into quarters, seeds removed

A small piece of red chilli, finely chopped

A handful of basil leaves

400 g/14 oz farfalle

75 g/2½ oz fresh Parmesan

Sea salt and freshly ground black pepper

Butternut squash

One of the winter squashes, so called because they can be stored, their skins hardening in the process, butternut squash has a lovely, sweet, flavour at once grounded and voluptuous, full and female.

It hails from the Americas, its name being a derivative of the Native American *askutasquash* and it can usually substitute for pumpkin. It roasts wonderfully in or out of its skin, its sugars concentrating into thick, sticky juices. It makes delicious velvety soups, griddled warm salads or a radiant topping for bruschetta, and caramelises beautifully with sugar or maple syrup – a few slivered almonds crisp with it – served with crème fraîche or a tangy goat's cheese slicing through the flavour. It is also wonderful with noodles and in risotto.

A halved butternut squash, basted with a marinade of olive oil, tamari, crushed garlic and chilli roasts in 30 minutes or so. Fill it with braised shallots and tender green beans for a stunning main course.

When needed, the peel can be easily removed using a vegetable peeler, it will come off in no time.

OTHER RECIPES USING BUTTERNUT SQUASH

Roasted butternut squash, wild mushrooms and spinach lasagne

Of the dozen or so recipes for lasagne I have come up with over the years, I probably like this best of all, though I cannot say that I've made even this one exactly the same twice in a row. The crème fraîche is lighter and cleaner-tasting with a hint of sharpness, but I recently made it with a mature Cheddar béchamel and grilled courgette slices instead of spinach. We polished it off in gluttonous moments.

Begin by roasting the butternut squash slices in a preheated oven at 230°C/450°F/gas mark 8 using 2 tablespoons olive oil and some salt and pepper. They should be tender and gently caramelised around the edge in about 20 minutes. Allow them to cool for just a few minutes before gently turning in the pesto. Meanwhile cook the pasta sheets in plenty of salted, oiled boiling water, following manufacturer's instructions.

When the pasta is ready, lift it out carefully and lie flat on a board, ideally lined with baking parchment. Keep the sheets covered with more paper or a damp tea towel till you are ready to assemble the lasagne.

Slice the cleaned mushrooms and fry them in 1 tablespoon olive oil with two-thirds of the finely chopped garlic and the teaspoon of tamari. When they are cooked and releasing some of their juices, add 1 tablespoon crème fraîche and simmer down for a couple of minutes. Set aside.

Wilt the spinach (no liquid added) over a gentle heat. Then cool, and squeeze out the excess liquid and add the grated Parmesan, remaining garlic, nutmeg, salt and pepper and 4 more tablespoons crème fraîche.

Preheat the oven to 190°C/375°F/gas mark 5.

To assemble the dish, place about two-thirds of the roasted butternut squash on the bottom of an ovenproof dish about 20x16-cm/9x6-inches. Cover this with 2 sheets of lasagne.

Continue, alternating the different vegetables with the pasta. Reserve a little of each vegetable as you go. Now cover the top sheet of pasta with these and the remaining 3 tablespoons crème fraîche.

Cover with the grated Gruyère or Emmenthal and bake in the oven for about 25 minutes until the cheese is gently melted and golden. Eat soon with a green salad.

Serves 4

900 g/2 lb butternut squash, peeled, cut in half lengthways, seeded and sliced into thin crescents

Olive oil

1 tbsp (generous) basil pesto

600 g/1 lb 5 oz mushrooms, any combination of chanterelles, porcini, pieds bleu, chestnut, shiitake, button, cleaned

6 lasagne sheets, good quality egg, or make your own (*see* p193)

3 garlic cloves, finely chopped

1 tsp tamari or soy sauce

8 tbsp crème fraîche

600 g/1 lb 5 oz spinach

30 g/1 oz Parmesan, grated

A pinch of freshly grated nutmeg

60 g/2 oz Gruyère or Emmenthal, finely grated

Sea salt and freshly ground black pepper

Glorious garlic bread

To make glorious, oozing garlic bread, use 1 baguette, 3 cloves of garlic, finely chopped or crushed, 125 g/4^1/2 oz butter and a good pinch of salt. Chopped parsley is an optional and attractive addition. Cut the baguette in finger-wide slices, not all the way through. Spread both sides with the mixed butter, garlic and salt. Wrap in foil, place on a baking tray and pop in the oven for last 8 minutes with the lasagne.

Homemade pasta pieces with tomatoes, spinach and black olives

This recipe uses about three-quarters of the pasta recipe so you could increase the sauce ingredients by about a quarter to make this enough for eight. You can use rocket instead of spinach and leave it out at the cooking stage, then pile onto each portion where it will pretty quickly wilt in the heat of the pasta. Ideally, your plates have been warmed first, as pasta goes cold alarmingly fast. Finally, if you are using baby spinach, add a smidgen of fresh nutmeg over each plateful before serving.

Roll the pasta thinly as always and cut it into squares about 8-cmx 3 ^{1}/4-inches. Leave them on your lightly semolina-dusted work surface while you make the deliberately quick and simple sauce.

Heat the olive oil in a pan and throw in the sliced garlic. When it is transparent, add the deseeded tomatoes. Fry for a few minutes until some of the tomatoes begin to fall apart but some are left pretty much intact. Add the black olives to warm through. Season to taste.

Meanwhile cook the pasta pieces in a generous pan of furiously boiling water. Add salt once it has come to the boil and not before; if this seems pedantic, I only suggest it because the salt is said to slightly lower the water's boiling point and you want it as close to a rolling boil as possible.

Drain the pasta properly and add it to the pan of mixed ingredients, still sparkling fresh. Lift through several times to evenly dress and serve at once with the shaved Parmesan, pine nuts and extra virgin olive oil. You can add the leaves to the tomatoes just before the pasta, warming them through to wilt. I would certainly do this with the spinach, though I'm often inclined to add the rocket on top in a whimsical mound.

Serves 6

1 quantity fresh pasta (*see* p193)

Semolina flour, for dusting

3–4 tbsp olive oil, plus a little extra virgin olive oil for serving

4 garlic cloves, finely sliced

1^3/4 kg/3^3/4 lb ripe vine tomatoes, quartered and deseeded

150 g/5 oz black olives, stones removed

100 g/4 oz Parmesan, shaved

A pinch of freshly grated nutmeg

30 g/1 oz pine nuts, lightly toasted (optional)

200 g/7 oz baby spinach or wild rocket, washed

Maldon sea salt and freshly ground black pepper

Pak choi

One of the so-called 'new vegetables', this is a staple of Asia and is now found alongside other Chinese greens such as *choi sum* (Chinese flowering cabbage) and *gai laan* (Chinese broccoli) in the Chinatowns of all major cities.

Pak choi, also known as bak choi and bok choi (probably the most popular), and many supermarkets now sell it. I like it best stir-fried with a slippery sauce of black beans, a sweet and sour sauce or, my favourite, with shiitake mushrooms and tamari accompanied by some well marinated fried tofu. It is also great with fried chunks of aubergine, sesame seeds and mirin (rice vinegar).

The large bud-like clusters, fleshy-leaved and crisp-stemmed, are best split in half before cooking. As usual for vegetables of the Brassica family, any yellowing indicates that it is past its best. Wash thoroughly in cold water to dislodge any small flies trapped within the leaves.

OTHER RECIPES USING PAK CHOI

Courgette koftas with an almond and tomato sauce 53

A quick and aromatic laksa 204

A quick, aromatic laksa

Much as I enjoy the razzmatazz of cooking and the more elaborate recipes, this simple, quickly prepared laksa features on my agenda more often than it might be wise to admit. It is comforting and about as instant as I ever need food to be. It happens in one pot and hardly makes a wave in the kitchen.

Mix and match the vegetables at your convenience: you can use sugar-snap peas instead of corn, spinach instead of or as well as pak choi. A tin of coconut milk, once opened, keeps in the fridge for 3–4 days, transferred to a lidded container or, if you're unlikely to use it so soon, you can freeze it until next time. Shiitake mushrooms offer a great boost to the immune system.

This serves two with seconds but nothing else besides.

Heat the oil in a large pan and throw in the pak choi. Toss it about quickly until it wilts, splashing it with a little tamari at the end.

Transfer to a dish and keep warm. In the same pan, add the carrot, baby corn and shiitake mushrooms. Toss over a fierce heat for a few seconds and pour in the stock, coconut milk, umeboshi paste, garlic, ginger juice and curry paste or red chilli.

Stir in the bouillon powder and throw in the smashed lemongrass stalks. Bring to the boil and add the noodles. Stir a few times to loosen the tangled threads, throw in the courgette, and boil again until the noodles are cooked, which should not take more than 4 minutes.

Retrieve the lemongrass and stir in the pale miso (the miso must never be added sooner than this or it loses its prized healing properties) and fresh coriander, reserving 2 sprigs for decoration.

Season with tamari and generally adjust the seasoning. Serve at once, piping hot, into large, wide laksa bowls if you have them, the pak choi, as well as a sprig of fresh coriander, set on top.

Serves 2

1 dsp sunflower oil

1 tightly budded head of pak choi, quartered

1 tbsp tamari, or more to taste

2 small carrots, thily sliced

100 g/4 oz baby corn, split down the middle

A handful of shiitake mushrooms, thickly sliced

1 litre/2 pints homemade or bought vegetable stock

200 ml/7 fl oz coconut milk

1 tsp umeboshi paste

2 garlic cloves, finely sliced

4-cm/2-inch piece of ginger, grated, squeezed and the resulting juice reserved

1 tbsp spicy red curry sauce (see courgette koftas p53), or a good-quality bought paste, or a couple of dried red chillis

1 tsp Marigold bouillon powder

2 stalks lemongrass, bashed and split

2 noodle nests or squares

1 courgette, finely diced

2 tbsp organic white miso, available from health-food shops

A small bunch of coriander

Linguine with walnuts, Dolcelatte and Marsala or Port

I usually have a small bottle of Marsala or Port kicking about the house and at certain appropriate times of the year (September to December), and walnuts in their shells. Of all the blue cheeses I find Dolcelatte the easiest, maybe because I am not an out-and-out blue cheese devotee.

Otherwise I suppose I'd be going for a Roquefort or a matured Stilton, but Dolcelatte has enough creamy sweetness to make the sharp veined mould easier on the palate than those two connoisseur's cheeses. My father used to drive miles when the Roquefort craving hit him, so I know all about it. If you think your palate is more like his than mine, then use a Roquefort instead. As usual I have to have my greens on the side, whether blanched-to-almost-soft, buttered broccoli; crisp green beans; steamed oily courgettes; buttery spinach; or simply wild rocket with little more than a shake of olive oil and balsamic vinegar.

My three-year-old son, who seems to have inherited quite some of his grandfather's characteristics, already loves this sauce. I would not have thought of it as particularly child-friendly, but he has proved me wrong. He also loves olives with almost the same passion as I do, and prefers strong flavours generally. So, as if I didn't already know it, I think all those plastic children's foods are way off the mark.

Bring a large pan of salted water to the boil. Plunge in the pasta, give it a whirl and cook it according to packet instructions. Always check a couple of minutes before they say – I like my pasta just on the other side of *al dente*, when it has just lost its chalky centre. Drain immediately, but not too fanatically. Shell and chop the walnuts finely and set aside.

Place the double cream, Marsala or Port and Dolcelatte in a saucepan and bring to the boil over a gentle heat. The Dolcelatte will take 3 minutes or so longer to melt. I don't even bother to cut it up into small pieces but I dare say that if I did, it would be melted by the time the cream had boiled.

Since there's little in it, do as you please. Also taste the sauce before serving. I like it on the gentler side, but if you want a more in-your-face 'blueness' to it, then add more Dolcelatte, or add more Marsala or Port if you want a more definite alcohol kick. Season with pepper and salt, despite the saltiness of the cheese, which is greatly attenuated by the cream. Mix with the pasta and scatter the walnuts over each serving.

Serves 4
500 g/1 lb 2 oz dried linguine

4 whole walnuts

300 ml/10 fl oz double cream

8 tbsp Marsala or Port

225 g/8 oz Dolcelatte

Salt and freshly gound
black pepper

Walnut wonder
Walnuts can be kept fresh for longer by putting them in a bowl of sea salt.

Linguine with new courgettes, lemon and extra virgin olive oil

This is a dish to make in summer when courgettes are at their youngest. The baby courgettes, which you can buy in small cellophane-wrapped packets all year round, are a sad approximation of what we are after. They tend to veer unpleasantly between bitter and insipid, as do their fat ungainly relatives. But good, fresh, young courgettes are delicate and crisp, almost sweet and fruity, so do wait for their season.

Mix two-thirds of the olive oil with the lemon juice, lemon zest and grated Parmesan as well as some salt and pepper, beat until thick and creamy and set aside.

Meanwhile, cook the linguine in plenty of salted water following packet instructions. While it is cooking, prepare the courgettes. These look prettiest peeled in stripes and I do this with a potato peeler, taking off as much as I leave on.

Gently heat 2 tablespoons olive oil, add the garlic and move it around in the pan for a minute or so, not allowing it to colour at all. Add the courgettes, increasing the heat only slightly, frying them till they are softened and showing a little tan here and there.

When the linguine is ready, drain well and add the lemon and olive oil mixture as well as the courgettes and basil. Scatter abundantly with the pine nuts or almonds and eat at once.

Sunshine and friendly company are a bonus.

Slimmers selection

For a less pound-piling alternative, forget about the olive oil bar 2 tablespoons, ignore the Parmesan and turn to a whole 250 g/9 oz tub of creamy Ricotta. Fry the garlic and courgettes in the oil as above.

Stir into the linguine with the lemon juice and basil, salt and pepper then dot the Ricotta all over. Scatter with the nuts and serve, with the ricotta breaking up and coating the pasta as you do so.

Serves 2–4

100 ml/3^1/2 fl oz extra virgin olive oil

Juice of 1 lemon and its zest

100 g/4 oz Parmesan, freshly grated

175 g/6 oz linguine, dried or 250 g/9 oz, fresh

10 small, very firm courgettes, peeled in strips and cut into 1-cm/^{1}/2-inch rounds

3 garlic cloves, finely sliced

A handful of fresh basil

2 tbsp pine nuts or slivered almonds, toasted

Sea salt and freshly ground black pepper

Rocket

With its strong, peppery, blade-like leaves, rocket burst forth onto the English culinary scene about 12 years ago as the kind of Italian cooking pioneered by the River Cafe grabbed hold of the public's imagination.

It was as if it had never previously existed though its use goes back a long way and it grows well and fast here. I plant it in mid-April and pick it from June onwards, well into summer, and that's just in an old basket in my small garden. It makes a wonderful pesto and is fabulous in soups and risotti. In salads it needs to be lightly dressed and then at the last possible moment. Rocket and Parmesan salad is a classically simple salad where each ingredient – the oil, the balsamic vinegar, even the salt and pepper – should be chosen with care. Still, rocket remains ludicrously expensive and unless you have access to a merchant or a friendly deli or local Italian restaurant, you'd think it only came in little polythene bags.

I long for the day when I can just walk into a shop, a supermarket would do, and pick out a handful for myself, still wet with that morning's dew. I think I'll have to emigrate.

OTHER RECIPES USING ROCKET

Rocket pesto linguine and wild rocket

This is a 'whizz-whizz' affair. If you use a bag or two of supermarket fresh linguine, you'll be done in 10 minutes from start to finish and you'll have a restaurant-smart meal to boot. These days I keep a tub of sunblushed tomatoes in the fridge pretty much all the time.

A few pieces scattered over a bowl of this wild green provide a sweet sharp contrast. A few roughly chopped black olives are nice too but if you think the appeal is all in the restraint, then hold back.

Put a large pot of water to boil while you proceed with the following. You are in effect going to be making a rocket pesto so you need to start with roughly chopped garlic and grated Parmesan.

Then you can simply place everything except for the bird's eye chilli in the herb attachment of a food processor (and go easy on the black pepper). You'll probably find that you can't at first shove in all the rocket, so add what you can, give the whole thing a few pulses then add the rest and whizz again.

Don a pair of gloves and chop the bird's eye chilli to a red speckle, discarding the seeds as far as possible. Transfer the pesto to a bowl or jar and mix the chilli into it.

Plunge the pasta into the boiling water, salted by now, and give it a good poke and a prod to loosen the strands. Drain (a few drops of hot water left clinging helps to disperse the sauce) and return to the hot pan. Stir in about 10–12 tablespoons pesto.

Transfer to oven-warmed bowls with a generous scatter of rocket, tomato pieces, roughly chopped black olives, pine kernels and a few delicate slivers of Parmesan. Eat at once.

Pesto power

You can keep the pesto in the fridge for a month and more, in a screw-top jar. For a rocket and Parmesan risotto just add spoonfuls of the pesto to risotto rice about halfway through its cooking time.

This time though, stir the extra rocket into the rice moments before serving so that it wilts in the heat. More Parmesan is a good thing.

Serves 6
750 g/1 lb 11 oz fresh linguine

Sea salt and freshly ground black pepper

For the pesto
6 plump garlic cloves, roughly chopped

150 g/5 oz very good Parmesan, grated

100 g/4 oz wild rocket

200 ml/7 fl oz olive oil

A few basil leaves (optional)

1 tsp Maldon sea salt and freshly ground black pepper

$1/2$ tsp grain mustard

Juice of half a lemon

1–2 bird's eye chillies

To serve
An extra 100 g/4 oz rocket

100 g/4 oz sunblushed tomatoes

A few black olives, stoned and roughly chopped

30 g/1 oz pine kernels, lightly toasted

Extra Parmesan

Lemongrass

Otherwise known as citronella grass (the citronella and lemongrass plants are closely related), both names point to its mild lemony flavour, though its fragrance is more perfumed, more aromatic than lemons, a fact that both attracts and alienates people.

It is at its most refined in Thai cooking where it imparts a special and distinctive flavour. Modern chefs use it to flavour ice-cream and other sweet desserts and it does share this quality of being able to merge with sweet as well as savoury with lemons.

Pacific Rim cooking is slowly popularising its use, which is hardly surprising since it grows widely in Australia. It also grows in America but its uses there are limited to dishes of Asian origin.

It is a perennial grass and you should look for firm stalks with no browning or withering. The outside leaves should be removed if they do not seem perfectly fresh. The rest need to be chopped as finely as possible using a very sharp knife and added to Thai green curries and other South East Asian dishes.

OTHER RECIPES USING LEMONGRASS

Pumpkin noodles with coconut milk, lemongrass and lime

I eat this often – on my own, with other people. I want some now, and I can practically smell it as I write. You can add finely chopped lemongrass and a few more Kaffir lime leaves if you want it even more fragrantly Thai.

Preheat the oven to 220°C/425°F/gas mark 7.

Place the pumpkin chunks, carrots and 2 tablespoons oil in an ovenproof dish. Add a little of the garlic, salt, pepper and Tabasco. Repeat with the courgettes in a separate dish as they will take slightly less time to cook.

Roast the pumpkin in the oven for 20–25 minutes until browned and tender. If there's room in your oven, roast the courgettes at the same time, but check them after about 10 minutes and remove when browned.

Meanwhile, fry the onion in the remaining oil until golden and set aside. Cook the noodles in plenty of boiling water, salted with tamari, for about 4 minutes or according to packet instructions.

Drain and set aside.

When the vegetables are golden brown and tender, add to the fried onion and pour in the coconut milk. Add the whole lemongrass stalk and the lime leaves.

Simmer gently for 2 minutes and add the fresh coriander, chilli and lime juice, reserving some of the chilli and coriander for garnishing. Remove the lemongrass and the lime leaves.

Add the noodles, stir and serve at once scattered with fresh coriander and chilli. It's addictive!

Serves 6

500 g/1 lb 2 oz pumpkin, tough skin peeled, cut into $2^1/2$-cm/ 1-inch chunks

150 g/5 oz carrots, cut into $2^1/2$-cm/1-inch slices

100 ml/$3^1/2$ fl oz sunflower oil

3 garlic cloves, crushed

Salt and freshly ground black pepper

A dash of Tabasco

150 g/5 oz courgettes, cut into $2^1/2$-cm/1-inch slices

100 g/4 oz onions, diced

750 g/1 lb 11 oz udon or egg noodles

A dash of tamari

250 ml/9 fl oz coconut milk

1 stalk lemongrass, bashed with the back of a knife

2 Kaffir lime leaves

A handful of fresh coriander leaves

Half a fresh chilli, sliced very finely

Juice of 1 lime

Pappardelle with grilled aubergine and homemade pesto

This uses about half of the pasta dough recipe (see p193), but if you haven't got round to making it, use bought pappardelle; you will need more than one standard 250 g/9 oz packet to serve four comfortably.

I used some beautifully marbled purple and white aubergines because, by some miracle, they happened to be at my local supermarket. The skins do remain paler even on grilling and perhaps it was my imagination, but I fancied that the flesh did too.

As for the taste, it would take a more refined palate than mine to tell the difference. The aubergines are only oiled on one side, but grilled on both which minimises their usual thirst for oil. Besides, the pesto is quite rich enough to more than make up for it. This also works deliciously well with roasted butternut squash slices instead of aubergine.

Start by oiling the aubergine slices as described above and grill them under a hot grill until deeply coloured and soft right through. Immediately sprinkle the lemon juice over the aubergine.

Cook the pappardelle in plenty of salted boiling water with a few drops of oil added in. Drain carefully and gently stir in first the pesto, then the aubergine slices. Season to taste

Serve at once with Parmesan and maybe some extra virgin olive oil.

Serves 4

4 tbsp olive oil

2 medium aubergines, sliced into about 13 slices each

400 g/14 oz homemade (see p193) or 375 g/13 oz dried pappardelle

4 tbsp homemade (see p264–6) or very good-quality shop-bought pesto of your choice

Juice of half a lemon

Salt and freshly ground black pepper

To serve

30 g/1 oz Parmesan, grated

Extra virgin olive oil (optional)

Easy peasy tasty pasta

The simplest sauces can be prepared in minutes if not seconds and even the stubbiest of pasta shapes never takes more than 14 minutes to cook. We may not have taken to making our own pasta on anything but an occasional basis, but we don't differ greatly from the Italians in this as their ready-made pasta can be of such excellent quality.

Pasta made with hard durum wheat is the best, cooking without becoming soggy or glutinous with excess starch, and some commercially so-called homemade pastas are becoming much better.

These take 3–4 minutes to cook. Extra virgin olive oil, finely chopped garlic, fresh lemon juice, perhaps a tiny heap of finely shredded lemon zest, a fistful of basil leaves and a generous hand with Parmesan, finger-crunched sea salt flakes and a twist or two of freshly ground black pepper. Nothing could be simpler and little could be better.

Pasta shapes

More robust or creamy sauces suit sturdier pasta – penne, shells, bows etc. Thin, gliding shapes take lighter, more refined sauces.

Spaghetti with peas, Mascarpone and lemon

This is a simple, soothingly sweet and creamy pasta. At its most basic it can be assembled in minutes. Even with slightly more refined touches, it is still one you can assemble in peaceful mood. It has an aura of luxury and delicacy, especially when using fresh petit pois.

Cook the pasta in a large pot of boiling salted water.

If you are using fresh peas, cook them in boiling water for 6 minutes or until they are just tender, or drop the frozen petits pois in boiling water for about 4 minutes. Drain and refresh under cold water.

Heat half the oil or butter and fry the shallot and garlic until tender. Add the lettuce and a little salt and pepper and soften for a minute or so. Add the cooked petits pois, a tiny touch of soft brown or caster sugar and a pinch of bouillon. Stir through and remove from the heat.

Drain the pasta, holding it in the hot pan with around 5 tablespoons of the cooking water so it slides easily. Immediately add the cooked petits pois and lettuce as well as the Mascarpone, lemon juice (if using) and remaining olive oil or butter. Stir well, grating as much Parmesan as you like into the linguine. Season with extra salt and freshly ground black pepper and immediately serve in 4 warmed pasta bowls, with extra Parmesan, black pepper, the lemon zest and a few leaves of basil.

Serves 4

500 g/1 lb 2 oz dried spaghetti or 1 kg/2^1/4 lb, fresh

800 g/1 lb 12 oz fresh peas, unshelled weight, or 400 g/14 oz tiny frozen petits pois

5 tbsp olive oil, or 75 g/2^1/2 oz butter

1 shallot, finely sliced

1 garlic clove, very finely minced

1 Little Gem lettuce, finely shredded

A touch of sugar

A pinch of Marigold bouillon powder

250 g/9 oz Mascarpone

Juice and finely pared zest of half a small lemon (juice optional)

Fresh Parmesan

A few small basil leaves

Sea salt and freshly ground black pepper

Pasta pouches with pumpkin and mango chutney

In case you think I've gone mad here, I swear I haven't. Now the 'real' thing, by which I mean the Italian recipe, normally has *mostarda di Cremona* (crystallised fruit in sugar) in the filling and could I find any? No. Besides, who says I have to be religiously authentic?

Pumpkin and mango have a natural affinity that, because of their geography, the Italians could not have stumbled across, but the lucky Antipodeans have. On no account try to speed up the cooking process by boiling the pumpkin instead of roasting it. It will become horribly waterlogged. I've replaced the traditional Amaretti biscuits with ground almonds and, call me arrogant, but I do prefer this.

Toss the chopped pumpkin in the olive oil and roast at 200°C/400°F/gas mark 6 for about 25–30 minutes, until tender and just beginning to colour. Mash with a vegetable masher or a hand-held blender and if your pumpkin looks as if it is leaching out too much liquid, squeeze out the excess.

Add the ground almonds, Parmesan, breadcrumbs, nutmeg, salt, pepper, garlic and mango chutney and mix well. Set aside until cool before assembling the pouches.

Divide the pasta in two even pieces, then roll out the pasta in lengths and widths suitable for your work surface, the important thing being that it is as thin as you can make it: the edges will be two layers thick by the time you've finished and you will have to press them together. Then use a round cutter 6-cm/3-inches in diameter to mark out circles where the pouches will be. This will make around 50 pouches.

Don't cut through the pasta at this point but place teaspoons of the filling in each circle. Then very lightly brush around the markings with beaten egg and lay the second sheet of pasta on top, pressing down around each lump with your fingers and squeezing out any air bubbles which will otherwise explode the pouch on cooking.

Now re-apply the cutter, this time going all the way through. To seal the pasta quickly run the cutter around the inside edge, again not slicing right through but simply scoring the pasta. To avoid thick-edged pouches, press the edges together with the thumb and index finger, pinching gently all the way round.

Transfer the pouches carefully to trays lined with baking parchment,

Serves 4–6
For the filling
500 g/1 lb 2 oz pumpkin, peeled and roughly chopped

2 tbsp olive oil

5 tbsp ground almonds

2 tbsp grated Parmesan

6 tbsp fresh white breadcrumbs

Freshly grated nutmeg

Salt and freshly ground black pepper

2 garlic cloves, crushed

4 tsp good-quality mango chutney

For the pasta
1 quantity fresh pasta dough (*see* p193)

1 egg, beaten

Semolina flour, for dusting

To serve
100 g/4 oz butter, melted

Several small sprigs of rosemary

Juice of half a lemon

1 tbsp double cream (optional)

Sea salt and freshly ground black pepper

Parmesan shavings

generously dusted with fine semolina flour. If you are not going to use them immediately, leave them out to dry somewhere cool, rather than keeping them in the fridge where the pasta will absorb moisture and the bottoms will go disastrously soft. If, despite your best efforts, this does happen, carefully prize the pouches off the paper and dust them with more semolina. Once when this happened to me, I ran a hot hairdryer over them until they were dry once more and carried on. Unorthodox, but useful to know.

To cook, plunge the pouches into a pot of salted boiling water. Once they have risen to the surface, give them 30 seconds or so and then scoop them out (test one first).

Put straight into a warmed bowl of the hot melted butter with the sprigs of rosemary, a good squeeze of lemon, double cream, salt and pepper briefly whisked in.

Serve in flat bowls also properly warmed first – pasta has a terrible way of losing its heat quickly, so take the simple precautions, especially with something as laboured as this.

Serve with first-class Parmesan and follow with a mound of wild rocket, lightly dressed.

An over-the-top roasted veg lasagne

This is a lovely sloppy lasagne, not one of those stiff slabs that looks like it has been sitting around for an age and is usually cold and horribly dry. Lasagne needs to be rich and flowing with sauces, mixing and running into each other – not very refined or sophisticated but exceedingly good.

Begin by preheating your oven to its maximum setting, keeping the oven tray in there to heat up.

Baste the peppers, courgettes, fennel and aubergine generously in 125 ml/4 fl oz olive oil, season them with salt, pepper and a generous dash of Tabasco – enough to add piquancy, not inappropriately burning heat – and place them in the hot tray. If you need more than one tray to carry all the vegetables, check occasionally to satisfy yourself that they are cooking at the same rate, or turn the trays around as necessary. Roast for about 35 minutes until well browned.

Meanwhile make the béchamel (*see* p217).

Firstly melt the butter in a small heavy-bottomed pan without letting it colour. Add the flour and stir vigorously with a wooden spoon to make a roux, literally a ring or wheel of butter and flour, well held together, matt rather than dry, soft but not wet.

Stir it like this for 30 seconds or so, enough to give a slight nuttiness. Then ideally pour milk warmed to scalding in a slow and even fashion while you continue to stir vigorously. If I've forgotten to heat up the milk first which happens to me often enough, I pour it into the roux pan and let it heat up first before even thinking of stirring it in. It's that or lumps.

Once all the milk is stirred in, cook gently on a soft flame, still stirring all the time. Taste to make sure there's not the slightest trace of flouriness – if there is, carry on cooking. Then remove from the heat and stir in the egg yolk, half the grated cheese, a few scrapings from a whole nutmeg and some salt and pepper.

Keep it warm so that it will pour easily and cover with a piece of baking parchment if you see danger of a skin forming as this could again cause lumps. These can be beaten out with a whisk or the magic electric stick but it is still best to avoid them if you can.

Cook the pasta sheets. I do this briefly even to the so-called 'non-cook' variety; it makes all the difference between a light and slippery pasta and a soft and stodgy one. Keep them from drying out by placing them between sheets of baking parchment while you wait for the remaining components to be finished.

Next, make the tomato concasse. Chop the deseeded, skinned tomatoes and fry them in the olive oil for about 20 minutes. Add the garlic and salt and pepper at the same time, but keep the sprigs of basil to add in the last few minutes only. The tomatoes should become thick and sweet, add $1/2$ teaspoon of sugar if they are not.

Add the roasted vegetables to the tomato concasse, stirring them in gently so they don't break up and then spoon or ladle one-third of the mixture into a large dish to cover the bottom. Follow this with 4 sheets of pasta, then another third of the vegetables, then half the béchamel, another layer of pasta as before. Top with the final third of the vegetables and remaining béchamel.

Finish with the remaining grated cheese, then bake in the oven for 30 minutes until golden, bubbling perfection. Allow to cool for a few minutes before serving or you'll burn the top of your palate. Serve with garlic bread (*see* p202) and a green salad (*see* p22). What more could anyone want?

Serves 6

3 red peppers, cut into 4-cm/ 2-inch squares

3 medium to large courgettes, chopped into 2-cm/$3/4$-inch chunks

2 fennel bulbs, each cut into 8 pieces

2 aubergines, cut into 3-cm/ $1^1/3$-inch chunks

125 ml/4 fl oz olive oil, plus extra for the pasta water

Salt and freshly ground black pepper

A dash of Tabasco

8–10 lasagne sheets, cooked according to packet instructions

For the tomato concasse

$1^3/4$ kg/$3^3/4$ lb tomatoes, blanched, deseeded and skins removed

75 ml/$2^1/2$ fl oz olive oil

3 garlic cloves, finely chopped

A small handful of fresh basil

Sugar

Salt and freshly ground black pepper

For the béchamel

40 g/$1^1/2$ oz butter

40 g/$1^1/2$ oz plain white flour

500 ml/18 fl oz milk

1 organic, free-range egg yolk

100 g/4 oz mature Cheddar, grated

Freshly grated nutmeg

Salt and freshly ground black pepper

Spinach pasta rolled with wild mushrooms

As a vegetarian, I sometimes miss the sense of occasion that comes from lifting a weighty tray from the oven or bearing to the table a ceremonial dish, laden with some extravagant preparation. Well, this dish satisfies that feeling. It has obviously not been just thrown together; on the contrary it's clear that you've worked at this, and it's worth it.

To write the recipe, I made this in September – hence the use of autumnal mushrooms. Besides I had just spent 10 days in the Alps not far from Leysin in Switzerland. High up on an almost unbeaten track, lies a tiny, shambolic restaurant. Alex, the chef-proprietor has a passion for mushrooms, which he says is about the only thing that will get him out of bed in the mornings.

The restaurant is strung with huge dried morels, ceps and chanterelles. One night, after we had trekked up, bad knees and all, and having pushed a pushchair all the way to the top, he took pity on us and made us a pasta roll very like this, rewarding us for our dedication with some of his prize mushrooms. In less cornucopian times, some regular mushrooms, livened up with dried porcini, will do fine.

Actually I don't own a fish kettle and, though I suggest one in the recipe, I use an oval Le Creuset cast-iron pan. A fish kettle would be elegant if you have one – you would get a longer, more impressive roll. Ricotta would be more Italian and I don't know what Alex used, but I like to use Boursin in this more than anywhere else.

Make the pasta dough first and allow it to rest in the fridge while you make the filling. Let the filling cool before rolling out the pasta and filling.

Melt the butter over a delicate heat and gently fry the chestnut mushrooms and most of the garlic for about 5 minutes. Then add the pieds bleus and continue in the same manner for 2–3 minutes, then the soaked porcini (reserving the soaking liquid) and the brandy. Finally add the more delicate chanterelles for another 2 minutes. Then strain the fried mushrooms of any liquid and reserve this.

Serves 4–6

Half the pasta dough recipe (*see* p193)

Salt and freshly ground black pepper

For the filling

30 g/1 oz butter

150 g/5 oz baby chestnut mushrooms, thinly sliced

2 garlic cloves, thinly sliced

175 g/6 oz pieds bleu mushrooms, thinly sliced

30 g/1 oz dried porcini, soaked in 200 ml/7 fl oz hot water

1 tbsp brandy

150 g/5 oz chanterelles

350 g/12 oz baby spinach

A pinch of nutmeg

225 g/8 oz Boursin (garlic or pepper)

Salt and freshly ground black pepper

To serve

200 ml/7 fl oz double cream

1 tsp tamari

A splash of brandy

30 g/1 oz Gruyère, grated

Basil leaves

Season with salt and pepper to taste.

Pick out a few of each of the mushrooms and set them aside for a moment. Wilt the spinach in a dry pan, adding a splash or so of water if necessary, but not if you have just washed it as the water clinging to it is more than adequate for the job.

Then squeeze the spinach in a sieve to discard any excess liquid and add the drained spinach, seasoned with nutmeg, salt and pepper, to the bulk of the mushrooms. When this is cool, add the Boursin and mix well.

Roll out the pasta very thinly to no more than $1^1/2$-mm/around $^1/_{16}$-inch thick, to a rectangle about 36x30-cm/$14^1/_2$x12-inches, and spread it evenly with the cooled mushrooms, spinach and cheese. Roll it gently lengthways like a Swiss roll or fat sausage, working away from you.

Wrap the roll tightly in a piece of muslin or a clean linen tea towel and tie the ends with string. You can secure the roll with string at regular intervals too. Lift carefully into a fish kettle, or oval, cast-iron pan full of lightly salted boiling water and cook at a rolling boil for about 20 minutes. I have also placed the roll in cold water and allowed it to come gently to the boil. Both methods work.

While the pasta roll is cooking, place the double cream, the rest of the garlic, the reserved porcini soaking liquid and the rest of the mushroom liquid, the tamari and the brandy in a pan.

Add the reserved mushroom pieces and simmer till reduced by about a third. Then lift the pasta roll on to a large warmed plate, remove the string and ease out of its muslin. Pour the hot cream sauce all over it.

Sprinkle the grated Gruyère on top and flash under a hot grill, just long enough to melt the cheese. Scatter lots of small basil leaves over it and season with pepper, slicing into 3 or 4x1-cm/$^1/_2$-inch thick slices per person into soup plates, using a very sharp knife, and spoon the sauce generously into each.

rice

& some other grains

rice recipes

I wish I could give you Sri Owen's *The Rice Book* (Frances Lincoln, 1993) on a microchip and slip it in between these pages – you would find in it so much that is marvellous. Here's a taste in my words: in many cultures, the rice spirit is female, with stories of unbridled laughter unlocking secrets and revealing what someone was endeavouring to hide – vulnerability and shyness. Take this as your inspiration the very next time you serve an exotically spiced pilaff, an endlessly comforting risotto or a simple bowl of softly cooked brown rice. There is more to this food business you know, than making bones grow.

The plainer the better –
how to get rice right

Some people tell you to add exactly twice as much water as volume of rice but I don't find this necessary. Sometimes you can be left with a thin crust of rice at the bottom of the pan. If you don't want this, simply add a spoonful of oil to the water before boiling.

Some recipes ask you to soak the rice first. This slightly increases the moisture content of the rice and then makes it easier for the cooking water to penetrate, so the rice is in less danger of falling apart.

Alternatively, you may be asked just to wash the rice first and then proceed. Generally speaking, this is only necessary with old rice which is recognisable by its dustier, more opaque look. Younger rice appears more translucent. Practice makes perfect. By the way, you should never wash rice for a risotto or you will lose the all-important creaminess.

Lastly, some add their rice to salted boiling water – twice the volume of water to the volume of rice. At the end the rice is drained. I find this method messier, more dangerous and less likely to result in perfectly fluffy rice so I don't use it myself. There are many roads to perfect rice. Here is my favourite. It serves six.

Fill a measuring jug to 450 ml/16 fl oz with long-grain American or Basmati rice and pour into a pan. Add 750 ml/1¼ pints cold water and a pinch of salt (optional at this stage). Bring to the boil with the lid on.

From the moment it has come to the boil, cook on a very delicate heat for 14 minutes, no peeking. It is also possible to cook rice in just its own volume of water but you really need to keep the heat very low. It gives a good dry rice for pilaffs and other occasions where the rice has to go through further cooking processes.

Take the pot off the heat and leave covered and undisturbed for about 8 minutes. There will be the characteristic small air holes all over. Carefully fluff the rice with a fork while you transfer to another bowl.

Alternative

One simple, effective treatment is to separately fry 1 teaspoon brown mustard seeds in 2 tablespoons light olive oil for a few seconds and throw them over the cooked rice, adding the juice and zest of a lime and mixing gently.

A slow-cooked rice with all the trimmings

Here is a vegetarian version of *dafina* – the Moroccan dish cooked by Jews in anticipation of the Sabbath (*see* p226).

This method takes barely 20 minutes to assemble, a couple of hours in a very hot oven (200°C/400°F/gas mark 6) or a steady simmer on top of the stove to start and then a slow, night-long simmer in a very low oven at 110°C/225°F/gas mark 1/4. When she makes this, my mother leaves it overnight on a hot plate instead. By lunchtime the next day, it is reduced to a dark, intense stew, the potatoes, waxy and brown as toffee.

Shelling the eggs is a revelation as the whites also turn a deep, fudgy brown. For a relevant way of serving this dish, I suggest an old-fashioned wintry Sunday when there is a gathering of family (or friends), a leisurely, appetite-inducing late lunch, followed by an amble in the park.

I give you a recipe for four but it doubles easily. You will need a very large pot or casserole dish with a good lid and if you want to tap into more of the folklore of this gargantuan meal, you should use an enamel pot. The quantities here are as they were given to me – a glass of rice and a glass of chickpeas each weigh about 200 g/7 oz, the equivalent of an American cup measure. As for the seasoning, well there is nothing remotely Moroccan about the marmite, or tamari or Marigold bouillon or porcini, but by the time you're done you'll think there is. It works.

I urge you to try this timeless dish.

Begin the day before you want to cook this by soaking the chickpeas overnight. The next day, preheat the oven to 200°C/400°F/gas mark 6 and roughly chop the onion and fry until brown in 1 1/2 tablespoons olive oil, placed in your chosen casserole dish.

Add the carrots, cut into long quarters as well as the leek, cut into 3 stumpier pieces. They should begin to brown a little before you add the garlic and chickpeas, covered with at least 1 1/2-litres/2 1/2-pints water. Remove the pot from the heat while you continue to assemble.

Next add the eggs, rinsed under cold water first and dried carefully, and the peeled potatoes. Then add the rest of the seasoning – the crumbled vegetable stock cube, Marmite, stirred in, saffron, nutmeg, bouillon and Tabasco. The dish is not meant to be spicy, so go easy – once again, it is only used to round off the taste.

Serves 4

1 glass of dried chickpeas

1 good-sized onion

5 tbsp olive oil

2 carrots, peeled

1 leek, trimmed

5–6 plump garlic cloves

1 1/2–2 litres/2 1/2–3 1/2 pints water

4 large organic, free-range eggs

8 potatoes, about 60 g/2 oz each, about the size of a small child's fist

1 dark vegetable stock cube

1 1/2 tsp Marmite

1 pinch of saffron, plus 1 extra pinch for the rice and 1 very generous pinch for the stock

A pinch of freshly grated nutmeg

1 tsp Marigold bouillon powder

A couple of dashes of Tabasco

2 bay leaves

A few dried porcini

A small date or a dried prune

1 glass of pudding rice

Salt and freshly ground black pepper

Finally add the bay leaves, dried porcini, date or prune and you'll see how the natural sugars seep into the broth and add to its deep intensity.

Place the rice in a bowl and moisten it with 1 tablespoon extra virgin olive oil. Stir in 1 tablespoon boiling water, into which you have crumbled a pinch of saffron filaments, a pinch of sea salt, a dash of Tabasco and a pinch of bouillon. Tear off a generous piece of foil, about 20-x25-cm/ 8-x10-inches and place the rice in the middle. Traditionally, this would have been muslin and you can do this if you like, though foil works surprisingly well despite its apparent impenetrability.

Roll the foil around the rice tightly folding the edges together over and over, so that the rice has room to swell as it cooks.

Put the rice in the pot on top of the chickpeas, topping up with water so that it is immersed. Add the remaining olive oil. Cover with a heavy lid and either set upon the stove over a minimal heat so that it comes slowly to the boil and then simmers steadily there for 2 hours. Or if you want to go out and don't want to worry about it, place it in the oven set at for 2 hours.

Next turn the heat right down to 110°C/225°F/gas mark $^1/_4$ and leave there for at least 8 hours and up to 18. My mother puts it in the oven at 7 PM on Friday night, turns the heat down 2 hours later and serves it for Saturday lunch. You can check it occasionally if you like, and if it seems to be running a little dry, add some boiling water. Similarly, check just before serving.

Addition

Typically the potatoes and peeled eggs are served first with a little of the broth, then the rice, stuffing and meat (but forget the last bit) and finally the chickpeas in plenty of soupy broth this time.

There is also a stuffing usually made for the *dafina* and for over two decades, my mother has made me this fantastic vegetarian version. Fry 1 chopped onion until very soft and brown. Add 1 chopped garlic clove, 3 tablespoons matza meal (available from all supermarkets), 3 tablespoons ground almonds, a few strands of saffron, a pinch of nutmeg, 1 small grated carrot, a few raisins, 1 tablespoon finely chopped parsley, 1 beaten egg and some salt and pepper. Oil a piece of foil and wrap in the same way as the rice.

Place in the pot with all the other things, also immersed and cook.

Timely tradition

Once upon a not so long ago time, *dafina* was cooked overnight in huge, walk-in communal ovens. This is not as horrifying as it sounds – the doors are sealed when everyone who has booked his or her place has delivered a pot and tipped handsomely to guarantee the best and hottest spot for their own dish in the oven. Each family's pot is marked appropriately so there can be no confusion when collecting on the way back from synagogue. I sometimes used to accompany my grandmother there and my grandfather back the next day.

A bowl of brown rice, dressed up

I think of brown rice as the quintessential food of the meditator. Certainly it seems to demand silence, attention, solitude. It is not something for raucous company, so eat it alone or make sure your companion is of the same quiet disposition. Meditation in action.

On a more pragmatic note, if you have over-indulged, nothing will sort you out faster than eating nothing but brown rice for a day or two. Organic short-grain Italian brown rice is by far the best, so it's worth visiting the health-food shop especially for it.

A bowl of cooked brown rice is not obviously pretty, but read on. In nothing is tenderness as important as here. To be good enough to eat, it needs to be at the point of collapse and almost creamy in its stickiness. It takes 45 minutes to get it suitably soft and digestible. Macro rice (short for macrobiotic) was a mainstay of Cranks, dressed with tahini, tamari, finely chopped parsley and toasted sesame seeds.

Bring the rice to the boil in a pan with the water and tamari. Boil vigorously for 5 minutes in an open pan, then simmer patiently for 40 minutes in a lidded pan. A heat-diffuser mat helps, though if the heat is gentle enough, the rice should not stick to the bottom. A pressure cooker will give you the same result in about 30–35 minutes.

Serves 2

1 cup organic short grain Italian brown rice, about 200 g/8 oz

3 cups water, about 600 ml/1 pint

1 tsp tamari

Dressed up

Tahini, thin and creamy; poured over with a dash of tamari.

Sesame seeds, toasted gold; finely chopped chives; tamari.

Sunflower seeds, toasted with a little crushed sea salt.

Mature Cheddar, grated, an optional addition for a child's bowl.

Hiziki seaweed and stir-fried marinated tofu, the one rich in iodine, iron and calcium, the other in phyto-oestrogen and hence especially good for women. The rice itself is rich in vitamin B.

A crushed dried chilli or two, to spice up your pleasures and comforts.

Olive oil, to lubricate.

Butter – it doesn't necessarily defeat the object.

A clove of crushed garlic, a squeeze of lemon, a twist of pepper.

Chickpeas or Puy lentils for a perfectly balanced herby, spicy meal.

A bowl of greens or some stir-fried veg.

Almost any braised or stoved vegetable to turn it into a feast.

A gentle fennel or celery gratin for body and bite and refinement.

Carrot rice

This is from Sri Owen's wonderful *The Rice Book* (Frances Lincoln, 1993). The recipe is of Persian origin and it is unusual on many counts. For a start the rice is cooked in milk. I also tried it with coconut milk to replace some of the milk which, being something of an addict, I prefer, but it does completely change the nature of the dish.

The rice also forms a golden crust above and below. She calls this 'intip'. It looks like what you thought was the overcooked bit, but it is delicious. You must use a short-grain white rice for this. I also could not resist adding a finely sliced garlic clove to round things off.

Preheat your oven to 180°C/350°F/gas mark 4.

Soak the rice in plenty of cold water for 1–2 hours. Then drain it and mix it in a large bowl with everything but the milk and butter. Season with salt and pepper.

Butter a soufflé dish big enough for the uncooked rice and milk to half fill it. Put the rice mixture into it and shake it gently to make sure the rice is evenly settled. Then pour the milk in slowly, disturbing the other ingredients as little as possible. Scatter the butter cut into small pieces all over the surface.

Transfer the dish to the oven and cook for 1 hour, by which time there will be a golden crust on top and, though of course you can't see it, one on the bottom too.

I ate it with some olive-oil-lubricated spinach and toasted cashew nuts because I really could think of nothing better and because carrots and cashews are simply one of those heaven-made matches.

Serves 4

350 g/12 oz short-grain rice

450 g/1 lb carrots, peeled and finely grated

Seeds from 4–5 cardamom pods

A pinch of ground nutmeg

1 garlic clove, sliced

Salt and freshly ground black pepper

600 ml/1 pint milk

30 g/1 oz butter, plus extra for greasing

Coconut rice

This lovely delicate rice can be used with all kinds of stir-fries and curries, Thai or Indian. To make it more festive, you can first fry a couple of shallots with a good fat pinch each of turmeric, ground coriander and cumin before adding the rice, and then briefly add a cinnamon stick and a Kaffir lime leaf to the coconut milk. Then do exactly as described below.

To make this into a one-pot meal, I sometimes add a whole bag of baby spinach and let it wilt in the heat. On one occasion, I roughly chopped a couple of courgettes, fried the pieces in some hot groundnut oil until nicely browned and added those to the rice.

Finally I often make this with organic, short-grain, Italian brown rice, cooking the rice in plenty of water in a pressure cooker. When it is all but cooked – about 30 minutes – and there is still a little water in the pan, I add the contents of 1 can coconut milk and cook the whole lot on a fast simmer until the rice is fully cooked (about another 12 minutes).

Expanded by the milk, this rice is soupy and rich. I add 1 tablespoon tamari, then the rest of the seasonings and my green veg *du jour*.

Heat the oil and/or butter in a saucepan and fry the rice for 3 minutes until it becomes translucent. Add the coconut milk, bay leaf, lemongrass and salt. Bring to the boil unlidded, then reduce the heat and cook slowly until the liquid is all but absorbed.

Then turn the heat to very low, cover the pan and continue to cook, or more precisely steam the rice for another 10–12 minutes, until tender and swollen with coconut milk. Cast out the bay leaf and lemongrass stalks and adorn with the fresh coriander and chopped chilli.

Serve with a Thai-inspired stir-fry and eat with contemplation.

Serves 4–6

2 tbsp light olive oil or sunflower oil or 1 tbsp oil and 1 tbsp butter

450 g/1 lb Basmati rice, soaked for 1 hour, washed and drained

800 ml/1½ pints coconut milk

1 bay leaf

2 stalks lemongrass, bashed with the back of a knife and left whole

1 tsp salt

A few coriander leaves to garnish

1 small bird's eye chilli, very finely chopped

Mustard

It isn't safe to have a pot of mustard on the table with me around. I'll do my best at first, but then sure enough, off comes the lid and in goes the spoon or tip of a finger.

I just can't resist, be it the tear-jerkingly strong English mustard I think so good in vinaigrette, or the mild, whole-grain *moutarde de Meaux*, whose little grains pop and burst against the tongue, or the slightly sweet and famous Dijon mustard. I eat some sort of mustard every day since a day does not go by without a salad dressed in a mixture of mustard, oil and vinegar. I add it to soups, especially creamy ones like leek and potato or cauliflower and corn chowder. Sometimes it's just a dab, enough to raise the temperature of a dish and give it oomph.

The ancient Greeks and Romans loved mustard, and Europeans have made the most of this indigenous plant, always readily available and cheap.

In India it is the seeds, yellow or black which are used, fried first to nuttiness rather than fierce heat. Other spices provide the heat there. One thinks of mustard most in the context of steak and sausages, but as a vegetarian I have never lacked opportunities to use it. A béchamel is transformed by it, mashed potato takes to it, steamed vegetables are divine with it and it makes salads positively hum.

OTHER RECIPES USING MUSTARD

Egg-fried rice

How many times have you ordered egg-fried rice in a Chinese or Indian restaurant and been presented with a pile of sticky, tasteless goo? True, you want something mild and absorbent of the stronger flavours and the idea sounds good, but if complete simplicity is what you're after, go for a well-made plain rice.

At home you can make a much more seductive egg-fried rice by spending a few moments longer on it. If the fancy takes you, a bowl of it on its own is more than palatable fuel, dressed with a mound of wilted spinach and a decorative swirl of anything from mango chutney (at the predictable end of the culinary spectrum, given its Eastern connection) to pesto or olive paste loosened in a little olive oil (at the other).

Serves 4–6

2 tbsp olive oil plus another 1 tsp

1 large (about 150 g/5 oz) onion, peeled and finely chopped

1 tbsp black mustard seeds

1 dsp ground turmeric

500 g/1 lb 2 oz Basmati rice

750ml/1^1/4 pints water

5 organic, free-range eggs, beaten

Salt and freshly ground black pepper

Heat 2 tablespoons olive oil in a large frying or sauteuse pan and add the finely chopped onion. Fry for a moment to soften and then continue until golden brown and soft together with the mustard seeds and turmeric. Season with salt and pepper before transferring to a separate bowl, then add the remaining oil to the frying pan. Don't bother to wash it in between – any residue spice will be welcomed by the rice.

Pour the rice into the hot oil and stir to coat. Now add the cold water and cover with a lid. Bring to the boil and continue to cook on a low heat for about 14 minutes or until all the water is absorbed and the rice cooked.

Still on a gentle flame, fluff up with 2 forks, mixing well with the fried onion mixture. Then push the rice to the sides so you can see a good gap in the middle. Pour the eggs slowly into it, stirring all the while with a fork or wooden spoon until the egg starts to scramble. Bring the rice back into the middle, stirring it steadily with the egg so that this is well dispersed in lumps of varying size. Adjust the seasoning. I am deliberate about the size of the lumps of egg because I can't abide mean strings of the stuff.

Serve at once (though in fact it reheats pretty well, the scrambled egg notwithstanding). Quickly blanched petits pois (100 g/4 oz) could go into the finished rice for colour as much as anything. Whether or not you bother, you'll get hooked on this rice anyway.

Saffron rice

I like these really simple recipes. Sometimes restraint is the judge of a good cook. It's so easy to add a bit of this and a bit of that, but sometimes backing off is the wisest thing. Warmly aromatic, saffron rice is perfect with any of the Moorish or Arabic recipes in this book, for instance the spinach with almonds (*see* p141).

Tiny pestle and mortars can be found in oriental food shops, usually made of heavy copper. I have one which belonged to my grandmother and no doubt came from an Arab *souk*, and it's perfect for grinding saffron. This rice, like the Italian risotti, likes a few minutes' rest before being served so that the grains can become fluffier and more separate.

Bring the stock to the boil. Crush the saffron in your mortar and add it to the hot stock.

Heat the oil in a heavy-bottomed saucepan, add the rice and stir until it is transparent. Pour in the saffron stock and a little salt and stir well. Bring to the boil, then reduce the heat to as low as possible and, still lidded, cook for 14–15 minutes or until the rice is tender and the liquid evaporated or absorbed. It will be cratered with small holes when you lift the lid.

Stir in the butter or olive oil if using, fluffing the rice up with a fork as you go, and remove from the heat. Sprinkle the nuts on top if you like and serve.

Zest for rice

Lemon rice is in the same simple vein. Cook the rice as above, adding cardamom pods and bay leaves to the boiling water. Discard these when the rice is cooked but add the juice of several lemons, to taste, and fluff up with 2 forks. Do away with the nuts in this one and replace with a few threads of lemon zest.

Serves 6

750 ml/1^{1}/$_{4}$ pints vegetable stock

^{1}/$_{2}$ tsp saffron threads

3 tbsp sunflower oil or very light olive oil

500 g/1 lb 2 oz Basmati rice

2 tbsp butter or extra olive oil

60 g/2 oz almonds, pine nuts or pistachios, toasted and roughly broken (optional)

Sea salt

Saffron

Russet to reddish brown filaments, gleaned from a million autumn crocuses – the true figure is 70,000 crocuses for 450g/1 lb of saffron – wrapped in precious small, dark packages and sold at an exorbitant price, you'd think I was speaking of some illicit drug but such is its preciousness.

My mother always has her little stash of it, hidden where the light can't get to it. She adds almost boiling water to the filaments (briefly dried first), waiting till it runs to rust before adding it to her braises, soups, casseroles. It imparts a lingering, aromatic, pungent, spicy and even bitter flavour (though this often reveals an undisciplined hand) and a deep-orange hue to the food it touches, *risotto à la Milanese* is the best example of this.

The Moghuls of Persia took it with them to India, where Kashmir remains a major producer. Indian supermarkets are the cheapest place to buy saffron – it is not as good as the prized Spanish, nor as the Iranian, but even by using a little more then I normally would, it does work out less expensively. Talking of Persia, the pilaffs I love so much, the layers of sweet and savoury, bitter and sour have their origins in the lavish feasts and banquets of that almost mythic place.

England was once a great grower of the precious flowers (saffron cakes and yeast breads were a commonplace). Saffron Walden in Essex is eponymously named. Couldn't someone have another go?

OTHER RECIPES USING SAFFRON

Rice bites

I wouldn't make all three of these for one sitting. The risotto croquettes are the most versatile and since all they do is use up left-over risotto, you won't need drinks or friends round or any excuse, though a few napkinned children's fingers would help.

The dolmades are better with a Greek or Middle Eastern meal to follow or just as part of a huge mezze platter that everyone can dig into.

Make the sushi to enter into a sedate, cross-legged Japanese affair. Try a simple miso soup, the cold Japanese salad (*see* p196) and a sizzling, transparent, tongue-scalding tempura.

Risotto croquettes

One portion of cooked cold risotto makes a good baker's dozen of golf-sized balls or elongated croquettes. If you are making more than one portion, it's worth adding a small beaten egg to the risotto, if not, I wouldn't bother as you can get away without it.

Make the croquettes or rice balls more interesting by drilling a hole into them halfway through with your index finger. Each one uses 1 tablespoon rice. Gently hide a morsel of Dolcelatte or a knob of garlic butter or a small piece of Mozzarella inside, bringing the rice over and rolling back into a little round rice ball. Obviously, the nicer the risotto you start with, the better these will be. A porcini risotto makes particularly exquisite rice bites.

Roll in dried white breadcrumbs bought from a baker or made yourself – about 4 crust-trimmed slices is enough for this quantity – so that they are evenly covered. Heat 1 litre/2 pints sunflower oil in a small pan.

Test that the oil is hot enough by seeing that a small piece of risotto floats straight back up to the top. It helps to have them all rolled and ready to go. Lower them in a few at a time and adjust the heat so it is hot enough but not at a furious and dangerous bubble.

Wait until they are a rich golden colour and lift out with 2 forks on to layers of kitchen paper, waiting to blot out the excess oil. Sprinkle with salt and lemon juice and eat with dancing fingers, blowing and puffing as you do.

Dolmades

When I was a child, our beloved neighbours the Savvas, he Cypriot, she Austrian (and owners of Richmond's once grandest Indian restaurant), would come each September to pick fresh young vine leaves from our garden for the dolmades she had learned to make for him.

Mrs Savvas' version had meat in them so this is my version, though to tell you the truth the recipe on the back of a packet of vine leaves is pretty good, too!

Separate out the vine leaves and plunge them into a large pan filled with boiling water. Simmer very gently for about 20 minutes, as much to tenderise them as to rid them of their unpleasant brininess. Then rinse them out in several washes of cold water.

While the leaves are cooking, toast the pine nuts in a dry frying pan. When they are starting to brown and still over a very low flame, crush them with a potato masher. Immediately transfer to a bowl and set aside.

Prepare the onion and fry it in the light olive oil, together with the garlic. Add the cumin, allspice, nutmeg and a generous crushing of sea salt flakes. Add a little of whatever spicy ingredient you have nearest to hand, such as Tabasco, cayenne, crushed dried chilli or harissa. You can also add a quartered tomato or 2 if you like.

Bring the rice to the boil in a pan and, when it is cooked, add it to the spicy, fragrant onion. If by any chance you have some left-over cooked brown rice – as I did when I last made these – then go for a 50/50 mixture of white and brown. It really improves the texture.

Mix thoroughly, also adding the crushed pine nuts and the parsley. When this is cool enough to handle, take tablespoon-size amounts in the palm of your hand and shape into chipolatas. As someone who spent so many years in productions on a grand scale, I tend to do such things in a production-line manner – first all the fillings, then all the assembly. It does tend to save time, but you should keep a damp cloth over them as you work to keep them soft.

Take a leaf, vein side up, place a rice sausage on it and roll the sides in and over tightly into a stumpy cigar. If your leaves are tender enough to begin with, you can just place the dolmades on a plate drizzled with olive oil and a little squeezed lemon. Or you can place them in an ovenproof dish and just cover them with equal proportions of water and oil, again seasoned with lemon juice, a small roughly chopped onion and a chopped tomato. Place them in a preheated oven at 200°C/400°F/gas mark 6 for around 20 minutes, until much of the liquid is reduced and the dolmades very soft and tender. Serve warm or at room temperature.

Serves 6

A packet of vine leaves (about 40)

2 tbsp pine nuts

1 large onion, finely sliced

1 (generous) tbsp light olive oil

1 garlic clove, finely minced

1/2 tsp ground cumin

1/2 tsp allspice

A pinch of freshly ground nutmeg

Sea salt

Tabasco or cayenne or crushed dried chilli or 1/2 tsp harissa

1 or 2 tomatoes, quartered (optional)

350g/12 oz Basmati or long-grain white rice

2 tbsp finely chopped parsley

Sushi

No, these do not contain fish and they are so easy to make a child could do it, and no special implements, training or ego required. Only the slicing with a razor sharp knife or an electric knife is over to you. You can buy sachets of sushi seasoning in Japanese shops and, recently, in some supermarkets. It is basically dried vinegar and sugar that gives sushi its distinctive delicate sweetness, with a hint of sharpness.

Place the tamari, ume-su (balsamic vinegar or diluted umeboshi paste would substitute), Tabasco and garlic in a shallow bowl. Toss the green beans and red pepper or carrot strips in this for a few minutes, then remove and reserve the juices. Cut the tofu into thin strips and drop into a frying pan with 1–2 tablespoons light olive oil, mixed with sesame oil if you have some. Add the sesame seeds and fry until brown and sticky, also adding the left-over tamari and ume-su marinade. Stir on a high heat until it is evaporated. The tofu should become both crisp and chewy as well as dark-golden brown.

Then place the rice in a saucepan with the cold water. Bring to the boil uncovered. Cover, reduce the heat and cook for 12 minutes until the water is absorbed and the rice cooked. Allow to cool for a few minutes, then stir in the vinegar and sugar or the powdered packet mix so it is well incorporated.

I find it easier to work with still slightly warm rice. Either way, you must keep a bowl of hot water by your side as you work, so you can keep your fingers clean. Put a mound of rice in the middle of a sheet of seaweed, the lines lying parallel to a board underneath. Flatten with the palm of a damp hand, spreading right up to the very edges on the left- and right-hand sides, but leaving a 2-cm/1-inch gap, top and bottom.

Run a little umeboshi paste along the bottom edge, using a teaspoon and your finger and lay down a row of each filling (the green beans, red pepper or carrot, fried tofu and avocado) closely packed together. Roll tightly like a Swiss roll, moving away from you. Moisten the end bit of seaweed with a little water to seal the roll shut. Repeat with the rest of the seaweed, rice and fillings. When you are ready to serve, trim the end bits, cut in half and then in half again to give you 8 perfect pieces, each revealing their multi-coloured fillings. You can make these up to a couple of days in advance, wrapping each roll in cling film, twisting the ends shut.

Serve with a dipping sauce made by mixing 100 ml/3^1/$_2$ fl oz tamari, diluted with 2 tablespoons of water, a good dash of Tabasco, a piece of ginger, freshly sliced or pink pickled, a few slanted slivers of spring onions and a couple of floreted slices of carrot floating like lotus flowers on top.

Makes 40–48 pieces

450 g/1 lb pudding or Arborio rice

600 ml/1 pint water

1 sachet sushi seasoning or
2 tbsp white wine vinegar and

1 tbsp caster sugar

6 sheets nori seaweed

For the filling

1 tbsp tamari

1 tbsp ume-su

A dash of Tabasco

1 garlic clove, very finely chopped

About 10 green beans, blanched until tender

Half a red pepper, roasted, peeled and cut into thin strips, or 1 carrot, cut into fat julienne strips

100 g/4 oz smoked tofu

1–2 tbsp light olive oil and a few drops sesame oil mixed in

1 tbsp sesame seeds

1–2 tbsp umeboshi paste

1 small or half a large ripe avocado, peeled and stoned and cut into thin strips

Biryani

A far cry from the pilaff-like biryani of Indian restaurants. This is a grand affair – Persian in origin, with all the elaborate trimmings and show of wealth, typical of the Moghuls. Some biryani are gilded with silver leaf. The spicing is complex yet delicate, saffron being essential to the fine hue and generous flavour; curry powder or garam masala won't do here. The careful layering of scented rice beneath, pale and delicate yoghurt lightly embellished above, and rich vegetable sauce in between makes for a splendid and sumptuous meal.

Heat the butter and half the oil and fry the onion over a medium heat for 8–10 minutes, until light brown. Add the cardamom, cumin, coriander, ginger, mustard seeds, cloves and chilli. Fry for a few seconds, then add the garlic and continue to fry for 2 minutes, adding a little water to stop the garlic from burning. Add the potatoes and fry for 8 minutes. Then add the carrots and half the tomatoes, which will dissolve to make a sauce.

Add the rest of the oil little by little from now on as you continue to cook the curry. Add the cauliflower and cook for 5 minutes, adding more water as you go along (about 150 ml/5 fl oz each time) to prevent the vegetables from sticking but making sure that it is all absorbed to maintain the curry's thick and rich consistency. Season with salt.

Add the saffron, courgette, coconut and tamarind juice and stir until dissolved. Simmer for 20–25 minutes, stirring frequently and adding a little more water. Finally, add the rest of the tomatoes and the coriander and fold in gently for just a couple of minutes before serving.

Meanwhile, cook the Basmati rice in 375 ml/13 fl oz water. Lid, bring to the boil and lower to a simmer for about 14 minutes until cooked.

In a separate pan, heat the oil and fry onion until transparent. Add the mustard seeds and crushed cardamom seeds and continue to fry for about 8 minutes until pale golden brown. Add the raisins, almonds, saffron threads, finely chopped chilli and coconut flakes and fry for a further 5–6 minutes, stirring regularly. Finally add the cooked rice and stir well so that the flavours mingle and the rice is speckled with the orange hue of the saffron.

Preheat the oven to 190°C/375°F/gas mark 5. Put the rice into an ovenproof dish and pour over the curried vegetables. Top with 500 ml/18 fl oz plain yoghurt and sprinkle on 1 tablespoon almonds, 1¹/2 teaspoons coconut flakes, zest of 1 lime and 1 tablespoon raisins. Bake gently for 15–20 minutes so that the yoghurt sets slightly on top and serve.

Serves 6

30 g/1 oz butter

200 ml/7 fl oz olive oil

300 g/11 oz onions, diced

4 cardamom pods, seeds scooped out and pounded in a pestle and mortar

1 tbsp ground cumin

1 heaped tsp ground coriander

1 heaped tsp ground ginger

¹/4 tsp mustard seeds

3–4 cloves

¹/4 tsp dried red chilli, finely chopped

4 garlic cloves, crushed

750 ml/1¹/4 pints water

250 g/9 oz potatoes, diced

250 g/9 oz carrots, peeled and cut in half lengthways and cut into half moons 1-cm/¹/2-inch thick

3 medium tomatoes, quartered

500 g/1 lb 2oz cauliflower, separated into small florets

A large pinch of saffron threads

250 g/9 oz small courgettes (as carrots)

60 g/2 oz creamed coconut

A few drops of tamarind juice

1 bunch fresh coriander, chopped

Salt

For the rice

250 g/9 oz basmati rice

25 ml/scant 1 fl oz sunflower oil

100 g/4 oz onion, diced

1 tbsp mustard seeds

4 cardamom pods (as above)

90 g/3¹/2 oz raisins

60 g/2 oz whole almonds, chopped

A pinch of saffron threads

1 piece red chilli, finely chopped

90 g/3¹/2 oz coconut flakes

Broad bean pilaff with raisins and almonds

This is my all-time favourite rice dish and I know that if I make it once then I'll be making it every week for a month – there 's something so addictive about its salty, pungent sweetness. A little lemony yoghurt by the side, some braised carrots with cumin (see p96), a small smoked aubergine and garlic, strong and doused in rich olive oil (see p47) – this is the quintessential (vegetarian) food of the Moors. And, served exactly as described, it is one of my 'can't-go-wrong dinner-party' meals and gatherings. It's informal, intense and, with the rice piled high in a mound, the carrots served in a warmed tagine, and aubergines glistening side by side and nose-to-tail on a painted platter, it answers my need for feast. When food is this good, it sings.

The pilaff can be prepared ahead of time, the flavours deepening with every passing moment and reheated quickly which is always a god send.

I do go in for a bit of atmosphere with this kind of food. Create your own feast with music from the Kasbah, a blown rose or two scattered about, and some sugary mint tea poured from a great height into gilt-edged glasses. Follow with any one of the Middle Eastern desserts.

Put the rice in a saucepan and cover with its volume in water and cook as instructed (see right). Once cooked, rest the rice off the heat and bring some water to the boil in a separate pan. Salt the water and boil the broad beans for 8 minutes or so. The beans will cook in the same time as the rice. Drain and refresh and, if you have the patience in you, slip the bright green kernels from their tough grey-green skins.

Heat the oil in a large frying pan and fry the shallots (or onion if you have no shallots to hand) for 6 or 7 minutes until they are richly coloured and crisp in places. Stir pretty much continuously, adding the garlic about halfway through. I don't add it in any earlier – in the heat required to turn the shallots their pale teak colour, the garlic has the tendency to burn. Neither do I add salt until the shallots are done as that draws out the water; it ends up broiling rather than frying and never turning brown at all. The cumin seeds go in for the last minute or so of well-stirred cooking.

Add the cooked rice, the broad beans and the raisins. Return to a safe heat and stir them together over and over, watching as the onion lends its golden tinge to the rice. Sprinkle with the almonds and serve.

Serves 4

250 g/9 oz Basmati rice

200 g/7 oz frozen broad beans

2 tbsp olive oil

3–4 large shallots, finely sliced

3 garlic cloves, finely sliced

1 tbsp cumin seeds

2 tbsp plump raisins

30 g/1 oz whole almonds, sliced into fine slivers and toasted until pale gold

Salt and freshly ground black pepper

Cooking rice

This method of cooking rice in its equal volume of water requires a couple of small precautions: that you keep the pot lidded, that you reduce the heat to a low simmer the very moment that the water comes to the boil and that you take it off the heat after 14 minutes or so, keeping the lid on for another 8 minutes, so that it can steam in its own heat. As a child I always wanted to lift the lid to check for the characteristic holes and I still like this simple proof that I've got it right. It is the least messy way of cooking rice I know. The suggested method produces a perfectly dry rice with independent grains, which will take the frying and stirring that's to follow without going mushy or falling apart.

Buckwheat

You could be forgiven for thinking buckwheat a grain like all other grains. But it is a plant of the same family as sorrel, rhubarb and dock and is mostly grown for its seeds which, while resembling cereal, are visually and nutritionally akin to grains such as rice.

Buckwheat grows in climates and conditions which would not support rice-growing – the mountainous regions of Japan, the northernmost parts of India and now predominantly in Russia, home of the most famous buckwheat dish, *kasha*; and to the well-known blini.

I enjoy the texture and taste of buckwheat so much that I wish it would catch on better here, but it seems never to have moved further than the health-food shop. It contains amino acids, potassium, magnesium, zinc, vitamin B6, iron, folic acid, calcium and lysine and is said to be good for dealing with high blood pressure. For many, it is also more easily digestible than rice. In macrobiotic terms, it is considered 'yang' – a good foil to the 'over-yin' – the over-sweet, over-processed diet on which most of us exist. If I didn't earn my daily crust by cooking, eating and writing, I would have to say that in my other guise, I would be a Zen monk, subsisting on simple food like this.

Buckwheat's Japanese name, soba, is given to the noodles made with it, used in the simple fresh-tasting, cold Japanese noodle salad.

OTHER RECIPES USING BUCKWHEAT

Buckwheat with petits pois

Actually the title is just a guideline because I don't see why you shouldn't add to this virtually anything you might be tempted to add to rice. The simplest way is with masses of finely chopped parsley, lemon juice (optional) and olive oil (advised). Or, if you can bear to be such a pleb and I assure you I can, the same amount of almost dry, butter-fried sweetcorn, gently browned and rather shrivelled, a stick of celery chopped up finely and softened too. Next, why not think about an aubergine cut into chunks and fried until soft, golden and succulent and mixed in with a few slivered sundried tomatoes or made more Asian with a dash of teriyaki sauce, a generosity of toasted sesame seeds and some slivered, deeply browned smoked tofu.

Talking of seeds, what would be wrong with all the seeds you know, toasted in a dry frying pan with salt. I hate the one-time vegetarian restaurant staple of tamari-fried seeds where the tamari burns and is embittered. Yuk. I'm talking pumpkin seeds, sunflower seeds, sesame seeds – but I wouldn't bother with poppy.

Next, try loads of chestnut mushrooms sliced and fried in a minimum of oil until dark and chewy, then moistened with tamari and a little garlic at the end. Then there's spinach, wilted in its own juices, seasoned with salt, pepper and nutmeg, perhaps with an egg scrambled in at the same time.

Am I running out of ideas? Not likely. Grate a mound of strong cheese, such as Cheddar, into a bowl of hot buckwheat and watch it melt. How about a mound of pitted olives, a can of drained chickpeas or a quickly-blitzed hummus, or even some other pulse – lentils and fried onions with raisins and toasted almonds in imitation of a proper pilaff. Oh and it's fabulous with finely sliced spring onions, and soaked Hiziki seaweed. Over to you.

To cook the buckwheat, heat 1 tablespoon light olive oil in a heavy-bottomed frying pan. Add 250 g/9 oz buckwheat and fry, tossing continually until browned, nutty and earthily aromatic. Cover with twice the volume of water. Lid and reduce the heat to a gentle simmer.

Cook for about 15 minutes until the buckwheat is quite, quite soft and all the water absorbed.

Meanwhile blanch the peas in salted, boiling water, drain and mix into the buckwheat.

Onions

Where would we be without onions? In the desert, that's where. Though even the Ancient Egyptians ate them, albeit raw. I grew up with the sweet smell of frying onion as an almost constant companion. My mother always fried them for an age until they were brown and caramelised.

I didn't discover that you can fry an onion to transparent until much later. Her rich braises and casseroles, her sauces and gravies all had the lavish look of the patiently, lovingly coaxed. One year, I went into mass production of mushroom Wellingtons. The first step of that recipe is to fry a whole load of onions until very soft and brown. We prepared vatfuls, and the smell would bring all the other budding entrepreneurs from their various small industrial units, noses twitching and mouths salivating.

If you've cried over an onion, spare a thought.... Now I have finally come across a reliable tip for onion tears. You simply refrigerate the onions before chopping them. This reduces the volatility of the offending allicin.

My favourite thing to do with onions is braise them and for this I use baby onions or shallots. A spoonful of sugar and a little oil are used to brown them initially and then some light stock, cooked at first on a fierce heat, then left to simmer until almost like a delectable jam. You can add prunes or soaked dried apricots, blanched almonds or (bar the sugar), green olives and preserved lemons. Delicious.

OTHER RECIPES USING ONIONS

Middle Eastern rice with lentils and fried onions

This is a pretty standard Middle Eastern rice dish which I have only customised by using Puy lentils instead of traditional brown or green ones. Smarter by far. It's a blessedly easy dish, despite the double-stage process with the onions, and it elegantly shatters the entrenched notions of worthy rice and lentils, which I think must have come about from ill-judged bastardisations of this staple food. It has universal appeal by dint of its simplicity and its far-reaching flavour.

I can make a meal of it alone or accompanied by Middle Eastern braised or grilled vegetables.

For those of you nutritionally rather than gastronomically motivated (or both), the combined action of the rice carbohydrate and the lentils, are turned to a 'complete' and perfect protein by the body. So let's not hear any more about vegetarians suffering from lack of protein. We need only eat this once in a while to be more then well-fed.

Cook the rice in 750 ml/1¼ pints cold water, bringing it to the boil in a lidded pan. Simmer for about 14 minutes until the water is absorbed. Sorry to sound pedantic but I do find that it is a touch under the full 15 minutes, but it will depend to some extent on your flame.

Bring the Puy lentils to the boil in a separate pan with the bay leaves and garlic cloves, and simmer for 40–45 minutes until tender. Meanwhile fry the onions in the oil with the cumin and mustard seeds until they are a rich golden colour. Remove half the onion with a slotted spoon and continue frying the rest until crisp. Set aside on kitchen paper.

When the lentils are tender, add them and the first lot of onion to a large frying pan. Stir over a moderate heat for a couple of minutes and then add the rice. Stir very well so that, while remaining intact, the rice and lentils merge to richer, deeper layers of flavour.

Season to taste and serve with the crispy fried onion laid on top. Drizzle with olive oil and garnish with the coriander leaves if using.

Serves 6

500 g/1 lb 2 oz Basmati rice

180 g/6 oz Puy lentils

2 bay leaves

3 garlic cloves

400 g/14 oz onions, finely sliced

8 tbsp olive oil, plus extra for serving

2 tsp ground cumin

1 tbsp brown mustard seeds

Salt and freshly ground black pepper

A small bunch of coriander, leaves separated (optional)

Paella

When I was writing *Cranks Fast Food* (C&C, 2000), I used quick-cook brown rice in an attempt to cut down on the cooking time. To my pleasant surprise this was a resounding success, both in texture and taste. Long-grain rice on the other hand, either white or brown, simply does not have the plumpness you need, nor can it swell to absorb the many vegetable flavours of this dish. The cumin is not typical but together with the wine, the olives and the sundried tomatoes, the flavour is as full and as redolent of the tapas bar as any you will taste in the cobbled alleys of Madrid.

This is definitely worth inviting people over for – preferably on a noisy, laid-back occasion. And, since we're talking Spain, you could do much worse than to serve poached quinces for dessert (*see* p315).

Place the rice and 450 ml/16 fl oz water in a large saucepan. Add 1 teaspoon tamari to the water. Cover, bring to the boil, then reduce the heat and cook until all the water is absorbed and the rice plump and tender (about 15 minutes). There should be not a trace of chalkiness left to it, nor any excess liquid. Remember too that the rice will continue to absorb liquid as it fries with the vegetables.

Meanwhile, heat 3 tablespoons olive oil in your largest sauté pan, frying pan or wok. Add the paprika and cumin, stir and fry for a minute on a closely watched heat. Then add the garlic, stir and fry for a further minute. Now slowly add tablespoons of the hot stock as well as the wine, stirring between additions, until you've used about half the liquid and the spices form a thin paste in the pan. Now stir in the Tabasco.

Add the carrots, stirring until they are coated in the sauce, then fry for a couple of minutes, always taking care that the spices do not burn, yet keeping the heat adequate. Next add the courgettes which must also become dressed in the sauce. Then the petits pois and corn kernels.

Sauté for a few minutes until the vegetables are tender but still firm. Remove from the heat.

Baste the red and yellow peppers in the remaining olive oil. Fry on a griddle pan until charred in places, or whole over a gas flame. Set aside.

When the rice is cooked, add it to the vegetable pan placed over a low heat. Stir continuously. If it looks at all dry, add the remaining stock as necessary. Then add the sundried tomatoes and black olives, stirring until they are well distributed. Finally, season, stir in the chopped parsley reserving a little for the top, and scatter the griddled peppers casually over the aromatic rice. Serve in the pan as is.

Serves 4

300 g/11 oz quick-cook brown rice or proper Arborio rice

1 scant tsp tamari or soy sauce

4 tbsp olive oil

2 tbsp bright red paprika

2 tbsp ground cumin

5 garlic cloves, crushed

200 ml/7 fl oz hot vegetable stock, made with a small pinch of Marigold bouillon powder and a pinch of saffron threads

3 tbsp white wine

$^1/_2$ tsp Tabasco

125 g/4$^1/_2$ oz carrots, peeled and sliced 5-mm/$^1/_4$-inch thick

125 g/4$^1/_2$ oz courgettes (as carrots)

150 g/5 oz petits pois

1 corn on the cob, stripped

1 small red pepper, deseeded, pith removed and cut into 8 fat strips

1 small yellow pepper, prepared as above

6 sundried tomatoes in olive oil, drained

12 black olives, stoned

1 tbsp chopped flat-leaf parsley

Sea salt and freshly ground black pepper

Risi e bisi

If you can create this with fresh young, delicate peas, still sugar sweet, you will see what a treat it is. And even if you resort to frozen peas – or rather petits pois – and turn this into a last-minute standby, you won't go wrong either. Some add fresh mint to the cooked rice and peas, but I find this a little too strong; a handful of sweet basil is harmonious and unobtrusive enough. In the most ancient of recipes, fennel seeds are used instead of the parsley and this is probably my favourite option of all.

Risi e bisi is a revered Venetian dish and more liquid than other risotti. The Italians think of it as a soup and as a recipe of their *cucina poveri* (food of the poor). Anna Del Conte, who writes simply and clearly about Italian food, calls it the aristocrat among rice dishes and I think she is nearer the mark. Try this in June or July when the home-grown peas in their pods hit the shops.

Pop the fresh peas from their pods.

Fry the shallots and garlic in the butter and oil until pale-blond, then stir in the fresh peas, parsley and enough of the hot stock to just cover the ingredients. Simmer for a couple of minutes, longer if necessary depending on how tender the peas are. Frozen peas only need to go into the rice about three-quarters of the way through cooking.

Add the rice and stir until transparent, then add most of the wine and a little freshly ground black pepper.

Then, ladleful by ladleful, add the remaining hot stock, stirring well between each addition until it is nearly all absorbed and the rice is creamy. Add the remaining wine, stir in the salt and Parmesan and remove from the heat.

Finally, cover with a lid and allow the rice to rest for a minute. If using fennel seeds, add them only a few minutes before the rice is done.

Just before serving stir in a ladle of hot water or stock if you have any left over as this needs to be heavenly molten.

Serve on warmed plates and pass around the Parmesan and glasses of the same wine.

Serves 4

1 kg/2^1/4 lbs fresh pea pods, young, tender and sweet or 250 g/9 oz frozen petits pois

6 shallots, finely sliced

2 garlic cloves, finely chopped

60 g/2 oz unsalted butter

2 tbsp olive oil

A small handful of fresh flat-leaf parsley, chopped, or 1 tsp fennel seeds

250 g/9 oz vialone nano risotto rice

125 ml/4^1/2 fl oz good dry white wine

1^1/2 litres/2^1/2 pints hot homemade stock

60 g/2 oz Parmesan, freshly grated, plus extra for serving

Sea salt and freshly ground black pepper

Barley risotto with wild mushrooms and red wine

I used to use barley only rarely, in a thick broth perhaps but not more than once in a blue moon. Yet I like its chewy texture, its delicate alkalising sweetness and, since a soft, creamy risotto with a chewy bite to it makes excellent use of this old-fashioned grain, I now use it exactly as I would Arborio and add the stock in the same slow, steady fashion.

I've partnered it with pumpkin and sage, with wild mushrooms and red wine and also with fresh artichokes. Croquettes made from the left-overs are particularly good (see p235). Use 2 teaspoons thyme or marjoram, too, if you wish.

If you want to make this with pumpkin, use 450 g/1 lb peeled and chopped to 350 g/12 oz barley or 2 raw artichoke hearts, chokes removed, thinly sliced and fried in a little butter and lemon juice before adding to the risotto two-thirds of the way through.

Keep the stock on the back burner at a steady, low simmer and use 150 ml/5 fl oz of it to soak the porcini for 20 minutes. Then drain them, reserving the liquid.

Heat half the butter in a heavy-based pan. Add the shallots or onion and garlic and fry for about 5 minutes until softened. Heat the remaining butter in another pan and add the porcini (checked for grit). Stir-fry for about 5 minutes before adding the remaining mushrooms. Remove from the heat when they are nicely browned. Set aside.

While the mushrooms are cooking, add the tamari and 1 tablespoon red wine to bring out their flavour. Then add the barley to the fried onion and fry for about a minute, stirring all the while until the grains are glistening and starting to go transparent.

Add a ladleful of hot stock and half the remaining wine and, when it is nearly all absorbed, add another ladle of stock. Continue until the barley is thoroughly cooked. A few minutes before it looks ready, add the mushrooms and the remaining wine, stirring gently but pretty much continuously. Stop when the risotto is quite sloppy, the grains bound by a rich, creamy sauce.

Season and stir in the Parmesan and parsley. Check the seasoning and serve with the Mascarpone, if using, stirred in or served separately.

Serves 4

1.2 litres/scant 2 pints dark vegetable stock

15 g/^{1}/2 oz dried porcini

60 g/2 oz butter

2 shallots or 1 small red onion, finely sliced

2 garlic cloves, finely chopped

450 g/1 lb mixed fresh mushrooms to include shiitake, chanterelles, chestnut, a prize morel if you can, blewits in season, and so on

A dash of tamari

6 tbsp red wine or Marsala

350 g/12 oz pearl barley

Salt and freshly ground black pepper

60 g/2 oz Parmesan, finely grated

2 tbsp finely chopped parsley

2 tbsp Mascarpone (optional)

Tomato risotto with basil and a tomato oil

A modern risotto, this is lighter and tastes fresher than most butter-rich risotti. I first made it from *I Risotti* by Anna Del Conte (Pavilion, 1993), part of a series of precious little books, designed as a gift set and delightfully illustrated by Flo Bailey.

You'll understand just what a precious gift the series really was when I tell you that I have cooked every one of the (vegetarian) recipes in it. In all things Italian, Anna Del Conte remains one of my most treasured sources of inspiration and information.

Set your stock to simmer gently while you work. Peel the tomatoes with a sharp serrated paring knife. You can add the peel to the simmering stock. Cut the tomatoes in half, discarding about half the seeds, chop them roughly and add them to 4 tablespoons olive oil and the garlic, warming over a gentle heat. Now increase the heat to a brisk simmer and stir for a couple of minutes. Add the rice to the pan and again stir continuously for about 2 minutes.

Pour over a ladleful of hot stock and continue cooking, adding more stock, a ladleful at a time, until the rice is tender with a little bite. Stir in half the basil and keep the rest for garnish. Season with salt and pepper and stir in the rest of the olive oil.

For the aubergine strips, heat 2 tbsp olive oil in a pan and fry with the Tabasco until they are golden brown. Salt them at once and keep them warm, covered with foil in a hot oven if necessary. Scatter a few over each serving with the Pecorino or Parmesan.

Alternatives

I used to make a cold tomato and aubergine timbale, the sides of a spring-form tin lined first with cling film then with fried aubergine slices – you'll need 2–3 large aubergines – and filled with the cold tomato risotto, a layer of fried aubergine in the middle. Pressed down, then turned out, it looks impressive, cuts easily and gives off all the flavours of the Mediterranean. You can serve crème fraîche or Mascarpone on the side, quite plain or lemon-and-garlic scented. This is useful for a cold table and a crowd of people.

Serves 4

1 1/2 litres/2 1/2 pints vegetable stock

750 g/1 lb 11 oz ripe tomatoes

150 ml/5 fl oz extra virgin olive oil

4 plump garlic cloves, thickly cut

350 g/12 oz Carnaroli or other risotto rice

A generous handful of fresh basil

Salt and freshly ground black pepper

To serve

Pecorino or Parmesan, finely grated

1 small aubergine, cut into slices and then into strips

2 tbsp olive oil (optional)

A dash of Tabasco

Tomato oil

If you want to make a tomato oil, heat some olive oil (in this case about 100 ml/3 1/2 fl oz or a little more) in a frying pan, add a chopped tomato and a dab of tomato purée, sundried if possible. Also add a thinly sliced garlic clove and warm until the tomato is completely soft and the oil turning a russet red. Drain through a small fine-meshed sieve and use this, drizzled through each serving, instead of the olive oil at the end.

Beetroot

Jane Grigson (whom I otherwise worship – her warmth) thought beetroot a dull vegetable and wondered how anyone could count it among their favourites.

Coming from a family of beetroot lovers, this is heresy. So forget the overpoweringly pickled kind and opt for freshly cooked. And, when you do add vinegar, which is an undoubted trusted accomplice, make sure it is judiciously. Do as the Moroccans do by marinating with a little ground cumin at the same time, as well as some finely diced onion.

A good borscht, zinging with vodka and lemon, is fantastic, especially with its customary dollop of sour cream and its little mound of sautéed potatoes, served by the side. A tray of roasted vegetables, including carrots, beetroots, shallots, small turnips, small chunks of butternut squash or sweet potatoes and tiny new potatoes is absolutely wonderful, bound in the final stages of roasting with a little tamarind and served with a garlic-rich crème fraîche.

I am not in the least squeamish about beetroot's vermilion juices or that it turns any yoghurt or cream sauce a particularly striking shade of fuchsia – that is all part of the fun. Try it in risotto for instance. Horseradish is another classic accompaniment, and anything sharp – a grain-mustard vinaigrette for instance – has the same effect and is a perfect balance to this vegetable's sweet, staining earthiness.

OTHER RECIPES USING BEETROOT

Beetroot risotto

I ate this unlikely sounding combination at Coast in London when it first opened. I was on 'a date' with an old friend. Enough said about that. About the risotto, however, I'll regale you with the details. A more lurid, shocking plateful I don't think I had ever seen (or maybe it was my delicate mood and I wasn't going to elaborate on that). But to my utter amazement, each mouthful was as exquisitely, upliftingly strange and perfect as the last. I ate it very slowly, almost grain by dissolving grain. There must have been something in it. There is vodka in this risotto, which is very un-Italian except in its sheer passion.

Peel (I use a potato peeler which removes it sparingly) and chop the beetroot into small chunks. Peel and chop the onion and then add it to the butter melted in a large saucepan. Fry the onion until transparent and add the beetroot. Stir rhythmically for about 10 minutes to coat in the butter and to soften slightly.

Then add the rice and garlic and, still stirring, fry for several minutes on a heat gentle enough not to colour the rice but simply to turn it translucent and readier to absorb the stock and pink juices of the beetroot. Now add a ladleful of the hot stock and stir steadily until it is all absorbed and you are ready to add the next ladleful.

Continue in this way for about 20 minutes until you have used up all the stock and the rice is tender, creamy and almost fuchsia pink. The beetroot should be soft, though perhaps with just a hint of bite to it.

Add the vodka and lemon juice in the last few moments, season with salt and pepper and add about half the Parmesan. Stir it a couple of times then let the risotto sit still for a few minutes, protectively lidded.

I always hold back a little stock for this stage or even a little boiling water just to loosen it slightly before serving. Serve with the rest of the Parmesan and the parsley if you wish. Personally I think I prefer it without, letting the freshness of the lemon sing through instead.

At the end, bring out a glass bowlful of frisée, torn to sizeable pieces and dressed with a palate-closing Dijon mustard dressing. As I write, I realise that I've never served dessert after this. There is such an integral balance of sweet and savoury in the risotto that nothing else seems really necessary.

Now if someone else was eating a velvety smooth crème brûlée (*see* p347) and I could have just a mouthful, that would do nicely.

Serves 4

400 g/14 oz raw beetroot

1 medium onion

30 g/1 oz butter

400 g/14 oz Arborio rice

3 garlic cloves, finely chopped

1.2 litres/2$^{1}/_{4}$ pints light vegetable stock made with 1 scant tsp Marigold bouillon powder, kept hot

50 ml/scant 2 fl oz vodka or dry sherry

Juice of half a lemon, plus $^{1}/_{2}$ tsp zest

90 g/3$^{1}/_{2}$ oz Parmesan, finely shredded to tangled threads

1 tbsp finely minced parsley (optional)

Salt and freshly ground black pepper

Parsley

Parsley is used in the Middle East, Europe and in its place of origin, the eastern Mediterranean. It is deep and grassy, yet somehow safe and reassuring.

It is very much at home with lemon. For some reason, curly-leaved parsley, less sweet and less potent (or maybe that's why), is or was more popular in England then elsewhere, used predominantly and rather sadly as a garnish. That's a shame since finely minced flat-leaf parsley adds flavour and natural, intrinsic adornment to stews, casseroles, salads, vegetables, risottos and paellas. One only has to take a look at a Lebanese tabbouleh where the herb is used with liberal abandon to experience a very different, far less fearful attitude. English parsley sauce, gentle and even elegant, is in better keeping, and the Italian *soffritto* combines parsley, garlic, onion and celery as a perfect basis for soups and sauces.

The stalks harbour most of the flavour and are very good in stocks and soups, though there is no reason why, chopped very small, they should not go into salads, together with the young leaves. I once ate a parsley sauce at The Oak Room, Marco Pierre White's restaurant in London, and it was pure essence of parsley, the most verdant green I have ever seen. I have made it several times since, frying or rather softening a mass of fresh parsley in butter until completely crumpled, then blending it and sieving it to a regal green velvet. Eat it with tender, lemoned baby vegetables and go to heaven.

OTHER RECIPES USING PARSLEY

Spring vegetables with butter, lemon and parsley 63

Parsley soup 74

Jerusalem artichoke, lemon and parsley salad with green olives and pistachios 83

Carrots with parsley, garlic and lemon in a walnut pastry tart 99

Root vegetable casserole with herb dumplings 151

Harira – chickpea soup 162

Cannellini beans with roasted garlic, sundried tomatoes and black olives 185

Pumpkin and parsley risotto with white wine 255

Chermoula 268

Pumpkin and parsley risotto
with white wine

'...To swell the gourd, and plump the hazel shells
With a sweet kernel; to set budding more'
To Autumn by John Keats

You could use a more aromatic herb than parsley, such as marjoram or oregano if, unlike me, you are fond of it. It may just depend on your mood, but please do capture a little of the fullness of autumn.

Preheated the oven to 220°C/425°F/gas mark 7.

Peel the pumpkin and cut into 3-cm/1½-inch chunks. Brush with oil, salt and pepper and roast in the oven for about 30 minutes until browned on the outside and soft inside. Remove from the oven and reserve.

Melt half the butter and the remaining olive oil in a large, heavy-bottomed saucepan and fry the onion until soft and transparent.

Season with salt and pepper. Add the garlic and the rice. Reduce the heat to very low and stir for a minute until the rice is well coated and translucent. Turn the heat up for a moment as you add a couple of ladlefuls of hot stock, then down again. I do play about quite a bit with temperature when I am cooking: the alternating rhythms of fast and slow, hard and soft lead you to a better conclusion. You have to feel it out, look and listen; this will sometimes work better than I can describe by giving clock-measured timings. It's a dance: one leads, the other follows, one follows, the other leads. So simmer away and let your instincts guide you.

Stir continuously until nearly all the liquid is absorbed by the rice, before adding the next ladle, 'nearly' being the operative word. If you let all the liquid dry out each time, you can end up with a lumpen and stodgy risotto.

Continue in this fashion until all the stock is used up which will take about 17 minutes or perhaps 20. Add the remaining butter, cut up into small pieces, the pumpkin and wine as well as half the parsley and half the Parmesan. Stir or rather turn over gently a couple of times. Let it rest for a moment or two, then serve with no further ado than the remaining Parmesan and parsley.

Serves 4

850 g/1 lb 14 oz very bright orange pumpkin, including skin

5 tbsp olive oil

150 g/5 oz butter

1 medium red onion, very finely diced

Sea salt and freshly ground black pepper

2 garlic cloves, very finely chopped

300 g/11 oz Carnaroli rice

1 litre/2 pints hot vegetable stock

75 ml/2½ fl oz dry white wine

75 g/2½ oz parsley leaves picked off the stalk and finely chopped

175 g/6 oz Parmesan, freshly grated

A radicchio risotto from the Veneto

This started off as the search for *risi e bisi*. Let me explain. I was in Venice for a few days and quite determined to eat *risi e bisi*, made by a real Italian. I asked and I looked and I asked some more. Finally a *padrone* put me out of my misery. 'But,' she said, 'it is not the "season",' and of course in early December, as we were, it was not. Silly me.

There, as here, the tiny peas are an early summer harvest. Of course I should have known but in the misplaced hope, excitement and anticipation, I went through seasonal amnesia. Now there was treviso around in great abundance. I had seen it on every market square and heaped high in the tiny shops, carved out of every nook and cranny of the labyrinthine streets. And it advertised itself proudly on every restaurant board, *risotto di treviso*. I did the inevitable and enjoyed every bittersweet mouthful. I can only ever get treviso by putting a special order with my local deli or with a specialist supplier, so this recipe is with the more easily obtainable radicchio.

The Dolcelatte is an addition I prevaricate over – sometimes yes, sometimes no – stirred in at the end with the pan just off the heat. It depends on how bitter you can take it.

Melt the butter in a large pan and fry the shallots until transparent. Add the garlic and fry on a gentle heat for a few minutes. Then add the rice and fry for a few minutes, stirring the whole time, until it loses its opacity and becomes transparent.

Add 1 ladle stock and stir it in over a low heat until well absorbed. Continue with the next. And the next. Then add the radicchio. It will soon lose its ruby red and turn brown. I regret this but it is completely unavoidable and you can always reserve a little of the fresh leaf to shred finely on top for colour. Braise for a few minutes, add half the Marsala and continue to stir. The wine and the radicchio will impart a dusky pink to the risotto.

Continue adding the stock until the rice is just tender, yet quite intact and held together in a pink, fragrant creaminess. Venetian risottos are wetter and creamier than others, somewhere between a soup and a risotto. I find myself nearly always making risotto this way now, just a little soupier, whatever its provenance.

Stir in the Dolcelatte, until it is all melted, plus the rest of the wine. Season with salt and pepper and stir briskly a few more times until perfectly ready. Serve as soon as possible, with grated Parmesan.

Serves 4

60 g/2 oz butter

3 shallots, finely sliced

3 garlic cloves, finely sliced

1/2 medium head radicchio, shredded

300 g/11 oz Arborio rice

1.2 litres/2¼ pints hot vegetable stock

100 ml/3½ fl oz Marsala

60 g/2 oz Dolcelatte

Salt and freshly ground black pepper

To serve

Parmesan

Ways with quinoa

When the early settlers arrived in America, they found a healthy, well-fed (and, it has to be said, well-lubricated) self-sufficient people. They made, and still make, a hot beverage, *chincha*, flavoured with dried apples and berries and also a lethal alcoholic drink.

The settlers couldn't be doing with that so they proceeded to burn vast stretches of quinoa fields to the ground. That way they enslaved the people and, through their malnutrition, made them totally dependent on their new masters.

Recently, some of the land has been bought back and the grain planted anew. It is a delightfully simple thing to look at, a little like millet. When cooked, however, the outer husk breaks off like thousands of tiny Saturn rings. It is gently nutty, as easy to eat as couscous, and there are the inevitable claims that it promotes a long and healthy life. In fact weight for weight quinoa is richer in protein than meat and contains all eight amino acids.

Quinoa cooks in about one and a half times its own volume of water, brought to the boil in a lidded pan as you would rice. It is then simmered gently for 20 minutes; its diminutive size may tempt you to cook it for less, but perfection comes in tenderness, so don't rush it.

For two people, use 200 g/7 oz of quinoa, cooked in 300 ml/10 fl oz of water. This will give you a full 500 g/1 lb 2 oz of fluffed-up, ready-to-eat beady grain. Then you can use it as you would bulgur for a herb-rich summer tabbouleh or instead of basmati rice with plump cooked chickpeas, olive oil, garlic and finely chopped parsley.

Add the cooked quinoa to 1 tablespoon hot, light olive oil, a garlic clove, finely chopped, and stir before adding the not-quite-drained can of chickpeas. Stir again, adding a good dash of tamari and Tabasco and a tablespoon or so of finely minced parsley. It is a take on rice and beans but an infinitely more soothing, more easily absorbed version.

Quinoa is also great in that other 'health-freak' bowl – all seeded and sprouted. Add salt-roasted sesame seeds, sunflower seeds and pumpkin seeds. Add mung bean sprouts, a web of alfalfa, not forgetting the obligatory soy sauce or tamari and a swirl of olive oil. Eat very fresh, the seeds crackling and exploding straight from the pan.

Everyone but everyone needs to eat like this sometimes. Especially if they eat like the rest of this book the rest of the time.

dressings oils & vinegars

dressings etc recipes

This book is gently bathed in olive oil and it's often the best extra virgin. The 'in-the-mouth feel of fat' is a hideous expression of the low-fat food industry but reflects what we all know in our hearts to be true. Food needs healthy, high-quality fat to taste good. I know there are other condiments and powerfully flavoured agents and you will find them in this chapter. But learning to use oil is an essential of excellent cooking. Add it at the end to simmering soups and stews to preserve its health benefits.

Which oils for what?

Groundnut, sunflower or rapeseed oil

for deep-frying and any Asian cooking. Light olive oil for general cooking of anything Middle Eastern or Mediterranean.

Extra virgin olive oil

for use on expensive leaves with first-class vinegars or on its own with fine fresh bread or with goat's cheese and a little sea salt.

Olive oil

for roasting, grilling or griddling anything from an aubergine to a zucchini, frying vegetables for a ratatouille or onions for the myriad reasons I fry onions. Frying rice for a pilaff or adding a film of it to a ball of homemade dough. I do not need the oil to look, much less taste, as if it has just come off the press. This is just perfect.

Walnut oil

in never more than a 50/50 ratio with light olive oil for salad dressings.

Argan oil

if it is ever available, for Moroccan cooking – very rare and very delicate.

Sesame oil

in homeopathic droplets added to organic sunflower oil in some sesame-seeded stir-fries.

Almond oil

for lining baking sheets and parchment before making biscuits and cakes.

Vegetable oil

for nothing.

Soya oil

for nothing.

Coconut oil

for your hair.

Basil

Italian food just wouldn't be the same without sweet, delicate, gentle, calming basil, the principal ingredient of *pesto alla Genovese*. It is deeply soothing to the stomach and mildly sedative.

It is potently aromatic and the subject of both erotic and funerary folklore. More surprising is that despite being native to India, it makes only infrequent appearances in that country's vast culinary repertoire, apparently because of its sacred association with the Hindu God, Vishnu.

In Britain, we are most familiar with the small-leafed variety, which is the most aromatic. But there is also a lovely lemon-scented basil and a purple-leafed variety, which seems to make only occasional fashionable appearances. All are delicious in mixed herb salads, and a well watered pot will keep beautifully on a sunny window-sill. Fridge-cold leaves won't release anything like the same perfume. Burying my nose in a pot of basil is yet another of the kitchen's heavenly experiences.

Basil grows best in warm, sunny climates, hence the difficulty experienced by most British home growers who invariably end up with toughened, rather bitter leaves.

OTHER RECIPES USING BASIL

Basil pesto

Using a pestle and mortar, pound the garlic and pine nuts together, then add the basil leaves and stems, a few at a time, grinding them to a pulp against the side of the bowl. Stir in the grated cheese, then slowly add the olive oil, beating as you do so. Season with a little sea salt.

Serves 4–6

2 plump garlic cloves, very finely chopped

60 g/2 oz pine nuts

60 g/2 oz very fresh basil, including stems

60 g/2 oz Parmesan, freshly grated

150 ml/5 fl oz light olive oil

Sea salt

Coriander pesto

Chop the coriander with a very sharp knife. Pound the almonds in a pestle and mortar or chop in a food processor. Mix with the garlic and then add the remaining ingredients and a pinch of salt. Stir into plain rice or eat with fried tortillas and feta cheese or as an accompaniment to the smoked aubergines (*see* p47).

Serves 4–6

1 large bunch of coriander (about 175 g/6 oz), leaves only

2 tbsp whole almonds

6 garlic cloves, finely chopped or crushed

4 tbsp light olive oil

Juice of 1 lime

1–2 tsp Tabasco

1-cm/$\frac{1}{2}$-inch piece of red chilli, chopped very small

Sea salt

Quick tomato pesto

Blend the tomatoes, Parmesan, oil and garlic. Tear the basil and scatter over the top, and add salt and pepper. Use instead of tomato sauce for pasta, as a garnish to soups or on ciabatta toast. This makes about 150 g/5 oz or two generous servings.

Serves 4

12 slow-roasted tomato quarters

30 g/1 oz Parmesan, freshly grated

1 tbsp olive oil

2 garlic cloves, crushed

4 or 5 basil leaves

Sea salt and freshly ground black pepper

Watercress pesto

I prefer to mix this by hand as I don't want it to become too much of a purée. Mix all the ingredients and serve with pasta, on grilled vegetables, on toast or as a spoonful in soup, especially carrot or leek.

Serves 4–6

90 g/3^1/$_2$ oz watercress, tough stalks removed, chopped

4 tbsp light olive oil

1 tsp balsamic vinegar

4–6 garlic cloves, chopped

1 shallot, very finely chopped

1 tbsp ground almonds (optional)

Sea salt

A classic vinaigrette

Place all the ingredients in a screw-top jar and shake as vigorously as required. You can add half as much hot water as oil, which allows the oil to be suspended in golden droplets and can look pretty on a plated salad of, say, blanched baby leeks and translucently thin garlic.

At the other extreme you can add half as much double cream as oil, season with a little finely milled pepper and use on stronger leaves, such as Cos, iceberg or radicchio, used together or separately and topped with shaven Pecorino or Parmesan.

Serves 4

125 ml/4 fl oz light olive oil

40 ml/1^1/$_2$ fl oz white wine vinegar

Sea salt and freshly ground black pepper

My mother's vinaigrette

This makes a thick, yellow, mustardy dressing quite unlike most people's perceptions of vinaigrette. It transforms plain iceberg lettuce into something rather more interesting and is great with artichokes or asparagus. I make a batch every week or so and keep it in a large jar. If you want to do the same, simply triple or quadruple the quantities given.

Put the mustard in a bowl and trickle in the oil very slowly, beating continuously with a fork until thoroughly mixed in. Add the garlic and vinegar and beat vigorously. Season lightly with salt and pepper.

For a quick method, place all the ingredients in a jar with a tight lid and shake well.

Serves 4

1 dsp English mustard

4 tbsp light olive oil

1 garlic clove, crushed

1 tsp white wine vinegar

A small pinch each of sea salt and freshly ground black pepper

Vinaigrette with olive oil, balsamic vinegar and grain mustard

Add the vinegar to the mustard in a jar or bottle, then pour in the oil, season with salt and pepper and shake. Add a sprig of tarragon and the garlic if required. Use sparingly on rocket or watercress.

Serves 4

1 tsp balsamic vinegar

1 dsp grain mustard

4 tbsp olive oil

A small pinch each of salt and freshly ground black pepper

A sprig of tarragon (optional)

1 garlic clove, crushed (optional)

A less-oil-rich vinaigrette

Simply mix all the ingredients together and whisk well. Customise this dressing with toasted cumin or caraway seeds or *sumac* – a sour, red-berry spice powder available from Middle Eastern shops

Serves 6

4 tbsp olive oil, cold pressed

4 tbsp vinegar

4 tbsp water

Juice of 1 small lemon

2 tbsp grain mustard

2 tbsp snipped chives

2 garlic cloves, finely chopped

3 tbsp chopped basil or coriander

A dash of Tabasco

A dash of tamari (optional)

A yoghurt dressing with herbs

Another low-fat salad dressing, as I am well aware that there are times when one needs (well, I need anyway) to eat more salads than usual and all the good intentions are compromised by the delicious, but unarguably fattening dressings that inevitably go on top.

Simply mix all the ingredients together in a bowl. You can add a pinch of suger to taste, too, if you prefer.

Serves 6

150 ml/5 fl oz plain bio yoghurt

1 garlic clove, finely minced

1 tbsp each freshly chopped parsley, coriander and chives

Salt and freshly ground black pepper

A pinch of sugar (optional)

Chermoula

The most magnificent and multi-dimensional of all sauces, chermoula opens up a whole new world of culinary exploration, and can only have been concocted by someone privy to the secrets of *A Thousand and One Nights*. It contains practically every element of the Middle Eastern kitchen blended together in a rich and complex marriage.

It's designed to go with fish, but I cannot think of any vegetable that it doesn't elevate. As with the harissa, it is best used with some discretion, though I always have extra in a bowl, and it disappears quickly enough. It stands its ground alongside other dips such as hummus, bissara (broad bean purée), aubergine purée, tzatziki, home-cooked bowls of fat chickpeas, and can be used over grilled or roasted vegetables, dribbled over frittatas and tortillas (Spanish egg version or Mexican flour tortillas). Indeed whenever you might be tempted to anoint with olive oil, you can bring out the chermoula instead.

As with all these mass-produced recipes, there's really no point in making just a thimbleful – it keeps so well you might as well make a tumbler-full. So I use the large bunches of herbs, not the tiny plastic coffins I'm always ranting against. Where there is the option to go big or small with a quantity, I tend to err on the side of largesse. Store in a well-sealed jar, a film of oil resting protectively on top, and keep refrigerated to increase its usage.

Mix all the ingredients together using a fork so that the oil and spices make a paste loosened by the lemon juice and roughened up by the herbs and garlic.

You could stick it all in the food processor and it would take seconds, but this and the Thai curry paste (which is much longer work) are two items I just love to make by hand. I know I'm mad but I love the growing mounds of herb and spice releasing ever more intense scents and aromas. I don't do it very often, so there's some ceremony involved.

Serves 6–8

1 large bunch coriander, tough stalks removed, roughly chopped

1 large bunch parsley, tough stalks removed, roughly chopped

6 large garlic cloves, very finely chopped or crushed

2 tbsp ground cumin

1 tbsp sweet paprika

1 tsp harissa (*see* p273)

1 small bird's eye chilli, very finely chopped

Juice of 2 lemons

300 ml/10 fl oz extra virgin olive oil, and more

Coriander

Coriander resembles flat-leaf parsley, though it is a paler green and its leaves are softer, sweeter and more delicate.

Its pervasive flavour is not to everyone's liking. I know people who liken it to a compost heap and won't go near it, though they give up the joys of almost all cooking outside Europe in the process.

I mean, imagine a Thai curry without coriander – I don't understand it, but you can't argue tastes and colours. Despite its extreme reception, it's possibly the most universally used herb of all. It is crucial to the cooking of the Middle East, parts of the Mediterranean, Asia and South America, always added at the end of cooking to maximise its sweetness and freshness.

The similarity with parsley does betray a common familial heritage, both being umbelliferous, but while one is earthy and quite subtle, the other is much more in your face, much more likely to please or to appal.

The seeds and plant have distinctively different tastes, the former spicier and with greater usage in Europe, and the latter more commonly used in the Middle East and Asia where it is more important than parsley.

Increasingly these assumptions no longer mean much when so many of us have adopted the food of different cultures into our own. Thai green curry paste and chermoula are fantastic examples of how best to use it.

OTHER RECIPES USING CORIANDER

Courgette koftas with an almond and tomato sauce 53

Thai green curry 157

Harira – chickpea soup 162

Chickpea salad with coriander, sunblushed tomatoes and Haloumi 176

Chickpea fritters with tikka yoghurt sauce 178

Biryani 238

Middle Eastern rice with lentils and fried onions 245

Coriander pesto 264

Chermoula 268

Cumin, coriander and garlic cream 271

Cumin, coriander and garlic cream

Around the corner from where I live is a no-frills Moroccan restaurant which serves accomplished food, sometimes too swimming in oil but nonetheless delicious.

As a starter I ate artichoke with coriander and cumin sauce. Michel, the chef, barked a list of ingredients at me *in lieu* of a recipe, but here is the sauce, pretty much as it is served.

Blend the peeled garlic cloves and cumin with a little of the oil and a little hot water to form a thick paste.

Mix in the coriander and then drizzle in most of the rest of the olive oil very slowly, followed by the lemon juice and finally the last of the oil.

Season with salt and pepper and serve.

Serves 6–8

2 large super fresh garlic heads

1 tbsp ground cumin

250 ml/9 fl oz extra virgin olive oil

1 large bunch coriander, stalks removed, finely chopped

1 tsp lemon juice

Sea salt and freshly ground black pepper

An orange and coriander dressing

Simply mix all the ingredients together.

This is perfect served over a small fennel bulb, very finely sliced; 2 large oranges, peeled and segmented; 1 perfect avocado, peeled and sliced; 1 tablespoon of blueberries; a walnut or two, taken out of their shell and broken very small, and a very finely chopped piece of red chilli.

Mix the orange juice with the rest of the ingredients, add to the salad and scatter over the orange zest.

Serves 4

Juice of 1 orange and zest of half

1 garlic clove, finely minced

2 tbsp finely chopped fresh coriander

1 tbsp olive oil

A few drops of balsamic vinegar

2 tsp teriyaki sauce

Chilli

Chillies originate in Mexico, having grown there for at least 9,000 years – Chilli con Carne famously celebrates them. Columbus probably brought chillies back to Europe with the rest of his spoils and, within a few years, some of his compatriots had taken them to Asia and then to the Middle East.

Everyone knows the story of poor Becky in *Vanity Fair* who, having just eaten a palate-raising hot curry, pounced on the cool-sounding green chillies only to double her anguish. The offending chemical compound capsaicin is not water-soluble, so her suffering was again prolonged by the ill-judged glass of water. Plain yoghurt or a salty lassi – capsaicin is fat soluble – would have helped. I have had my own salutary experiences with chilli and would not dream now of preparing any quantity without first donning a pair of surgical gloves.

Chillies vary enormously in strength – the heat is in inverse proportion to size – so the poetically named bird's eye chillies are the most fierce. People who eat chillies consistently do become inured somewhat to their effect, requiring ever bigger amounts to experience the same eye-stinging, nose-dripping hit. No wonder they are thought to be addictive. Tabasco peppers are amongst the hottest and make up the well-known sauce. They give heat, warm sweetness and complex flavour. Dried chillies should be respected – only a couple will give you quite the kick you need.

OTHER RECIPES USING CHILLI

Harissa

This fiery hot paste is one of Morocco's (also Tunisia's and Algeria's) exotic treasures. It brings tears to people's eyes but I fancy these are not entirely because of the chilli. There is something so very perfect about it, dabbed discreetly over vegetables, couscous or salads. The great thing about making your own is that you can regulate the heat to suit your palate. I've seen my father add a carefully judged spoonful (he would call it *un soupçon*) of ketchup to add soothing sweetness to the fiery blast! I offer it as a humorous option.

I am also quite attached to the yellow and red toothpaste tubes of harissa. I remember them from Arabic shops and markets and they look the same now as they did 35 years ago.

To make my own I buy the chillies from Indian supermarkets or Middle Eastern grocers where spices are sold in bags meant for people who actually cook and use their spices, not in under-sized jars that suggest a purely decorative purpose. The cumin is not strictly authentic (though I do know others who use it), but I like it too much in this to call it optional.

You should wear rubber gloves to make this, because it's practically impossible not to burn your skin otherwise. You can buy close-fitting surgical gloves from a chemist and you'll be pleased to have them.

Remove the stems and seeds from the chillies and soak in enough warm water to cover for about half an hour.

Drain and place in a mortar. Then pound with a pestle together with the peeled garlic, coriander seeds, caraway or fennel seeds, mint, if using, fresh coriander, cumin and salt.

Moisten with the olive oil and the ketchup if desired, both stirred in to make a thick and vibrant paste. If it seems too thick, moisten with a little water.

Makes 350 g/12 oz

250 g/9 oz dried fiery red chillies

1 medium-sized whole head of garlic

1 tbsp coriander seeds

1 tbsp caraway or fennel seeds

1 tbsp finely chopped fresh mint (optional)

3 tbsp fresh coriander leaves (or to taste)

1 tsp ground cumin

1 tbsp sea salt

1 tbsp olive oil

1 tsp tomato ketchup (optional)

Harissa made with fresh chillies

This has all the spark and sparkle of a crackling, newly lit fire. It will set your taste-buds searingly alive, make your eyes water and your nose run, but not before it has lulled you into a sweet sense of security – the red chillies mild before they hit you in the face.

But a dab of harissa, judiciously added here and there like fine perfume, is enticingly fabulous. Just stir it into a bowl of couscous and see.

Slit the chillies in half, remove their seeds and pith and chop roughly. You can hold back a few of the white seeds if you want a really raging fire. I try to keep the paste itself as fiery red as possible so don't blend the seeds in at the same time as the flesh.

Mix the olive oil, garlic cloves, coriander seeds, caraway, mint, coriander leaves, cumin and salt. Put in a pestle and mortar or a food processor with herb-processing attachment and grind or pulse firmly several times. Combine with the chilli.

This will give you 8 tablespoons or 150 g/5 oz of harissa and it keeps for a couple of weeks and more in a screw-top jar stored in the refrigerator.

Chilli batter

Try adding a little finely chopped red chilli to a batter containing dessicated coconut and roughly chopped almonds and macadamia nuts.

Makes 140 g/ 4^1/$_2$ oz

6 chillies, fat, bright red and superfresh

2 tbsp olive oil

3–4 plump garlic cloves

1 tsp coriander seeds

1 tsp caraway seeds

1 tsp dried mint

1^1/$_2$ tbsp fresh coriander leaves

1 scant tsp ground cumin

1 tsp sea salt

Mayonnaise

I watched my mother make mayonnaise from a very young age, including the splits (curdling), accidents and remedies. Later, I headed the large kitchen of a 300-strong community and there, in my industrial Robot Coupe (extra-large food processor), I made oil-drums full of the stuff. So, believe me I speak from experience, especially when I say that though you may wish to martyr yourself to the hand-whisk option, making it in an electric blender is so much easier.

What matters is that you add the oil in drop by amalgamated drop, especially at the beginning. Then when it is already very thick, add the vinegar and continue to add the oil in a steady but extremely thin stream.

Now to the remedies. If – and this will happen to you at least once in your life – the mayonnaise splits, simply place a fresh egg yolk in a new clean bowl and, drop by drop, add first the curdled mixture then the rest of the oil until emulsified once more. An even simpler method is to add 1 tablespoon boiling water to the split mess, and carry on. No one will ever know.

Finally you can make mayonnaise with a bland sunflower or rapeseed oil, with extra virgin olive oil (I prefer to use half light olive oil and half rapeseed or sunflower oil) or with peanut oil and you can easily incorporate other ingredients into it. Try chopped green olives, chopped garlic, saffron, basil, additional lemon or lemongrass or tomato purée and red peppers to make a rouille – you don't need to eat fish to enjoy this. Use judiciously in a fat-conscious way.

And, since you are going to be eating raw egg, insist on organic, free-range – much better all round.

Makes around 450 ml/16 fl oz

2 large organic, free-range egg yolks

1 tbsp Dijon mustard

1 garlic clove, crushed or very finely chopped

450 ml/16 fl oz oil

1 tbsp white wine vinegar or lemon juice

Sea salt and freshly ground black pepper

Place the egg yolks, mustard, garlic, salt and pepper in a blender and whizz for about 10 seconds. Then increase the speed and add 1 teaspoon olive oil.

Only when this is perfectly amalgamated, add the rest of the oil, drop by drop at first.

Then add the vinegar, blend in and continue to add the oil in a thin and steady stream until it is all used, emulsified and you have a good bowl-full of gleaming thick mayonnaise. It will keep in the refrigerator, covered with cling film, for about a week.

Olive oil

Ages ago, when I was catering to the rich and famous, I unpacked my boxes in someone's kitchen ready for the big night (a New Year's Eve, I think) to be greeted with incredulity as I brought out my bottles of Sainsbury's own-brand olive oil. 'But your food is so good and you use that?' the host exclaimed.

Quite apart from the fact that I would have had to charge about twice as much if I'd bought vintage bottles instead, I stick to that habit. It's not to say that I don't enjoy a small bottle of the dark, green, throat-rasping stuff sometimes, or a delicate, fruity Ligurian oil, but for most things basic quality suffices. Reserve top-quality oils for eating neat – at the most a spoonful of soft goat curd with it, a slice of warm bread, toast (and I could tell you a few stories about the reactions I've had from people who have seen me doing that) or some robust leaves.

Heavy oils collapse delicate greens, so use lighter styles. But, drizzle a rich oil on to a soft and deserving polenta or pasta dressed with little else, however, remember it can overpower the flavour of other ingredients.

In Italy my idea of heaven is dunking pieces of fresh bread into thick, bitter oil, sprinkling salt on every piece. Far from refined, this oil is as dark as ink, thick and heavy, with detritus settling on the bottom. True, they might not win any prizes, but somehow you know that's how they have been for 1,000 years and I would make them my first choice any day.

OTHER RECIPES USING OLIVE OIL

Olive oil and lemon dressing

You hardly need a recipe for this though it is useful to know just how much lemon can be diluted and still give its indelible tart fragrance. Three tablespoons of the juice, roughly equivalent to half a large and juicy lemon, can be quadrupled in volume by olive oil, one that is not too strong, dark or peppery.

Such oil is best left to its own powerful devices. But a lemon and olive oil dressing can be poured on to leaves, grains, beans, potatoes or pasta without a moment's thought and is useful indeed. Soft, collapsing broccoli, stirred into a bowl of linguine and an egg-cup full of this will restore your flagging spirits, satisfy your appetite and cheer you up.

When you put these ingredients in a screw-top jar and shake, you will immediately have a thick, viscous syrup like a thin liquid lemon curd. Keep it for a few days somewhere cool and dark and use as a lifeline.

Makes 225 ml/9 fl oz

3 tbsp lemon juice

12 tbsp olive oil

1 plump garlic clove, very finely minced

1 scant tsp sea salt

3 droplets Tabasco

Roasted garlic and other tales

Try whole heads of garlic roasted, with just their tops cut off. Bake in a low oven at 180°C/350°F/gas mark 4 for just over 1 hour, doused in olive oil – butter too if you want an especially honeyed goo at the end – and cover with foil. Squeeze the golden cream into soups, on to toast.

For a paler, creamier thing still, blanch several peeled heads in a little water till soft. Blend and add a light olive oil till they won't absorb any more, or even some single cream. By the way, it's true about the green bit; it really does give you indigestion, heartburn, the works. Flick it out with the point of a knife.

But, probably my favourite way, my gentle best with garlic, is to slowly cook it in soups and sauces. Much as I always start a tomato sauce with a fried onion and some chopped garlic, it is adding a couple (or more) whole peeled cloves to the sauce which I think gives it the sweetest, richest, most benevolent, still unmistakably garlicky flavour of all.

Pick bulbs which are firm and plump with pristine skins. Buy fresh young summer garlic when it's in season and if you are very lucky, the exquisite purple-skinned specimen.

But you might have to go to France for those.

Rouille

Add the garlic cloves, tomato purée, Dijon mustard, paprika, red pepper, lemon juice and a pinch of cayenne pepper to the egg yolks.

Blend thoroughly, adding the first spoonful of oil and blending fast until incorporated.

Proceed with the rest of the olive oil, as for mayonnaise (*see* p275). Add salt to taste as well as extra cayenne if necessary. A homemade mayonnaise will keep in the fridge for a week as will this rouille.

This is used in the celeriac soup (*see* p70), but it is good in other soups too. Omlettes welcome it gladly, as does a bean salad of cannelini and green beans, served with a simple chunk of warm bread.

Makes around 450 ml/16 fl oz

5 garlic cloves, crushed

1 tsp tomato purée

1 tsp Dijon mustard

1 tsp paprika

2 tbsp finely chopped red pepper

1 tbsp lemon juice

A pinch of cayenne pepper

2 large organic, free-range egg yolks

450 ml/16 fl oz olive oil, a little of which should be extra virgin

Sea salt

Tamari, lemon and balsamic dressing with chilli and garlic

I seem to live on salads and chocolate. So when I don't reach out for the vinaigrette like a robot, I make the following dressing.

Mix 1 tablespoon dark, almost syrup-thick soy sauce or tamari with 3 tablespoons water, 1 tablespoon lemon juice and balsamic vinegar mixed, a loose shake from the Tabasco bottle or a tiny bit of finely chopped red chilli, and a small garlic clove, minced with a cleaver.

Finally, squeeze the juice from a small pile of coarsely shredded ginger for all it's worth and mix this in.

You'll only need 2 or 3 tablespoons of this mixture to resonantly dress a huge bowl of leaves and harder vegetables. You can use carrots, fennel sliced carpaccio-thin, shards of celery, plump, juicy corn kernels sliced from the cob, mung beans newly sprouted and potent with 'chi', cracked oily olives, a baby avocado almost falling out of its skin, a handful of toasted sunflower seeds and a muslin-fine pile of alfalfa sprouts.

All this makes me a happy girl.

Skorthalia

Skorthalia is a thick bread-and-nut-based Greek sauce, akin to a dip. It goes very well with raw vegetables, cut into sticks, or on any simply prepared vegetables, and it offers an interesting alternative to hummus on a summer table, laden with Mediterranean dishes. Blanched broccoli florets spring to mind – I have often partnered them this way – or fried aubergine slices which always appreciate a good strong dose of lemon and garlic. You can sandwich slices of fried and kitchen-paper-dried aubergines into stacks with the skorthalia.

I have made the skorthalia in identical proportions with pistachio nuts, the subtlety of which I prefer over the traditional walnuts – the colour is prettier and the taste more delicate.

Trim the slices of bread and soak them in the water for about 10 minutes. They will sponge up most of it, but drain off the excess.

Crush the garlic and salt together in a pestle and mortar to make a paste. Then put the bread, garlic paste, pepper, Tabasco and lemon juice in a blender and whizz together for a few seconds.

On a fairly high speed, add the olive oil in a thin stream. Finally add the walnuts or pistachios and process for a few seconds. The sauce should be both creamy and nutty and you can adjust the consistency with a little water and lemon juice. It keeps for a week, if not longer, in a cold fridge.

Oily origins

A few years ago I saw the whole olive-oil making process with my own eyes in, of all places, a small, mainly Arab town in Israel.

My cousin Danny who lives on a *moshav* had collected baskets full of ripe olives from the trees in his garden and we took them to an old man in a dark nook of the local market. There he had a round stone olive press that was as ancient as the hills. He used it to crush the olives without breaking the stones (or that was the theory) and extract the oils. We came back for our bottles a couple of days later.

Certainly the oil was not refined – my cousin apologised for its crudeness and said it looked like the stuff he put in his car. In fact it was pretty close I should think to the olive oil I'd heard derided throughout my childhood, but it seemed magical to me.

Serves 6

3 thick slices stale white bread, crusts removed (about 100 g/4 oz with crusts, 75 g/3 oz without)

250 ml/9 fl oz water

3 garlic cloves, finely chopped

$^1/_2$ tsp sea salt

A pinch of white pepper

A dash of Tabasco

Juice of half a lemon

4 tbsp olive oil

50 g/scant 2 oz walnut or pistachio kernels

fruit & nuts

fruit & nut recipes

When I am working, I often find myself grazing rather than eating a proper meal. I eat a ripe medjool date here, a brain-boosting almond there, an apple or three and, in the summer, embarrassing numbers of nectarines and cherries. I would be delighted if everyone did the same. This does not mean that I don't look forward to turning my hand to these delights in rather more sophisticated and epicurean modes. Just look at the apricot and almond tart or the quinces slowly poached with rose water and cardamom or the syrup-drenched baklava or the English strawberries with Cointreau in my version of Eton mess.

Apricots

We have a hard time finding good, ripe fresh apricots in this weather-blighted country of ours and most of the ones available in the shops are probably best roasted with sugar or stewed to bring out their juices.

Despite this, they have been cultivated here since the 16th century though most are now imported and, by modern necessity, picked when not fully ripe. The well-developed orange hue often hides a fruit sadly short of its potential. Imagine instead the unparalleled delights of a Provençal summer market. Sun-warmed, deep-coloured apricots that fall apart in the hand-dripping luscious, sweet, honeyed, almost toffee-like juices. In England, we fare better with dried apricots from eastern Turkey. At least these we can steep in alcohol or soften by gentle simmering.

Apricots, both fresh and dried, feature widely in the cooking of the Middle East and the Mediterranean, though they actually hail from China. They are used for jams and compotes, for summer tarts in France and Italy, with pumpkin as an accompaniment to couscous in Tunisia, cooked in savoury sauces in Morocco, for apricot and walnut puddings, among a myriad other uses, including 'apricot leathers' in Turkey and in Indian curries...the list goes on and on. With dried apricots the darker and more caramelised the better, hence the popularity of the unprepossessing brown and leathery though very sweet *hunza*.

OTHER RECIPES USING APRICOT

Apricot and almond tart

This is a take on the classic pear and almond tart but made with summer fruit instead. In the *River Cafe Cook Book Green* (Ebury Press, 2000), the authors suggest a very practical way of handling pastry: instead of rolling it, which would be difficult straight from the fridge, they grate it through the largest holes of a cheese grater, then press it in to the sides and base of the tin. An ingenious way of making sure the pastry remains cold, yet easy to handle. It is so very buttery that it needs to stay this cold. Even then, the base is returned to the fridge for half an hour before baking. I give several pastry recipes throughout the book and this is the most buttery. I absolutely adore the fragility of it and the knowledge that you have taken it as far you can.

It seems almost a wonder that the featherlight and delicate piece holds together at all.

Either by hand or in a food processor, turn the flour and butter to a mixture resembling coarse breadcrumbs. For me, doing this with anything but the lightest of fingers – 'God's knives and forks' as a beloved aunt of mine used to say – seems almost sacrilegious. Sorry to sound evangelical but I am about pastry as some are about bread. It may not be quite the staff of life but it is one of the kitchen's richest and simplest offerings.

Add the sugar, salt and egg yolks and mix until the mixture just leaves the sides of the bowl clean. Shape into a ball and refrigerate for at least 1 hour.

Lightly butter and flour a 30-cm/12-inch loose-bottomed, fluted tin, and press in the pastry as described above. Chill for 30 minutes.

Preheat the oven to 180°C/350°F/gas mark 4 and blind-bake the pastry case in whichever way suits you best (*see* above) for 20 minutes until pale golden brown. Allow to cool completely.

For the filling, cut the apricots in half and stone them. Place them cut side down in the cold tart case.

Cream the butter and sugar until pale and light, then add the ground almonds, brandy and, one at a time, the eggs, stirring to a smooth and shiny mix, which drops weightily from a spoon.

Pour this mixture around the apricots and a little over and bake in the oven for 40 minutes until lightly set. Remove from the heat and allow to relax and ease into itself.

Serve just warm with the sour note of crème fraîche acting as a foil to the sweetness of the tart.

Serves 6

For the pastry

350 g/12 oz plain flour

225 g/8 oz unsalted butter, cold and cut into pieces

100 g/3^1/$_2$ oz caster sugar

A pinch of salt

3 large, organic, free-range egg yolks

For the filling

450 g/1 lb ripe, fresh apricots

300 g/11 oz unsalted butter

300 g/11 oz caster sugar

300 g/11 oz whole blanched almonds, ground

2 tbsp brandy

3 large, organic, free-range eggs

Poached apricots with crème fraîche and pistachios

I ate these for the first time in a Lebanese restaurant, then just about identically at a friend's house, prepared according to Nigella Lawson's recipe. Then I made them myself, a quicker way. You'll wonder how you ever managed without.

Place the apricots in a pan and add water to cover, the lemon juice, cardamom, orange oil or water and caster sugar and simmer for about 20 minutes until the apricots are even more tender and juicy than before and there is ample syrup in the bottom of the pan.

Lift them out carefully. You can mash or break up any that are collapsed into the syrup later. When they are a little cooled, open them out, then fill them with the crème fraîche, using a teaspoon, so they become rotund with it.

Close them up again and place them on a festive plate with the syrup poured all over. Just before serving, sprinkle the pistachios over the crème fraîche.

Serves 4

250 g/9 oz soft, ready-to-eat, semi-dried apricots

Juice of half a lemon

12 cardamom pods, seeds only

1/2 tsp orange-flower oil or 2 tbsp orange-flower water

2 tbsp caster sugar

To serve

200 ml/7 fl oz crème fraîche

2 tbsp chopped and lightly toasted pistachio nuts

Perfect partners

I've served this with a date and walnut loaf, cut into thin slices. Another time I served them with a lemon cake, and my friend Harriet put them with a simple almond sponge, gilded with real gold leaf.

A healthy way to start the day

The typical Greek breakfast of thick yoghurt, doused with honey and topped with chopped almonds is a summer holiday luxury that is easily copied at home. And however rich the yoghurt seems, it still only has half the fat of double cream or créme fraîche.

Frozen yoghurt is yet another possibility and is so simple it is also a delight to make. Just churn the yoghurt with the fruit of your choice and freeze it.

Blackberry crumble and crème anglaise

I think of this as one of the quintessentially English desserts. Most of us could pick enough blackberries growing wild to make a crumble or pie on at least one late summer night.

Preheat the oven to 200°C/400°F/gas mark 6. Mix the flour, butter, sugar and salt till they resemble fine breadcrumbs. I positively enjoy doing this with my fingers and can't usually be bothered to go through the palaver of getting out the food processor, setting it up, using it, cleaning it and putting it away again. Who needs it?

Mix the berries and sugar together and place in an ovenproof pie dish. Top with the crumble mixture and bake for about 30 minutes until golden all over. Serve with crème anglaise and/or cream.

Crème anglaise

This is a classic crème anglaise which is thinner, paler, and more delicate than custard. It also goes well with the apricot and almond tart (*see* p285), the ginger chocolate tart (*see* p344) and the chocolate cakes (*see* p338). As long as you work on a very gentle heat and stir all the time without taking your eye off it, it's really one of the very simplest things to make.

Place the egg yolks and sugar in a rounded bowl and beat until pale and creamy. Bring the milk to the boil, remove from the heat and pour over the egg and sugar. Stir to dissolve properly, return to the pan and heat through very slowly, stirring continuously with a wooden spoon until the mixture thickens enough to coat the back of the spoon.

Remove from the heat and pass through a fine sieve into a bowl, set in a sink of cold water, which arrests the cooking. Cover with a piece of cling film to prevent a skin from forming and allow to cool, though you can serve it warm, too, if you wish.

You can also infuse the milk with a vanilla pod, which you can then remove, wipe dry and use again.

Serves 4

At least 450 g/1 lb freshly picked juicy blackberries

About 3 tbsp caster sugar, or more depending on the sweetness and ripeness of the fruit

For the topping

225 g/8 oz plain flour

150 g/5 oz butter, chilled and cut into pieces

90 g/3$\frac{1}{2}$ oz caster sugar

A pinch of salt

Serves 4–6

6 organic, free-range egg yolks

125 g/4$\frac{1}{2}$ oz caster sugar

500 ml/18 fl oz organic milk

Coconut pound cake

Having given you my mother's birthday cake recipe (*see* p334), I think I have a right to give you mine. It is as simple as hers is grand and, in a vain attempt to curb my son's inherited chocoholicism, I have made it for each of his birthdays so far.

I make a triple quantity and fill a number mould with it. I omit the icing, as I then cover every millimetre with slices of strawberry and they turn the icing immediately to syrup and slide down faster than he can blow out a candle. Nowadays, I brush the cake with the very lightest film of strawberry jam instead and the slices are as if superglued.

This is a classical pound cake and an easy way to think of it is equal amounts of each of the main ingredients, plus 4 small eggs. Traditionally it would have been mixed all at once (and by hand!), but I think you get a better and lighter result by taking the slightly lengthier route described below. If you want to give this a more Germanic feel, add 2 tablespoons flaked almonds and 2 tablespoons raisins and press these into the sides of a fluted, funneled Kugelhopf tin before pouring in the cake mixture.

Serves 8–10

175 g/6 oz plain flour, plus extra for dusting

1 tsp baking powder

175 g/6 oz butter, plus extra for greasing

175 g/6 oz caster sugar

3 large or 4 small, organic, free-range eggs

90 g/3$^{1}/_{2}$ oz flaked or desiccated coconut

Zest of 1 lime or lemon

For the icing

100 g/4 oz icing sugar

Juice of $^{1}/_{2}$–1 lime or lemon

Preheat an oven to 180°C/350°F/gas mark 4.

Start by sifting the flour and baking powder twice. Then cream the butter, cut up small, with 125 g/4$^{1}/_{2}$ oz caster sugar in an electric mixer, until it is pale, light and fluffy and leaves a trail when you lift the beaters.

Whisk in 2 eggs (1 if large) at high speed until well mixed. Separate the remaining egg(s) and add the yolk and zest to the mixture. Beat in one-third of the flour mixture until only just incorporated. Then beat in the rest of the flour and the coconut, again taking care not to overdo it – you don't want a heavy, stodgy cake.

Whisk the remaining egg white until stiff, sift over the last of the sugar and whisk just long enough for the mixture to become glossy. Fold a spoonful of this into the batter, then all of the rest. A metal spoon cuts through the egg white without flattening it.

Pour into a lightly buttered and flour-dusted 20-cm/8-inch spring-form tin. Bake for about 1 hour, until a skewer comes out clean. Allow to sit for about 10 minutes, then run the point of a small knife round the edge. Remove the tin and turn out to cool on a wire rack.

For the icing, add the lime or lemon juice to the sugar and mix to a thickish paste. Prick holes all over the surface of the still-warm cake and pour the icing on top. Serve soon with raspberries or filled poached apricots (*see* p286).

Raisins

This word comes in the same breath as sultana and currant and describes one variety of dried grape. When I use the term in this book I always refer to the full, gorgeous, winey Muscatel raisins from Spain or Australia.

I do not bother, if I can help it, with the little shrivelled 'flies' as my three-year-old calls them, all crunch and no flesh.

Of all sultanas, I prefer the golden-yellow, seedless ones, which you can buy in large bags or vacuum-packed boxes in Middle Eastern grocery stores. They can be as big as a squashed grape.

I don't go in much for currants, though these have the longest history in British cooking. They are fine enough amongst other dried fruit in mincemeat and Christmas pudding, but for pilaffs, which is where I use them most, they are too small and dry.

The Australian Lexia raisins are plump and generous to a fault; you can still taste the grape and the caramelised sugars, and a few go a long way.

OTHER RECIPES USING RAISINS

A typical Algerian couscous 105

Middle Eastern potatoes with saffron and raisins 137

Spinach with slivered almonds, raisins and fried onion 141

Biryani 238

Broad bean pilaff with raisins and almonds 240

A celebratory carrot cake 291

Spiced mango chutney 327

Cantuccini 358

Walnut and raisin loaf 365

A celebratory carrot cake

The original Cranks carrot cake takes some beating and the recipe for it appears both in *The New Cranks Recipe Book* (W&N, 1996). But beaten it is by this version which comes to you via the *Vegetable Book* (Conran Octopus, 1995), by the illustrious Colin Spencer, its progeny going right back to *Laurel's Kitchen*, the vegetarian classic of the 1970s.

Not content with this, I have replaced the rum he adds with brandy, rum is just not my favourite tipple. On top of this I enjoy honey only very occasionally but could eat maple syrup every day, so have used the latter instead. Finally, just so that you can see the tortuous route a recipe sometimes travels to become what it is, I have kept to the coconut of the original Cranks version.

If you were expecting a virtuous sort of a cake, think again. I have given the traditional cream-cheese frosting recipe, but I prefer it with a turned spoon of thick crème fraîche.

Preheat the oven to 180°C/350°F/gas mark 4.

In a saucepan, heat the maple syrup, orange zest and juice, brandy, water and carrots, butter, raisins, dates, coconut, cinnamon and nutmeg. Boil for 5 minutes, then leave to cool until lukewarm. You can speed this up by placing the pan in a sink part filled with cold water.

Sift the wholemeal flour into a bowl and lightly fold the bran back into it, adding a pinch of salt at the same time. Add the bicarbonate of soda and finally the walnuts or pecans. Make a well in the middle and pour in the carrot mixture, blending well.

Lightly butter and flour a 25-cm/10-inch cake tin, pour in the mixture and bake for about 1 hour or perhaps a little more depending on the efficiency of your oven, until a skewer comes clean out of the cake. Leave in the tin for 10 minutes before turning it out on to a wire cooling rack.

To make the topping, cream the cheese and crème fraîche together and mix in the softened butter. Beat in the icing sugar and vanilla. Spread this over the cooled cake and serve. If there is to be a delay, wrap the un-iced cake in foil and finish later.

Serves 8–10

300 ml/10 fl oz maple syrup

Juice and zest of 1 orange

175 ml/6 fl oz brandy

110 ml/4 fl oz water

125 g/4^1/2 oz carrots

100 g/4 oz butter

100 g/4 oz Muscatel raisins

90 g/3^1/2 oz chopped dates

2 tbsp desiccated coconut

1 tsp ground cinnamon

^{1}/2 tsp freshly grated nutmeg

225 g/8 oz wholemeal self-raising flour

A pinch of sea salt

2 tsp bicarbonate of soda

120 g/4^1/2 oz shelled walnuts or pecan nuts

For the topping

150 g/5 oz cream cheese

150 g/5 oz crème fraîche

2 tbsp softened butter

3 tbsp icing sugar

1 tsp vanilla extract

Sticky-date pudding with brandy and pecans

This version is not steamed but baked, and takes only 20 minutes. The puddings freeze very well, the best way to reheat them being to place them in the oven, straight from frozen, covered with a piece of foil, in a tray filled with hot water so that it reaches halfway up the sides.

Two date stories for you – one short and sweet, the other mad. When I was a child my father once brought home a wooden crate of yellow dates in big fat bunches. They were inedible at first, but we hung them in a store room and picked them over the next weeks as they ripened. They were called *ableuh* and had come all the way from Marrakech. I must have been about six or seven years old at the time, but the memory came rushing back recently when my local Asian shop suddenly had a stall heaped with them.

The second is a (slightly) more recent story. I must have been about 20 and taking a holiday in Israel when I decided to embark on a five-day fast, at the same time as trekking through the desert. I allowed myself water and cucumber. I thought I might have a mystical experience or something. Mad, I know. I arrived half-dead at Deganya, the first of Israel's kibbutzim, where I was lovingly tended. The next morning, still very weakened, I half strolled, half stumbled to the date grove and watched as athletic young men and women all but flew up the tall palms and cut off the huge bunches which they then lowered to the ground in nets. Loose ripe dates rained all around. I gorged myself and hardly need tell you how very ill I became.

Ripe dark dates are the only food I have ever found that rival chocolate for sheer orgiastic pleasure.

Preheat the oven to 180°C/35°F/gas mark 4 and butter 4 ramekins.

Beat the butter, sugar and orange-flower water until pale and creamy. Beat in the eggs, then fold in the flour and baking powder. Strain the dates and blend with 2 tablespoons brandy, either in a food processor or simply mash with a fork. Mix witht the batter and spoon the mixture into the ramekins so that it nearly reaches the tops.Place on a baking sheet.

Bake for 20 minutes or until well risen and just firm to the touch.

Meanwhile, make the sauce by gently heating the butter, sugar, maple syrup and cream in a small pan for about 5 minutes. Add the toasted pecans at the last moment.

Serves 6

100 g/4 oz butter, softened

100 g/4 oz soft light brown sugar

1 tsp orange-flower water

2 large, organic, free-range eggs

100 g/4 oz plain flour

1 1/2 tsp baking powder

2 tbsp brandy

250 g/9 oz stoned dates, softened in hot water

For the sauce

60 g/2 oz butter

90 g/3 1/2 oz soft dark brown sugar

1 tbsp maple syrup

2–3 tbsp single cream

8 pecan halves, thinly sliced and very lightly toasted

To serve

Cream or ice-cream

Let the puddings cool down for 5 minutes, then run the point of a blade all the way round and loosen them on to plates with the sauce poured over. I am childishly excited by ice-cream with hot puddings, but what extravagance you go for here is entirely up to you.

Perhaps surprisingly, these puddings are great freezer standbys. To warm simply place in a tray of boiling water so it reaches halfway up the sides and bake for about 20 minutes in an oven at the same temperature as before.

Greengage fool

In memory of a greengage tree.

I have a nostalgic (and very real) affection for greengages. When I was a child we had an enormous greengage tree, which year after generous year, yielded a hundred pounds of fruit or more. My brothers and I would climb into the tree and indulge ourselves in the unbelievably sweet ripe fruit, and, as my mother made jam to last the year, neighbours shared in our bounty. Then one day, while I was away at university, the beloved tree split down the middle, collapsed and died. I returned to a sad bare patch in the middle of the garden. To this day, my guests are entertained by discourses that begin, 'We used to have a greengage tree...'.

Serves 6

675 g/1^1/$_2$ lb ripe greengages

150 g/5 oz caster sugar

300 ml/a generous 10 fl oz double cream

Halve the greengages and remove the stones. Place in a stainless-steel saucepan with 3 tablespoons water and the sugar. Cover with a lid and simmer over a gentle heat, stirring occasionally, for about 10 minutes or until the fruit is soft.

Purée until smooth, using a hand-held electric blender and strain through a sieve. Cover with a cloth and allow to cool, before placing in the fridge to chill properly.

Whisk the cream to soft peaks and fold delicately into the fruit purée, swirling it in to reveal a marbled bi-coloured fool.

Spoon into tall glasses almost to overflowing and serve.

Figs

The fig is a strange and delightful fruit from a tree whose antecedents may be 4,000 years old. I have eaten them best in Italy, where they have been highly regarded since the Romans.

Even then the finest of them were considered an expensive delicacy. And I have enjoyed them in Israel where I picked bags full from an ancient tree, so sun warmed, so swollen and so ready to burst that the dark-purple skin fell off in my fingers. It is hard to describe the sweetness of the dark-pink filaments, the fullness of the flesh or the obvious eroticism. When you have eaten them like this how can you settle for less?

Amongst the trays of individually protected fruit, there are usually one or two that are at the magical point of near collapse. Pick those up and don't wait until you get home to savour their luscious sweetness. If you are not so blessed, then ripen on your sunniest window-sill.

I have made an exquisite salad of figs, gently prized open, with balls of labne placed among them, both doused in a little barely thinned down and sweetened pomegranate molasses. I dislike grilled figs as they so quickly lose that vibrancy. But I have baked them with a syrup of sugar, brandy or Cointreau, a splash of orange-flower water, crystallised ginger, sliced thin and still in its thick sweet juice and served them with fig ice-cream or a jug of double cream. Well, I hardly need tell you how they were received.

OTHER RECIPES USING FIGS

Dried figs caramelised with kumquats, Mascarpone and ginger 295

Fresh fig and Port sorbet 296

Fig and rose water double-cream ice-cream 299

Dried figs caramelised with kumquats, Mascarpone and ginger

This is a recipe I've been making for years and it is in my first book, *Secrets from a Vegetarian Kitchen* (Pavilion, 1996). You can make it in minutes but it's incredibly sophisticated, though not remotely complicated, very pretty and seductively delicious, the sourness of the kumquats only remaining as a distant wake-up call. Though this is gorgeous as it is, you'll find that it dresses up a number of simple and richer cakes

Cut the kumquats in half. If they are inordinately stuffed full with pips, scoop them out, taking care not to discard the flesh too.

Remove the tough stalk from the figs and soak in the warm water, orange-flower water, orange juice and brandy for about 10 minutes until the figs are a little softened and plumped up.

Transfer the soaked figs, soaking liquid and all, to a saucepan and add the kumquats and sugar. Simmer gently for 7–8 minutes until the kumquats are soft but still their own pretty shape and luminous orange, with their topsy-turvy tastes – the sweet skins and the sour insides – fully brought out. Add a little water or extra orange juice to prevent drying out and sticking during cooking.

Mix the crystallised ginger with the Mascarpone, dust lightly with a little cinnamon and serve.

Partners in crime

This goes fabulously with any type of sponge cake; chocolate cake; sweet tarts and ice-cream.

Also for a glorified crêpe Suzette, put inside or on top of a lazy crêpe and flambé in brandy – and say a little prayer for me.

Serves 4–6

225 g/8 oz kumquats

225 g/8 oz very good dried Turkish figs

3 tbsp warm water

1 tsp orange-flower water (optional)

2 tbsp orange juice

2 tbsp brandy

2 tsp soft brown sugar

To serve

225 g/8 oz Mascarpone

1–2 pieces crystallised ginger, finely chopped

A pinch of ground cinnamon (optional)

Fresh fig and Port sorbet

This is the simplest way to make a sorbet. There is no glucose syrup, no whisked egg white and no special thermometer. You just boil the fruit with the sugar, chill, blend and freeze. You can use Marsala or even brandy instead of Port if you like.

Having extolled the wonders of fresh figs, please don't think I'm recanting in suggesting this sorbet. The brief boil concentrates the sugar, juice and colour. I once made a huge heart-shaped chocolate casket (*see* right) and filled it like a fairy-tale treasure trove, with dozens of the iridescent ruby baubles, scooped out to suitable size with a melon baller.

I think the first magazine article I ever wrote featured the sorbet in individual chocolate heart-shaped boxes. No prizes for guessing the occasion, though to be frank September would be a more appropriate month to get the best-quality figs.

To make the sorbet, peel the figs with a sharp knife, then cut into quarters. I have made this with the skins left on and the result is slightly cloudier and darker. But if the figs are very ripe, that shouldn't matter.

Combine the sugar, Port and figs in a saucepan and bring to the boil. As soon as the mixture bubbles, lower the heat and simmer gently for 5 minutes. Remove from the heat and allow to cool completely. Then blend the figs and their poaching liquid for a couple of minutes in a blender, together with the lemon juice.

Pass through a fine, wire-meshed sieve. Transfer to a suitable container or bowl and freeze. A couple of hours later, or just before it is fully frozen, whisk the mixture again and return to the freezer. If you have an electric, hand-held whisk, use this to whisk lightness and air into the sorbet. Otherwise do it in a mixer bowl. I tend to repeat this operation one more time before letting it freeze right through.

About 10 minutes before serving, transfer the sorbet to the fridge, so it can relax into scoopable softness, then scoop into sugar-rimed Champagne cups or the chocolate caskets. If you haven't made these, I urge you to bring some crisp black dark chocolate into the equation somehow, either as thin rounds you have made yourself or a bowl of melted dark chocolate which freezes to a brittle shell as soon as you drizzle it on top.

Serves 6

700 g/1 lb 9 oz very ripe fresh figs

100 g/4 oz caster sugar

300 ml/10 fl oz Port

Juice of half a lemon

Dark chocolate, to serve

Chocolate treasure

All you do for the casket is turn a heart-shaped tin upside down, cover it tightly with foil, very lightly brushed with a bland oil (you can even use cling film which saves you the bother), and paint melted chocolate over it. You freeze this and then repeat the process a couple of times. The foil or film is easily peeled off. To make the lid, trace the outline of the tin on to a piece of baking parchment, cut it out and paint this in several layers of chocolate, also freezing inbetween. Peel carefully and set jauntily on top of the sorbet.

Rose water

I confess to a grand passion here: rose water makes me swoon. I know some people respond in quite the opposite way, so I don't know whether to contain my enthusiasm or write a lyric verse.

My love affair with it did not start in the kitchen but in the bath and on the massage table and that sums up why I love it and others don't. They think it should remain there. I want it everywhere. I add it to creams and quinces, baklavas and sugar syrups and every time, I feel like a queen, bringing a little godliness to earth. I would like to breathe it in and hold the sumptuous fragrance in my every pore. OK, you want me to stop now?

Most rose water nowadays comes from the Valley of the Roses in Bulgaria; *Rosa damascena* is the name of the rose, probably introduced there by the Ottoman Turks.

The petals can be steeped in oil, water or alcohol to release the subtle, fragrant essential oil. Jams are made from it, preserves and jellies, oils and waters. These are (or were) used in the East with none of the self-consciousness nor sentimentality to which over-marketing makes the rest of us prone.

OTHER RECIPES USING ROSE WATER

Fig and rose water double-cream ice-cream

'You cannot think what figs
My teeth have met in'
Goblin Market by Christina Rossetti

I cannot resist giving you another ice-cream recipe and one I know you won't be able to buy. Yet this is child's play – I made it with my three-year-old boy by my side and for once didn't go mad. He watched me in total silence, thought my cheap little whirring ice-cream maker was magic, stood on his small chair and watched the beaters churn lazily away for an age. He knew what was coming and he knew it was worth waiting for.

Pour the cream and milk if using (the full-double-cream version is extravagantly dense) into a saucepan and slowly heat just to boiling point. Remove from the heat as soon as you see the merest hint of a bubble breaking the surface.

In a bowl, beat the egg yolks and sugar together with an electric whisk until they are thick and creamy and then still beating, though with a fork or a hand whisk this time, pour into the cream.

Return the pan to a gentle heat, stirring constantly with a wooden spoon until the mixture leaves a film on the back of it. This will take less time with the thick cream than with the milk and cream. Do not let it boil or it will separate. Add the figs towards the end and cook for about 2 minutes.

Remove the pan from the heat and let it go cold. Add the rose water, then pour it into your ice-cream machine and churn for about 25 minutes or according to the manufacturer's instructions until set.

Makes about 750 ml/1¹/₄ pints

600 ml/1 pint organic double cream (or half cream, half milk)

4 large, organic, free-range egg yolks

100 g/4 oz caster sugar

5 semi-dried figs, finely chopped

1 tbsp rose water

Added joy

Quinces in rose syrup: I had a bowl of them in the fridge and they matched pretty well.

Very dark chocolate melted over a pan of boiling water. This cut through some of the sweetness – very exotic.

Toasted slivered almonds add a simple but elegant touch.

A trickle of single cream – not bad but who needs it?

A tablespoon of Muscat – is there no end to this madness?

Lemon

The Middle East, Asia, Europe, there is hardly a kitchen that doesn't use the special sour, tart hit of lemon. It was Arab traders that spread the use of lemons throughout the Mediterranean, taking them as far eastwards as China.

Southern Italian market stalls laden with huge, thick-skinned, juicy lemons from Sicily, their leaves still attached, are a wonderful sight to behold. I once spent a holiday in Amalfi continuously drawing lemons, as if to take back to England some of that fragrance, that essence of summer.

Lemons are unique in their ability to marry with both sweet and savoury flavours. They can be dried or preserved in salt – a Middle Eastern practice. The zest, which releases an aromatic essential oil, is as important as the juice, and the high pectin content is useful for jam making. Mixing lemon with olive oil is the simplest and often most effective dressing, and more complex egg and lemon sauces can do wonders.

Preserved lemon and green olive sauces are intense and amazingly good, while on the dessert table few things can parallel a well made fresh lemon tart, fairly zinging with zest. As if you didn't know, lemons are also a rich source of vitamin C and were used medicinally long before they entered the world's kitchens. I use them so much that I often keep a whole bowl of them on the table. I go for unwaxed organic lemons when I can but then keep a beady eye on them.

OTHER RECIPES USING LEMON

Lemon tart

I can't write a book with desserts in it that doesn't include a lemon tart. Besides, if I were you, I'm sure I would want it right here in company with other classics.

Many of you probably have a recipe for it somewhere, but if it isn't this generous-to-a-fault one, leave it alone. There's no point in making a lemon tart unless it really is as quintessentially lemony or as creamy as this one. I like it best served quite pristinely, with just a dusting of icing sugar on its pastry edge and, since I'm not interested in anything which detracts from it, I don't serve cream or anything with it. It's too, too perfect just the way it is.

If this has too much the ring of zeal for you, please adulterate away.

Begin by heating the cream to boiling point. Then add the lemon zest and let its scent infuse the cream for several hours or even overnight if possible. Sift the flour into a bowl and add the butter and sugar to it. Rub them in with light fingers so that they are turned to fine crumbs.

Bring the dough together with the beaten egg yolk and just enough ice-cold water to bind – add it by the tablespoon to be safe. Again, I remind you to reserve a small lump of pastry to patch up any cracks that may appear on baking the pastry blind, the exquisite custard is far too precious to allow escape in rivulets through the cracks.

Preheat the oven to 125ºC/255ºF/gas mark 1/2.

Butter and flour a 28-cm/11-inch loose-bottomed tart tin and chill the pastry. The 15 minutes in the freezer compartment trick is particularly appropriate here, as you can then grate the pastry into the tin and press it with your fingers into the sides, which is easier than rolling out such a soft dough. Chill again before blind-baking, lined with baking parchment and baking beans if that suits you or left bare if you prefer. Make sure the pastry is golden and cooked right through. Allow it to cool, then patch up if necessary.

To make the filling, whisk together the eggs and sugar and stir in the lemon juice, zest and cream. At this point, I sometimes remove some of the lemon zest, squeezing it out first; too much does tend to sink heavily to the bottom, and I make sure that what I leave in is well mixed through.

Place the pastry-lined tart tin on a baking tray and set it on an oven shelf, pulled part way out of the oven. Transfer the cream and lemon mix to a pouring jug and carefully fill the tart case to the rim. Gingerly move the shelf back into the oven.

Serves 8–10
200 g/7 oz plain flour

100 g/3 1/2 oz butter, cubed and cold

30 g/1 oz caster sugar

1 organic, free-range egg yolk, beaten

Iced water

Icing sugar for sprinkling

For the filling
250 ml/9 fl oz double cream

200 ml/7 fl oz lemon juice (4–5 lemons), and the lemon zest

9 organic, free-range eggs

275 g/10 oz caster sugar

Bake in the oven for 1–1¹/₂ hours until set.

If after about 45 minutes, the filling still looks and feels like tepid liquid, turn the heat up a smidgin, but turn it down if it appears to be cooking too quickly.

Remove from the oven as soon as it is set so that it doesn't colour or toughen. Chill to room temperature and sprinkle icing sugar over the pastry rim. Serve soon.

Lemon pudding

Buttermilk replaces the usual milk and cream in this recipe and works brilliantly to create a light, mousse-textured sponge with an oozing lemon sauce beneath. I worked out this light version for *Cranks Light* (W&N, 1998) when I was under pain of death (or at the very least, loss of my job) to create lower-fat recipes. What can I say – it was part of my growth. But do you know what? It works.

Preheat the oven to 180°C/350°F/gas mark 4. Very lightly brush with oil a 30-x20-cm/12-x8-inch ovenproof glass dish and place it in a 5-cm/2-inch deep roasting tin. Bring a kettle of water to the boil.

Sift the flour and baking powder into a large bowl and mix in just over half the sugar. Add the buttermilk, lemon juice and zest, and egg yolks, stir to mix and set aside.

Whisk the egg whites to soft peaks, then add the salt and beat until stiff. Beat in the remaining sugar. Gently fold the egg whites into the buttermilk mixture, then spoon into the oiled dish.

Pour boiling water into the roasting tin to come halfway up the sides of the dish. Bake for 30–35 minutes, until well risen and golden with a layer of sauce beneath.

Serves 6

Oil for greasing

50 g/scant 2 oz unbleached white flour

2 tsp baking powder

325 g/11 oz caster sugar

375 ml/13 fl oz buttermilk

125 ml/4¹/₂ fl oz fresh lemon juice (2¹/₂ lemons)

2 tsp grated lemon zest

2 organic, free-range egg yolks, lightly beaten

4 organic, free-range egg whites

A pinch of salt

Lemon drizzle cake

It seemed so easy to make this organically (or as near as – the buttermilk isn't, but there's nothing to stop you substituting it with organic yoghurt, though if the lower fat of the buttermilk is what draws you to this, stick with it).

Buttermilk is a good old-fashioned thing that all but disappeared off the shelves for years, but is enjoying a minor revival. The health benefits apart – and they only interest me peripherally – it does make for an incredible lightness of baking.

I've made many versions of lemon drizzle cake, any lemon dessert coming high up on my list of favourites, creaming the butter and sugar first, or the flour and butter first as in this one. You have the option of pouring the lemon juice and caster sugar straight on to the hot cake as below or adding icing sugar to the lemon instead so that it sets to a light icing consistency. I do as the mood takes me.

Line a 23-cm/9-inch diameter spring-form tin with baking parchment. Preheat the oven to 180°C/350°F/gas mark 4.

Sift the flour, caster sugar and baking powder into a large bowl. Add the butter and turn it to the texture of fine breadcrumbs through 5 minutes of beating with an electric hand whisk.

Beating all the while, slowly add the buttermilk, the juice of half a lemon, the lemon zest and all the eggs. Pour into the prepared tin and bake in the middle of the oven for 1¼ hours or until a skewer comes out of it clean.

While the cake is still hot make the icing. Mix the caster sugar with the lemon juice, and warm through until the sugar is dissolved. Then, prick the warm cake all over with a skewer and pour over the icing.

Let the cake cool down for 30–40 minutes and eat with crème fraîche, Greek yoghurt or double cream.

Serves 8–10

400 g/14 oz plain flour, sifted
400 g/14 oz caster sugar, plus
5 tbsp to glaze
4 tsp baking powder
A pinch of salt
250 g/9 oz butter, at room temperature
1x284 ml carton buttermilk, at room temperature
Juice of ½ large lemon
Zest from 2 large lemons
2 large eggs, beaten
4 large egg yolks, beaten

For the icing

5 tbsp caster sugar
Juice of 2½ lemons

Passion-fruit ice-cream

Several of the recipes in this book hark back to my catering days and this is one. I remember making baby baths full of it. Actually, you would want to bathe and wallow in the lingering, symphonic fragrance of it.

In *The New Cranks Recipe Book* (W&N, 1996), there is a recipe for passion-fruit cheesecake, which is also worth remembering.

Bring the milk and half the cream to the boil in a saucepan and immediately remove from the heat. Whisk the egg yolks and caster sugar either in the bowl of an electric mixer or with a good, hand-held electric whisk, until the mixture is thick, pale and doubled in volume.

Slowly pour the scalded milk over the egg mixture, stirring all the while and then return the lot to the pan. I wash and dry the pan first to remove any residue as this can so easily catch and burn. Stir continuously for about 10 minutes over a low heat until it is thickened to a thin custard or crème anglaise. Do not let it boil or it will curdle and be nigh on impossible to salvage.

Pass through a fine-mesh sieve into a bowl sitting in a sink of cold water. Stir occasionally until the mixture is completely cool to prevent a skin from forming, or else just cover it with a piece of cling film. Fold in the rest of the cream, softly whipped.

Sieve the passion-fruit pulp and seeds into the ice-cream mixture so that it is infused with the exquisite fragrance and the tropical hue. You will be left with a load of seeds. Keep rubbing these until you have loosened and removed all the fruity fibre and fold about half the black seeds into the custard. Discard the rest.

Pour the very cold mixture into your ice-cream maker if you have one. If you don't, then freeze the mixture for about 4 hours, transferring it to a food processor at the end of every hour and blitzing it until completely smooth. All the tiny ice crystals should be broken down and the seeds dispersed. Return to the freezer until set. Now, transfer from the freezer to the fridge for about 10 minutes before serving. Nothing more complicated than a thin almond tuile is necessary with this.

Serves 6

375 ml/13 fl oz milk

375 ml/13 fl oz double cream

6 large organic, free-range egg yolks

150 g/5 oz caster sugar

8 passion-fruit

Pecan pie

America was bound to come up with a dessert to celebrate its abundance of pecan trees. The nut, sweeter, oilier and milder-flavoured then the walnut it resembles, can replace it in any recipe but it's particularly good in this all American pie.

I often add toasted pecans to apples, cooked in maple syrup, or caramelised as I would for a tarte tatin and set upon lacy pancakes. Home-made vanilla ice-cream sometimes goes on top. That may seem a bit OTT but somehow pecans, America and OTT all go together. By the way, I put in twice as many pecans as any recipe that I found for it, let abundance be a byword of your cooking and you cannot go wrong. If you're wondering why the pastry has no sugar, trust me when I say the filling is as sweet as can be, though less oppressively so with maple syrup than with the more common golden syrup. The hint of saltiness is one of the tart's special appeals.

This is also a good opportunity to tell you another thing about pastry. There is a mantra that those of us who ever did home economics (if there ever was a more alienating name for the art of cooking) at school were taught – pastry equals half fat to flour. Mediocre pastry perhaps. Good pastry equals at least 60 per cent fat to flour. Now that's worth getting your fingers sticky for.

Sieve the flour into a bowl and add the salt. Rub the cold butter into the flour until it resembles fine breadcrumbs and add the cold water to bring it together into a ball. Refrigerate for 30 minutes or freeze for 15 minutes.

Then, on a lightly floured surface, roll out very thinly and use to line a buttered and floured 28-cm/11-inch loose-based tin, preferably fluted. Press it firmly into the sides, leaving a slight overhang.

Preheat the oven to 200°C/400°F/gas mark 7.

Chill again as before and then blind-bake in the oven for 10–15 minutes until crisp but still pale. Mix all the filling ingredients together and pour into the pie shell. Lower the oven heat to 180°C/350°F/gas mark 4 and bake for about 1 hour. Remove from the oven and allow to cool to just warm before serving.

Serves 8

100 g/4 oz plain flour

A pinch of salt

60 g/2 oz cold butter, cut into pieces

2 tbsp ice-cold water

For the filling

3 large organic, free-range eggs

125 g/4^1/2 oz pecan kernels

60 g/2 oz butter, melted and cooled

200 ml/7 fl oz maple syrup

1 tbsp lemon juice

Freeze frame

I did once happen to freeze this. Should you wish to do so, place it straight from the freezer into a preheated oven. This will return it to its essential crispness of base and moistness of filling. I wouldn't eat it straight from the fridge either but would give it a blast of heat first. Ice-cream or whipped cream are mandatory.

Plum jam

My parents are both avid jam makers. I think it started off with them making marmalade for the Passover feast. At this time there are even more dietary restrictions than usual and my parents, though not particularly religious, like to make their own jam. To this day, homemade marmalade on oven-warmed matza is synonymous with Passover in my mind.

Then there are the grape jams my father painstakingly makes from his tiny garden-grown black grapes. I have watched his patient fingers clean the grapes of insects and remove – I can hardly bring myself to say it – every single seed hour after hour. He ends up with mountains of deseeded grapes and jars of the most intense purple, grapey fruitiness I have ever tasted. The plum jam – this one with Victoria plums – is my easy way out.

Wash, stone and cut the plums into 8 sections. Place them in a large pan with the sugar, water and lemon and ginger juices. I throw the stones in too as they release more pectin but I am meticulous about removing them afterwards, so maybe I have a trace of my father in me after all.

Cook on a steady simmer for 1^1/$_2$ hours, stirring regularly to prevent sticking. Test for readiness by pouring a little onto a small saucer and placing it in the fridge to cool. It then needs to wrinkle as you push it gently with your finger. Watch it carefully at this point, reducing the heat if necessary. Sometimes it sets in just the time it's taken your first sample to cool.

While the jam is cooking, wash your preserving jars thoroughly. Dry them and pour boiling water into them. Then empty them and let them dry in the air before filling them with the hot jam. Place a circle cut from baking parchment to seal the top and close.

Enjoy for weeks or months to come.

Makes 1.5 kg/3 lb 5 oz

1.25 kg/2 lb 14 oz plums

750 g/1 lb 11 oz caster sugar

200 ml/7 fl oz water

Juice of 1 lemon

4-cm/2-inch piece of ginger, grated, juice squeezed out and reserved

Plum cake

This wonderful plum cake is an heirloom of Stephanie Alexander's wonderful plum cake. I've omitted the cinnamon, though I know many of you won't thank me for that economy. I prefer my fruit fruity and I avoid adding another layer to the sharp sweetness of plums. The only exception is ginger but even that is not appropriate in this gentle, homely, afternoon cake.

When I last made this cake I found that I had run out of plain flour, so I added Farina 00 instead. I've since played around with the plain flour proportions, in one instance replacing it with ground almonds and once half Farina 00 and half a carefully sifted wholemeal flour – however well sifted it is, it leaves a fine residue of bran which adds colour and texture.

I couldn't resist a few toasted slivered almonds on top. I grind my own whole almonds to a texture of fine powder and small grits. Ready-ground almonds are fine though. The softness of the plums with the soft sweet sponge has the same direct appeal as hot apple crumble. I know it will be around in my family for at least another 40 years. It's that sort of cake.

Preheat the oven to 180°C/350°F/gas mark 4 and lightly butter a 28-cm/ 11-inch spring-form tin.

For the cake, cream the butter and sugar together in the bowl of an electric mixer at high speed until light and fluffy. Then mix in the flours and salt, slowing the speed right down, so the flour doesn't go flying alarmingly round the kitchen. Add the beaten eggs and milk to make a soft dough which drops easily from the spoon. Spoon this mixture into the prepared tin so that it reaches no further than a quarter of the way up the tin – the cake rises impressively. Then sprinkle the ground almonds over and arrange the plums, cut side up, on top, starting around the outside and working towards the centre.

To make the topping, melt the butter and stir in the sugar, then allow to cool. Whisk the eggs well and stir into the cooled butter to make a thick fudgy-looking mixture. Spoon over and around the plums.

Bake for 1 hour or until a skewer or cocktail stick comes out clean from the centre. Add the almond slivers for the last few minutes only.

Serve warm with cream, crème fraîche or ice-cream. If not using until the next day – it will actually keep for a week, wrapped up and in a cool place – wrap in foil and warm through at the same temperature as before for about 15 minutes.

Serves 8

275 g/10 oz softened butter, plus extra for greasing

250 g/9 oz caster or soft brown sugar

200 g/7 oz Farina 00

200 g/7 oz self-raising flour

A pinch of salt

3 organic, free-range eggs, lightly beaten

100 ml/3^{1}/$_{2}$ fl oz milk

125 g/4^{1}/$_{2}$ oz gritty ground almonds

20 ripe red plums, halved and stoned

For the topping

125 g/4^{1}/$_{2}$ oz butter

200 g/7 oz soft brown sugar

4 organic, free-range eggs

1 tbsp almonds, slivered

Roasted plums with orange water and crystallised-ginger crème fraîche

Sweet, ripe, yellow plums, sweet purple plums, sweet greengages, tiny mirabelle plums. All these together or apart make a shining dessert, glistening like warm sunshine in the sweet fragrant syrup.

I also make this with ripe fresh figs, their tough stalks snipped off with scissors, then halved part of the way through to reveal the luscious vermilion flesh. Baste them like the precious babies they are, spooning the syrup and juices over and over. If you have some frozen berries in the freezer, sprinkle a generous amount into and over the cut figs. They will soften in the heat and add to the fruity, alcoholic syrup. I've used ginger cordial or spiced ginger drink in place of the stem ginger syrup. Anything sweet, sticky and peppery like this will do just fine.

Provide Mascarpone or thick double cream, excellent vanilla ice-cream or Greek yoghurt for the more parsimonious, though it's hardly a deprivation. The sensation of puddings such as these is so gorgeous, the taste so multi-layered, it masks how very little you've actually had to do. Be attentive time-wise though, as the plums should not stay longer than 15 minutes in the oven or their purity and delicacy is marred. And let them cool just a little first before serving.

Sometimes I add thick rounds of very short, buttery biscuits, which practically dissolve as they absorb the juices. Sometimes, I just lick the plate.

Preheat the oven to 200°C/400°F/gas mark 6.

Place the plums in an ovenproof dish with the sugar, orange-blossom water, brandy or Cointreau, ginger juice and ginger syrup. Bake for 10–20 minutes, until the plums are softened and the skins blistered and split. Meanwhile mix the chopped stem ginger with the crème fraîche. Serve the plums warm or at room temperature with the crème fraîche on the side.

Serves 6

750 g/1 lb 11 oz plums, halved and stoned

3–4 tbsp pale soft brown sugar or caster sugar

1 tbsp orange-blossom water

2 tbsp brandy or Cointreau

4-cm/2-inch piece of fresh ginger, grated and squeezed, and the resulting juice reserved

4–5 tbsp stem ginger syrup

4 pieces stem ginger, roughly chopped

150 g/5 oz crème fraîche

Clafoutis Limousin

The cherry season is brief and in the UK we don't live in a climate where we're likely to experience a glut. Still, this is one of my favourites and once a year, I don't mind sacrificing a load of glistening claret-red or purple-black marbles to this simple and delicious dessert.

Besides, once you have made it the original, classical way, there is nothing to stop you experimenting with other fruit – full-bodied ripe apricots are a perfect alternative and nectarines and plums also work a treat. In the winter, turn to 3–4 fragrant Cox apples instead, sliced into fine crescents.

Butter a shallow baking dish and sprinkle with a tablespoon caster sugar. Preheat the oven to 190°C/375°F/gas mark 5.

Stone the cherries and lay them in the buttered dish.

To make the batter, sift the flour, salt and remaining sugar together in a bowl. Beat in the whole eggs, 2 at a time, alternating with the milk or milk and cream if using.

Beat in the egg yolks and pour the smooth batter over the cherries. Spoon the Cognac on top.

Bake for 30–40 minutes or until the clafoutis is risen and golden. Sprinkle with icing sugar and serve warm.

Serves 6

15 g/^{1}/$_2$ oz butter

450 g/1 lb small black cherries, washed

2 tbsp plain flour or potato flour

A pinch of sea salt

60 g/2 oz caster sugar

4 organic, free-range eggs

600 ml/1 pint milk, or ^{1}/$_2$ milk/ ^{1}/$_2$ double cream

2 organic, free-range egg yolks

4 tbsp Cognac

Icing sugar

Chocolate-stuffed prunes
in an almond tart

For Harriet

For this recipe I actually used the fat, juicy mi-cuit (half-cooked) plums, for which the word prune is too mean and manky, and stuffed them full of chocolate, then set them in a gritty frangipane made with almonds I had roughly ground.

I always grind my own almonds now, my only exception being when I use them as a replacement for flour or a thickener in soups. There cannot be any comparison to the shop-bought powdered stuff.

The combination of prunes, almonds and chocolate is a well-loved classic, but I have to admit to a certain pride in planting them like this in a tart. Instead of Armagnac, you can always use brandy – it doesn't need to be the most expensive.

First make the pastry by crumbling the butter into the flour, sugar and salt until you arrive at a texture like fine breadcrumbs. Then bring together with the egg yolks. Roll the ball around the bowl a couple of times until it is smooth and the colour of polenta. Then wrap in cling film and refrigerate for a good half hour.

Preheat the oven to 180°C/350°F/gas mark 4.

Prepare the 28-cm/11-inch tart tin by smearing it with butter and a fine dusting of flour. Grate the pastry into the tin and press it down easily. Refrigerate again for 20 minutes or so, then blind-bake for about 10–15 minutes until pale golden.

To make the filling, tuck the plums into a small pan with 1 tablespoon caster sugar and 60 ml/2 fl oz of the Armagnac. Simmer gently for about 5 minutes (longer and more slowly if you are using regular prunes), turning each plum at least once in the process, so that all the brandy is absorbed and the plums are coated in a thin layer of sticky syrup.

Allow them to cool and then stuff them full of chocolate.

Meanwhile place the almonds and the rest of the caster sugar in the herb-chopping attachment of a hand-held mixer or in a food processor and grind together until they are broken up into a mixture of fine and coarser grits.

Serves 8–10
For the pastry
90 g/3 oz butter, cold and diced, plus extra for greasing

175 g/6 oz plain flour, sifted, plus extra for dusting

60 g/2 oz caster sugar

A pinch of salt

2 organic, free-range egg yolks

For the filling
300 g/11 oz semi-dried plums, stones removed, or 225 g/8 oz soft prunes

175 g/6 oz caster sugar

175 ml/6 fl oz brandy, Armagnac if possible

90 g/3 oz very good quality dark chocolate, broken into pieces

175 g/6 oz whole almonds

175 g/6 oz butter, at room temperature

2 organic, free-range eggs

Beat the almonds, sugar and butter together – by hand or with a hand-held whisk and break in the eggs one at a time, continuing to blend. Finally, add the remaining Armagnac, lowering the speed of the beaters. The mixture is almost bound to split and to look curdled, but don't become alarmed by this as it will come together again in the oven heat.

Lay the stuffed prunes on to the pastry and spread the almond mixture all the way round – it will spread and fill in the gaps on cooking. Bake in the oven for about 30 minutes until crisp on top, moist in the middle, the chocolate melting inside the prunes. Serve warm.

Advance moves

If you are preparing it in advance, return the tart to the oven for a few minutes before serving, so that the chocolate remains molten inside the soft plums or prunes.

The tart is rich and dark and sophisticated without, but you might like a fine drizzle of double cream to gently mute the sweetness.

Summer pudding

I have previously given a recipe for a layered summer pudding, made in a rectangular dish in *The New Cranks Recipe Book* (W&N, 1996) as this suits the vagaries and necessities of cooking for large numbers. This one is made in the more traditional pudding basin, which is lined with the bread slices and then stuffed full of the fruit. Gently cooking the berries first releases their bloody juices so that the bread can be truly engorged.

Blackberries will make the juice darker in colour, so if you prefer a true-red pudding, stick to red berries. You can use frozen berries if you like, though it rather defeats the object which is to use summer fruit at its ripest and sweetest stage. But frozen ones do release pools of juice and you may want to eat this outside its prescribed season. Just remove every single strawberry – I don't know why anyone bothers to freeze them in the first place as they become unbearably water-logged, soggy and discoloured.

Serves 6

1 kg/2^1/$_4$ lb mixed berries, including blueberries, redcurrants or blackcurrants, blackberries and raspberries

225 g/8 oz caster sugar

3 tbsp water

10 medium slices good-quality white bread, crusts removed

A few mint leaves for garnish

Mix the clean blueberries, currants and blackberries, if using, together and place in a large stainless-steel saucepan. Add the sugar and water.

Cover with a lid and heat very gently for 5 minutes so that the sugar dissolves completely and the fruit releases its gorgeous juice. Stir in the raspberries and continue to simmer for another couple of minutes. Remove from the heat and allow to cool.

Lightly oil an 850-ml/1^1/$_2$-pint pudding basin. Cut the bread into neat triangles, reserving 2 slices from which to cut circles for the base and lid. Line the base with one circle and the sides with the triangular pieces, so that they lie snugly side by side, leaving no gaps for leakage or your pudding will fall apart on inversion.

Tightly pack the fruit into the lined basin and fold the top of the bread slices down to hold the fruit in place. Complete by adding the remaining circle of bread and cover with a saucer, laden with a heavy weight. Save any remaining fruit for later.

Place the pudding in a dish to catch any overflowing juices and leave in the fridge overnight or for at least 8 hours.

To serve, carefully run the rounded point of a knife around the basin's rim and turn the pudding out on to a plate, giving it a sharp tap. Pour the escaped juices and any extra fruit all over. Garnish with the mint leaves and serve with crème fraîche or double cream.

Cardamom

Up there with the greats, cardamom is another elusive, subtle, feminine, delicate spice, probably accidentally dropped down to earth by gods and goddesses wishing to tease and seduce us, play with our taste-buds.

You catch it on a pale and mysterious green whiff but it helps if your eyes are shut and the lights are turned down low. Have you tried it in crème brûlée, a perfectly churned ice-cream, a powdery lemon biscuit? Have you cooked quinces with it and its celestial partner rose water? Have you been to India and smelled it in the vats of roadside *chai*? And have you cracked the seeds from their husks and pounded them, their distant peppery note released by your pestle and simply breathed?

For the *Diwali* festival, Hindus paint them silver and shower them like confetti. I can think of ay least one other calander event where this practice would not be out of place.

OTHER RECIPES USING CARDAMOM

Fennel and almond soup with cardamom 12

Carrot rice 228

Biryani 238

Poached apricots with crème fraîche and pistachios 286

Quinces slowly poached with rose water and cardamom 315

Baklava fit for a queen 320

White chocolate chip and pistachio cookies with cardamom 345

Crème brûlée 347

Coconut and cardamom rice pudding 348

Quinces slowly poached with rose water and cardamom

'And they dined on mince and slices of quince, which they ate with a runcible spoon.' And who could blame the Owl and the Pussycat?

But I hope they took the trouble to cook them first, lovingly and at length, releasing their sweet, romantic fragrance, and their burnt-pink, sticky, sweet juices. A little rose water and a hint of delicate pepperiness from the cardamom add to the occasion.

But who knows? Perhaps they were too much in love and had no time for such fuss. Maybe, instead, they pared them down with a bone-handled knife, paper thin and crisp, Aphrodite having made sure they had picked a rare sweet one, so that they might 'dance by the light of the moon, the moon'.

Wash the quinces and slice them vertically very thinly indeed, not more than 3 mm/1/8-inch, you'll need the sharpest knife and you'll still wonder at the exertion required, since the quince certainly protects its delights well.

Leave the seeds where they are, picking up any that drop out and adding them to the pan since they also release the surprisingly intense clear-ruby-pink colour. As for coring, I'd wait till they're cooked and already soft.

Cover the quinces with the water and add the cardamom pods and 2 teaspoons lemon juice. Bring to the boil and add the sugar. Cover and simmer steadily for about 2 hours until the slices are divinely soft and fragrant. Your home will smell wonderful for hours.

Add the rose water and the Muscat, if using, only towards the end of cooking – it goes slightly bitter otherwise and in something this sublime that would be travesty indeed. You can remove the quince cores and seeds at this stage.

Serve the slices set upon a jewel-coloured plate with quenelles of homemade vanilla ice-cream and douse with the syrup. Eat in precious and small doses.

Serves 4

2 perfect unblemished quinces

450 ml/16 fl oz water

6 whole cardamom pods

Juice of 1 small lemon

150 g/5 oz caster sugar

1 tbsp rose water

2 tbsp Muscat wine (optional)

Tarte tatin

If I had to pick my favourite apple dessert, it would have to be tarte tatin, the queen of all apple tarts, an accolade not in the least tainted by its popularity. For any of you who might worry at the lack of a special tatin pie dish or think you have to rush out and buy one, please don't.

I simply fry the apple quarters in a large frying pan, then nuzzle them, bottom down, into a round ovenproof dish, scooping every drop of juice from the pan with a spatula and covering the pie with thinly rolled-out pastry.

I look forward to the moment when I lower the apples into the butter and sugar mix. They release some of their juice and there is the kind of hiss and sizzle that is part of the music and sound effect of cooking. I get a little flutter every time.

There now exists a superb organic shortcrust pastry in supermarkets and recently I have started to use it for my tatins. It is unsweetened but short and buttery enough to work perfectly. I spend so long over the apples that I value this bit of help. Otherwise, you can make a 60 per cent butter-to-flour pastry, only very lightly sweetened and bound together with an egg yolk. Chill it well before using it.

First make the pastry, and chill it. Then peel the apples, cut them into quarters or six if they are big. Use a small knife to remove the cores, if you have an apple corer and can centre it well enough, use that.

Place the sugar, brandy and apple juice in a large frying pan over a low heat. Stir to dissolve the sugar. Add the butter and allow to melt until bubbling, then add the apples and cook over a low heat for 45 minutes. After a few minutes of leaving them to themselves, turn the apples over, spooning the sugar and butter sauce over and over, sometimes increasing the heat slightly until you feel they simply cannot take any more and they are sitting in the pan just drenched in dark, almost black sugars. That famous edge again.

Next, transfer the apples to a shallow dish – even a shallow cake tin will do – and arrange them neatly. Roll the pastry delicately thin to a circle traced around your tin and lift it carefully over a rolling pin, then cosily over the apples, tucked in here and there.

Bake in a preheated oven on 200°C/400°F/gas mark 6 for about 25–30 minutes until the pastry is golden and the apples even more caramelised than ever, with the juices bubbling up at the sides.

Serves 4–6

160g/5^1/2 oz shortcrust pastry (*see* p285), with as much butter added as you feel comfortable with

8 or more Cox apples or other very fragrant eating apple

100 g/4 oz caster sugar, golden if available

3 tbsp brandy

3 tbsp apple juice

60 g/2 oz butter

Alternative apple

If you need a quick alternative and apple is what you must have, try this. Take an all-butter puff-pastry disc, rolled as thin as can be and pricked with a fork. Cover it, apart from a 1-cm/1/2-inch wide safety rim, with the thinnest sliced apple crescents arranged in overlapping concentric rings, dredged with caster sugar and dotted with butter.

In not much more than 10 minutes of baking in a very hot oven, you have a crisp, golden tart, the sugar caramelised and tinged with a brûlée darkness. I was served just such a thing in Madrid with a cinnamon-scented double-cream ice-cream and I can't get it out of my mind.

Coconut and passion-fruit tart

Speaking in culinary terms, few things will alienate me more from someone than a dislike of coconut. Do they have a missing gene or what? Or maybe it's all those Bounty bars. I made this tart when my baby was born, for my 40th birthday and for my mother's 70th, so I have a special affection for it.

Make the shortcrust pastry (*see* p285), adding the coconut to the flour with the lemon zest and sugar before rubbing in the butter. Chill.

Preheat the oven to 170°C/325°F/gas mark 3.

Blind-bake the pastry for 10–15 minutes until crisp but still pale

To make the filling, mix the eggs and caster sugar very well. Gently mix in the cream, then the passion-fruit juice. Then fold in about half the seeds, passion-fruit pulp and desiccated coconut.

Pour into the pastry shell and bake for about 30 minutes, until it is just set but the delicate paleness is maintained. Allow to cool for about 1 hour, allowing it to become a little firm.

Serve at room temperature.

Serves 8–10
For the pastry
500 g/1 lb 2 oz plain flour

2 tbsp desiccated coconut

2 tsp finely grated lemon zest

200 g/7 oz icing sugar

300 g/11 oz unsalted butter

50 ml/scant 2 fl oz cold water

For the filling
2 organic, free-range eggs

60 g/2 oz caster sugar

375 ml/13 fl oz double cream

10 passion-fruit, liquid strained and seeds reserved

90 g/3 oz desiccated coconut

Mango cake with passion-fruit and coconut

Breakfast may not strike you as the obvious time to eat this moist, fragrant cake (or a version thereof), but then on the shores of a ferocious Tasman sea, anything is possible even at 6AM and especially after a dawn rising, a brisk walk, yoga on the beach.

And when the restaurant is called Mermaids and the menu trips elegantly from eggs Benedict to white chocolate and pistachio muffins, mango cake is the least you can do. It's served enticingly warm, the mango and passion-fruit sharp through the sweetness.

I have made this cake with finely chopped almonds instead of the coconut and with self-raising flour instead of half or even all the almonds but somehow lime, coconut, passion-fruit, mango – it all seems to make such perfect sense. Taste the syrup and adjust the sourness to suit you.

Preheat the oven to 180°C/350°F/gas mark 4.

In a large bowl, mix the egg yolks with the sugar, lime zest, cardamom, almonds and coconut.

In the bowl of an electric mixer, whisk the egg whites until stiff and fold them into the mixture quite firmly using a metal spoon so that they are well incorporated but the mixture remains light and aerated.

Pour this into a buttered and floured 20-cm/8-inch non-stick cake tin (or lined with buttered and lightly floured baking parchment), or into a spring-form tin. Bake for 45–50 minutes or until a skewer or toothpick inserted into the centre of the cake comes out clean. Let the cake cool and transfer on to a plate large enough to contain the copious syrup.

To make the topping, peel and slice the mango into even slivers. Keep the stone and add to the scooped-out juice and seeds from the passion-fruit as well as the sugar, fruit and lime juices, orange oil and butter.

Place all these into a saucepan and bring to the boil slowly. Then add the mango slices and simmer together for a good 10 minutes. Remove the stone and pour the syrup over the cake after you have made little holes in the top with a fork, at the same time holding back the mango slices.

Arrange the mango slices on top of the cake like the closely packed petals of a sunflower. If you push the passion-fruit seeds towards the middle of the cake, the sunshine-flower look is complete.

Serve slightly warm, with a bowl of Greek yoghurt or crème fraîche by the side, and a little of the oozing syrup with each slice.

Serves 8

6 organic, free-range eggs, separated

175g/6 oz golden caster sugar

Grated zest of 2 limes

2–3 cardamom pods, seeds removed and finely crushed

75 g/2^1/2 oz ground almonds

75 g/2^1/2 oz desiccated coconut

For the topping

1 large ripe mango

8 passion-fruit

200 ml/7 fl oz orange or apple and mango juice

Juice of 1 lime

1 tsp orange-flower oil or 1 tbsp orange-flower water (optional, but delicious)

75 g/2^1/2 oz golden caster sugar

25 g/scant 1 oz butter

Praline ice-cream

The original French praline is made uniquely with almonds, drenched and coated in caramel – or boiled sugar – and this is my undoubted favourite. However, you can replace half the almonds with hazelnuts, also roasted and with their skins removed as best you can.

Usually, rubbing and shaking in a clean tea towel and discarding the debris is the most effective way. Pecan nuts are another more than acceptable alternative to the almonds. The nuts may be ground to different degrees of finesse, though in a dish like this, a coarse 'nut brittle' is best.

Later, when you come to chopping the caramelised nuts, some powderiness is inevitable and that's fine as long as there is a good balance of powder and glass-like shards. You could add brandy to the ice-cream but not more than 4 tablespoons per 250 ml/9 fl oz double cream or you will have trouble freezing it.

I made ice-cream for years without the aid of an ice-cream maker and achieved pretty good results by stirring at regular intervals – about every 2–3 hours with a hand-held electric mixer and repeating the exercise at least 3 or 4 times. But even I, luddite that I am, have to admit that even the most basic electric ice-cream machine does the job better.

Serves 6–8
For the praline
300 g/11 oz whole unblanched almonds

400 g/14 oz caster sugar

Oil for greasing

For the ice-cream
250 g/9 oz caster sugar

350 ml/12 fl oz milk

8 large, organic, free-range egg yolks

200 ml/7 fl oz double cream

Preheat the oven to 190°C/375°F/gas mark 5.

First make the praline. Blanch the almonds in boiling water for a few minutes and quickly slip off the skins. Roast in the oven for a precise 8 minutes until golden all over.

Roughly grind or chop the nuts and set aside.

Oil a baking sheet lightly and put to one side. Then set a large, heavy-bottomed pot over a low heat and pour the sugar into it, letting it sit undisturbed until the caramel starts to form in large bubbles at the sides of the pan.

Stir gently and let it sit again for a few more minutes. Then stir again and continue in this fashion until you have a clear caramel, deep amber in colour. Tip in the broken nuts and mix well, then spread on to the oiled sheet. When cooled and set, break and grind to a mixture of powder, filaments and shards.

To make the ice-cream, place a large heavy-bottomed pan on a low heat to warm and make the caramel, slowly melting all the sugar and, as for the praline, not letting it scorch at all.

Meanwhile, add a little of the milk to the egg yolks, mix well and add the rest of the milk. Set aside.

Then add the cream to the bubbling, caramel sugar and immediately stand back as it will spit and splutter furiously. Once the cream and caramel are well amalgamated, pour in the milk and egg mixture and cook the custard until fully thickened, stirring all the while. The mixture should coat the back of a wooden spoon.

Strain through a fine-meshed sieve into a bowl sitting in ice and stir frequently, to prevent curdling. Churn in an ice-cream maker according to manufacturer's instructions. Serve with the praline on top.

Baklava fit for a queen

There is little to compare between this and the commercial, lacklustre baklava, sitting in polystyrene trays in the windows of the local Greek bakery. For a start the filling is nothing like as mealy – I just don't grind the nuts so finely and I am generous with them. Plus I don't want the syrup to taste of nothing but sugar.

I want the full femininity of the rose water, the subtle spicing of the cardamom and the gentle lift of the lemon. It needs to be just stars-over-an-eastern-sky perfect. If you can eat it fresh, with the pastry still *croustillante*, it will be as I intended it.

Begin by roasting the almonds and/or pistachios in a medium oven for no longer than 7–8 minutes. Allow to cool, then chop roughly; some will inevitably turn to powder and that's fine. If you are able to find unsalted pistachios, please note that they will take even less time to crisp up slightly – they do not need to colour.

Set aside and prepare the sugar syrup by simmering the sugar, water, cardamom and half the lemon juice, until it coats a spoon. Transfer to a jug or bowl when cool. Add the remaining lemon juice and the rose water. Place in the fridge to cool and keep the pan for later.

Preheat the oven to 170°C/325°F/gas mark 3.

Serves 8–10

375 g/13 oz unsalted pistachios, or half almonds and half pistachios

175 g/6 oz best unsalted butter

450 g/1 lb filo pastry

For the syrup

300 g/11 oz caster sugar

200 ml/7 fl oz water

5–6 cardamom pods, crushed open but left whole

Juice of half a lemon

2 tbsp rose water

Assemble the baklava by first melting the butter and keeping it warm so that it stays melted to the end. Butter the sides of a shallow dish, then lay down one sheet of filo. Brush generously with melted butter, add another sheet at 90 degrees to the first, folding it in at one end if it's too big. Repeat at least a further 3 times.

Then tip the nuts into the saucepan in which you have made the syrup, adding a spoonful or so of the syrup itself. Mix well and tip these coated nuts over the pastry, spreading them evenly. There is no real need to pre-bake the bottom layer, though I often do so to a very pale-brown only, then allow it to cool first before adding the nuts.

Cover with the rest of the pastry, overlapping and buttering as before. Score the pastry in diagonal strips, first one way and then the opposite way, going all the way through to the bottom, to form diamond-shaped lozenges. Brush the top layer generously with butter.

Bake in the oven for 45 minutes, then raise the heat to 220°C/425°F/ gas mark 7 for a further 15 minutes until puffed and pale golden. The diamond shapes will be all the more prominent by now, and when you pour the cold strained syrup over the hot baklava it will flow in rivulets into the grooves as well as soaking the pastry.

Follow your previous scorings with the point of a sharp knife and lift out the individual diamond shapes on to a silver platter or clear glass plate. For a final flourish, set on a table scattered with fresh or dried rose petals.

Cornes de gazelle

These may be unfamiliar to some of you but if you have become fascinated by the cooking of the Middle East, then these delicate 'gazelle's horns' might become a regular festive feature. Try them instead of mince pies sometime.

My Aunt Stella, who was the finest of cooks (she cooked regularly for the Aga Khan), was famous for her delicate *cornes*. I used to help by making the almond 'fingers' for the filling. Don't be alarmed by the generous amount of icing sugar on top as the filling itself is quite restrained. The pastry has to be as thin as possible and you'll see that the oil instead of butter makes it particularly crisp.

Preheat the oven to 190°C/375°F/gas mark 5.

To make the pastry, add the beaten eggs and oil to the flour and mix until all of a piece, using enough of the water and orange-flower water to bind it to a smooth, soft, but not sticky dough. Dust with a little extra flour if too sticky or a few extra drops of water if dryness is the problem. Wrap in cling film and refrigerate for half an hour.

Mix the filling ingredients to a soft paste and and set aside while you roll out the pastry into the thinnest possible sheets; it will be easier for you to do this in batches. With a very sharp knife, cut the pastry into squares, slightly under 10-cms/4-inches.

Break off a piece of almond paste and roll it into a finger shape about 4-cm/2-inches long. Place an almond finger diagonally across the square of pastry, leaving a gap all the way round. Fold the pastry over the filling and roll tightly. The remaining paste can be frozen or used to stuff mejdool dates.

Then carefully curve into a crescent, with the corner point on the outside of the crescent so the corne looks like a small and skinny croissant. Repeat until all the filling is used up. Pinch the ends tightly together and trim with a sharp knife.

Place on oiled baking sheets or trays lined with baking parchment and bake for about 15 minutes until just beginning to colour. When they are cool and firm – the pastry should break clean and sharp – roll them in the icing sugar.

Serve with coffee or, for greater authenticity, sweet mint tea.

Makes 50
For the pastry

2 organic, free-range eggs, lightly beaten

125 ml/4 fl oz vegetable oil

500 g/1 lb 2 oz plain flour

6 tbsp water

3 tbsp orange-flower water

For the filling

350 g/12 oz whole almonds, ground to fine but not factory-fine grits

200 g/7 oz caster sugar

1 organic, free-range egg, lightly beaten

1 organic, free-range egg yolk

Grated zest of 1 lemon and 1 lime

Juice of half a lemon or lime

1 tbsp rose water

To serve

Lots of icing sugar

Eton mess

I enjoy this very English dessert so much and sometimes part-freeze it to make something akin to a *semi-freddo*. Not a summer goes by without it.

You can do it with shop-bought meringue nests but they will not have the necessary marshmallowness, unless you live next to a very posh deli or something. Anyway meringues take moments to make in these sorts of quantities. You can do a hundred things or nothing while they cook.

It seems that only in this country are strawberries so ubiquitously eaten with cream, a fact that shocks most English people. I was brought up on strawberries, dusted with caster sugar and impregnated with Cointreau. It brings out the flavour of the strawberries like nothing you have ever tasted. If you have never tried it, you must. I won't give you a quantity – start with a dessertpoon each and build up from there.

Ice-cold is my twist on it. This will soon lead you on to another family tradition – Cointreau in the fruit salad. There! you are privy to all the secrets now.

First prepare a baking sheet by lining it with baking parchment and preheat the oven to 140°C/275°F/gas mark 1.

Whisk the egg whites until stiff and then add the caster sugar a spoonful at a time. The egg whites will become shiny. Drop large spoonfuls of the mixture at well-spaced intervals on the parchment and bake for 1–1½ hours until they are dry and crisp.

Meanwhile macerate the strawberries in a bowl with 2 tablespoons sugar. Beat the remaining sugar into the cream or yoghurt or Mascarpone (or both), as well as the vanilla pod seeds and ground in a pestle and mortar, if using.

When the meringues are cooled, crush them a little and fold them into the cheese/yoghurt/cream and stir in the strawberries, reserving a few to scatter over the top.

Chill and serve with glasses of Champagne or elderflower cordial.

Serves 2

4 egg whites

225 g/8 oz caster sugar, plus 4 tbsp for the strawberries and cream

350 g/12 oz strawberries

200 g/7 oz Mascarpone or Greek yoghurt or a mixture of the two, or double cream, lightly whipped

1 vanilla pod, seeds scraped out (optional)

Yoghurt

Yoghurt can be made from cow's milk as well as from goat's, sheep and buffalo, the latter said to be particularly rich and delicious (I first tried it in a remote kashmiri village). It is a universal food originally from Asia though it reached Europe through Turkey (it is a Turkish word) and the Balkans.

My Bulgarian friend bemoans English yoghurt as lacking the typical 'farmhouse' flavour of Bulgarian yoghurt with its unique and inimitable micro-organism. Greek yoghurt, made from whole, full-fat milk comes closest. In the Middle East it is used as a sauce, poured over rice dishes, in India too, biryani being the best-known example. Its lower fat content makes it unstable in cooking though, and even the richest is apt to split and curdle. This can be remedied by mixing it with a little cornflour first.

Labne is a Lebanese speciality – pressed yoghurt-cheese that comes in little balls steeped in olive oil. It has a soured, sometimes slightly fizzy taste that can take some getting used to. But on warm Arabic bread, with plenty of extra virgin olive oil and a little salt and pepper, it can be very good. It is cheap and lasts up to a year in a jar in the fridge. In India *lassis* (thin, watered-down yoghurt drinks) are popular, either salted to have with curry (cooling the chilli), or sweetened with rose water or cardamom.

Yoghurt cools the blood so is ideal in the hot climate of the East. Plain yoghurt aids digestion, and can suit people with lactose intolerance.

OTHER RECIPES USING YOGHURT

Bulgarian pumpkin and cinnamon coil

A Bulgarian friend extols the wonders of her native food. Once, when I made her pumpkin filo ring, she lectured me endlessly about how I should have made my own filo pastry.

After about my fouth attempt at the ring, it did finally begin to meet with her approval. She had a point. Most of the mass-produced orange-skinned pumpkins are waterlogged and bland, the flesh drained of its carotene intensity. See if you can get a genuine Italian specimen – a hard, grey, hollow-sounding carapace without, and dense, bright, sweet flesh within. Bulgarians eat this at any time of day including breakfast, and it is at this meal that it has come into its own in my house, served warm with Greek yoghurt and sometimes, less typically, maple syrup.

Preheat the oven to 200°C/400°F/gas mark 6.

Peel and coarsely grate the pumpkin flesh and squeeze out the excess liquid. Add about two-thirds of the sugar, and the nutmeg, cinnamon and ginger juice. The sugar seems to have the ability to draw out yet more juice, so squeeze out again if necessary.

Melt the butter and set aside. Then lightly brush an oven tray with oil or a little of the melted butter and set one sheet of filo on it, making sure that the rest is not exposed to the air so it runs no risk of drying out.

Brush the sheet with some of the melted butter and, taking up some of the grated pumpkin mixture, shape it into a generous sausage. Place that at the furthest left-hand edge of the pastry and continue adding sausages of pumpkin end to end to make one long sausage.

Roll tightly in the pastry, push the ends in like an accordion and coil the whole thing like a sleeping snake. Don't worry if it splits, if you've pushed as suggested any tearing will be minimal.

Repeat with the second sheet, this time carrying on where you left off to make an increasingly large spiral. Continue with the final sheet. By now you will have a coil about 25–30-cm/10–12-inches in diameter. Brush with any remaining butter. Any splits can be patched up with small pieces of filo pastry, torn from a larger sheet and 'glued' on with melted butter.

Finally sprinkle with the remaining sugar and the chopped walnut kernels. Place in the hot oven for 25–30 minutes until a deep-golden brown, the sugar melted and caramelised with the nuts.

Allow to cool slightly (it's also great cold) and eat, either conventionally cut into wedges or simply tear pieces off the coil.

Serve on its own or with cream or yoghurt.

Serves 6

1 kg/2¼ lb pumpkin

160 g/5½ oz pale golden caster sugar or light muscovado

Freshly grated nutmeg, to taste

½ tsp ground cinnamon

8-cm/4-inch piece of ginger, grated, squeezed out and resulting juice reserved

60 g/2 oz butter

3 large sheets filo pastry

60 g/2 oz walnut kernels, roughly chopped

Alternative

I once squeezed out so much pumpkin juice, that I placed it in a saucepan with sugar to taste, a good fat knob of butter and a generous swirl of double cream. I set them to a steady simmer for about 10–15 minutes, by which time I had a slick, pumpkin-rich, fudgy sauce. Not remotely Bulgarian, but delicious all the same.

Spiced mango chutney

I never for a moment imagined that I would find myself making preserving jars full of mango chutney. For all that I am drawn to it in the more generous Indian restaurants, where they bring it on a spinning tray with other brightly coloured dips, sauces and poppadoms, I've always thought this kind of thing is best left to the experts. But when I realised that a chutney is in effect a glorified jam, I lost my trepidation. I'm one of those awful people that picks out all the fat juicy bits. So in my own chutney, I thought I'd better go for chunkiness with an unstinting hand.

The moment came quite by chance and I actually had three ripe mangoes at my disposal (left over from cooking for a party of 60). I seized the day. The smell of vinegar as you cook is quite alarming and I kept thinking I must have misread instructions, but in fact it all comes together more harmoniously than you might think.

Makes enough to fill a 750 g/ 1³/₄ lb preserving jar

3 ripe mangoes, peeled and chopped into chunks

1 large onion, finely chopped

125 g/4¹/₂ oz large Muscatel raisins (optional)

1 large apple, peeled, cored and cut into chunks (optional)

9-cm/4-inch piece of fresh ginger

3 garlic cloves, finely sliced

500 ml/18 fl oz white wine vinegar

2 tsp yellow mustard seeds

1 tsp ground turmeric

1¹/₂ tsp cayenne pepper

1 tsp salt

450 g/1 lb soft brown sugar

Place all the ingredients apart from the sugar in a large saucepan and bring to the boil. Reduce the heat and add the sugar, stirring continuously until it has all dissolved.

Continue to cook for about 1¹/₂ hours, stirring regularly to stop it sticking to the bottom. It should become thick and shiny with enough chunks for the greedy.

While the chutney is simmering, pour boiling water into the jar (or jars) and swill round. Once empty and dry, pour in the hot jam or, in this case, chutney. Seal immediately and leave in a cool dark place for about a month before eating.

Serve with poppadoms you take out of a packet and fry yourself, or even ready-fried ones, crisped up for a moment in a hot oven.

Marmalade

Homemade marmalade is a habit I retain from my childhood, eaten on warmed matza at Passover, and I have Claudia Roden to thank for linking this ritual to my culinary roots.

It seems that, since antiquity, Jews were responsible for the cultivation of citrus throughout the Mediterranean. Certainly my grandmother had no end of recipes for orange preserves and cakes, including a favourite – candied peel of oranges. More than once I remember sneaking one out of her fridge, curled on a cocktail stick and dripping with sticky syrup.

This marmalade is a deep, dark, thick-cut, adult dish – definitely not a jelly, whichever side of the ocean you come from. A kilo of Seville oranges, bought in February, will keep you in jam for several months and it will be better than anything you can buy.

We appreciate and enjoy jam in this household though none of us is quite an addict, so a morning's work sees us through from one year to the next, sealed in those timeless, sealed preserving jars. We also like sending people home with a jar. When I last made this, I used soft brown sugar. I feared it would turn out too dark, even for my liking, but it just added to the rich, caramel fullness of it. The proportions here are my preference, but you can add up to another 300 g/11 oz sugar if you like.

Sometimes I add brandy to the marmalade, a little at the beginning, a little at the end. I know oranges in brandy are a cliché, but not through failure of imagination. Besides I am rather tired of the clever self-consciousness that attends these things – in the kitchen, of all places, you do things with your heart and soul or you don't do them at all.

Makes 2³/₄ litres/4¹/₃ pints

1 kg/2¹/₄ lb Seville oranges

1.5 kg/3 lb 5 oz caster sugar or soft brown sugar

Water

Peel the oranges as thinly as possible and then peel off the pith, removing every last bit you can, and set aside.

Cut up the orange flesh into small pieces, catching all the juices in a bowl. Reserve the flesh and juices. Remove the seeds, add to the reserved pith and place in a small pan. Cover with water and set to a gentle simmer for about 10–12 minutes.

Leave to sit while you slice the thin peel into strips. Place the flesh, juice, strips of peel and sugar in a large pot. Tie the cooked pith, seeds and jelly-like pectin from the seeds in a piece of muslin and add that in too. Alternatively, strain and discard the pith and seeds, adding the left-over pectin-rich, jelly-like substance to the rest of the fruit.

Bring to the boil, then simmer steadily for about 1¹/₂ hours until the jam thickens and a small amount of it placed on a saucer and cooled, puckers when you push it with your finger. Have ready three 1-litre/ 1³/₄-fl oz preserving jars or several jam jars, washed and rinsed in boiling water and allowed to dry. Pour the hot marmalade into them. Cover with circles of baking parchment and wait until the marmalade is completely cold before closing the jars.

Marmalade and slivered-almond muffins

In *Cranks Fast Food* (C&C, 2000) I mentioned a vast quantity of marmalade that I'd made one day. It's still this same lot I am talking about now and the marmalade muffins I referred to are these. As usual go for the light touch, be light-wristed when adding wet to dry and, soothing as the movement is, stop after 10–12 lifts and turns, no more. Lumps in the mix don't matter – in fact they are a sign of lightness to come.

You can treat this recipe, bar the marmalade, as a basic mix and replace the marmalade and orange juice with about 125 g/4¹/₂ oz fresh blueberries, raspberries or blackberries. I've often made them with frozen raspberries, just thawed. We used to make hundreds of these every day at Cranks. If you only have one muffin tin, you'll need to make this recipe in two batches, but it's probably worth buying a second so you're always easily able to make the full batch, freezing half if you don't think you'll get through them all in one go.

Reheated from frozen they'll seem fantastically fresh and right at any time of day from breakfast through to tea.

Preheat the oven to 190°C/375°F/gas mark 5.

Sift the flour and baking powder into a large bowl, with the salt.

Beat the eggs, buttermilk, orange juice, marmalade and maple syrup in a separate bowl and add the melted butter. Then stir lightly into the flour mixture. Pour into lightly buttered and floured muffin tins. Mix the topping ingredients together and spoon over each muffin.

Bake in the preheated oven for 25 minutes until the muffins are well risen and golden and the marmalade is bubbling on top.

Remove from the heat and allow to cool in the tins for 5 minutes before transferring to a wire rack. Serve warm.

Makes 12

300 g/11 oz self-raising flour, plus extra for dusting

¹/₂ tsp baking powder

A pinch of salt

2 medium eggs, beaten

100 ml/3¹/₂ fl oz buttermilk, or ¹/₂ buttermilk/¹/₂ cream

2 tbsp orange juice, made fresh if you can

100 g/4 oz marmalade

4 tbsp maple syrup

110 g/scant 4¹/₂ oz unsalted butter, melted, plus extra for greasing

For the topping

60 g/2 oz marmalade

30 g/1 oz light brown sugar

30 g/1 oz almonds, slivered and toasted

chocolate & cream

chocolate & cream recipes

Nothing does it like chocolate. It gets under your skin. The biochemical euphoria is only part of its deep, dark intensity. How can you eat truly good chocolate without lowering your lids and being brought almost deliriously into the scintillating present? But please, please use it like this and for this and not as a cheap, adulterated, spot-making quick fix – 70 per cent cocoa solids content is the sublime best. I think of chocolate as 'occasion food', it both marks and makes celebrations. As for cream, it rises to the top, so is in good company here.

Chocolate brownies

Delia Smith says that 8 minutes in a preheated oven is the perfect time to roast nuts and she's right. No guesswork though, a moment later and they turn – perfect to imperfect. Brownies are perfection when the insides are soft and squidgy, a little as you'd expect undercooked cake mixture to look, and slightly crisp on the outside. Warm chocolate brownies and vanilla ice-cream served together make one heavenly treat.

Line an 18x28-cm/7x11-inch tin with baking parchment, allowing the paper to come 2-cm/1-inch above the tin.

Preheat the oven to 180°C/350°F/gas mark 4.

Chop the nuts roughly so they're still quite chunky and roast them in the preheated oven for 8 minutes, timed.

Meanwhile put the butter and chocolate in a metal bowl placed over a pan half-filled with barely simmering water. Allow the chocolate to melt, then beat until smooth. Remove from the heat and stir in the other ingredients, including the nuts, until thoroughly mixed. Spread the mixture evenly into the prepared tin and bake in the middle of the preheated oven for 30 minutes or until it is slightly springy in the middle.

Take the brownies out of the oven and allow them to cool for 10 minutes before cutting into about 15 squares. Then use a palette knife to transfer to a wire cooling rack and serve when cool or still just slightly warm.

Makes 15

100g /4 oz almonds, pecans, walnuts and pistachios, or as many as you think you can stuff into the mix (ditto the extra chocolate)

100 g/4 oz unsalted butter

100 g/4 oz (70 per cent) chocolate, broken into small chunks, plus extra

2 organic, free-range eggs

225 g/8 oz granulated sugar

50 g/scant 2 oz plain flour

1 level tsp baking powder

1/4 tsp salt

Chocolate and almond meringue

This is my version of one of the two cakes that my mother makes for birthdays. The recipe has existed on her mother's side of the family for around 100 years and, though I knew the great aunt who gave it to my mother, I have no idea where she got it from.

Cake is an inadequate term for the rich layers of this recipe. We used to alternately call it *gâteau russe*, and French pâtisseries still sell it as *progrès* (an apt term, given that the cake is made of a progression of layers). We don't make it with that kind of precision though. It's just extravagant and looks it. The chocolate mousse, which isn't really a mousse since it's made with cocoa powder, is completely delicious served on its own and is much easier to make than a proper mousse.

Chocolate

Appropriately for chocoholics, the Latin name for chocolate really does mean 'food of the Gods'. Columbus, apparently unaware of its established use as a beverage, first brought it back to the Old World, from Latin America and then simply used it as a currency with great bartering potential.

Spain was the first European country to adopt it, the rich and famous quickly becoming addicted to the drink, mixed in the ancient style with chilli and other spices. Spanish Jews introduced it to France, where once again the rich took to it. The French added sugar, the English added milk and manufacturers worked on a greater maleability, gloss and flavour. By the 19th century, Europe was producing chocolate as we know it today.

Long-imbued with near mystical, mood-enhancing properties and considered an aphrodisiac, it was soon linked with obesity. Indeed many console themselves by pleading its high iron content to compensate for its high fat and sugar. I don't know of any chocoholic who could not tell you of the naturally occurring phenylethylamine, the chemical responsible for the euphoric feelings associated with being in love. I've even heard say that chocolate is the best – nay – the only cure for unrequited love. All this makes the blending, roasting, grinding, refining and conching (to develop flavour and texture) worthwhile and this from trees which only yield half to one kilo of dried beans per year. There must be something in it.

OTHER RECIPES USING CHOCOLATE

I have even made it with good-quality drinking chocolate, no sugar. I once made it for the buyer at Fauchon in Paris, who claimed it was better than theirs!

Preheat the oven to 120°C/250°F/gas mark 1/2. Draw a 20-cm/8-inch diameter circle, using an upturned plate or cake tin as a guide, on three separate pieces of baking parchment. Lightly brush each with oil and set aside.

To make the meringue, place the egg whites in a large, clean mixing bowl and reserve the egg yolks for use in the chocolate mousse. Weigh out the sugar and have it easily to hand.

Begin by whisking the egg whites at a gentle speed so they break down completely, and then turn to the fastest speed until they stand in stiff peaks. Immediately add 1 tablespoon caster sugar until it is thoroughly whisked in and then slowly, spoon by spoon, add the rest of the sugar, mixed with the cornflour. It is essential that each spoonful is well incorporated before you add another.

Cover one circle of paper with a third of this plain meringue, using a large metal spoon to lift the mixture on to the paper, and lightly swirl the surface with a clean skewer or lines with a fork. Add the nuts to the remaining meringue mixture and divide between the other two paper circles, spreading evenly and swirling as before.

Place in the oven and allow to dry out for 1 hour, or more if necessary, until the meringue is dry and crisp. Remove from the oven. Turn each meringue layer upside down on to a large flat plate and carefully peel off the paper.

While the meringue is in the oven, make the chocolate mousse. Whip the cream with the icing sugar until it just holds stiff peaks. Set aside. Place the softened butter, cocoa powder and caster sugar in a large mixer bowl. Add the egg yolks and brandy and whisk, slowly at first as otherwise the cocoa powder will rise in a cloud. When evenly blended, increase the speed and whisk for several minutes until the mixture is smooth and voluminous and there is no trace of powderiness. Fold the sweetened whipped cream into the mousse mixture and set aside.

Make the chantilly by whipping the cream and sugar together.

To assemble, place one layer of almond meringue, smooth side up, on a large flat serving plate or cake stand. Spread carefully with half the chocolate mousse, taking the mixture up to the edges but thinly enough so that it does not ooze out when you add the next layer. Cover with the layer of plain meringue. Spread over the remaining chocolate mousse and then the Chantilly. Set the third layer of almond meringue on top.

Serves 8
For the meringue
8 organic, free-range egg whites (size 3), at room temperature

450 g/1 lb caster sugar

1/2 tsp cornflour

100 g/4 oz toasted whole almonds, coarsely chopped

For the chocolate mousse
200 ml/7 fl oz double or whipping cream

1 tbsp icing sugar

250 g/9 oz unsalted butter, lightly softened

100 g/4 oz very good quality cocoa powder

125 g/4 1/2 oz caster sugar

6 organic, free-range egg yolks (size 3)

2 tbsp brandy

For the Chantilly cream
200 ml/7 fl oz whipping cream, chilled

1 tbsp icing sugar

Freeze frame
Both the meringue and chocolate mousse freeze very well. The chocolate mousse will have to be thawed out first, but the meringue can be used straight from the freezer. Alternatively, freeze the assembled dessert and eat it while it is still very cold.

Two chocolate cakes

Everyone needs at least two chocolate cake recipes – one 'spongy' and one 'moussey'. This 'spongy' recipe is based on almonds and the 'moussey' one is baked and is almost a fudgy soufflé since it doesn't contain flour. In fact neither of them do.

Chocolate mousse cake

I believe it was Ursula Ferrigno who called out the ingredients for this recipe to me as she was running out of Books For Cooks one lunchtime to rescue her car from the unwelcome attentions of a traffic warden. The four-year-old piece of crumpled paper has stayed in my box all this time.

Over the years I have tinkered with it. Though I started with a full complement of 70–75 per cent dark chocolate, I now use half of this and half at about 53 per cent. I found the almost caffeine-like bitterness of the purer alternative just too much to handle except in the very smallest of doses and only by the most devoted aficionados.

I also remember once belting back to the Cranks kitchen and making it in double-quick time for someone's birthday. Despite blast-chilling it, it was still not quite cool enough to set and the centre oozed thick and gungy chocolate sauce. But I don't remember anyone complaining, it was just fabulously rich and luscious.

If it gives you kittens to think of this, all you need to do is to leave it to cool in its tin, even in the fridge once it's no longer piping hot. The wobbliest of cake will firm up in the cold and cut like butter if you take a knife dipped in hot water to it. I now bake it for longer than it says in my notes, however.

I enjoy melting chocolate much as any more hands-on kitchen work. You know a chocoholic speaks when she describes watching the squares collapse, turn to molten velvet and shine like satin.

Serve it at room temperature with a mound of raspberries and a jug of thin pouring cream. I may sound like a kill-joy, but I now serve jugfuls of water with anything as sweet and rich as this.

Preheat the oven to 180°C/350°F/gas mark 4. Butter a 23-cm/9-inch non-stick spring-form tin.

Place the chocolate and the butter in a bowl set over a pan of simmering water – the bottom of the bowl should not touch the water or the chocolate risks burning. However, as usual, if you work quickly enough, you can save or rescue just about anything in the kitchen – a dollop of butter or a drizzle of bland oil stirred in usually does the trick, should you be fortunate.

When the chocolate and butter are both melted, give them a good stir with a spoon. In the meantime, you will have been able to whisk the egg yolks and sugar to a pale creamy consistency, the beaters leaving a thick ribbony trail in their wake when lifted.

Separately whisk the egg whites until stiff.

Add the chocolate and butter to the egg and sugar, then pour in the cream and mix well. Finally, fold in the egg whites until well incorporated.

Pour the mixture, swiping a fingerful for yourself, into the prepared tin and bake in the oven for about 25 minutes. The cake should register a gentle tremor on the Richter scale but if it's a full-on earthquake, return it to the oven for a few minutes. Let it cool completely.

Run the point of a knife all the way round and the ring will spring off cleanly and painlessly. Cut into refined slices and serve, lightly misted with icing sugar if desired.

Rich and silky

Afficionados insist that you should never use anything with less than 70 per cent cocoa solids, but in some moods you may find that too bitter, not to mention too mood altering. Certainly using anything with less than 55 per cent is a waste of time and money so it's always worth buying the best you can afford. And give chocolate-flavoured anything a wide berth.

Serves 8–10

400 g/1 lb plain chocolate (*see* below)

100 g/4 oz unsalted butter

5 large organic, free-range eggs, separated

100 g/4 oz soft brown caster sugar

150 ml/5 fl oz double cream

Icing sugar (optional)

Chocolate almond cake

Here you have a deeply luxurious cake in a shiny, velvety chocolate mantle. I have lost count of the times I have made this cake for a wedding. Three-tiered on an American wedding cake stand, its chrome curves ribboned and draped in a garland of fresh flowers, the top of each cake elegant with gilt-edged chocolate rose leaves or fairly dripping with sugared roses, this is as Bacchanalian a cake as any you could dream of.

Line a 25-cm/10-inch cake tin with baking parchment. Grease with butter and dust lightly with flour. Or use a non-stick spring-form tin, which takes away all the uncertainty about turning the cake on its head.

Preheat the oven to 190°C/375°F/gas mark 5.

Melt the chocolate for the cake in a bowl placed over a pan of gently simmering water, not allowing the bowl to touch the water. Remove from the heat and allow to cool for a few minutes.

Cut the softened butter into small pieces and place in the bowl of an electric mixer. Add the sugar and beat with a whisk attachment on the highest setting until pale and creamy. Add one egg at a time, waiting for each to be well incorporated before adding the next. Do not be alarmed if this combination now looks curdled, it will come back together again as soon as you pour in the melted chocolate. You can do this now, and then slowly fold in the ground almonds and finally the fresh breadcrumbs for a softly textured mixture.

Pour into the tin and bake for 40–45 minutes, or until firm – a skewer inserted into the middle of the cake should come out pretty clean.

Run the point of a knife around the cake to loosen it and turn it out on to a wire rack to cool. Prick the surface with a fork and pour the brandy over so that it soaks into the cake.

While the cake is baking, make the chocolate icing. Melt the broken chocolate, honey and butter in a bowl set over a pan of boiling water. When they have melted, stir well with a metal spoon until smooth, dark and deeply glossy.

Put the cooled cake on a plate. Lift in the palm of one hand so you can manoeuvre the cake round and pour the hot and still molten icing over, turning the cake as you pour to make an even layer. You should try to do this in one continuous, sweeping movement; any attempt to smooth the mixture, say with a palette knife, will backfire and the almost-reflective quality of the icing will be lost.

Serves 8–10

250 g/9 oz unsalted butter, softened, plus extra for greasing

Flour for dusting

250 g/9 oz plain dark chocolate

250 g/9 oz caster sugar

6 organic, free-range, size 3 eggs

250 g/9 oz ground almonds

100 g/4 oz fresh white breadcrumbs

2 tbsp brandy

For the icing

150 g/5 oz dark chocolate, broken into small pieces

1 tbsp clear honey

75 g/2½ oz unsalted butter

Tip of the icing

I have sometimes placed the cake in the freezer for half an hour or so first. The hot icing poured over the cold surface immediately seizes into mirror-like smoothness. You do need to keep on your toes as it's all over in the blink of an eye and you'll feel either elated or stilled, depending on your temperament.

Chocolate ice-cream and pistachio sauce

Once I started making ice-cream I couldn't stop and no one wanted me to. So here is a fabulous version, smooth as silk satin, served with a pistachio sauce for good measure, the pale, new-shoot-green looks exquisite with the sophisticated black. It helps if you can rub at least some of the skins off the pistachios and you can do this in a tea towel.

To make the ice-cream whisk the yolks in a bowl with the caster sugar till thick, pale and creamy and leaving a ribbon trail when you lift the beaters. Bring the milk and half the cream to the boil and beat it into the egg and sugar cream.

Meanwhile, melt the chocolate, broken into pieces, in a bowl set over a pan of boiling water, as usual not allowing the bowl to touch the water. Whisk it, the cocoa and sugar into the eggs and milk and return to a pan set over a gentle heat. Stir carefully and meditatively until the custard coats the back of a wooden spoon – when you run a finger through the mixture, it should leave a clear path.

Turn the dark chocolate cream into a bowl set in a sink of cold water and keep stirring. When it is cool, stir in the rest of the cream. Refrigerate first before transferring to your ice-cream maker. Churn according to manufacturer's instructions. Serve to the kind of people who piously declare they don't really like ice-cream and just watch their faces.

Make the pistachio paste, mix the ground pistachios with 60 g/2 oz caster sugar and the egg white, it's difficult to process in a smaller quantity. This makes more than you need, but you can keep the remaining paste in the fridge, stored in a screw-top jar for a couple of weeks. Or you can freeze it until next time.

For the sauce, put half the paste in a saucepan with the milk and bring to the boil. Remove from the heat and leave to infuse for at least 5 minutes.

Whisk the egg yolks and remaining caster sugar together until thick and creamy, add to the milk and mix well until smooth. Stir gently and continuously over a moderate heat until lightly thickened. It is delicious hot, warm or cold. Try it also instead of cream with either of the two chocolate cakes.

Serves 6
4 large, organic, free-range egg yolks

125 g/4^1/$_2$ oz caster sugar

250 ml/9 fl oz milk

250 ml/9 fl oz double cream

100 g/4 oz very best dark chocolate

40 g/1^1/$_2$ oz cocoa powder

2 tbsp dark Muscovado sugar

For the pistachio sauce
50 g/2 oz pistachios, finely ground in a food processor

175 g/6 oz caster sugar

1 organic, free-range egg white

600 ml/1 pint full-fat milk

4 organic, free-range egg yolks

Chocolate tart with crystallised ginger

This simple to make but very smart tart appeared in *The New Cranks Recipe Book* (W&N, 1996), except that in this version I add crystallised ginger. Enjoy the intrigue.

To make the pastry, mix the flour, salt and sugar in a bowl and make a well in the centre. Use your fingertips to work the egg yolks into the butter and then this into the flour to form a smooth dough. Wrap in cling film and refrigerate for 20 minutes or freeze for 10.

Preheat the oven to 200°C/400°F/gas mark 6.

Butter a 28-cm/11-inch loose-based tart tin and sprinkle with 1 tablespoon flour, shaking out any excess. Roll out the pastry and line the tin with it, prick with a fork and refrigerate or freeze again, then blind-bake for about 15 minutes until pale gold.

To make the filling, melt the chocolate with the butter in a bowl over a pan of simmering water (the bowl must not touch the water). Whisk the eggs, yolks and sugar with an electric whisk for at least 5 minutes or till doubled in volume, thick, pale and leaves a trail when the beaters are lifted. Gently pour in the melted chocolate and fold together carefully. Also fold in the crystallised ginger and syrup.

Pour the mixture into the pastry shell and bake in the hot oven for 10–12 minutes or until just set – the top will have a friable, meringue-like crust and the centre will still be wobbly, though it will become firmer as it cools. Remove the tart from the tin and ideally serve while still just warm. Just one whole crystallised piece of ginger splayed out in the middle is pretty and if you are feeling really sumptuous, you can gild it in real gold leaf.

Crème fraîche goes wonderfully well but for a superbly vibrant accompaniment, try the caramelised figs (*see* p295).

Serves 8

For the pastry

250 g/9 oz plain flour

A pinch of salt

75 g/2^1/2 oz caster sugar

2 organic, free-range egg yolks, lightly beaten

125 g/4^1/2 oz unsalted butter, diced

For the filling

325 g/11^1/2 oz very good dark chocolate, broken into pieces

200 g/7 oz unsalted butter, cut into pieces

2 organic, free-range eggs

4 organic, free-range egg yolks

75g/2^1/2 oz caster sugar

A quarter of a jar of crystalised ginger pieces, thinly sliced, plus 3 tbsp of the syrup (reserve 1 whole lump for decoration)

White chocolate chip and pistachio cookies with cardamom

I tried out many recipes before plumping for this one. Some were too soft, some were too crumbly, some were too dark or too bitter. This one, given to me by Cucina (one of the few decent restaurants in Hampstead), is delicate, crisp and decadent and, I warn you now, addictive.

Preheat the oven to 180°C/350°F/gas mark 4 and line a large baking sheet with baking parchment.

Then cream the butter together with the caster and demerara sugar until light and fluffy and slowly add the flour, salt and baking powder, alternating with the beaten egg.

Add the cardamom or vanilla extract and stir well. Then mix in the pistachios and the chocolate buttons and refrigerate the mixture for at least 10 minutes. When you are ready, spoon dollops of it on to the baking parchment, leaving plenty of space all the way round. In fact you will probably only manage 4 cookies per standard size baking sheet.

They will end up being a gargantuan 15-cm/6-inches in diameter, though delectably thin and crisp.

Bake for almost 10 minutes or until just set and still pale. They will continue to firm up in their own heat when you take them out of the oven.

Darker desires

To make a dark chocolate version, do exactly as above, replacing the white chocolate drops with dark and the pistachios with 100 g/3^1/$_2$ oz walnuts, hazelnuts or pecans. I also went mad and made them with both white and dark chocolate.

I don't have much of a restrained hand around chocolate. In fact I sometimes think that if I didn't eat chocolate, I'd be as skinny as a rake – well, that's the fantasy, anyway.

Makes 8

200 g/7 oz unsalted butter, at room temperature

200 g/7 oz caster sugar

175 g/6 oz demerara sugar

200 g/7 oz plain flour

1 tsp salt

3 tsp baking powder

2 organic, free-range eggs, beaten

1 tsp ground cardamom

175 g/6 oz pistachios, skins rubbed off

300 g/11 oz good quality white chocolate buttons

Cream

At nearly 50 per cent fat, cream is the richest of foods and often just a little goes a long way. A spoonful or two of luxurious double cream, or even so-called extra thick double cream, which is so thick that you can cut it with a knife, added to a soup immediately transforms it.

But you have to be careful to add it only after the soup has boiled so that it doesn't curdle. Hot pasta gliding with a coating of cream and perhaps a little garlic and lemon is one of life's most sensual and delicious pleasures.

Mustard is another natural partner and eggs, of course, are greatly enhanced by cream. Single cream is not designed for cooking at all. Reserve it for pouring on hot dessert pies and on summer fruit, strawberries and cream being the obvious. The French crème fraîche has a hint of sourness to it which can offset the sweetness of a rich dessert perfectly. The singularly English clotted cream (though it is believed to have exotic ancient Phoenician links) seems as if born to the perfect tea-house scone and homemade strawberry jam.

Homemade ice-creams using the best double cream leave most commercial brands standing and, for perfection twice over, a dark homemade chocolate ice-cream with a crown of feather-light whipped cream, adding lightness to every mouthful.

OTHER RECIPES USING CREAM

Roasted tomato soup with garlic cream 16

Artichoke with saffron and green olives bound with cream in a puff pastry pie 36

Beetroot in sour cream 87

Fig and rose water double-cream ice-cream 299

Passion-fruit ice-cream 304

Praline ice-cream 319

Chocolate ice-cream and pistachio sauce 342

Crème brûlée 347

Crème brûlée

People play around with this divinely rich, silken dessert in ways and for reasons quite beyond me. They add bananas or raspberries, coconut or passion-fruit, nuts to the caramel, cardamom (oh okay, I give in to that one) and so on.

But once in a while, don't you just long for something pure?

Preheat the oven to 140°C/275°F/gas mark 1.

Mix the caster sugar with the egg yolks in an electric mixer on a low speed until thick and creamy. Gently heat the milk and double cream together with the vanilla or cardamom pods and seeds, taking care that it does not boil. Strain and remove the pods.

With the mixer turned even lower, gradually add the milk and cream to the beaten egg mixture. Now pour this into a large rectangular ovenproof glass dish and place it in a *bain marie* or large roasting tin one-third filled with water.

Bake in the oven for about 1 hour or until set. Place in the fridge to chill and firm to a thick spoonable cream.

When ready to serve, sprinkle the demerara sugar evenly over the surface and caramelise under a very hot grill, or use a blow torch if you have one. Watch carefully to make sure that the bubbling sugar doesn't burn. When it has set to luminescent, amber glass, wait a few moments for it to cool, then serve.

Serves 8

150 g/5 oz caster sugar

10 organic, free-range egg yolks

100 ml/4^1/$_2$ fl oz milk

900 ml/a scant 2 pints double cream

2 vanilla pods or 8 cardamoms

150 g/5 oz demerara sugar

Coconut and cardamom rice pudding

Technically this really shouldn't appear here, but I just had to make a point about the intense creamy texture and lusciousness that defies any use of cream.

This stove-cooked rice pudding is not unlike a sweet risotto. It doesn't contain cream or eggs and is considerably lower both in calories and fat than that version. Many who are not great fans of the traditional rice pudding have enjoyed this. You must stir continuously and stop exactly as you would with a risotto – that is, when the grains are creamy but still separate and with a hint of bite to them.

Although I used to make this with ordinary pudding rice, I now use Arborio which is so much creamier and firmer. Sophie Grigson adds a brulée caramel topping to her rice pudding and I recommend it.

Finally, there is nothing to stop you adding a little chopped, soft or stewed apricot; some plump Muscatel raisins or roasted plums to the rice. But even without, this is delicate, gentle and subtly aromatic.

Heat the milk to just below boiling point. Pour in the rice, sugar, nutmeg, cardamom and coconut and stir over a low heat for about 25 minutes until the rice is tender, the milk thick and creamy and the grains of rice still separate.

Divide between pudding plates or bowls and serve hot or cold. Garnish with roughly chopped toasted pistachios.

To make the brûlée sprinkle the demerara sugar over the puddings – about 1 tablespoon per serving (on top of the nuts is fine). Place under a hot grill (or use a blow torch if you have one) for 3–5 minutes. Leave to cool so that the sugar forms a hard crust, then serve.

Serves 4–6

1.2 litres/2 1/4 pints milk

150 g/5 oz Arborio rice

60 g/2 oz caster sugar

A pinch of freshly grated nutmeg

4–5 cardamom pods, seeds removed and pounded in a pestle and mortar

40 g/1 1/2 oz creamed coconut

40 g/1 1/2 oz pistachios, toasted, skins slipped off and roughly chopped

100 g/4 oz demerara sugar, for brûlée topping (optional)

bread, biscuits & baking

baking etc recipes

These recipes are simple and extremely rewarding. There's hardly a time-consuming or labour-intensive one among them, but the satisfaction is great, especially as the yeasty, fruity smells waft through the house. It takes around 5 minutes to assemble the mix for a tray of scones or muffins and even some of the yeasted breads don't require kneading, though for those who appreciate that particular quietening, grounding, hands-on therapy, there are some that do. This is probably the best chapter for weaning children on to the art of cooking and for imbuing them with a balanced, integrated view of the kitchen.

Basic pizza dough and toppings

This is the classic Neapolitan pizza dough. You can make it richer by replacing about 125 g/4¹/2 oz of the plain flour with either rye flour or semolina flour. About 60 ml/2 fl oz of the warm water can also be replaced with warm milk and you may add a little more olive oil to the dough so that it becomes amalgamated into it on kneading.

Whichever you choose, your oven must be as hot as possible and, to replicate the feel of the wood-fired bakers' oven at home, invest in a pizza stone. This distributes the heat more evenly and creates a crisper crust on the underside by absorbing moisture. Sprinkle the stone with a little cornmeal before placing the dough on top.

Another useful implement is the 'pizza peel' – a thin wooden board with a long handle. If you watch them make pizza in a traditional pizzeria, it's the long wooden paddle with which the rolled-out dough is transferred into the oven. You'll soon get the hang of it.

Alternatively a little dextrous flipping of the dough on to your lightly cornfloured or oatmealed hands will do the trick.

Put the flour in a large bowl with the salt. Crumble and dissolve the fresh yeast in about half a glass of the measured water with a pinch of sugar to activate the yeast. Follow packet instructions if using dried yeast.

When it begins to froth, pour the yeast mixture into the flour, then gradually pour in the rest of the warm water, mixing first with a wooden spoon and then working the flour into the liquid with your hands. The dough just needs to hold together into a ball, though a stickier mixture will give a crisper crust.

Knead lightly for 10–15 minutes, either by hand (or in a mixer with a dough-hook attachment, though you probably know by now how I feel about this).

Pour 1–2 tablespoons olive oil into a bowl and turn the ball of dough in it so that it does not form a dry crust as it rises, and drizzle a little olive oil over the top. Cover the bowl with a damp cloth (or cling film which speeds up the process) and leave to rise in a warm spot – an airing or boiler cupboard for instance – for up to 2 hours, until doubled in size.

Knock the dough back and knead for a couple of minutes, then return to the bowl to rise for a further 40 minutes or so.

Preheat the oven to 200°C/400°F/gas mark 6.

Makes 4

500 g/1 lb/2 oz sifted plain flour, plus extra for dusting

A good pinch of Maldon sea salt

25 g/scant 1 oz fresh yeast or 15 g/¹/2 oz dried yeast

250 ml/9 fl oz warm water (approximately)

A pinch of sugar, if necessary

3–4 tbsp olive oil for the bowl

Divide the dough into six small balls to make six individual pizzas. Roll out on a lightly floured surface as thinly as possible to a diameter of about 23-cm/9-inches. Add your topping (*see* below) and bake for about 15 minutes, until the crust is blistered black here and there.

Suggested toppings

Paper-thin white onion, drizzled with olive or truffle oil, seasoned with salt, pepper, chopped garlic and a few shavings of black or white truffle.

A concasse of fresh tomatoes, some shrivelled black olives, and thick rounds of Mozzarella.

Paper-thin potato slices, golden fried onion, fried sliced mushrooms, baked until the base is crisp and the potatoes succulent. Fresh thyme or marjoram. A rivulet of olive oil.

Fine rings of sautéed baby courgettes and their butter-wilted flowers to cover the base. Homemade tomato sauce and Mozzarella melting on top.

A thin layer of tomato sauce, charred fennel, aubergine, red pepper and red onion. More Mozzarella and olive oil. Basil. Garlic. Salt. Pepper.

A mound of wilted spinach, goat's cheese and pecans.

Spinach with an egg nestling in the middle. Double cream. Parmesan.

Calzone

Add 4 tablespoons olive oil with the warm water to the flour and follow the dough recipe as above.

Preheat the oven to 220°C/425°F/gas mark 8.

For the filling, roast the aubergine in the oven, together with the courgette, all well basted in the oil and seasoned with a little salt and pepper. While they are roasting, mix together the remaining ingredients.

Calzone are usually off-puttingly gargantuan so I make mine smaller. I use a 12-cm/4^1/$_2$-inch saucer as a template and cut 12 circles from my thinly rolled dough. Divide the filling equally between the circles, brush the rims of one-half with water, fold over and press to seal, crimping with a fork to make the whole thing more secure.

Now either brush generously with olive oil and bake in the oven for about 15–20 minutes, or more quickly (and seductively) deep-fry in at least 1 litre/2 pints very hot sunflower oil till golden all round. Be vigilant here and turn them over with 2 forks so they are evenly cooked.

Transfer to a plate lined with kitchen paper, then serve at once.

Makes 12 (small)

90 ml/3 fl oz light olive oil

1 average-sized aubergine, cut into small chunks

1 courgette, cut in small chunks

Sea salt and freshly ground black pepper

1 ball of Mozzarella, torn into small pieces

1^1/$_2$ tbsp each lightly toasted pine nuts, well-drained capers and raisins

1 tbsp sundried tomato purée

150 g/5 oz black olives

2 ripe tomatoes, chopped small

1 garlic clove, crushed

Bulgarian filo coil with three cheeses

I'll prove to you that there's nothing new under the sun. I made this prompted by the filo coil with pumpkin (*see* p326) and decided to include it here because each of my several attempts met with widespread approval – and because it's so easy.

Then at the 11th hour, I picked up my pretty well-thumbed copy of Claudia Roden's *A History of Jewish Food* (Viking, 1997), which is actually the only cookery book I have ever taken to bed, and what do you know, it opened at a whole section on filo coils. On the subject of taking cookery books to bed, I rarely do. I know people do and that it is so often regarded as a sign of being a true foodie. But I cook in the kitchen, not in my head, and I did not begin to cook using books.

My mother did not even own a cookery book, unless you count her time-worn, kitchen-spattered notebook, the one with recipes from aunts long gone, friends now dispersed to the four corners of the earth, cutouts from 40- and 50-year-old newspapers. There was nothing intellectual about my first attempts and I hope there isn't now. I cook because I have to and I don't mean have to in the sense that my mother had to or her mother before her but because it is one of the ways in which I love.

Serves 4–6

450 g/1 lb Ricotta, well-drained

275 g/10 oz feta, crumbled into generous lumps

150 g/5 oz mature Cheddar, coarsely grated

Roughly 4 large, organic, free-range egg yolks (judge amount needed by texture of mix)

Freshly grated nutmeg

1 tbsp chopped chives

1 garlic clove, finely chopped (optional)

3 tbsp olive oil or more

3 large sheets filo pastry

1 tbsp sesame seeds

Freshly ground black pepper

Preheat the oven to 200°C/400°F/gas mark 6.

Empty the Ricotta, the feta and the Cheddar into a good-sized bowl and beat the egg yolks into the mix. Season with a well-judged grating of nutmeg (to taste) and some black pepper as well as the chives. I doubt that you'll need salt with the feta, but you decide. As for the garlic, sometimes I include it, sometimes not. The mixture should be soft and moist and hold together when you shape it into a roll with your hands.

Take out your largest oven tray and brush it generously with oil. Lay one sheet of filo out on it, keeping the others protected from the drying elements with a damp tea towel. Brush this with oil and place a long sausage of cheese mixture along the bottom (the longest edge). Roll it up tightly and push the ends in like a concertina (I got that bit from Claudia – thank you), then twist into a coil. If it splits anyway, you can patch it up with spare bits later. Repeat with the rest of the mix and filo sheets, taking up where you left off and pressing the 'sausages' together, end to end, until you have one large Catherine-wheel-shaped coil.

Brush the top with more oil and sprinkle the sesame seeds all over.

Bake for about 30 minutes until golden, crisp and delicious. Eat hot although it tastes fabulous cold, too.

Cantuccini

This recipe is usually referred to as biscotti, the very hard little biscuits that are delicious dipped in *vin santo* or in tea or coffee. But I prefer this longer grander-looking version, baked for slightly less time than usual, so that they are crisp on the outside and have a touch of cakiness to the insides. By all means experiment with the cooking times, as different occasions may colour your judgement as to what's best for you. As an accompaniment to roasted fruits and compotes, cantuccini are absolutely delicious, especially served with crème fraîche or Mascarpone.

Preheat the oven to 180°C/350°F/gas mark 4.

Mix the flour, sugar and baking powder in a large bowl. Add half the beaten eggs and mix well, then add half of what's left and mix again. Then add the final batch, a little at a time, until the dough sticks together without being too wet. Please note, you may not need to add all the remaining egg.

Add the chopped fruit, nuts and lemon zest and mix well.

At this stage you can roll the dough into six sausage shapes, about 2$\frac{1}{2}$-cm/1-inches in diameter, or fill a 2$\frac{1}{2}$-cm/1-inch-deep tray lined with baking parchment with the mixture. If doing the former, place the sausage shapes on to a tray lined with baking parchment, wet your hands with water to shape the dough to prevent it from sticking to you and lightly flatten the sausages, baking them for about 20–30 minutes or until golden brown. Remove from the oven and leave for 10 minutes to cool and firm up.

If you are not making the sausage shapes, then cut deep into the baked mixture to make six long strips and allow to cool.

Lower the oven temperature to 140°C/275°F/gas mark 1 and, with a serrated knife, cut the dough into pieces about 10-cm/4-inches long (or, for small biscotti, into slices about 5-mm/$\frac{1}{4}$-inch thick).

Return them to the oven and cook for 12 minutes. For a crisper, harder finish, turn them over and cook until a pale golden colour, a further 10–15 minutes.

Remove from the oven when ready and cool on wire racks. Store in really airtight jars for up to 3 months, or less for the less-cooked version.

Makes loads

500 g/1 lb 2 oz plain flour

500 g/1 lb 2 oz unrefined caster sugar

1 tbsp baking powder

5 organic, free-range eggs, lightly beaten

100 g/4 oz Muscatel raisins or other plump raisin

100 g/4 oz soft dried apricots, sliced

100 g/4 oz pitted dates, chopped

100 g/4 oz shelled pistachio nuts

100 g/4 oz whole blanched almonds

100 g/4 oz shelled hazelnuts

Zest of 2 lemons

Olives

I hold certain foods in almost hallowed place. Olives are one such. I don't know if it is possible to have these things in the blood but I do experience a certain programming or blueprint – a predisposition to loving them.

Why this should be true of mediterranean types like me, I can understand but I find the way they've been taken up by cooler blooded Northerners quite extraordinary. Certainly, I still occasionally meet someone who says they don't like olives but to most people, they have become symbol for sun and sea and probably sex as well. It's a shame that Athena, the goddess of wisdom who is said to have brought the tree to earth has been honoured only symbolically by the proferring – not always sincerely – of an olive branch. Peace on earth or not, an olive tree, gnarled and still yielding annual crops can survive for several hundred years and perhaps in this lies its timelessness.

Olives are harvested at different degrees of ripeness and cured appropriately to make them suitable for eating. This involves soaking them in different media (water, oil, brine, salt and even a caustic soda solution) for many months at a time. They vary in size from the tiny Niçoise to the practically walnut-sized, meaty, green queen olives. There are juicy ones and dried ones, lip puckeringly salty ones and herb redolent ones, oily ones, chilli hot and spicy ones, mild tasting and bitter ones.

OTHER RECIPES USING OLIVES

Artichoke and sundried tomatoes and preserved lemon dressing 32

Artichoke with saffron and green olives bound with cream in a puff pastry pie 36

Carpacio of fennel with black olives and tomato 59

Jerusalem artichoke, lemon and parsley salad with green olives and pistachios 83

Cannelini and garlic purée and tabbouleh 185

Homemade pasta pieces with tomatoes, spinach and black olives 202

Feta and sunblushed-tomato scones with black olives 361

Feta and sunblushed-tomato scones with black olives

These are a departure from the mammoth sized scones of the Cranks of old. Those were a meal in themselves and you'll find the recipe in *The New Cranks Recipe Book* (W&N 1996). There I did say that if you could bear to play around with something as quintessentially English as a scone you could stuff them full of contemporary additions such as feta, sundried (or in this case sunblushed) tomatoes and juicy Kalamata olives.

But I didn't tell you how, so here goes. By the way, these scones are tea-time size and quite dainty for all their robust flavour. Like all bakery products, they freeze excellently so make them in a spare moment and heat them straight from frozen in a very hot oven till they look and smell as good as new.

Begin by preheating the oven to 220°C/425°F/gas mark 7.

Take a large bowl and sift the flours and baking powder into it, folding the bran back in. Then add the oil, chilli and mustard and work loosely with a fork until the mixture turns to small lumps. Stir in the feta, sunblushed tomatoes, olives and basil.

Separately, beat the egg and milk together and gradually pour into the flour mixture, bringing the whole thing lightly together with your fingers until you have a ball of soft, but not sticky, dough.

Roll out on a floured surface to a depth of 2-cm/1-inch and cut out with a 5-cm/2-inch round, fluted cutter.

Line a tray with baking parchment and place the scones in rows on it, brush them lightly with milk and bake on the oven's highest shelf for 12–15 minutes until golden brown. Transfer to a wire rack and eat them when still just warm.

And a little more on olives

Stuff olives with blanched almonds, peppers, garlic, or blend them into pastes and purées with basil or a fuggier herb, garlic, a dash of Cognac (in imitation of the French tapenade) and a spoonful of whipped cream to lighten it if you wish. Spread onto crostini, add a spoonful to soups or stir into a tangle of linguine.

Makes 8

175 g/6 oz self-raising flour, plus extra for dusting

60 g/2 oz wholemeal flour

$1/4$ tsp baking powder

2 tbsp extra virgin olive oil

A small piece of red chilli, very finely chopped

$1/2$ tsp English mustard

75 g/$2^1/2$ oz feta, cut in small cubes

60 g/2 oz sunblushed tomatoes, drained and roughly chopped

10 Kalamata olives, pitted and roughly chopped

Several basil leaves, roughly torn

1 organic, free-range egg

2 tbsp milk, plus extra for the top

Goat's cheese, olive and sunblushed-tomato muffins

Just about everyone thinks 'American' these days when they hear the word muffin. They forget the yeast-leavened squat, spongy English muffins, which I am suddenly tempted to try for the first time in ages. They were favourite breakfast fare in my family, the warm dough accepting the melting butter almost too hungrily.

This recipe is a grand meal-in-a-muffin sort of affair. Even after a week kept in a knotted plastic bag in the fridge, they were softer by half then some purported to have been made that very morning. Once again, I stuffed them full of titbits. I hate to have to search for a solitary piece of olive or the odd flake of tomato, so if these muffins seem to be bursting with goodies, that's how they are meant to be. Eat warm and, if you are thinking of freezing, remember the golden rule – always bake straight from frozen.

Herbamare, which I use instead of salt here, is a dried vegetable salt, comprised of 85 per cent salt and 15 per cent vegetable. Consuming 15 per cent less salt may not seem to amount to much in these hardened-artery days but it's a step in the right direction. I use sunblushed tomatoes, they are sweeter, softer and brighter and I like them better than their more leathery sundried predecessors.

Makes 9

225 g/8 oz plain flour or Farina 00

1 tbsp baking powder

1/2 tsp garlic salt or Herbamare

Freshly ground black pepper

30 g/1 oz butter

100 g/4 oz cheese, half Cheddar and half goat's cheese, cut into small pieces

60 g/2 oz black olives, pitted, chopped and patted dry

90 g/3 1/2 oz sunblushed tomatoes, chopped

1 tbsp chopped basil

1 large egg, beaten

250 ml/9 fl oz milk

Preheat the oven to 220°C/425°F/gas mark 7.

Sift the flour, baking powder, salt and pepper into a large bowl. Rub in the butter and add two-thirds of the Cheddar and goat's cheese, olives, tomatoes and basil, reserving the remaining third for the topping. Mix well.

Beat the egg and milk together and add to the dry ingredients, working quickly and lightly with a large fork until the flour is just incorporated. I keep my movements large to allow as much air as possible into the mix and am very careful not to over-beat – less than 30 seconds is enough.

Lightly butter and flour the muffin tin (or line with muffin papers) and fill each two-thirds full, sprinkling the remaining bits on top.

Bake in the middle of the oven for 18–20 minutes until well risen and golden. Remove from the oven and allow them to cool for 5 minutes before loosening with the tip of a knife and transferring to a wire rack.

Eat warm.

In plain English

For a plain English muffin, blend together 15 g/¹/₂ oz fresh yeast with 250 ml/9 fl oz of hand-hot milk and 1 teaspoon caster sugar. Beat 1 egg and 30 g/1 oz butter together. Then sift 450 g/1 lb flour with a pinch of salt into a bowl. Make a well in the centre and pour in the yeast mixture and the butter and egg mixture. Mix to a dough.

Turn out on to a clean surface and knead till smooth and elastic. Cover and leave in a warm place for about 40 minutes to double in size. Turn out and pummel lightly. Roll out on a lightly floured surface to a thickness of about 1-cm/¹/₂-inch. Use a floured, round cutter and cut into 6-cm/2¹/₂-inch rounds. You can knead the left-over trimmings and roll them out, too. Place the muffins on a lightly oiled and heated griddle pan and fry them for about 6 minutes on each side until golden brown. You can bake them if you like, first 5 minutes on one side and then 10 minutes on the other. Serve warm with butter.

Pain perdu

I hadn't planned to include this recipe in this book, except that I am writing this on a freezing-cold, snow-covered early morning and there is (or was) a loaf of wholemeal bread with hardly a slice eaten from it on my kitchen counter. It had been sitting there for a week and had turned hard all around. On top of that I'd run out of yoghurt – a cardinal sin in my household – and breakfast threatened to be a pretty frugal affair.

So I cut 4-cm/2-inch thick slices from the loaf, dipped them in 400 ml/14 fl oz organic milk, poured into a large shallow dish, till they were heavy with it, then dipped the wobbly slices in 3 beaten, large, organic, free-range eggs.

I put 100 ml/3¹/₂ fl oz of sunflower oil in a large frying pan and, on a hot flame, fried 2 slices at a time, a minute on each side. No sooner fished out of the hot oil, than they were drenched in maple syrup and placed straight on to the breakfast table in the time it has taken me to write this and you to read it. I only wish I had gone for a run beforehand – and afterwards, for that matter.

I liked the nuttiness of the wholemeal bread, but you could do the same with some stale *chollah* or brioche or an uneaten cottage loaf (how so?). It will be even speedier to cook, but won't let you off the need for exercise.

Walnut and raisin loaf

This is my favourite bread – except it's a loaf. So I make a couple of loaves and freeze one. When I next need it, it goes into a heated oven for about 20–25 minutes until it is warm and crisp on top. Or I slice it before freezing so that I can pull out a slice or two whenever I want.

It's the perfect base for all kinds of fast lunch toppings, for example, roasted butternut squash with watercress pesto, or avocado with roasted tomatoes. It's easier to make the bread by mixing the wet ingredients in a bowl and adding the flour to them.

But if making bread just isn't the same for you unless you have a mountain of flour on your worktop, with a well dug out of the centre as receptacle for the wet ingredients, then do it this way. What matters is that the ingredients are well and truly mixed.

You can do the restaurant thing and serve several types of bread or loaf in one basket, assuming you are making them for a party or large gathering. Otherwise it's a good thing to have wrapped up in the fridge or cupboard for a few days as it will take you through from breakfast to teatime and back again.

Preheat the oven to 200°C/400°F/gas mark 6 and line a 25-cm/10-inch loaf tin with baking parchment. In a large bowl mix the milk, eggs, sugar and yeast and leave to sit in a warm place for 10 minutes.

Sift the flour and salt into the bowl and mix well. Add the nuts and raisins and mix again so that they are well distributed. Pour into the prepared loaf tin and put in a warm place to prove for 30–45 minutes.

When the dough has risen to 1-cm/$1/2$-inch above the top of the tin, brush with the glaze and place in the oven. About 5 minutes later, turn the temperature down to 160°C/325°F/gas mark 3 and bake for a further 25 minutes. Cover loosely with a piece of foil or baking parchment if you see any danger of the top burning.

A hollow sound when the bread is gently tapped on the bottom tells you that it is ready. Cool, first in the tin for 5 minutes, then on a wire rack. Then, take the first warm slice, spread it with butter and sink your teeth into it. You know you deserve it.

Makes 2
200 ml/7 fl oz milk

1 organic, free-range egg

3 organic, free-range egg yolks

30 g/1 oz brown sugar

20 g/$3/4$ oz fresh yeast

300 g/11 oz plain flour

$1/2$ tsp salt

250 g/9 oz fresh walnut halves

200 g/7 oz large Muscatel raisins, soaked in a little warm water

For the glaze
1 egg white, mixed with

2 tbsp milk

Butter, flour, sugar

The French make the finest, creamiest unsalted butter in the world. My mother tells the story that when England was about to join the Common Market, members of her office were up in arms because they were afraid that they were going to lose English salted butter.

Their fears have proved unfounded, so you can still slather it on to hot toast to your heart's content. But these days, thank goodness, anyone interested in cooking recognises the superior virtues of unsalted. *Beurre D'Isigny* is rightly considered the best and I use it whenever possible.

It makes luxury of the simplest vegetable dish, the simplest white loaf, the simplest oat cracker. Don't fall into the other English habit of keeping it out on the kitchen counter. It soon loses its freshness, turns yellow and even rancid. *Quelle horreur*!

I always use unbleached flours and, now that they are more easily available, organic ones. The only exception is Farina 00 the Italian pasta flour, which is also remarkably good in cakes and muffins.

Very finely milled wholemeal flours are good to add in small doses to pastry mixes, some loaf cakes and breads. Although flour keeps for a long time, it is best to store it in a cool dark place and not to leave little odds and ends lying around. Self-raising flour is particularly prone to deterioration and will lose its raising ability (created by the addition of baking powder) if kept too long.

Strong bread flour, on the other hand, improves on keeping, giving a softer, fuller loaf. The best of these are stone ground in methods still close to the ancient ones, archaeological evidence of which are found all around the eastern Mediterranean.

With rare exceptions, I now only use unrefined pale golden caster sugar.

There might be the odd dusting of icing sugar and the occasional use of dark muscovado sugar, with its strong, treacly, caramelised flavour.

But even meringues I would once only have made with white caster seem to me better these days with pale golden, the loss of the pure-white confection compensated for by the deeper, more interesting taste.

OTHER RECIPES USING BUTTER, FLOUR AND SUGAR

Pumpkin loaf

I said that the walnut loaf is my favourite, but it's a closely run thing. While everyone else was hollowing out the seasonal pumpkins and sticking candles in them to celebrate Hallowe'en, I used to make special trips to Sally Clarke's shop in Kensington to buy her pumpkin bread, which became the inspiration for this recipe. Her window is piled high with these luxurious loaves.

While you are at it, you may as well make two, but make sure that the pumpkin is deeply coloured and therefore tasty enough to start with. The green-skinned Crown Prince is the best.

Preheat the oven to 200°C/400°F/gas mark 6.

Roast the pumpkin in a little olive oil, salt and pepper for 30 minutes until tender and gently browned.

Bring the milk to the boil in a covered saucepan. Then remove the lid, reduce to a soft simmer and reduce the milk by about half. Transfer to a bowl to cool until lukewarm.

Dissolve the yeast in the water and mix into the milk with the roasted pumpkin, then add the flours, salt and pumpkin seeds, reserving a few for the top, and knead for 5 minutes. Make sure that some whole pieces of pumpkin remain, however. The dough should be soft but not sticky, so you may need to add a little extra flour. Leave in a warm place to rise for about an hour so that it doubles in size.

When it has risen, knock the dough back by punching it with your fists and divide it into two lumps. Roll each into a long sausage shape and place on a baking sheet, either lightly floured or lined with baking parchment. The loaves now need to rise and double in size one final time, so again place in a warm spot until they have done so.

Preheat the oven to 180°C/350°F/gas mark 4.

Brush the loaves with a little water or milk and sprinkle with a little coarse sea salt and the remaining pumpkin seeds. Place in the hottest part of your oven to bake for 20 minutes, by which time it should sound hollow when tapped on the bottom. If it doesn't yet, then give it another few minutes until it does. Remove from the oven and cool on a wire rack.

Makes 2

600 g/1 lb 4 oz pumpkin or butternut squash, peeled and cut into 2-cm/1-inch pieces

Olive oil

400 ml/14 fl oz milk

20 g/¾ oz fresh yeast (or 3 tsp dried yeast)

50 ml/scant 2 fl oz warm water

600 g/1 lb 5 oz strong white flour

200 g/7 oz strong wholemeal flour

1 tsp sea salt for the dough plus more to sprinkle on top

60 g/2 oz pumpkin seeds

Freshly ground black pepper

Cranks wholemeal bread

This is the famous, densely textured bread, as popular now as when it first saw light, more than 40 years ago. If you are even remotely intimidated by the process of bread making, one of its undoubted advantages is that it requires no kneading.

This makes a 450g/1 lb loaf, baked in a tin or as a fat sausage or in baps, with the traditional grated cheese melting on top as it bakes. The baps are wonderful split and buttered while still warm and stuffed full of mustard and cress or, even more seductively, a whole butter-fried field mushroom, tamari-doused, garlic and basil or finely chopped parsley added abundantly as well as a dash of Tabasco for pep. Squash the mushroom into the bap, letting its juices soak through the bread – you may not even need the butter as you can wipe every last drop from the pan. Then take the biggest handful of squeakily fresh watercress and ram it into the bap so it is hinged open by your unstinting generosity.

Preheat the oven to 200°C/400°F/gas mark 6.

Mix the flour with the salt in a large bowl or set in a mound on a lightly floured surface. In very cold weather, warm the flour slightly by leaving it to stand over a warm stove for a few minutes.

Mix the yeast and sugar in a small bowl with 150 ml/5 fl oz of the warm water. Leave in a warm place for 10 minutes or so to froth up. Pour the yeasty liquid into a well in the flour and gradually add the rest of the water. Gradually draw the flour into the water and mix well.

Divide the dough into six even-sized lumps. Roll the lumps into balls, then oil a baking sheet and flatten each lump with the palm of your hand on to it. Cover with a cloth and leave in a warm place to rise for about 15 minutes.

Brush with milk and transfer to the hot oven to bake for 20–25 minutes. Turn one over and tap to test for the hollow, drum-like sound. Cool on a wire rack. Split. Butter. Eat.

Makes 6 burger-sized baps

450 g/1 lb organic wholemeal flour

1 generous tsp salt

15 g/^{1}/$_2$ oz fresh yeast

1 tsp brown sugar

300–400 ml/10–14 fl oz warm water

Oil for greasing

Milk to glaze

For the sandwich
Serves 6

60 g/2 oz butter

6 garlic cloves (yes, 6), thinly sliced

6 large field mushrooms

2 dsp tamari

A small handful of basil or tarragon, marjoram or thyme

A dash of Tabasco

1–2 large bunches watercress

Mushroom sandwich

Melt the butter in a large frying pan, add the garlic and move about in the pan gently for a few minutes, the heat kept prudently low.

Add the mushrooms and, when they have begun to soften and to weep, add the tamari. Keep frying quite gently until the mushrooms are limp and juicy. Add the herbs to the pan for a rich herby, garlicky liquor, and a dash of Tabasco. Eat with the baps and watercress.

Irish soda bread

This gives all the satisfaction of homemade bread in a fraction of the time and is a good way to ground yourself or deal with conflicting emotions – they do say the kitchen is the place to burn up karma.

It so forces you to be here and now.

Preheat the oven to 200°C/400°F/gas mark 6.

Sift the wholemeal flour together with the salt and bicarbonate of soda into a large bowl. Fold the bran back into the flour and rub the butter into the flour mixture. Next, add the buttermilk and honey and mix gently with a fork into a dough.

You can shape into one large loaf, or try making two smaller sausage-shape loaves – giving a slightly lighter texture to the bread. Set straight on to a lightly greased baking tray. Make a cross in the top of the larger loaf, if making, so that by the time it's baked it has the characteristic four-section look to it.

Place in the oven and bake for 40–45 minutes until the bottom sounds hollow when tapped. Transfer to a cooling rack and serve with a little warmth left.

Serve with butter, soft goat's cheese or any other cream cheese. Or simply do as the Irish hermits did and eat it with watercress.

Makes 1

450 g/1 lb wholemeal flour

1 tsp salt

1 tsp bicarbonate of soda

30 g/1 oz butter, chilled

284 ml/approximately 10 fl oz tub of buttermilk

1 tsp honey (optional)

Oil for greasing

Simple white bread

I've given you wholemeal bread, fruit loaves, scones and muffins, crêpes, pizza dough and pasta, so how can I not give you this?

You can substitute olive oil for the butter if you like and you can treat this as the basis for other loaves. For instance, you could go 50/50 white and wholemeal flour or two-thirds wholemeal and one-third white.

You can even add bits and pieces – olives, fried onion, roast pumpkin, sundried tomatoes. But if you do, chuck them in by the handful as there's nothing worse than getting a loaf advertising itself by some glamorous-sounding name and then finding out you need a magnifying glass to find the booty. Like life really, it's all or nothing.

Use this recipe to make lots of different shapes and sizes – from 1 large, crowd-feeding loaf to up to 50 rolls. I used to make hundreds of these tiny rolls when I was catering for parties. One year there was an almost daily production.

Makes 1 loaf, or 24–50 rolls

1 kg/2^1/$_4$ lb strong bread flour

30 g/1 oz sea salt, pounded fine

30 g/1 oz butter or 2 tbsp olive oil

600–750 ml /1–1^1/$_4$ pints lukewarm water

30 g/1 oz fresh yeast, or 15g/^{1}/$_2$ oz dried yeast

1 tbsp honey or soft brown sugar

A little milk to glaze (optional)

Place the flour and salt in your largest bowl.

Melt the butter in the lukewarm water set over a very gentle heat or warm the oil and water together until lukewarm. Add the yeast and honey or sugar to about one-quarter of the buttery or oily liquid, stirring it in to dissolve.

Make a well in the centre of the flour, pour the liquid into it, sprinkle a little flour over the top and leave in a warm place for about 10 minutes until bubbly and spongy. Then mix to a soft, pliable dough with the remaining liquid. You'll have to judge the exact amount of water, but the dough should be soft and pliable.

Knead the dough for about 10 minutes on a floured surface. After a while, you'll get into quite a pleasant turn-fold-push rhythm and the dough will feel soft, supple, alive and should come away cleanly in your hand and from the sides of the bowl. A little extra flour soon sorts out a dough that's still a little sticky; a little added water will lighten up dough that feels heavy and lifeless.

Someone once told me that she took out all her anger on the dough, killing ex-boyfriends and traffic wardens in the process. Well I must be angrier because mine just went a bit dead when I tried it. So do give it some of your life and soul, but keep the vibes positive and laid back.

Anyway, shape into a ball, cut a cross into the top, put back into the bowl, covered with a warm, floured cloth. Leave in a warm place (a boiler cupboard or on top of the stove with the oven on) to prove or double in size. This may take up to 2 hours, depending on quite where it is and how old your flour and your yeast are. You shouldn't hurry it.

The way to tell when it is ready is when the dough springs back as you touch it with a floured finger.

Preheat the oven to 240°C/475°F/gas mark 9.

Knock the dough back a few times and bring it back into a ball. Place on a floured baking sheet or, if you prefer, into 2x1.2-litre/scant 2-pint tins. After about 30 minutes, it will have risen over the edge of the tin or spread over the baking sheet in rather daunting fashion. It should be about twice as big as before.

Gently ease the loaf back into some sort of neat ball. You can leave it like this or make a cut down the centre which will give you that gaping wound look on top, although I've heard this more kindly called a 'kissing crust'.

Brush it lightly with the milk and, now that gentleness is the new order of the day, lift the tray into the very hot oven, closing the oven door softly behind. I like to turn the heat down after about 10 minutes, to about 220°C/425°F/gas mark 7 for the next 30 minutes or so, though if you forget it shouldn't matter. You can check to see if it's done a few minutes before that.

Tap it on the bottom to make sure it sounds hollow – that is a satisfying sound if ever I heard one. If there's no resonance to it, return it to the oven for a few more minutes. Then ease it on to a wire rack and let it cool and settle for a while before cutting into it – the best bit at last.

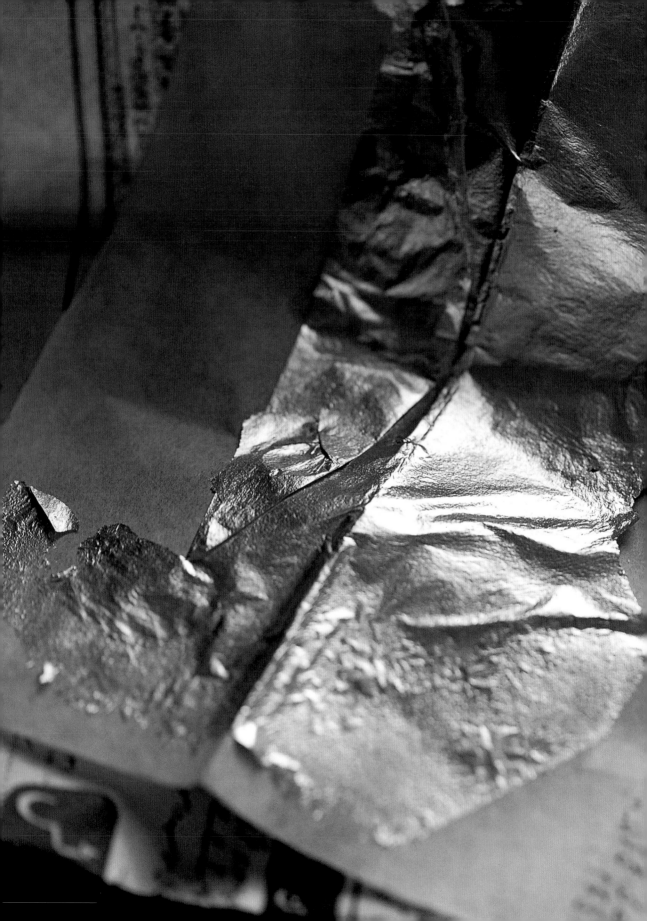

Bibliography

Abensur Nadine *Secrets from a Vegetarean Kitchen* Pavilion 1996

Alexander Stephanie *The Cook's Companion* Viking 1996

Bareham Lindsey *In Praise of the Potato* Michael Joseph 1989

Bell Annie *Annie Bell's Vegetable Book* Michael Joseph 1997

Carluccio Antonio *Antonio Carlucio's Vegetables* Headline 2000

Costas Margaret *Margaret Costa's Four Season's Cookery Book*
    Nelson 1970; Grub Street 1999

Cranks *The New Cranks Recipe Book* Weidenfeld & Nicolson 1996

Cranks *Cranks Light* Weidenfeld & Nicolson 1996

Cranks *Cranks Fast Food* Cassell & Co 2000

David Elizabeth French *Provincial Cooking* Penguin 1960

Davidson Alan *The Oxford Companion To Food* Oxford University Press 1999

Del Conte Anna *I Risotti* Pavilion 1993

Escoffier Auguste *The Illustrated Escoffier* Conran Octopus and
    William Heineman Ltd Heinemann 1987

Grigson Jane *Jane Grigson's Vegetable Book* Michael Joseph 1978

Grigson Sophie *Sophie Grigson's Feasts For a Fiver* BBC Worldwide Ltd 1999

Good Housekeeping *Step By Step Vegetarian Cookbook* Ebury Press 1997

Gordon Peter *The Sugar Club Cookbook* Hodder and Sloughton 1997

Gray Rose and Rogers Ruth *River Café Cook Book* Ebury Press 1995

Gray Rose and Rogers Ruth *River Café Cook Book Two* Ebury Press 1997

Gray Rose and Rogers Ruth *River Café Cook Book Green* Ebury Press 2000

Jaffrey Madhur *World Vegetarian* Ebury Press 1998

Kapoor Sybil *Simply British* Penguin 1998

Lawson Nigella *How To Eat* Chatto and Windus 1998

Mosimann Anton *Naturally* Ebury Press 1991

Owen Sri *The Rice Book* Frances Lincoln 1993

Roden Claudia *A New Book Of Middle Eastern Food* Nelson 1968

Roden Claudia *Meditarranean Cookery* BBC 1987

Roden Claudia *The Food of Italy* Chatto and Windus 1989

Roden Claudia *The Book Of Jewish Food* Viking 1997

Rosengarten David with Joel Dean and Giorgio DeLuca
    The Dean and Deluca Cookbook Ebury Press 1997

Sahni Julie *Classic Indian Vegetarian Cooking* Dorling Kindersley 1987

Spencer Colin *Colin Spencer's Cordon Vert* Guild Publishing 1985

Spencer Colin *Colin Spencer's Vegetable Book* Conran Octopus 1995

Slater Nigel *Real Fast Food* Penguin 1992

Trotter Charlie *Charlie Trotter's Vegetables* Chicago Ten Speed Press 1996

White Marco Pierre *Wild Food From Land And Sea* Ebury Press 1994

Angels at my table

Hilary Lumsden worked indefatigably, imaginatively and sweet-naturedly throughout, sprinkling gems, golden nuggets and wisdom with her graceful wand and softly spoken authority.

Annabel Ford once again aided and abetted in the kitchen, completely taking the load off my shoulders since she shopped and chopped, enduring my non-stop chatter and enjoying the food.

Eluned Jones edited, catching the ones that got away. I love what her lively headings and sub-headings have done for the text.

Charlotte Coleman-Smith came late to the table but she was the awaited guest whose gifts added the final touch. And I am eternally grateful to her for helping me to make the right phone call to the right person at the right time.

My mother was, as ever, on the other end of the phone, answering my every question and query. I only wish we had remembered to photograph her blue notebook as we had planned to do. It is precious.

Jason Lowe took the wonderful, evocative photos working more quickly, spontaneously and originally than I would have thought possible.

Peter Dawson brought his truly fine eye to the design and final exquisite look of the book. It has made all the difference.

Ross arrived from Sydney on Saturday to prepare the food for photography on Monday. That takes guts.

Giles Kendall, managing director at Cranks, has all my gratitude. I hope you will agree that he was right to allow me complete *carte blanche*. I had waited a very long time.

Digby allowed the house to be turned into a big kitchen laboratory and practically gave up any claim to the office, month after month.

Noah, my beloved boy, dragged me away from pan and pen whenever he could. Thank you darling.

And a posse of yoga teachers – Cathy, Louise, Nadia and Marisol among them – kept me in some sort of shape in the distracted months of this book.

To you all with love.

Nadine Abensur
February 2001

Index